Untimely Ruins

Untimely Ruins

NICK YABLON

An Archaeology of American
Urban Modernity, 1819–1919

The University of Chicago Press

Chicago and London

NICK YABLON is associate professor of American studies at the University of Iowa.

Publication of this book has been aided by a grant from the Neil Harris Endowment Fund, which honors the innovative scholarship of Neil Harris, the Preston and Sterling Morton Professor Emeritus of History at the University of Chicago. The Fund is supported by contributions from the students, colleagues, and friends of Neil Harris.

The University of Chicago Press, Chicago 60637
The University of Chicago Press, Ltd., London
© 2009 by The University of Chicago
All rights reserved. Published 2009
Printed in the United States of America

18 17 16 15 14 13 12 11 10 09   1 2 3 4 5

ISBN-13: 978-0-226-94663-4   (cloth)
ISBN-13: 978-0-226-94664-1   (paper)
ISBN-10: 0-226-94663-0   (cloth)
ISBN-10: 0-226-94664-9   (paper)

Library of Congress Cataloging-in-Publication Data

Yablon, Nick.
    Untimely ruins : an archaeology of American urban modernity, 1819–1919 / Nick Yablon.
        p. cm.
    Includes bibliographical references and index.
    ISBN-13: 978-0-226-94663-4 (cloth: alk. paper)
    ISBN-13: 978-0-226-94664-1 (pbk.: alk. paper)
    ISBN-10: 0-226-94663-0 (cloth: alk. paper)
    ISBN-10: 0-226-94664-9 (pbk.: alk. paper)
1. Cities and towns—United States—History—19th cenrury. 2. New York (N.Y.)—In literature. 3. Cairo (Ill.)—History—19th century. 4. San Francisco (Calif.)—History—20th century. 5. American literature—19th century—History and criticism. 6. Ruins in literature. 7. Ruins in art. I. Title.
    HT123.Y33 2010
    307.760973—dc22

                                                              2009017799

Contents

Illustrations

Acknowledgments

This book began at the University of Chicago, under the guidance of Neil Harris, Amy Dru Stanley, and Bill Brown. I am deeply indebted to them— both directly, for their probing questions and constructive suggestions at those early stages, and indirectly, for the inspiration their scholarship provided, and continues to provide. Neil Harris's studies of American visual and consumer culture—which I discovered as an undergraduate at the University of Birmingham, England—were the main reason I decided to cross the Atlantic. Neil turned out to be an ideal academic mentor, serving as an inexhaustible source of encouragement, insightful criticism, and bibliographic recommendations.

I am also grateful to the many librarians and archivists who provided invaluable research assistance, particularly those at the American Antiquarian Society; the Bancroft Library at the University of California, Berkeley; the Beinecke Library at Yale University; the California Historical Society (San Francisco branch); the California Museum of Photography at the University of California, Riverside; the California State Library at Sacramento; the Fine Arts Museums of San Francisco's American Art Study Center; the Foundation Archive of Science Fiction at the University of Liverpool; the Getty Research Center; the Henry E. Huntington Library; HSBC Archives, Canary Wharf, London; the Library of Congress; the MetLife Archives; the New York Public Library; the St. Louis Historical Society; and, closer to home, the University of Chicago and University of Iowa libraries and special collections.

In the past six years, I have had additional research assistance from several American studies graduate students at the University of Iowa; Wayne Anderson, Craig Eley, Brian Hallstoos, Erica Hannickel, Eric Johnson, Richard Landon, Beth Marino, and Steven Williams all proved exceptionally skillful in hunting down obscure sources and images. In addition, Katie Hoffer and

Emily Traw helped out with image editing, Katharine Dale answered some particularly difficult research queries, and Craig Eley produced the index and checked the proofs.

Early versions of the chapters were presented at various venues, and benefited from the responses of audiences at the Johns Hopkins University's Humanities Center; Columbia University's Buell Colloquium on American Architecture; the Newberry Library; the American Antiquarian Society; CUNY's Gotham Center for New York City History; Wayne State University's Department of American Studies; University of Birmingham's "Engaging the New American Studies" conference; the University of Iowa Museum of Art; and the annual meetings of the American Studies Association, the British Association of American Studies, the Organization of American Historians, and the Society for Cinema and Media Studies. Parts of chapter 6 also appeared as "The Metropolitan Life in Ruins: Architectural and Fictional Speculations in New York, 1909–1919," *American Quarterly* 56, no. 2 (2004): 308–47, and I thank that journal for granting permission to reproduce it here, and its anonymous readers for their helpful suggestions.

During the revisions of the manuscript, I have benefited immensely from the responses of some incisive readers. Neil Hertz, Kim Marra, Alexis McCrossen, Lauren Rabinovitz, John Raeburn, and Laura Rigal generously took the time to read the entire manuscript, and their comments helped me to improve it. I am also grateful to those who read and responded to individual chapters, including David Depew, Joni Kinsey, Max Page, John Peters, Susan Scheckel, Russell Valentino, Nigel Wheatley, Vershawn Young, and the members of the Social History Workshop and Mass Culture Workshops at the University of Chicago, and of the Project on Rhetoric of Inquiry Workshop at the University of Iowa. I also learned much from discussions with Joel Brattin, Ken Cmiel (who is sadly missed), Kasten Fitz, Bridget Ford, Bob Gross, Sabine Haenni, Janet Headley, Joseph Heathcott, Glenn Hendler, Jerry Herron, Tom Hill, Linda Kerber, Kevin Mumford, Eliza Richards, Jim Sidbury, Matt Smerdon, Reiner Smolinski, and Alan Wallach. The final shape of the manuscript owes a great deal to Carl Smith and Ann Fabian, who wrote detailed reader reports recommending numerous ways to hone its argument and structure.

Various sources of financial assistance enabled me to research, write, and revise this book, including a Getty Postdoctoral Fellowship; an AAS–National Endowment of the Humanities Postdoctoral Fellowship for a year of research at the American Antiquarian Society; an Andrew Mellon Dissertation Writing Fellowship; an Andrew Mellon Summer Research Fellowship for research at the Huntington Library; and an Old Gold Summer Fellowship and a semester of research leave from the University of Iowa. Generous grants from the Neil

Harris Endowment Fund, the University of Iowa Office of the Vice President for Research, and the Department of American Studies at the University of Iowa helped to defray the costs of acquiring images and permissions, thereby allowing the book to be amply illustrated.

My editor Robert Devens deserves special thanks, both for his astute editorial advice and for his general enthusiasm for the project. The patience and meticulousness of his editorial assistant Anne Summers Goldberg also eased the process of turning the manuscript into a book. And I was lucky to have an expert copyeditor in Dawn Hall.

From the distance of London, and on regular visits to the Midwest (scheduled—not always successfully—to avoid climatic extremes), my family provided great support. I thank my parents Rosemary and Tony Yablon, my sister and brother-in-law Emma and Jeremy Parlons, my late grandfather Harold Steel, and my grandmother (and intellectual inspiration) Doris Steel. Thanks are also extended even farther afield, to Melbourne, Australia, where Marie, Peter, Martin, Lisa, Nicole, and Danielle Amad warmly welcomed me into their family.

But the deepest debt of gratitude I owe is to my wife Paula Amad. This book would not have been possible without her intellectual contributions at every stage, her companionship, and her love. It is therefore dedicated to her.

Abbreviations

The following abbreviations are used to refer to archives and special collections:

AAS — American Antiquarian Society, Worcester, Massachusetts

Banc — Bancroft Library, University of California, Berkeley

Beinecke — Beinecke Rare Book and Manuscript Library, Yale University

CaHS — California Historical Society, San Francisco

CMP — California Museum of Photography, University of California, Riverside

CSL — California State Library, Sacramento

FASF — Foundation Archive of Science Fiction, University of Liverpool, England

Getty — Getty Research Center, Los Angeles

HEH — The Henry E. Huntington Library, San Marino, California

HSBC — John Wright & Co. Archives, HSBC Holdings, Canary Wharf, London

LC — Library of Congress, Washington, DC

MCSF — Museum of the City of San Francisco, San Francisco

MLICA — Metropolitan Life Insurance Company Archives, Long Island City, New York

NYPL — New York Public Library, New York

NYSL — New York State Library, Albany

SLHS — St. Louis Historical Society, St. Louis, Missouri

Of Light Bulbs and Bathtubs:
Excavating the Modern City

In 1925, the *New York Times* invited readers to imagine their city as
it would appear to a "dark-skinned" archaeologist in some distant
time when its skyscrapers have been eroded by rain, snow, ice, wind,
and rust, when the Public Library's marble lions have become en-
twined with creepers, and when Penn Station's glass roof has caved
in. The *Times* was by no means indulging in a frivolous fantasy,
but rather assessing the material and cultural durability of contemporary New York—a question that absorbed even the professors
and professionals the newspaper interviewed. Representing diverse
fields of knowledge from archaeology, anthropology, mineralogy,
and geology to architecture, engineering, and construction, these
experts envisioned very different futures for their city. They could
not even agree exactly how long it would take to reduce it to ruins, whether two or three millennia or less than a century. And they
were equally uncertain which buildings would survive the longest:
the newer skyscrapers of steel and glass or an older neo-Gothic
church of solid masonry walls. If skyscrapers did survive would
they do so intact and upright, thanks to their cement mortar and
paint-protected girders, or would their porous limestone facades
and soft, rust-prone steel reduce them to scattered mounds or cones

of debris? After all, as short-term investments, skyscrapers were hardly built "to
last 3,000 years." The question of which structures survived impinged on the
kinds of artifacts available to this future archaeologist. Would he discover the
treasures of the Metropolitan Museum or a tile from the fireplace of a Harlem
apartment; literary works printed on paper or some legal diploma inscribed on
parchment; a painting in a nightclub, "miraculously preserved like murals at
Pompeii," or a cowboy movie recorded on some "strange strip of film"? When
deciding *where* to begin his dig, should he proceed to the island's southern tip
to excavate "traces of city over city as man of today has found in ancient Troy,"
to a refuse dump with its cache of nondegradable bottles and crockery, or to a
cemetery with its well-embalmed remains? But above all the *Times* remained
uncertain whether this archaeologist, possibly untrained in the English language, could reconstruct the lost civilization from any of these surviving ruins
and relics. The evidence might be too fragmentary to illuminate its technological, let alone cultural accomplishments. He might mistake its subways
(possibly flooded by then) for the legendary labyrinth of the Minotaur, and
its skyscrapers for "temple[s] of a forgotten god." In deciphering those ruins,
moreover, he would not necessarily be able to draw on local knowledge. Like
Pompeii and Troy, Manhattan might well remain a depopulated site, its only
inhabitants some carrion birds or wolves, or the occasional fish found swim-
ming in "ingenious machines which long ago sold chocolate for a penny." Even
as simple a technological artifact as a light bulb might thus become a mystery
of the ages (fig. I.1).[1]

Readers and moviegoers of the early twenty-first century have become familiar with such visions of an American city—typically but not exclusively
New York—transfigured through ruination and depopulation into a potentially fruitful yet inscrutable site for archaeologists. Imagined ruinscapes,
populated variously by cyborgs, gangs, vampires, zombies, or survivalists, have
served as a stock backdrop to postapocalyptic science-fiction cinema, novels,
comics, and video games. Meanwhile, images of the actual ruins of postwar
inner cities have been widely disseminated through news media and photography books, shaping contemporary debates about crime, housing, riots, and
gentrification.[2] This book, however, explores the distinctive urban imaginary
of dereliction and decay in its period of emergence: the hundred years *preceding* the *Times* article. During that century of rapid demographic and economic
growth, the city-in-ruins paradoxically became a common trope and reality,
invoked in politicians' speeches and tourists' journals, narrated in classic literary works and popular magazine fiction, and depicted by painters, illustrators,
cartoonists, photographers, and cinematographers. The causes of imagined
and actual desolation varied widely. In some cases, ruins were the outcome of

Fig. I.1. W. F. White, "He Finds Now a Treasure, a Globe of Thin Glass as Big as a Pear." Illustration from "When History Has Forgotten New York," *New York Times*, May 31, 1925, Sunday Magazine, 12.

natural forces: from earthquakes and fires to the more extreme cataclysms of volcanoes, tidal waves, planetary explosions, and cometary collisions. In others, the ruins were man-made, the work of anarchist mobs or counterinsurgent agents, military invasions or civil wars. In still others, they were economic in origin, brought about by misguided speculations or apparently uncontrollable (and thus quasi-natural) capitalist forces. Cutting across these disparate scenarios, however, was a common preoccupation with how cities would look, not so much in moments of actual destruction or abandonment as in their distant aftermath. To picture a metropolis buried in rubble, protruding through sand or vegetation, or submerged beneath an ocean, was to project it into another order of existence and to view it in a very different light. What was it about the social, economic, or political conditions of nineteenth-century American cities that prompted inhabitants and visitors to experience or envisage them as dilapidated and deserted, or even condemned—like Troy and Pompeii—to centuries of oblivion before being rediscovered and disinterred? Or, more succinctly, how did urban modernity come to be imagined as the classical antiquity of the future?

A fundamental premise of this book is that visions of modern cities in ruins were not necessarily expressions of cultural pessimism or nihilism, or even of antipathy toward modernity or urbanism as such. Since at least the seventeenth century, ruins—both real and imagined—have elicited pleasure as much as gloom. They have yielded pleasure through their historical associations, as objects that testify to the glories of a specific empire or civilization— and of empire and civilization in general—or that conversely commemorate the fortunate endurance of Christianity over barbaric paganism (in the case of Roman ruins), or of democratic enlightenment over feudal tyranny (as in gothic ones). So too have ruins served as vehicles of spiritual pleasure, above all in Baroque religious allegories of the divine immortality transcending earthly transience. Since at least the eighteenth century they have also been embraced aesthetically, insofar as their irregular forms and rough surfaces conform to the formal principles introduced by the "picturesque" movement. Even those ruins haunted by robbers and spirits would become, in the Gothic imagination, conduits of pleasurable melancholy or sublime terror.

The pleasure of the ruin may be even more deep-seated. The German philosopher Georg Simmel's 1911 essay "Die Ruine" probes the underlying reasons why a crumbling building—unlike, say, a broken statue, damaged painting, or half-lost poem—could be construed as delightful and meaningful rather than "sad" or "negative and degrading."[3] Bracketing questions of historical association, religious meaning, and aesthetic form altogether, he sought to grasp ruins phenomenologically, that is, as they are directly experienced by the mind. When confronted with a ruin, one does not behold a formless "heap of stones," but something distinct and coherent (261). If the original building had once represented a specific configuration of human intention and natural materials, so too does the ruin—except that in the former, nature had remained subordinate to the will of man, while in the latter it has become "master" over it (259). The ascendancy of nature is thus understood not as an arbitrary or "senseles[s]" perversion of the building from without, as in the destructive erosion of wind and rain or the creeping overgrowth of ivy or moss, so much as a "realization of a tendency inherent" *within* it (263). Nature is simply reasserting a "rightful claim to this work" that it had harbored all along (262). But natural forces have not gone as far as to erase *all* human traces, at least not yet. In the ruin, the "brute, downward-dragging, corroding, crumbling power of nature" (*Natur*) is still held in check by the "striving upward" of the human spirit (*Geist*) (261, 263). It is this ongoing balance, this sense of being delicately poised "between the not-yet and the no-longer," that renders the ruin dynamic rather than static, alive rather inert (262). In fact, the ruin may even represent the *reconciliation* of nature and culture, the sublation of those erstwhile antagonists into a new, albeit unstable synthesis (266). Where *Geist* had once "violated" *Natur* (259), it now coexists peacefully with it. Having scaled the "peak," it now "descends to its home," into the arms, so to speak, of Mother Nature (262). One may even glimpse a sense of the secret affinity between *Geist* and *Natur*, as forces growing from a "common root," in the way that decaying building materials merge seamlessly into the "surrounding landscape," sometimes even taking on the color of the ground in which they stand

(260, 263–64). This is why the ruin, for all its gnarled and battered appearance, "conveys the impression of peace" and exudes an aura of serenity (264). Simmel's affirmation of the ruin found an echo in the work of his influential students, such as the Marxist philosophers and literary theorists Walter Benjamin and Ernst Bloch. For Benjamin, ruins—whether as motifs in Baroque culture or as outmoded commodities in a run-down shopping arcade—could preserve the redemptive potential of the past in such a way as to unmask the conceits of the present, while for Bloch they were exemplary "wishful images" that resonate with a utopian longing for some kind of apotheosis.[4]

Such a sensitivity to the allure of the ruin—whether aesthetic, historical, religious, or philosophical—has been deemed lacking in the United States. Since the founding of the nation, its supposed inhospitality to the cult of the ruin has becoming a defining myth. For the nineteenth-century aesthetician John Ruskin, the "charm of romantic association" could "hardly be felt in America" because of the absence of physical "traces" of a long and heroic past, or what he called the "precursorship of eventful history." English travelers of his generation who did acknowledge the presence of such traces, such as prehistoric burial mounds or eighteenth-century military forts, invariably pronounced their utilitarian, forward-looking hosts culturally immune to their melancholic meanings.[5] These observations were supposedly reinscribed, albeit as positive attributes, by American writers hailing the dearth of ruins as the hallmark of a "Virgin Land," and flaunting their disregard for such decadent emblems as a sign of the "Adamic" innocence of a young republic unencumbered by the past—to invoke two founding texts of American studies.[6] More recent cultural historians have reaffirmed this exceptionalist notion that ruins were essentially "meaningless" to a nation securely oriented toward ideas of material progress, manifest destiny, and moral perfectibility.[7] If recognized at all, an American indulgence in the iconography of decay has been confined to a narrow circle of dissenting artists and writers. The last canvas of Thomas Cole's *Course of Empire* series (1836; see chapter 1, fig. 1.1), one of the few American paintings included in genealogies of the ruin in Western culture, has repeatedly been characterized by art historians as a jeremiad issued from outside of, and in opposition to, the Jacksonian mainstream—in other words, as an exception that proves the rule.[8]

Far from being absent or marginal, ruins were in fact ubiquitous across diverse cultures and landscapes of the United States during the nineteenth century. The first chapter of this book traces the gradual development through the Jacksonian period of an American taste for ruins of all kinds, including the classic monuments that increasing numbers of artists and writers venerated on their tours of Europe, the artificial ruins that landscape designers occasionally

borrowed from English folly gardens, and also the "authentic" home-grown
ruins of burial mounds and military forts that amateur archaeologists, travel
writers, poets, and artists promoted as vital attractions of an "American Grand
Tour." Americans sometimes perceived ruins when they were *not* there, hal-
lucinating ancient temples and cathedrals out of trees, mountains, or rock
formations—apparitions I call (here and elsewhere in the book) *ruin-effects*.
Moreover, far from being confined to the margins, the ruin was widely invoked
in many of the central political, social, and religious discourses of the antebellum years. Broken columns surfaced in the speeches of Democrats as well as
Whigs, in public enactments of patriotism as well as the private ceremonies
of Freemasons, and in the sermons of mainstream denominations as well as
millenarian sects. Subsequent chapters trace the further dissemination of
the ruin, as it was taken up by both English novelists and their American
readers (chapter 2), by members of both the bourgeois elite and the artisanal
classes (chapter 3), by native-born, conservative intellectuals and immigrant
radicals (chapter 4), by male amateur photographers and their female colleagues (chapter 5), and by a Boston Brahmin expatriate and an African American activist (chapter 6). Although they diverged widely over how to interpret
and represent the ruin, their mutual investment in this object provides a crucial point of convergence from which to delineate the political and cultural
dialogues of the nineteenth century. Even the very act of disavowing ruins as
"absent" or "meaningless" arguably betrays their implicit centrality to dominant constructions of national identity.

   A second myth about ruins this book interrogates is that of their trans-
historical status. It is often assumed that their appearance and significance
have remained constant over time, as artists, writers, and orators of different
periods inevitably appropriated a conventional iconography of classical columns and Gothic arches to convey certain universal, moral themes—chiefly
the impermanence of human life, and by extension civilizations, and thus the
folly and futility of overreaching ambitions and enterprises. Certainly, this was
the dominant conception of the ruin during the seventeenth century. According to Benjamin's dissertation on German tragic drama, the ruin was one of
several "characters of transience" in Baroque culture. The crumbling monuments of Roman antiquity, ripened through centuries of natural decay, were
the inorganic analogs to the human skulls in *vanitas* paintings and theatrical
scenery of the period. Both functioned as allegorical expressions of the limits
of earthly achievement, and as contrasts to the indifference of nature and the
eternal truth of God. Indeed, some Baroque emblems paired ruins and skeletons within the same image.[9]

But although this moral philosophy and classical iconography of decay persisted (with variations) into the eighteenth century, above all in the work of Enlightenment *philosophes* and academic landscape painters, by the nineteenth century the ruin had begun to acquire new, unfamiliar qualities and meanings. The Viennese art historian Alois Riegl, unlike his contemporary Simmel, foregrounded rather than bracketed the historicity of monuments, thereby providing a useful model for tracking the emergence of a "modern cult of the ruin" that was "fundamentally different" from that of the Baroque.[10] Whereas the term *ruin* had once been reserved for works of Roman architecture, with their unique associations of "earthly power and grandeur," with the advent of Romanticism it came to encompass the Gothic remains of abbeys and castles in Northern Europe (31). And whereas the only noteworthy ruins had been those possessing "commemorative value" (that is, memorializing a specific person, deity, or event) and subsequently "historical value" (documenting the achievements of a specific moment in time), the emergence of "age-value" allowed one to "embrace every artifact without regard to its original significance and purpose," provided it simply conveys a sense of the passage of time as such (26, 24). Consequently, rather than judging ruins from an objective aesthetic standpoint (that of classical antiquity), one could consume them subjectively for their sensory and emotional effects (26, 29, 24, 35). According to Riegl, this "modern cult of the ruin" (of which Simmel might be considered an adherent) remained devoted to natural, or quasi-natural, processes of decay over long periods of time (32, 44); evidence of instantaneous "destruction *by man*," as Simmel put it, would spoil the whole effect (260). But with the outbreak of revolutionary insurrections and military campaigns across Europe, even more unorthodox ruins materialized, ones that were entirely man-made and contemporary.[11] Further challenges to traditional conceptions arose from European encounters with nonclassical ruins in its colonies, such as the temple of Angkor Vat or the Amaravati marbles, "rediscovered" and photographed in the 1850s by French and British explorers respectively; and with differing articulations of the theme of decay in non-Western cultures such as China and Japan.[12]

It is within this larger history of the ruin—of the violation of its criteria and destabilization of its meanings—that the phenomenon of American ruins is to be situated. In stark contrast to the grandiose neoclassical piles conjured by its antebellum landscape painters and poets, the actual ruins found in the urbanizing landscapes of nineteenth-century America tended to be prosaic, even tawdry structures. The meditations on decay recounted in the various chapters of this book were prompted by the remains of abandoned log

cabins and defunct canal bridges (chapter 1); disreputable banks and unsound
town sites (chapter 2); half-demolished churches and cemeteries (chapter 3);
run-down tenements and dilapidated docks (chapter 4); earthquake and fire-
ravaged pipes and telegraph poles (chapter 5); and the first dismantled skyscrapers (chapter 6). Similarly, fictional (and nonfictional) speculations about
the postapocalyptic rediscovery of America rarely imagined the sacred vestiges
of its cathedrals or the official relics of its Congress or City Halls, but rather
the profane temples of its commercial-industrial everyday: shopping arcades,
office buildings, subways, factories, power plants, and railroad stations. These
vernacular ruins—whether actual or imagined—would neither memorialize
epoch-defining events and individuals nor embody the period's highest aesthetic standards. On the contrary, they were banal, ambiguous, or obscure in
origin, unmediated by well-known legends or preeminent visual or literary representations, and thus unassimilable to the grand historical narratives concret-
ized by the classical and Gothic ruins of Europe.

Materials and styles of construction in the United States presented further
difficulties. Houses built of cheap materials such as wood, and with crude techniques such as the balloon frame, did not offer sufficient resistance to decay,
fire, or vegetative growth. Like the prehistoric earth mounds, they thus failed
to retain that equilibrium between structural integrity and natural processes
Simmel considered fundamental to the ruin.[13] Conversely, the newer industrial materials of steel, iron, glass, and concrete were too durable—liable only
to rust, shatter, or crack. Connoisseurs of ruin have instead favored stone (ideally marble) structures and bronze objects for the modulated way they register
the effects of time, as their forms disintegrate gradually, their surfaces accrue
a lustrous patina, and their crevices take in foliage. One can hear echoes of
Ruskin's refusal to count "the iron roofs and pillars of . . . railway stations" as
architecture, because "no builder has true command . . . over [their] modes
of decay," in the Nazi architect Albert Speer's renunciation of steel and concrete on account of their lack of "ruin value," and even in the anti-Nazi critic
Ernst Bloch's repudiation of the machine age for having produced "gadgets and
streets" incapable of acquiring an aura of antiquity: they "cannot grow old, but
only ro[t] in the course of the years" (386–87).[14]

But the problem with modern ruins was not simply their banality or de-
formity; even more troubling was their apparent illegibility. The Benjamin-
influenced, French literary historian Philippe Hamon distinguishes between
"the ancient ruin of the distant past" and "the modern ruin" that became a
leitmotif in the novels and newspapers of nineteenth-century Paris, such as ruins found on the site of riots, slums, or speculative construction. Whereas the
ancient ruin was "laden with history," the modern variant was "far more am-

biguous and far more difficult to interpret."[15] Such resistance to interpretation was even more pronounced with the American ruins described in this book, from the frontier log cabin and prehistoric mounds scrutinized by Alexis de Tocqueville in the first chapter, to the skyscrapers and bridges pondered by future travelers and explorers in the last. A certain amount of mystery is inherent in all ruins and has been an essential ingredient of their fascination. As Hamon observes, it was precisely this veil of obscurity—the cryptic quality, for instance, of a faded inscription engraved on a pediment or plinth—that enabled the antiquary or well-educated traveler to prove his (and they are almost invariably male) mastery of the art of decryption, a "semiotic prowess" distinguishing him from ignorant and indifferent locals (53, 55, 56). As a fragment that elicits such "acts of semantic completion," the ruin might be viewed as the master metaphor for that very act of cross-temporal interpretation known as hermeneutics (58). But in many of the "future ruin" scenarios discussed here, the archaeologists, explorers, and historians ultimately fail to display such semiotic prowess. Some draw absurd conclusions about the use and meaning of the monuments before them. Others simply abandon the task of interpretation altogether.

This incomprehensibility of America's ruins—and especially its future ruins—is in part a consequence of the backgrounds of those who discover them. Whereas scholars of ancient Rome (most famously Gibbon) had acknowledged their indebtedness to its civilization, the future scholars of ancient America—whether Maori, Turkish, Chinese, or, in the *Times*'s account, "dark-skinned"—turn out to be its cultural "others," unversed in, and thus unsympathetic to, its cultural, political, and linguistic traditions. Even those barbaric remnants of the American nation lingering in the ruins appear to have lost all memory of their original purpose or significance. But the collapse of meaning owes more to the nature of the ruins themselves. As vernacular archaeological sites containing artifactual evidence, they present numerous obstacles. Given the adoption of perishable materials such as pulp paper and photographs—as opposed to papyrus and parchment— writers expected much of the cultural patrimony of the United States to have crumbled or faded by the time it is exhumed. Moreover, those relics that are best preserved, in shopping arcades or sites of commercial entertainment, may not necessarily be the most significant. As everyday commodities or advertisements, they would represent the superficial scraps rather than highest specimens of civilization, and furthermore might be too culturally specific to be intelligible to others. How, to take just two examples from the 1925 *Times* article, is any archaeologist to make sense of a "taxidermist's stuffed poodle" recovered from the "wreckage" of a shop on Columbus Avenue, or a skyscraper whose only surviving inscription was some graffiti that reads, "Exeter Street Giants Are Champs"? Conversely, there were concerns about the lack of cultural specificity of America's future antiquities. With their voracious accumulation of material objects, art works, and literature from other cultures, American homes, museums, and libraries would reveal little about the people who had actually built them. "Will the stone sarcophagus in an Egyptian collection" at the Metropolitan Museum, the *Times* asked, "be taken for an American bathtub?" And will Cleopatra's Needle in Central Park, another author suggested, prompt a future explorer to conclude that America was invaded by Egyptians? Indeed, the idea of a monument first erected in the desert finding itself surrounded once again by desolation was an irony Benjamin relished, with respect to the obelisk in the Place de la Concorde.[16] Certainly, many cultural critics warned that the eclecticism of American buildings and monuments—their borrowings from the architectural vocabularies of other nations and periods—would result in a failure to bequeath a recognizable national style to posterity. It was in part to allay such concerns about cultural transmission, and to ensure the survival of at least a few exemplary tokens of American civilization, that the time capsule was pioneered in Philadelphia in the 1870s. But, as we will see, even this expedient aroused as much skepticism as confidence.

The most glaring anomalies of America's ruins, however, were their temporal properties, or what I call their *untimeliness*.[17] The actual ruins forged by the great fires that periodically ravaged its cities, by the scorched-earth tactics of General Sherman's rapid advance through the South, or by the equally swift and destructive swings of the capitalist economy, were all instantaneous and largely unanticipated, and thus radically different from those formed over time.[18] In addition to being produced in an instant, they were also consumed immediately, before they had time (even if they were made of stone) to attract foliage, accrue a patina, or merge into their surroundings. Such *day-old ruins*—a term coined, as we shall see in chapter 1, by Tocqueville himself—did not necessarily preclude affective responses. We will encounter several scenes in which natives of New York, such as the ex-mayor Philip Hone or the expatriate novelist Henry James, experienced strong emotions in the presence of the ruins of buildings they had inhabited or frequented in their lifetimes. But those emotions were generally disturbing rather than pleasant, involving a distressing sense of the writers' own mortality and displacement. Lacking the temporal distance and discontinuity afforded by ancient ruins, day-old ruins thwarted the pleasures of nostalgia and antiquarianism.[19] Nor did it appear likely that these structures would ever become ancient. In southern cities such as Naples, Italy, Bloch observed, modern ruins such as broken water pipes and abandoned railroad tracks are permitted to remain in place for years, and may even have unintended benefits (in this case, channeling water down the tracks into the drier districts).[20] But given the rapid and seemingly relentless process of capitalist urbanization in the United States, its ruins typically proved ephemeral. Despite some efforts to preserve them for future generations, the ruins of fires, earthquakes, or bankruptcies tended to disappear almost as quickly as they had materialized, recycled for their precious building materials, deployed as landfill, or simply erased to clear the way for new rounds of capital investment.

The evanescence of America's ruins extended to the types of media and genres through which they were disseminated. Through the mid-nineteenth century, the pleasures of architectural decay had been transmitted via the visual media of the canvas, engraving, or sketchbook, the three-dimensional media of the garden folly, theatrical prop, or trompe l'oeil "ruin room," and the print media of the poem, travelogue, or philosophical treatise. Indeed, this book begins by examining how Americans commandeered the vehicles of painting (chapter 1), travelogue (chapter 2), and fiction (chapter 3) to depict various ruins. But by the end of the century these were supplemented by modern media of representation that were apparently less durable, materially and culturally. Chapter 4 considers the depiction of American ruins in cartoons published in the weekly satire magazines, as well as in popular fiction. Chapter 5 investigates the use of instantaneous roll film and handheld Kodak cameras to photograph the ruins of the San Francisco earthquake and fire of 1906. And chapter 6 recovers the postapocalyptic science fiction narratives that appeared in the "all-story" or "pulp" magazines of Progressive-era New York, juxtaposing them with the urban ruins depicted in contemporaneous time-lapse films and magazine cartoons. These modern media were notable for their accessibility to mass audiences, their cheapness (Kodak Brownies costing a dollar, pulp magazines a dime), their interactivity (Kodakers forming clubs, while science fiction magazines published fan letters), and also for their temporal qualities. With their susceptibility to physical decay and cultural ephemerality, some critics were already suggesting, photographs and pulp magazines were unlikely to last much longer than the ruins they depicted.

The concept of "untimeliness" applies not only to the problematic duration of American ruins and their modes of representation, but also to the difficulty of situating them within received models of historical temporality. According to the "classical republican" philosophy of the eighteenth century, ruins were supposed to appear only in the final stage of the fixed life cycle of a nation, that moment of death and dissolution when the mantle of civilization was passed on, usually in a westward direction. How was one to account, then, for the materialization of ruins within a nation clearly still in its early stages of political, economic, territorial, and urban development? Did they represent the fatal signs of premature decline, or the first tentative steps toward greatness?

Although Tocqueville asked this question—"What! Ruins so soon!"—in the context of a deserted rural settlement, such premature or "untimely" ruins were even more discordant when they appeared in the heart of rapidly developing cities.[21] Standing out against (and sometimes even obstructing) the rapid redevelopment of American downtowns into exclusively business districts, holdovers from earlier periods—such as churches, cemeteries, mansions, or obsolete office buildings—acquired an air of antiquity. These holdouts—or in Bloch's terms, "non-contemporaneous elements"—testified to the unevenness of capitalist urbanization: the way in which one plot of land was developed while an abutting one was left barren, one neighborhood was "improved" while an adjacent one deteriorated, or the way in which one city (such as Chicago) could blossom into a metropolis while others in the region lagged or collapsed (as with St. Louis and Cairo, Illinois, respectively).[22] American urban ruins could also be untimely in the sense of preceding their own completion. Banks or city halls that were under construction, but delayed through budget overruns, political controversies, or financial panics, reminded more than one nineteenth-century commentator of inauspicious ruins—or what the 1960s earthworks artist Robert Smithson would call (in reference to a temporarily abandoned highway construction zone in Passaic, New Jersey) "ruins in reverse": structures that "don't fall into ruin after they are built but rather rise into ruin before they are built."[23] To some extent, all ruins exhibit a degree of nonsynchronicity. In such material remnants, Simmel wrote, one perceives "the present form of the past," or rather the past and present "fuse[d] . . . into one united form" (266), a temporal composite that belies any simple notion of a completed past or a self-contained present. But the anachronism and incongruity of American ruins—the way in which they erupted out of time and out of place—generated a particularly complex sense of temporality as multilayered and multidirectional. It was to convey their disruption of traditional conceptions of time that nineteenth-century witnesses coined such oxymoronic terms as *day-old ruins, temporary ruins,* or simply *modern ruins.*

The anomalies of these modern ruins in turn freed Americans from the traditional poetics and aesthetics of architectural decay. A third myth this book challenges, then, is that American articulations of the ruin amounted to little more than variations on a European theme. Those few cultural and literary historians who have acknowledged the rhetorical uses of the ruin in nineteenth-century America have described them as a litany of "conventional gestures," "standard enthusiasms," and "stock imagery."[24] So too have art historians characterized the enthusiasm of certain antebellum painters for ruins as an old-fashioned and short-lived vogue, picked up on their travels in Europe and taken up at home to assert the cultural maturity of their own nation. "Founded on an ideal of the picturesque, on an esthetic of the ruin, which belonged more properly to the late eighteenth and early nineteenth centuries," Barbara Novak has written, this genre of painting was destined to endure only for a few years before being replaced in the 1860s by a more appropriate "cult of nature."[25] To be sure, nineteenth-century American writers, painters, and gardeners were inspired by the classic ruins they visited in Europe. So too were they influenced by the classic European treatises on ruin, from the Comte de Volney's *Les Ruines* and Edward Gibbon's *Decline and Fall of the Roman Empire* to Reverend William Gilpin's *Observations* on the "Picturesque"—however freely they adapted those texts. And they continued to borrow their vocabulary and iconography of the ruin from their precursors in Europe, even after it had been written off there as an outmoded aesthetic fashion. Indeed, these are all further instances of the anachronism or untimeliness of the American ruin. But the broader cultural preoccupation with landscapes of decay in nineteenth-century America cannot be written off as a belated foreign import. Most of the diverse writers, artists, and audiences discussed in this book had neither visited the classic ruins of Europe nor viewed the work of European painters of ruin. Instead, ruins spoke to them because they resonated with more local issues and concerns.

Of all the issues and concerns that engendered an affinity for scenes of desolation, the most significant were those pertaining to urban modernity. The popularization of the ruin in nineteenth-century American culture was exactly coeval with the emergence of the modern city as an inescapable fact of the nation's social life. Whereas German Baroque allegories of ruin can be traced back to that period's religious strife and protracted wars (as Benjamin did), the modern American fascination with this motif needs to be located within a contrasting set of historical experiences, marked by a burgeoning population, a (largely) growing economy, proliferating cities, and rising skylines.[26] This book therefore provides an extensive, although not exhaustive, examination of the diverse processes of American urbanism as they played out across a number of different locations. Chapter 1 foregrounds the sheer rapidity of urban growth that took off in the 1820s, focusing on "inland cities" such as Rochester, Syracuse, and Buffalo that rose up—albeit haphazardly—along the Erie Canal. Chapter 2 turns to Cairo, Illinois, as a notorious example of the "paper cities" (or speculative town sites) that were touted as the next great metropolis of the West in the late 1830s and early 1840s, but frequently fell victim within months to the whims of British investors and the instability of American banks and paper money. Chapter 3 explores the radical transformations of urban space within antebellum Manhattan, as it became segmented along the lines of class, ethnicity, and land use, dominated by a new regime of landlordism and tenancy, and exposed to successive bouts of construction and demolition—processes that combined to create the modern problem of homelessness. Chapter 4 addresses the conflicts that simmered—and occasionally boiled over—in the industrial cities of the Gilded Age, especially Chicago, conflicts between striking labor unions and capitalist bosses, socialists and conservatives, and immigrants and nativists. Chapter 5 considers how the introduction of new technologies of transportation, communication, and construction, and the provision of gas, electricity, water, and sewerage, transformed a city like San Francisco, simultaneously rendering it all the more vulnerable to the natural disaster of an earthquake. Finally, chapter 6 returns to New York City during the Progressive Era to witness the birth of the skyscraper out of new technologies (the steel skeleton and the elevator), new practices of speculative construction (and demolition), and the new spatial demands of corporations that were hiring growing numbers of female clerks.

These various developments are related to visions of ruin in a number of ways. Contemporaries seized upon the motif in part simply to register the pace, scale, and intensity of American urbanization. It was as if the advent of the modern city could only be gauged retroactively, in the hindsight of future archaeologists and historians comparing it with other epochal chapters in human history; or as if America's departure from prior models of urban growth and development was revealed in the divergence of its steel and concrete ruins from classical models. But contemporaries also embraced the ruin as a device that might enable them to render complex urban phenomena visible, and thereby grasp their deeper significance. Through narratives and images of the abject barrenness of speculative town sites, the nocturnal desolation of financial districts, the technological detritus of earthquake-ravaged infrastructure, or the fleeting spectacle of dismantled skyscrapers, the American city emerged as a fragile entity, vulnerable not so much to the external forces that traditionally threatened cities (foreign armies or natural disasters), as to equally violent forces unleashed by the internal contradictions of capitalist urbanization. Such revelations of the unstable, uneven development of American cities belie those linear narratives of urban progress (or decline) more often cited by historians.

As a study of American urban modernity, however, this book is concerned not just with the outward processes of urbanization but also with their implications for what Simmel called the "inner life" of city dwellers. Indeed, for both him and his intellectual heirs, including Benjamin and Bloch, modern cities were distinct not only in terms of their geographic and demographic magnitude, or their economic and technological supremacy, but also at the more subtle level of individual experience. In a paper, "The Metropolis and Mental Life," that was originally delivered in Dresden in 1903 and would become the founding text of this tradition of urban theory, Simmel made few references to the physical settings of any city. Instead, he was concerned with how urban dwellers attempt to "accommodat[e]" themselves to its intensified sensory impact (the bombardment of vehicles and advertisements), its social complexity (the intricate division of labor and the corresponding dependency on anonymous others), its spatial constrictions (the confinement of the individual within dense crowds and cramped spaces), and above all its new temporal conditions (the acceleration and syncopation of the "rhythm of life," along with the coordination and subordination of time to precise schedules). City dwellers' defensive reactions to these excessive demands of the metropolis, Simmel argued, give rise in turn to new psychic disorders such as alienation, anomie, restlessness, and nervousness (and one might add, agoraphobia, melancholia, and nostalgia); to new configurations of the human sensorium such as exaggerated or attenuated sensitivity to external stimuli; and to new personality types such as the blasé, the reserved, or the dandy.[27] Although the context and occasion of Simmel's lecture was the dramatic development of German cities, especially his own Berlin, its observations resonated with American intellectuals confronting their experiences of modernity. Indeed, for Simmel, as for later German critics, cities like New York and Chicago represented the telos of technological and capitalist modernity known as *Amerikanismus* toward which Berlin—and for that matter, Paris and Moscow—seemed to be heading.[28] This book therefore illuminates the experiences of American urban dwellers by deploying Simmel, Benjamin, and Bloch not only in their guise as theorists of the ruin but also as theorists of urban modernity. In fact, their almost romantic meditations on ancient ruins need to be placed in dialogue with their more avant-garde analyses of modern cities. Does the struggle between nature and spirit that Simmel discerned in the ruin correspond to that between the emotions and the intellect within the modern city dweller?[29] Could we compare the "downward-dragging, corroding" forces of nature ("Ruin," 261) to the "overwhelming social forces," the "threatening currents" of the urban environment, and the "level[ing]" and "hollow[ing]" effects of money that conspire to wear down the "metropolitan man"? ("Metropolis," 174–75, 176, 178). And similarly, what lines of connection link Benjamin's earliest reflections on the Baroque ruins of seventeenth-century German tragic drama, to his final, unfinished work on the commodity culture of nineteenth-century Paris?

If images of crumbling ruins—rerouted through Simmel's "Metropolis and Mental Life"—can suggest the erosion of intimacy, community, and traditional ways of life in an age of capitalist urbanism, they might also be read in the light of German critical theory as utopian fantasies of some kind of postcapitalist or posturban future. As an expression of the "serene . . . synthesis" of *Geist* and *Natur* as well as their mutual "antagonism" (261, 265), Simmel's ruin provides a foil to the alienated and conflicted psyche of the metropolis, and thus holds out the possibility of attaining a more harmonious mode of existence.[30] Similarly, for Bloch, the ruin, which had been a "terror to unbroken ages," has come to "indicate meanings" and utopian longings that transcend the "everyday," and does so "most powerfully in empty ages" such as that of capitalist technology (*Principle of Hope*, 384, 386); while in Benjamin's formulation, the "destructive" process of ruination strips away the mythical pretensions of a commodity or building, bringing to light its hidden "truth content," that utopian "wish image" buried within it.[31] Along similar lines, the representations of urban ruin explored in this book serve not merely to register the actual scale and intensity of various processes of urbanization but also to generate new ways of envisioning and experiencing the city. To view one's everyday environment through the eyes of a future archaeologist or historian is to begin to view it in another light: an act of estrangement equivalent to that of returning to one's city after an extended absence, or to the critical illumination Benjamin identified with surrealism, dreams, *flâneurie*, hashish, child's play, or cinema. But unlike those other tropes through which the urban is made legible—the metropolis as inferno, prison, labyrinth, stage, or text—the city-in-ruins introduces a unique temporal perspective.

Thus, however inaccessible and indecipherable they might appear, American ruins were imagined in futurological speculations as unintended time capsules that could ultimately—if carefully excavated and interpreted—expose the hidden histories of nineteenth-century cities. Indeed, it is the least intelligible ruins that may turn out to harbor the profoundest truths. Moreover, for several writers from Tocqueville to Twain, the banal detritus of America's vernacular structures—unlike the grand monuments erected in honor of the leaders and gods of antiquity—would preserve the unofficial traces of history: the suppressed voices, secret hopes, and lived experiences of everyday people, even marginalized ones, who had built or passed through them. It is this revelatory potential of America's unintended monuments that gives rise, in some of the texts discussed here, to various utopias. Some of those utopias erected upon the ruins of American cities would be politically reactionary, predicated on the exclusion of ethnic or racial others, the subordination of women, or the overthrow of the republic in favor of a more authoritarian system of governance, whether monarchical or theocratic. But others would embody more progressive goals, such as the transcendence of class hierarchies, racial distinctions, or gender divisions—and, in at least one case, the simultaneous transcendence of all three. Even the process of ruination could function as a great social leveler. In the scenario predicted by the *Times* article with which we began, "Fifth Avenue is forgotten" while a Harlem apartment is remembered.

1

Crumbling Columns and Day-Old Ruins

Specters of Antiquity on the American Grand Tour,
1819–1837

Two contrasting scenes from 1835–36 exemplify the range of responses and representations that ruins can elicit. In *Desolation*, the
last canvas of his *Course of Empire* series, Thomas Cole depicted
the kinds of classical ruins that adorn the Mediterranean coastline
(fig. 1.1); in the first volume of *Democracy in America,* Alexis de
Tocqueville described some decidedly nonclassical ruins discovered in the wilderness of the American interior. While the painted
landscape is scattered with the imagined ruins of marble edifices
and anchored by a Corinthian column in the center foreground, the
narrated landscape is limited to a few modest traces of civilization,
such as an abandoned log cabin and the "blackened" stones that
represented the "ruins of a fallen chimney." The differences between
these ruins are accentuated by the kind of light, climate, and ecology in which they appear. Cole's are gently bathed in atmospheric
winter moonlight, their broken architectural forms complemented
by the sparse ivy growing out of the arid, Mediterranean soil; Tocqueville's are viewed in the glare of midday, midsummer sun, and
are marred by the "vigorous vegetation" that grows out of the "in-
comparable . . . soil" of the American forest, enveloping clearings
"with green branches and flowers," turning fences into "live hedges"

Fig. 1.1. Thomas Cole, *The Course of Empire: Desolation* (fifth in series of five canvases), 1836. Oil on canvas. 39 1/4 x 63 1/4 inches. Acc. #1858.5. Collection of The New-York Historical Society.

and causing tree stumps to "sprou[t] afresh." But above all the two ruinscapes are antithetical in their temporal implications. If the American painter more conventionally conveys the deep time of epochal history in the gradually eroding remains of some civilization that had risen steadily over time and long since fallen, the French traveler is struck by the radical contemporaneity of his ruins. These are only "day-old ruins" (*ces ruines d'un jour*), the remains of a settlement that was hastily built, hastily abandoned, and almost as hastily reclaimed by nature. And most anomalous of all is their presence in a country so recently founded, a discrepancy that causes him to exclaim repeatedly on leaving the scene: "What! Ruins so soon!"[1]

Taken together, however, these two scenes mark a decisive rupture in the history of the ruin. From the Enlightenment through the early nineteenth century, ruins were identified with the idea that every empire traversed a cyclical course. More specifically they denoted that cycle's final stage, the aftermath of its dissolution, by which time its legacy had passed on to an emerging empire elsewhere. As citizens of a republic that was at an earlier stage of its political, economic, territorial, and urban development, Americans assumed themselves—and were assumed by Europeans—to be spatially, temporally, and temperamentally distant from ruins, even if they still needed to heed their warnings. Not until this cyclical paradigm was superseded by new conceptions of temporality in the early nineteenth century did American ruins—and an American cult of the ruin—materialize. Paradoxically, the ascendancy of a new liberal confidence in infinite progress and a millennial faith in a glorious end-time excited interest in these melancholy emblems—above all, the broken or detached column—across a variety of spheres, from painting, poetry, and political oratory, to material culture, amateur archaeology, landscape design, and especially travel writing. It was while traveling through New York State on the Northern Tour, the American equivalent of the Grand Tour, that Americans and Europeans increasingly observed—or imagined—various scenes of ruin.

But despite their efforts to reconcile the ruin with new liberal and millennial visions of the nation's future, for instance by appropriating and adapting eighteenth-century aesthetic and political ideas, American artists and writers could not fully domesticate its meanings. The rapid urban and economic growth that followed the opening of the Erie Canal's first section in 1819 produced unintended ruins that resisted recuperation into dominant discourses of progress, or any recognized model of historical time. Accounts of these newer ruins littering the shores of the canal from Albany to Buffalo recur as disruptive moments within the narratives of European and American travelers.

The Cycles of Empire

Tocqueville's account of that "enchanted" site of a ruined clearing in the American wilderness could be—and has been—written off as the indulgence of a passing "romantic idea" peripheral to the more serious themes of *Democracy in America*. The letters, notebook entries, and drafts he wrote en route, but never published, imply that he and his companion Gustave de Beaumont, had taken a detour from their investigations of American democracy to satisfy a literary whim. As a child, Tocqueville had read a Romantic tale titled *Voyage . . . au lac Onéida*, based on an apocryphal account of an actual French nobleman—Louis des Watines—who had fled the 1789 Revolution with his wife and begun a new life in the New World wilderness. The unnamed island visited that day—July 8, 1831—was Frenchman's Island, on Lake Oneida in northwestern New York, confirmed by a local to have been the home of a French couple. The wife had since died, the husband mysteriously disappeared, and the cabin disintegrated. Satisfied that this was in fact the nobleman's refuge, the travelers lingered several hours, savoring the site's poetic sensations, "visit[ing] its smallest ruins, and listen[ing] to the icy silence that now reigns in its shadows" (fig. 1.2). They even observed the standard romantic ritual of engraving their names on a nearby plane tree before resuming their itinerary.[2] Recounted in *Democracy in America* four years later, these ruins were stripped of their historical context and presented as an accidental discovery, yet they

Fig. 1.2. Gustave de Beaumont, "View of Lake Oneida from Frenchman's Island" (dated July 8, 1831). Pen and ink. From Beaumont's Second Sketchbook, Box B.III.c, MS Vault Tocqueville, Beinecke Rare Book and Manuscript Library, Yale University.

still prompted similar romantic commonplaces about the triumph of nature, the ineluctability of time, and the "feebleness of man" (284).[3] Such effusions might be expected in accounts of Roman remains on the European Grand Tour, a rite of passage for young aristocrats, but not in a philosophical treatise on the political and social institutions of the United States.

But far from considering the episode a diversion from his itinerary and his larger inquiry, Tocqueville believed it crucial. In his pocket notebook that day he ranked it the "most vividly interest[ing] and mov[ing]" of all his travel experiences, and in a letter to his sister several days later insisted she would "dream of it for a week."[4] The excursion marked a critical reversal in the early weeks of his ten-month tour, when Tocqueville began to question his assumptions about the importance of natural resources—in this case, America's pristine, untapped landscapes—in perpetuating a democratic republic. The scene may initially have testified to the fecundity of nature there, indeed a nature so fecund it overwhelms man-made structures as violently as wars and revolutions had in Europe. But by the time it reappears in *Democracy in America*, the ruined cabin on Lake Oneida has come to represent less the natural conditions of America than the cultural habits of its population: specifically that spirit of restless acquisitiveness and rampant individualism that drives so many Americans to uproot themselves repeatedly, to break whatever "ties of attachment [they have] to their native soil" for new lands and profits farther west. The ruins are thus reenvisioned as the sign of "man advanc[ing] so quickly that the wilderness closes in again behind him" (283). If he had previously romanticized this spot as the final refuge of a French nobleman fleeing revolution, he now represents it as just one of many "ruined cabins in the remotest solitude" left behind by American settlers, merely for the "gamble" or "sensations" of movement (283). Whereas such "restless passions" would be considered "great social dangers" in Europe, this very spirit of mobility assures the republic a "long and peaceful future" by draining a growing population away from overcrowded eastern cities (284). Confirming this scene's importance, Tocqueville inserted it into what historians consider the book's most important chapter, the one that summarizes "The Main Causes Tending to Maintain a Democratic Republic in the United States" and ultimately emphasizes the role of cultural habits and customs (*moeurs*, or mores) over the material circumstances of climate and geography and the constitutional powers and laws of the state.[5]

If that desolate clearing on Lake Oneida designates a watershed in Tocqueville's thinking about the sustainability of the American democratic project, it may also indicate a turning point in the history of the ruin in Western culture, comparable to the discovery of Asian and Mesoamerican ruins. Neither the classic eighteenth-century treatises on the poetics, aesthetics, and philosophy of the ruin, nor his own account of Roman antiquities in his previous *Voyage en Sicile*, could have fully prepared him for the unexpected sight of ruins in the wilds of New York.[6] His erasure of the anecdote about the French nobleman betrays the difficulty of imposing conventional meanings and narratives upon the "day-old ruins" of the American frontier. A "modern wooden ruin" in the North American wilderness, observed a contemporaneous Canadian writer, departs from the classical ruins of Europe insofar as it bears "no historical importance," inspires no "poet" or "antiquary," and holds no aesthetic appeal (resembling a "mangled corpse" in its "rank and rapid decay"); it bespeaks only "recent use and temporary habitation."[7] But Tocqueville did not abandon the task of reading historical significance into American ruins. Whereas European ruins signified the tragic dissipation of empires or violent overthrow of monarchies or monasteries (the relentless advances of equality and democracy, "even now going forward amid the ruins it has itself created," aroused a "kind of religious dread" in Tocqueville [*Democracy*, 12]), American ruins appeared to embody the vital energy that guarantees "a long and peaceful future." They were signs not of past failures but of future profits. And while comparable to those barbarian "irruptions which caused the fall of the Roman Empire," this westward migration that scatters so many ruins in its wake is precisely the reverse: the descent not of barbarians upon a civilized land, but of "civilized" men upon a "barbarian" land (280–81, 302–3, 330–31).

Tocqueville's experience on Lake Oneida may thus have led him to question the moral and historical meanings ascribed to the ruin by the Enlightenment *philosophes* of the preceding century, some of whose works accompanied him on his American tour.[8] To the *philosophes*, and the Florentine Renaissance historians before them, ruins were intelligible only through a cyclical framework of universal history. According to historical laws of rise and decline that paralleled the natural laws of life and death, every great civilization is born, gradually approaches maturity, then succumbs to decrepitude and death. "Almost all the nations of the world travel this circle," wrote Montesquieu (whom Tocqueville read daily while in America); "to begin with, they are barbarous; they become conquerors and well-ordered nations; this order permits them to grow, and they become refined; refinement enfeebles them, and they return to barbarism" (101). This cyclical metahistory was at once disturbing in its constraints on the potentiality of nations, and yet comforting in its assurance of the future's predictability, an idea that departed from the medieval resignation to the random reversals of *fortuna*. Ruins served not only as memorials to past civilizations and reminders of the transience and *vanitas* [emptiness] of all worldly endeavors but also as specific object lessons for the present. Crumbling arches, weathered friezes, and above all broken columns, while derived from the architectural vocabulary of Ancient Greece and Rome, could convey timely warnings about the imminent dangers of virtue's corruption by commerce and luxury, the overextension of territories and armies, the division into separate classes and castes, the contagion of national hubris, and not least the expansion of large cities—with their scenes of profligacy, poverty, and depravity.[9]

According to that schedule of universal history, France still had some time to go before reaching its appointed hour of dissolution, and further centuries would be required to ripen its abandoned monuments into aesthetically satisfying ruins. For *philosophes* confident in the patterns of cyclical history, genuine ruins could not turn up unexpectedly in the present. The *Encyclopédiste* Denis Diderot reaffirmed this axiom in comparing the ruinscapes of two French painters at the Salon exhibition of the Royal Academy in 1767.[10] Hubert Robert, by skillfully depicting ancient Roman monuments in varying states of decay and reuse (fig. 1.3), provoked that metaphysical reverie unique to the "poetics of ruins," in which we "retreat into ourselves; we contemplate the ravages of time, and in our imagination we scatter the rubble of the very buildings in which we live" (197). His paintings thus stimulated those "grand" reflections about how "everything comes to nothing, everything perishes,

Fig. 1.3. Hubert Robert, *The Old Temple*, 1787/88. Oil on canvas, 100 x 88 inches. Gift of Adolphus C. Bartlett, 1900.382. Reproduction, The Art Institute of Chicago. This is a variation of the lost painting, *Large Gallery Lit from Its Far End* (1760), one of several ruinscapes Robert exhibited, and Diderot viewed, at the Salon of 1767. While commending this painting for its "sublime ruins," Diderot complained that there were "too many figures here," compromising the "effect of solitude and silence" (*Salon of 1767*, 198).

everything passes"—a "general law" of decay and dissolution that cannot be resisted by stone and bronze, let alone flesh (198, 199). But if Robert's ruinscapes transported Diderot at once into a distant past and a distant future, those of another academician, Pierre-Antoine de Machy, left him mired in the present. De Machy had unwisely chosen to depict the recent ruins of some half-demolished Parisian buildings of the 1760s (fig. 1.4). Even though he

Fig. 1.4. Pierre-Antoine De Machy, *Demolishing the* [buildings obscuring the] *Colonnade of the Louvre in 1764* (1764). © Gianni Dagli Orti/CORBIS. A similar version, titled *The Louvre Peristyle and the Demolition of the Hôtel de Rouille*, erased the *démolisseurs* and transformed the eviscerated building into an antique, enfoliated ruin. Exhibited at the Salon of 1767 alongside one of Robert's classical ruinscapes, it was reviewed (unfavorably) by Diderot.

had "intelligen[tly]" concealed signs of contemporaneity such as the "massive, tasteless, masonry foundation" of the Louvre in the background, effectively disguising a demolition site as a classical landscape, his *vedute* still struck Diderot as anomalous and anachronistic—out of place and time. The banal effect of such "brand new ruins," if they could be called ruins at all, was also a product of his literalistic style and bland palate of "grey or straw-yellow" (137–38). Whereas "de Machy's ruins are modern," Robert's are imaginatively conceived, fluently painted, skillfully illuminated, and above all "eroded by time" (220). In his advice to future "painters of ruins," Diderot encouraged even more scrupulous attention to locality and historicity. For all the restless pleasures of the imagination, representations of ruins must be properly rooted in space and time to avoid the confusion that marred de Machy's work. "Travel to the ends of the earth," he advised, "but make it so that I always know where you are, be it in Greece, in Egypt, in Alexandria, or in Rome . . . make it impossible for me to mistake the date of your monument . . . specify the place, morals, period, customs, and persons in question. Make sure that in this sense your ruins are informed by erudition" (217).

Of all the "ends of the earth," French philosophers would least have expected ruins at its westward end. If monarchical France was far from the final stages of its cycle, colonial America was even further. Its youthfulness was believed to be embodied in its "noble savages" and its pristine landscapes—indigenous mounds hardly counting as *ruins*, a term restricted in Diderot's *Encyclopédie* to "palaces, sumptuous tombs, or public monuments."[11] French travelers and settlers in America corroborated this notion of a transatlantic time lag. Hector St. John de Crèvecoeur's "farmer," writing on the eve of the Revolution, cited his minister's observation that Rome's "musty ruins" transport the imagination back to the ancient past, whereas America's "spectacle" of landscapes unscarred by "revolutions, desolations, and plagues" propels it "forward to the anticipated fields of future cultivation and improvement." Even the demolished buildings left behind by the British army in the 1780s were "the image of a transient misfortune," wrote the philosopher and general, the Marquis de Chastellux, not the ruins of "long adversity." As late as 1827, the Romantic traveler François-René de Chateaubriand, for whom the traumas of revolution inspired a new, post-Enlightenment sensitivity to recent as well as ancient ruins—could still find few of either in America. The United States was historically thin, he observed; its "society . . . has no past; the towns are new, the tombs are of yesterday."[12] It was Tocqueville's familiarity with these writings—especially those of his uncle, Chateaubriand—that would have prompted his surprise at finding "ruins so soon" in what he had imagined as a pristine landscape. In the very chapter that describes Oneida's ruins, Tocqueville reasserts that urban growth—another critical development through which "democratic republics" tend to "perish"—had hardly begun in the United States, a country still lacking "any great capital" or metropolis (278–79, and n.).

The association of ruins with a cyclical theory of history, and the belief that the United States remained unblemished by such stains of time, were ideas that Thomas Cole would also have recognized. In May 1835, while already at work on the *The Course of Empire*, he delivered a lecture to the New York Lyceum extolling "American Scenery" precisely for not being "besprinkled with venerated ruins." Its appeal lay in vast scenes of "wildness" that represent a "primitive" stage no longer visible in "civilized Europe," and in pastoral scenes of "flourishing towns, and neat villas" that conveyed future potentiality. The absence of ruins was not to be lamented but celebrated, as an index of the still uncorrupted state of the American republic: "You see no ruined tower to tell of outrage—no gorgeous temple to speak of ostentation; but freedom's offspring—peace, security, and happiness, dwell there, the spirits of the scene."[13]

It was the innocence of the national landscape, "that wilder image" of American scenery, that the poet William Cullen Bryant had famously urged Cole not to forget when, five years earlier, he embarked for the timeworn landscapes and "ruins" of Europe.[14] The counterpart to this vision was the certainty of ultimate corruption through the growth of cities and the decline of farming. In a rough, unpublished manuscript of a story that anticipates the science fiction apocalypses of this book's final chapter, Cole narrated the violence, anarchy, and sectarianism that would erupt at the end of the twentieth century, when America's "vast continent . . . was peopled with . . . hundreds of millions," its "last broad prairie" sacrificed to the plow, and its coastlines, lakefronts, and riverbanks crowded with "uncounted dwellings."[15]

At first glance, Cole's *Course of Empire* seems to be an unequivocal expression of this cyclical theory of history. In dramatizing some unspecified classical civilization in five acts—from its "savage" origins depicted in the prologue, through its "pastoral" phase and then its "consummation" as a prosperous, imperial state, to a finale of "destruction" and epilogue of "desolation"—he appears to have rendered Montesquieu's inexorable circle in visual, or rather theatrical, form. Cole would certainly have been familiar with the cyclical philosophy of history, if not from French *philosophes* then from British sources. His first three "States" closely conform, in compressed form, to the four stages of "hunting," "pasturage," "agriculture," and "commerce" theorized by Adam Ferguson, Lord Kames, and other figures of the late eighteenth-century Scottish Enlightenment.[16] His title directly acknowledges the Irish philosopher, Bishop Berkeley, whose poem "On the Prospect of Planting Arts and Learning in America" (1726) adapted the medieval concept of *translatio imperii* to assert that as one nation falls to ruin, its legacy is transferred to the "virgin earth" and "happy climes" of a new nation farther west, in accordance with the inexorable "course of empire."[17] The influence of subsequent poetic reinterpretations of the theme of imperial decline and fall are evident in Cole's motto for the series; he borrowed the words "First Freedom, and then Glory—when that fails, / Wealth, vice, corruption" from the fourth canto of Lord Byron's romantic epic, *Childe Harold's Pilgrimage* (1812–18), omitting (for reasons we will later surmise) the final words of the second line, "barbarism at last." His original working title, "The Cycle of Mutation," also suggests he was reflecting on the ephemerality of all civilizations.[18] And his iconography similarly follows precedent: the solitary column of *Desolation* was as conventional an emblem of the fallen empire as the shepherd was of its pastoral origins.

Cole was by no means the first to introduce this theme into American aesthetic or political culture. The French and British vocabulary of cyclical history had become embedded in the political language of eighteenth-century

Americans, providing the terms in which they articulated their independence. Patriots regularly denounced—and occasionally depicted—the British imperial monarchy in Montesquieuian terms, as an edifice despoiled by commerce or "luxury" and thus reduced to a "mighty ruin of a once noble fabrick." Although the colonies still retained their youthfulness—as evinced by their agricultural footing, low population density, truncated social structure, and above all small cities—they were in danger of becoming prematurely aged by the germs of decay infecting the mother country. To preserve their juvenescent virtue intact, they would have to seize the "Machiavellian moment"—that *kairotic* instant in which the formation or survival of a republic hung in the balance—and cut themselves free. And if the British Empire were not already a ruin, it would certainly become so with the secession of its colonies (fig. 1.5). Within this republican paradigm, such a "revolution" retained its original sense of a "rolling backward" (from the Latin *revolvere*). More than simply a radical upheaval, it denoted a setting back of the colonies' historical clock—not to a Lockean state of nature, but to that semideveloped phase in a republic's life history when agrarian virtue still held commercial corruption in check.[19]

Even after the revolution, Jeffersonian Republicans demanded unceasing vigilance against fresh agents of decay and ruin, whether in the guise of

Fig. 1.5. *The Royal Hunt, or a Prospect of the Year 1782*, 1782. Pen and wash. 9 x 13 inches. Courtesy National Maritime Museum, Greenwich, London. Sketch for a caricature published by R. Owen, of Fleet Street, London. Caption in the printed version reads: "The Temple of Fame, formerly the Wonder of the World, but now in Ruins." British politicians in the foreground witness the literal dismantling of the British Empire. America is one of the columns lying on the ground.

British mercantilism overseas or Federalist plans for large-scale manufacturing at home. If the former hindered America's efforts to sell its agricultural surpluses in foreign markets, the latter threatened to accelerate the emergence of those "great cities" whose "mobs" Jefferson famously likened to cankerous "sores." Republicans did retain some hope of slowing down the historical clock, or staying the hand of time, through various remedial policies. To prolong the agrarian stage, they called for the acquisition of new territories that could sustain future generations of yeoman farmers. Thus, despite Montesquieuian warnings about outsized republics and overextended empires, they advocated expansion across *space* as the means to decelerate development through *time*. Jefferson believed that if industrial and urban development were forestalled, the new republic could "remain virtuous for many centuries."[20] But ultimately these policies could only defer the inevitable. Sooner or later, he and others cautioned, they would come up against the ruinous effects of those natural and universal laws of commercial, demographic, and urban growth; not even the American republic could escape history altogether.[21] Thus, even as Americans celebrated the Roman Republic as a source for their own political oratory, sculptural iconography, and constitutional arrangements, they also cited the fate of the Roman Empire as a historical lesson of how liberty, by inducing imperial growth, ensures its own demise.[22]

Given this ongoing preoccupation with the fragility of republics, ruins functioned in postrevolutionary America more as emblems of political peril than objects of aesthetic pleasure. Political prints allegorized the task of forging a federal government architecturally, in terms of the urgent construction of a vast, usually domed, neoclassical edifice that would only be as strong as its supports, namely the columns representing each state. Thus, when Rhode Island initially rejected the constitution in 1788, a political cartoonist depicted it as a fallen and disintegrated pillar, while hoping (despite uncertainty regarding North Carolina's ratification) that the overarching "national DOME" "may yet be SAVED" by the soundness of its foundations (fig. 1.6). The more the ruin served as a cautionary trope for the political dangers of tyranny or dissension, the more its sentimental seductions needed to be disavowed. It became almost an oath of patriotism to denounce the veneration of ruins as decadent and aristocratic, and thus anathema to virtuous republicans. An indication of this renunciation may be gleaned from the American reprintings of John Aikin's *Letters from a Father to His Son* (1792–93). One letter warns the son against succumbing to the "extraordinary passion for ruins," an aesthetic taste that has become the "rage of a predominant fashion, and goes beyond all bounds of sober judgment." Only in an age of overrefinement could objects that once

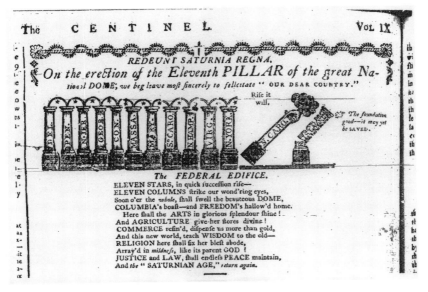

Fig. 1.6. "The Federal Edifice," *The Massachusetts Centinel* 9, no. 40 (1788): 160.

conveyed "waste, and desolation" come to be appreciated as objects of beauty, or "melancholy" become a "source of pleasure."[23]

It is this classical republican discourse, within which the ruin functioned not as a frivolous aesthetic diversion but as a solemn, didactic object signifying the ultimate fate of all republics, that art historians have consistently detected in Cole's *Course of Empire*. Drawing on his letters to patrons and statements outlining his program, and pointing to such pictorial elements as the waxing and waning of the sun and seasons from one canvas to the next, they have interpreted the series as the definitive allegorical restatement of that eighteenth-century philosophy of cyclical history.[24] This philosophy may have appealed to Cole, and for a variety of reasons. As a weighty and universal theme, it allowed him to elevate landscape painting—then considered less prestigious than religious or history painting—to the "higher style" of "*historical* landscape."[25] And as a theme that required not one canvas but several, it allowed him to demonstrate his versatile command of diverse European influences: Salvator Rosa's romantic wildernesses in the first canvas, Claude Lorrain's pastoral idylls in the second, John Martin's *Destruction of Tyre* in the fourth, and Turner's *Building of Carthage* and *Fall of Carthage* in the third and fifth. But above all, the theme is believed to have served a political purpose for Cole. It enabled him to voice his supposedly "pessimistic" sense of the current direction of the United States, now under threat of corruption not by the British monarchy but by the unrestrained economic expansion, social flux, and political factionalism he identified with Andrew Jackson's Democratic movement of the 1830s. The commander who triumphantly returns to the imperial capital in *Consummation*, laden with bounty and slaves, and honored with a spectacular parade of senators, priests, and civilians, has been identified as an allegory of Jackson himself, who similarly rose to power through his military conquests, presided over the distribution of the "spoils" of political office, and was branded a "King" or "Caesar" by his Whig opponents.[26] The architectural and engineering achievements that frame the scene (and recall the neoclassical structures then under construction in Washington) thus mark not the attainment of a state of perfection but the first seeds of decay and ruin. As expressions of imperial expansion and rampant materialism, such massive ornamental edifices are a perversion of the simple agrarian virtues of the *Pastoral State*, and as such, are already doomed. Situated within this cyclical framework of historical time, the solitary column of the final scene of *Desolation* stands as an apparent reminder of the fixed laws of rise and fall that govern all states, even the United States.

Sermons in Stone

Yet even as Jacksonian-era writers, orators, and artists reiterated the classical vocabulary and iconography of the cycles of empire and the ruins of time, the emergence of new political philosophies had subtly altered their meaning. As early as the 1780s, constitutional theorists such as James Madison had begun to chip away at the edifice of classical republicanism, undermining its foundational assumptions—chiefly, the embodiment of civic "virtue" by a "natural aristocracy" of disinterested, landed gentlemen acting on behalf of a larger public or "commonweal"—and constructing alongside it a new, liberal-democratic paradigm resting on an equilibrium of competing individuals acting in their own "interests," and on the subordination of politicians to the sovereignty of "the people."[27] But it was during the subsequent market revolution that the underlying republican equation of commerce with inevitable decay was ruthlessly dismantled. Unable to account for the sustained economic growth that began in the 1790s, the classical, historically derived models of political economy were discredited in favor of liberal models (chiefly Adam Smith's) that discerned a timeless nature and order in the workings of the market.[28] It now became possible to reconceptualize commerce as a dynamic, progressive force that was compatible with liberty, thus potentially releasing America altogether from the closed circle of republican temporality. At first, the enunciation of this more confident notion of time as endless progress was partial and hesitant, punctuated by frequent relapses into the entropic *mentalité* of classical republicanism. But by the 1810s, even some Jeffersonians—notably John Calhoun, Henry Clay, and DeWitt Clinton—embraced an essentially Federalist platform of enterprise, manufacturing, and internal improvements (or public works), leading to the formation of a pro-development, pro-urban National Republican Party in the late 1820s.[29] Proclaiming a new era of commercial expansion, these politicians were less likely to consider classical antiquity a direct template for future action. Some even went so far as to eschew the ruin altogether as politically as well as aesthetically irrelevant to their ascendant nation.[30]

Despite the collapse of its cyclical and metahistorical tenets, classical republicanism's rhetorical and iconographical investments—most notably in the figure of the ruin—were not jettisoned altogether but redeployed to a variety of new conceptions of temporality.[31] The rearticulation of the ruin can be discerned most clearly in the transformation of the meanings of *translatio imperii*, or the transit of empire. In speeches and sermons during and immediately after the revolution, the *translatio* connoted the immensity and urgency, as much as the historical legitimacy, of the task confronting Americans. That the "course" of civilization from "east to west" would eventuate in the "future glory of America" remained, for John Witherspoon, president of the College of New Jersey in 1776, "a matter rather of conjecture than certainty"; it would depend on the soundness of their "cause," "conduct," and "principles."[32] And whether contingent or guaranteed, the inheritance of Rome's legacy would likely be a mixed blessing. In the wake of the westerly drift of empire, wrote the scientist David Rittenhouse in 1775, there would blow the corrupting winds of "*luxury* and her constant follower *tyranny*." "Our connections with Europe" may bring about great "advances," he continued, "but by those connections too, in all probability, our fall will be premature."[33] As in the original conception of the ecclesiastical chroniclers of the Middle Ages, the *translatio* still implied a *cyclical* repetition of rising and declining empires (each one falling ever shorter of the glories of Rome), even as it claimed a *linear* trajectory of authority leading to and thus legitimating the present order: whether the Western or Eastern Roman Empire, the Holy Roman Empire, or the new Rome of the western hemisphere, Jefferson's "Empire of Liberty."

By the 1830s, however, authors and orators invoking the *translatio* placed greater emphasis on the vector of progress subtending the fluctuations of fortune. Bishop Berkeley's 1726 poem, with its unqualified declaration of faith in the New World as "Time's noblest offspring," thus became the exemplary expression of the *translatio*. Although written a century earlier to promote a college he hoped (but failed) to found in Bermuda, the poem was ubiquitously deployed in American patriotic schoolbooks, western booster treatises, commemorative orations, and amateur poems, as well as landscape paintings.[34] The Jacksonian *Democratic Review*, above all, set about realigning the ruin to this new faith in the future. The sight of "some lone column" on the site where "the stateliest palaces" once stood, wrote one of its essayists, may appear to embody only the vicissitudes of fortune, but in fact testifies to the "operation" of a higher "principle," namely "the great law of Progress." "One after another the generations may pass from the stage of action . . . —empires may sink in ruin—and whole nations be swept from the face of the earth . . . but the course of the whole race is still onward," culminating in the efflorescence of "freedom" in the New World. Thus, if human history could still be compared to a turning wheel, it was not the "mill-wheel which, impelled by the current, revolves for ever with ceaseless din, while remaining in one place," but rather "that which bore the Olympic charioteer . . . to the goal of his ardent desire." Instead of the cycles of empires rising and falling in succession, the author emphasized only the upward (and westward) spiral of progress.[35]

The *Democratic Review*, among other magazines, worked not only to linearize but also to Americanize the *translatio*. If that concept had once expressed the idea that each empire was simply another chapter in the book of universal history, this latest chapter was now considered worthy of a separate volume altogether. Writers marshaled a variety of reasons in support of this emerging exceptionalist claim that in crossing the Atlantic the transit of empire was entering a unique phase. As this was a transit not only of mature ideas and beliefs but also of already "civilized" people, America had no need to embark from a state of infancy but could "commenc[e]" its course "in manhood."[36] These distinguishing factors, combined with the buffer zone of the Atlantic Ocean, the superabundance and fertility of its land, and the invigorating climate, guaranteed that America would not merely emulate Rome but surpass it altogether. Ruins could thus be embraced as emblems of the very failures of past civilization that America was certain to overcome.

This nationalization of the *translatio* required further modifications to its spatial and temporal coordinates. In the first place, its geographical itinerary had to be rerouted. Brushing aside predictions that the circuit of empire would either terminate in Europe (as in Hegel's philosophy of world history), or else continue its circumnavigation all the way to China, perhaps even returning to its point of origin in Asia Minor, American proponents now insisted that it would come to its final resting point in their own country.[37] At the same time, they relaxed the temporal terms of the *translatio* so as to grant America immunity from the ultimate fate suffered by other empires. In an 1835 article,

"The Downfall of Nations," the *Knickerbocker Magazine* surveyed the ruins of Athens, Sparta, Rome, and Carthage, yet confidently concluded that "America will long bear evidence of the fact, that republics *can* endure: that the enlightened condition of a community insures the perpetuity of her institutions." Where earlier empires were content to erect monuments of degradable stone and mortar, intoned the *Boston Lyceum* in 1827, America fashioned hers out of the abstract ideal of "American freedom" itself, an ideal so pure that they would prove more durable than even the "storm-beaten pyramids of Egypt."[38] No material "misfortunes" wrought by wars, declared Webster five years later, but only the breakup of the Union could reduce the "well-proportioned columns of constitutional liberty" to ruin; and as irretrievable ruins, those fallen columns would arouse "bitterer tears" than those spilled over any Greek or Roman remains.[39] The potential indestructibility of the American republic was embodied in the figure of a solitary classical column, such as the one in the foreground of Cole's *Desolation*, which remains intact rather than broken. In an earlier Independence Day oration, the New York Democrat and early Zionist Mordecai Noah likened the American republic to "a golden column" that has been "spared by the hand of time." "Standing firmly erect," it is "surrounded by the crumbling fragments of other republics."[40]

The most crucial of all revisions of the *translatio*, however, was its recuperation into American millennial religious beliefs. Overcoming their misgivings about a discourse that foregrounded Rome rather than Jerusalem as the source and spirit of world history, millennialists set about reinterpreting the *translatio* as a prophecy of Christ's Second Coming in America.[41] This was a westward transit of the Gospel, propelled not by men or natural laws but by the grace of God. It was foretold both in New Testament allusions to "the lightning [that] cometh out of the east and shineth even unto the west" as signaling the return of Christ (Matthew 24:27), and in Old Testament references such as King Nebuchadnezzar's dream of a colossus made of gold, silver, brass, iron, and clay, interpreted by Daniel as representing the historical empires that would fall one by one, to be succeeded by a final "kingdom" of God that "shall stand forever" (Daniel 2:31–45). Virtue could now be imagined not as innately corruptible but as ultimately perfectible, consummated through apocalypse.

It was this religio-nationalist conception of history, more than the secular historiography of classical republicanism, that shaped contemporaneous interpretations of Cole's *Course of Empire*. Many antebellum critics took the series to depict the spiritual descent of past empires from the rustic religion of the *Pastoral State* to the opulent priesthood in the foreground of *Consummation*. Their downfall thus cleared the way for an American nation erected upon the secure bedrock of Protestant faith. The *New York Mirror*'s art correspondent advised American viewers to take comfort from the fact that "when the lust to destroy shall cease, and the arts, the sciences, and the ambition to excel in all good shall characterize man, instead of the pride of the triumph, or the desire of conquests, then will the empire of love be permanent." Even Cole's close friend Louis Legrand Noble situated *The Course of Empire* within a millennial framework. This "drama," he wrote, depicted the fate of "man acting only within the lines of this world, without a recognition of the future state brought to light in the gospel." Noble considered the series the prequel to Cole's final, unfinished religious allegories, which would close "not with the decay of ruins and the sleep of the tomb, but with the repose of Glory and Immortality." As a counterpoint to the monotonous cycles of earthly empires, he saw Cole's final canvases as charting the "Course of Sacred Empire."[42]

These viewers and reviewers, however, were not rewriting the intended meaning of *The Course of Empire*, but decoding the millennial signs Cole embedded within it. A devout Christian (although not an evangelical), Cole may have intended the last canvas of this series to represent the advent of the millennium, the actual moment when human history would take its final, apocalyptic turn.[43] Evidence of that intention is to be found in two key absences. By deciding not to include nomadic figures in *Desolation*, and deleting "barbarism at last" from his Byronic motto, Cole frustrates any attempt to imagine a further cycle of empire transpiring after the final act of this drama. He resists, that is, any expectation that the "Savage State" of a new nation would succeed the "Desolation" of the old.[44] The sense that this might be the conclusion to the last republic in history, the fulfillment of America's divine task of preparing the way for the Second Coming of Christ, is also supported by various smaller details Cole did include—millennial allusions overlooked by art historians. The bird nesting on top of the foreground column was an image conventionally associated with apocalyptic visions, most famously the biblical prophecy that Nineveh will be destroyed and "the cormorant and the bittern shall lodge in the upper lintels" of its columns (Zephaniah 2:14). The water level, noticeably higher than in the previous stages, suggests the advent of the Second Deluge identified in the Gospel of Matthew with the Second Coming (Matthew 24:34–39). And the loose boulder (or "rocking stone") crowning the mountain in the background of *Desolation*, as in the other four canvases, may well be the apocalyptic agent mentioned in the Book of Daniel: that massive stone, "cut out of the mountain without hands," that would at the appointed time descend and shatter the colossus representing the empires of human history (Daniel 2:45).

Resituated within this millennial framework, ruins no longer needed to be apprehended as melancholy emblems of the political and moral corruptibility of republics. The fall of the American republic would be a fortunate one, signaling the consummation of its spiritual errand. Several writers thus reclaimed the ruin as a device inducing sentimental rather than gloomy feelings in Christian minds. "*Ancient ruins*," wrote the *Christian Register* in 1829, were "among the inanimate objects that speak with the most powerful appeal to the imagination and feelings." But the emotions they conveyed were entirely positive: rather than evoking the "discord" of death, they resonated with the "harmony" of the afterlife; rather than signs of men's failures, they were gifts from God, "wisely and mercifully adapted to our happiness." Above all, decay threw into relief the immortality promised on the Day of Judgment. Man's architectural works may become irretrievable ruins, the *Western Luminary* proclaimed, but man's own bodily ruins are redeemable; with Christ's return, they "shall be restored" to life. Even the destruction of whole cities merely underscored the indestructibility of the City of God. This was the lesson derived by the *Christian Index* in an article reinterpreting the "course of empire" theme for a burgeoning Protestant nation. Anticipating Cole's series, its author outlined "Three States" that might be witnessed on a single, given "spot": first, of undefiled nature, then of urban sophistication, and finally of "decay and desolation." It is the last of these scenes, the only one that America does not "furnis[h]," that is most relevant to its Christian citizens. In a city's ruins they would "find lessons which its hour of holiday did not furnish," namely that "there is but one Being that is constant; one city that is immutable; one treasure that cannot corrode."[45]

Millennial meanings such as these made *The Course of Empire* surprisingly palatable to nineteenth-century Americans. Many critics found the final scene more pleasurable than those that preceded it, and one even singled it out as "one of the most remarkable productions of American art."[46] *Desolation* was sometimes detached from the series altogether, hung on its own in exhibitions, and effectively transformed into a self-contained devotional relic, a symbol of Protestant sentimental piety. When it was exhibited in 1848 at New York's American Art-Union Gallery, a critic noted how its "calm and holy stillness entered into our hearts," neglecting the violent depredations that had left this imperial city in ruins.[47] The celebration of that painting was rooted in a more general predilection for the sentimental associations of detached or broken columns. During these years, as sentimental rituals and accessories of mourning were supplanting Calvinist conceptions of death, the broken shaft was introduced into cemetery iconography—especially for tombstones of those who died young, their lives cut short (fig. 1.7).[48] A decaying column also served as an attribute of elderliness in paintings of the "ages of man," such as Asher Durand's *The Evening of Life* (1840) (fig. 1.8). And also at this time the broken

JOHN TAPPAN'S MONUMENT. LOT 307.

At the junction of Linden and Narcissus Paths is a broken shaft, as an emblem of an unfinished course of life; with a rose bush limb, from which five of its flowers and buds have been broken off, leaving five roses on the principal stem; betokening the number of the social circle alive and deceased.

Fig. 1.7. John Tappan's Monument, Mount Auburn Cemetery, Cambridge, Massachusetts. From Nathaniel S. Dearborn, *Dearborn's Guide through Mount Auburn* (Boston: Dearborn, 1857), 48.

Fig. 1.8. Asher B. Durand, *Evening of Life* (detail), 1840. Oil on canvas. 49 3/8 x 83 3/8 inches. National Academy Museum, New York, Gift of Mrs. Frederick J. Betts, 1911 (387-P).

column became a central hieroglyphic symbol of the Masonic movement, to which Cole belonged; appearing on ceremonial prints, bookplates, brooches, aprons, and carpets, and usually accompanied by an open book, hourglass, and weeping virgin, it denoted either the attainment of a master mason's degree, the death of a Masonic leader, or the antiquity of Masonry itself (fig. 1.9).[49] Whereas an earlier generation had preferred the Doric column's "republican simplicity" and "masculine vigor," Masonic iconography and Cole's *Desolation* featured the more luxurious and ornate Corinthian order, which evoked the "delicacy of form, and gaiety of dress of a Grecian maiden."[50] Together, this simultaneous sentimentalization, Christianization, and feminization of the ruin facilitated its gradual assimilation into middle-class American culture.

Fig. 1.9. Amos Doolittle, illustration of broken column, virgin, and Father Time, in R. W. Jeremy L. Cross, *The True Masonic Chart, Or Hieroglyphic Monitor* (1819; New Haven, CT: Cross, 1826), fig. 18. Courtesy University of Chicago Library, Special Collections Research Center.

Surrogate Antiquities: Answering the Trollopizers

Middle-class Americans' growing *Ruinenlust* was evident not only in the favorable reception of paintings such as Cole's but also in the practice of traveling to the actual sites of European remains. The same year Tocqueville was in
America, Cole was touring Europe, lured (like other American artists) as much
by its ruins as by its galleries. Of all the "things" in Rome, its antiquities "most
affect me," he declared in a letter to his parents; and he stressed the importance of viewing them in the flesh rather than mediated through second-hand
reproductions: "None but those who can see the remains can form an idea of
what Ancient Rome was." It was there, while sitting on "the fragments of a
column" one evening in a state of "silent, mournful pleasure," that he claimed
to have conceived, in Gibbonesque fashion, the epic that was to become *The
Course of Empire*.[51]

   The American art colonies that materialized across Europe in the late 1820s
and early 1830s provided a kind of liminal space in which the aesthetic and
poetic pleasures of the ruin could be indulged at a safe remove from more
suspicious compatriots.[52] Although by no means the first Americans to visit
monuments of Roman antiquity, these travelers and expatriates were arguably
the first to emphasize their intrinsic romance and beauty as ruins. When Jefferson wrote of being "nourished with the remains of Roman grandeur" during
his European travels of the late 1780s, his interest had been largely academic,
as he painstakingly reconstructed the orders of classical architecture from its
surviving fragments. He thus preferred the better-preserved Roman structures,
above all the temple known as the Maison Carrée in Nîmes, to those that were
reduced to "feeble remains," "defaced" by "Barbarians" of the Middle Ages, or
overgrown with vegetation.[53] But a generation later, American travelers articulated a fascination with the ruin for its own sake, as an object of beauty and
mystery not despite but because of its dilapidation. Affective responses thus
supplanted, or at least supplemented, intellectual and antiquarian ones.

   This trend conforms to a larger transformation in the perception of monuments in Western culture, as theorized in 1903 by Alois Riegl, a Viennese art
historian (and an influence on Walter Benjamin). Treasured since antiquity
for their "intentional commemorative value" as memorials to gods, rulers, and
generals, and since the Renaissance for their (art) "historical value" as exemplars
of significant moments in (art) history, monuments had begun to acquire—
with the advent of modernity—a third value, that of age. Viewed through the
lens of "age-value," monuments evoked not a specific moment *in* time, but the
general "passage *of* time."[54] By the nineteenth century it became possible to
savor the scattered fragments left behind by years of erosion and neglect with-

out lamenting the causes of ruin or reconstructing the lost whole. In fact, any attempt to restore a monument, or even halt its decay, would detract from the pleasure of witnessing the ongoing work of time (32). It was this emphasis on pleasure that distinguished the "modern cult of ruins" from its precursors. The earlier Baroque association of ruins with "regret" and "pathos" was utterly "alien" to this new sensibility (31). Instead, the appeal of age-value was to the senses and the subjective emotions (24). Dependent "on neither scholarly knowledge, nor historical education," and thus accessible to "the masses," this modern cult of monuments was a democratic one, appropriate to an age of individualism (24, 29).

American travelers' growing preference for visiting or depicting ruins at dusk or night provides one indication of this emergent modality of age-value. Instead of the clarity of the midday sun, which exposes architectural and epigraphic details, they increasingly favored the semi-obscurity of twilight or moonlight for the atmosphere it imparts. For the Yale graduate Theodore Dwight, recovering from illness in Italy, the deep shadows of a "setting sun" could transfigure a classical ruin on the Via Appia into a gothic vision of "fantastic forms" resembling "a mysterious assembly of gloomy spirits."[55] Cole also favored the luminous qualities of moonlight—what he called its "silvery lustre"—for many of his ruinscapes, including *Desolation*. This process of gothicization mitigated the pagan associations of Roman ruins, which had discouraged earlier American travelers. By 1853 the popular travel writer George Hillard could describe even the Coliseum, that notorious site of Christian martyrdom—and the subject of another painting by Cole—as having acquired through ruination and foliation the "variety of form and outline which we admire in a Gothic cathedral."[56]

Accompanying the rise of age-value, Riegl claimed, was a greater inclusiveness regarding what actually constituted a monument. If antiquity knew only of "intentional monuments" (those deliberately erected to preserve the memory of a person or event), the category was enlarged in the Renaissance to encompass certain objects not intended as monuments, but whose (art-) historical significance allowed them to be designated "historical monuments" (24). But age-value expanded the category still further to include any object, "without regard to its original significance and purpose, as long as it reveals the passage of a considerable period of time" (24). Whereas Jefferson had focused his attention on intentional monuments such as the Maison Carrée temple, a generation later Cole found inspiration in the aqueducts of the Roman Campagna, which as "unintentional monuments" circumvented those lingering Protestant and democratic misgivings about admiring structures erected to honor pagan gods or imperial tyrants. In terms similar to Simmel's contemporaneous definition of the ruin, Riegl described such "monuments of age-value" as "catalysts which trigger a sense . . . of the emergence of the particular from the general and its gradual but inevitable dissolution back in to the general" (24). This expansion of the category of monument was accompanied, moreover, by a relaxation of the emphasis on classical antiquity altogether. The ruin painters of the Baroque period had "almost exclusively" confined themselves to Roman remains, due to their singular associations with "earthly power and grandeur" (31). But for adherents of the modern cult of the ruin, the process of decay that produces age-value arose out of "natural laws . . . governing all artifacts" (31). Thus, Cole included in his European itinerary such non-Roman ruins as the remains of a medieval fortress in the Vaucluse and the "ivy-clad towers [and] roofless halls" of Kenilworth Castle.[57]

Out of this generalization of the category of ruin came the realization that such objects might be found beyond the borders of Europe and the Mediterranean, and even beyond the Atlantic. This new latitude in defining a ruin was what enabled Tocqueville to apply the term to the humble remains of a log cabin on the American frontier. Those remains on Lake Oneida were just one of several kinds of ruins that both American and foreign travelers were beginning to discover—and in some cases imaginatively insert—in rural New York during the 1820s and 1830s. In turn, these various "American ruins" contributed still further to the disintegration of the cyclical framework within which such emblems had conventionally been construed.

For the consumption of age-value, upstate New York was in some respects ideal. Travelers returning from Rome frequently complained that distractions had marred their enjoyment of its celebrated ruins. Overrun with beggars, looters, souvenir sellers, and other tourists, and strewn with "dirt and rubbish" (as the American painter Rembrandt Peale lamented in 1830), the Forum disenchanted many travelers hoping to find themselves alone in a Claudian landscape, or at least in the company of lute-playing goatherds.[58] The less celebrated ruins of Mayan cities, by contrast, were still considered too remote for amateur travelers, and were little known until the publication of John Lloyd Stephens's exploratory narratives of 1841–43.[59] A more favorable balance between convenience and isolation was to be found in New York's rural regions. The introduction of steamboats on the Hudson in 1807 (and the construction of canals in the 1820s and railroads in the 1830s) rendered rural sights accessible, while high fares and slow speeds maintained exclusivity to those with a degree of wealth and leisure.[60] Similarly, the elimination of the difficulties of travel—with the installation, for instance, of coil-spring suspensions and cushioned upholstery in horse-drawn and railroad carriages, and the introduction of hotels and pocket guidebooks—enabled tourists to experience the landscapes outside as aesthetically pleasurable; while the persistence of certain inconveniences, such as the "infernal" roads and older springless carriages Tocqueville encountered in upstate New York, retained the thrill of the secluded and the unfamiliar. If traveling for pleasure had been restricted to an aristocratic elite through the eighteenth century, by the 1820s a standardized American Grand Tour—also known as the Fashionable or Northern Tour, after the titles of the leading guidebooks by Gideon Davison, Theodore Dwight, and Henry Gilpin—had emerged as a bourgeois rite of passage.[61]

American efforts to locate (or project) ruins in the national landscape were in part a defensive reaction against the condescension of British writers and travelers who considered it devoid of aesthetic or historical interest, especially when judged from the Anglocentric standpoint of the "picturesque." Originally referring to a landscape's suitability for pictorial representation, the picturesque had acquired more precise definition in the travel "observations" of William Gilpin in the 1760s and 1770s and his followers' subsequent elaborations. In contrast to the smooth transitions and geometric regularity of "beautiful" landscapes (exemplified by French rectilinear gardens), picturesque landscapes presented rough textures and complex contrasts of light, color, and form. But they were also distinguishable from the "sublimity" of wilderness landscapes by the presence of more homely, man-made elements. The most valued of such artificial accessories were ruins, preferably Gothic rather than classical, and of stone rather than wood (wooden ruins, as Tocqueville discovered on Frenchman's Island, decay far too quickly). Gilpin valued ruins less for their moral meanings than for their irregularity of outline, their intimation of a centuries-old blending of nature and culture, and the richness of their literary or legendary associations. Such "natural, and artificial richness" was what he declared—in 1776, no less—lacking in the formless landscapes of America, as well as parts of Scotland and Wales.[62] Although Gilpin never visited the United States, his precepts resonated across numerous British travelogues, from Isaac Weld's complaint about the "unpicturesque appearance of the angular fences, and of the stiff wooden houses," to Frances Trollope's suggestion that the otherwise pleasing landscapes of the Ohio still needed "a ruined abbey, or feudal castle."[63] Even if ruins could be found there, its inhabitants did not possess (in the view of many English writers) the sensitivities and skills required for picturesque perception, above all that of transcending the utilitarian and the quotidian. "Oh, surely, there will come a time when this lovely land will be vocal with the sound of song," proclaimed the English actress Fanny Kemble on her tour up the Hudson River Valley in 1835. "Yet 'tis strange how marvelously unpoetical these people are! How swallowed up in life and its daily realities, wants and cares!"[64]

But in attempting to counter such trollopizing (as it became known), American travelers, artists, and novelists rarely repudiated the picturesque aesthetic itself, for all its Anglocentric biases. As a loose assortment of shifting and often conflicting tenets that were never fully codified, it was susceptible to appropriation and adaptation.[65] Gilpin himself admitted that few landscapes were picturesque enough to be transferred to sketchbook directly from observation; even English countryside needed to be viewed through the softening and tinting lens of a "Claude glass." Where bucolic features such as tree stumps or cottages were missing, he similarly advised the artist to insert imaginary ones; and if ruins were malformed, to simply "remove" the offending parts. Drawing books filled with samples of such features were published for that very purpose, and were widely used by American artists.[66] Taking these liberties further than Gilpin intended, American painters such as Thomas Doughty claimed artistic license to import ruined castles and classical temples into native landscapes; and nature writers such as Susan Fenimore Cooper, the poetic license to describe how a pastoral scene in upstate New York would look had it acquired the ruins of a Roman and medieval past.[67] The fictional relics her father James Fenimore Cooper inserted into the New York landscapes of his novels—the "picturesque ruin" of Tom Hutter's mock castle on Lake Glimmerglass in *Deerslayer*, or the "smouldering ruin" of Fort William Henry in *Last of the Mohicans*—similarly function as aestheticizing and historicizing accessories.[68]

Picturesque substitution assumed its most literal form in the practice of installing actual "mock ruins." Imported or fabricated remains had been popular as follies in English and French country gardens since the early eighteenth century. In the 1780s, Gilpin, concerned less with actual age than appearance of age, embraced them as appropriate elements in landscape design, provided they were visually convincing and harmoniously situated (too often, he complained, they turned out to be "ridiculous," "ill-stationed," and "absurd").[69] But it was not until the 1830s that any prominent ruin-follies were constructed in American gardens. Indeed, one of the first ruins visible to travelers taking the standard itinerary of the American Grand Tour, departing New York by steamboat up the Hudson, were the follies of Cruger's Island, just north of Poughkeepsie. Reportedly inspired by Cole's ruinscapes, the New York merchant John Church Cruger transformed his island retreat into a phantasmagorical landscape of desolation, featuring the broken arches of a church. He supplemented these Gothic ruins in 1842 with Mayan ones, recovered from the Yucatán by his friend, John Lloyd Stephens.[70] Despite this anachronistic *pasticcio*, which blatantly contravened both Gilpin's principle of congruence and Diderot's call for historical and geographical specificity, Cruger's Island became a popular attraction, recommended in guidebooks, depicted by painters and panorama artists, and admired by American and European travelers alike, including the Swedish feminist Fredrika Bremer, who considered the assemblage "in the best taste." It even inspired the erection of ruin-follies in nearby gardens, adorning the Hudson's shores with the kinds of ruins that Cole earlier associated with the Rhine.[71]

Beyond the Hudson Valley's manorial estates, however, American appropriations of the ruin-folly remained rare, its foreign and aristocratic associations at odds with the patriotic and democratic fervor of the Jacksonian period. In James Fenimore Cooper's *Home as Found* (1838), Eve Effingham's daydream about the transformation of Lake Otsego by "villas . . . church-towers . . . a castle or a crumbling ruin, and all the other accessories of an old state of society" she had recently witnessed in Europe, is interrupted by her suitor, Paul Powis, who hints at the native suspicion toward such "poet[ic]" ornaments. To render oneself "less liable to criticism," he later advises, one should "think less of the artificial and more of our natural excellences."[72] A more legitimate substitute for authentic historical antiquities were thus the "natural antiquities" of American mountains and trees such as those in the Catskills, another stopping point of the American Grand Tour, across the Hudson from Cruger's Island. On his earliest steamboat trips there (beginning in 1825), and later as resident, Cole found numerous surrogate ruins: dead trees represented in his earliest Catskill landscapes as shattered and moldering columns, some prostrate and others still standing; a frozen waterfall that he likened in his journal to the "tracery" and "ornament" of Saracenic or Gothic architecture; and the "everlasting hills" of the Catskills themselves, apotheosized in his paean to "American Scenery" as the "pillars" of a "great temple" (8).[73] In conjuring architectural fragments out of geological formations, Cole and his contemporaries could finally claim monuments of even greater antiquity than Europe's. That assertion was substantiated by European geologists who were beginning to question earlier assumptions about the newness of the American continent. While examining the ancient strata and fossils of the Hudson Valley in 1841, the Scottish uniformitarian geologist Charles Lyell "became convinced that we must turn to the *New World* if we wish to see in perfection the oldest monuments of the earth's history"—a conclusion endorsed five years later by his opponent, the Swiss catastrophist geologist Louis Agassiz.[74]

If America's mountains possessed greater antiquity than Europe's, so too might its forests. For D. J. Browne, writing in the *North American Review* in 1832, ancient trees were the proper "monuments of our country" and the perfect ripostes to "all future Trollopes." With their pleasurable and wholesome associations of nature's power to "strengthen and restore," these "Sylva

Americana" overshadowed *all* other ancient monuments, including the Great Wall of China (a "monument of . . . cowardice and weakness"), the Pyramids of Egypt ("ignorance, and . . . superstition"), and the cathedrals and castles of Europe ("corrupt religion" and a "barbarous" society, respectively).[75] Nevertheless, nineteenth-century Americans continued to dress theirs up in the borrowed garb of European forms. In his *Tour on the Prairies* (1835), Washington Irving transfigured a rock formation into a "ruined fortress," or "Moorish Castle," and a grove of trees into a cluster of "stately columns," their autumnal leaves simulating the "effect of sunshine" through the "stained windows" of a Gothic cathedral. And that same year Cole himself invoked the tradition (dating back to Vitruvius) of finding architectural correspondences in the natural world, by analogizing the indigenous hemlock to a "dark and ivy-mantled tower" in the way it "rises from the gloom of the forest" ("American Scenery," 10).[76]

The process by which American landscapes indirectly evoked European ones—as in the ruin-effects described above—was nonetheless a complex one in Cole's view, requiring sensitivity to the subtle play of associations in nature. Influenced by the "associationist" aesthetics of the Scottish philosopher Archibald Alison, Cole believed that the mind responds to objects in the natural world by following a chain of "harmonies and associations," a field of "magnetism" in which opposing ideas are "drawn together, and bound." Thus, a "mountain here" in the Catskills "sends one, in a thought, to a mountain in a foreign land," while a "streamlet, warbling at one's feet, is answered to by another on a far-off continent."[77] Through this transatlantic linkage, the "mind's eye" may travel through time as well as space, allowing it to "see far into futurity" to a time when American landscapes will be endowed with "temple and tower" ("American Scenery," 12). There is evidence that Cole intended his domestic and Italian-inspired landscapes to be hung side by side, as pendants, an arrangement that would have channeled this bidirectional flow of associations. Moving through the exhibition space, an imaginative viewer would transpose various elements (such as trees and columns) from one canvas to the other, thereby breaking down the frames between them. The installation of landscape paintings in Hudson River steamboats, interspersed between windows, similarly allowed travelers to extrapolate motifs onto the physical landscapes outside.[78] Even Cole's *Course of Empire* traversed the borders supposedly separating national landscapes. The ruins of Rome may well have inspired his series and provided his iconography of imperial decay, but it was the landscape of the Adirondacks (which he visited in 1835 "in search of the picturesque") that allegedly provided him with his backdrop and setting.[79]

Yet for all his emphasis on *natural* antiquities, Cole did not consider American landscapes entirely "destitute of historical and legendary associations"; there were many sites that had been "sanctified" by the "great struggle for freedom" ("American Scenery," 11). The ruined forts around Lake George, particularly Fort Ticonderoga, were becoming obligatory staging posts for picturesque travelers, as they continued their itinerary north of the Hudson valley. Controlled first by the French (1755–59), then by the British (1759–75), and finally by the American revolutionary army (1775 until succumbing to bombardment in 1777), Ticonderoga thereafter suffered neglect and decay until 1826, the year of Cole's visit.[80] Capitalizing on the publication earlier that year of Cooper's *Last of the Mohicans*, which sparked interest in the historical associations of the Lake George region, and on the recent completion of the Champlain Canal, which allowed steamboat travel beyond Albany, the New York merchant William Ferris Pell developed Ticonderoga into a tourist resort. He constructed a private steamboat landing, a luxurious Greek Revival inn, and an English-style landscape garden from which to view the ruins. But even amid that year's semicentennial celebrations, Ticonderoga was not yet sanctified as a specifically "American" ruin.[81] Cole embellished his *View near Ticonderoga* (1826) with a scene not from the Revolutionary but the French and Indian War, borrowed from "Gelyna," a historical romance by his friend Giulian C. Verplanck. Having flown the "flags of three nations" (in the words of another visitor of the period, Nathaniel Hawthorne), the fort could also be celebrated by European travelers, who projected their own meanings and memories onto it. For aristocratic French travelers, it represented a poignant cenotaph to that grand imperial project known as *la Nouvelle-France*, while for British travelers it marked the melancholy ground of their last military victory in North America.[82] This multinational status allowed American artists, writers, and travelers to revel in the legends of its ruins, while disavowing them as the relics of other empires. Accused by an English traveler of indulging in a European cult of the ruin, one American clarified that "our only ruins are British fortifications, and we go to see them because they remind us that we whipped the nation which whips all the world."[83] When they did celebrate the site as a birthplace of American nationhood, they tended to do so through the mediating figure of a surviving patriot. For those still ambivalent about the decadent pleasures of ruins, these war veterans were more appropriate objects of veneration. They were "a sort of living monumen[t]," enthused Dwight, as "exalted" as any "columns of antiquity."[84]

In the Northern Tour's middle stages, as travelers reached the westernmost regions of New York State, they could visit even more antiquated monuments. The mysterious earthworks or "mounds" of Onondaga and Ontario counties had been largely dismissed as historically and aesthetically insignificant until they were promoted by New York governor DeWitt Clinton in the 1810s as genuine "antiquities," worthy of investigation and preservation. Just as geologists were asserting the anteriority of America's physical landscapes, an emerging group of professional archaeologists led by the polymath and politician Samuel Mitchill, now submitted the mounds as evidence that their continent was also "the cradle of the human race." Responding to Clinton's paper, Mitchill playfully suggested telling European travelers that it was *they* who came from the "*new*" world." Indeed, by 1832, after the discovery of further mounds in the Ohio and Mississippi valleys, the western booster Timothy Flint could adduce them to refute foreigners' claims that Americans had "no monuments, no ruins . . . nothing to connect the imagination and the heart with the past."[85]

But when compared with European ruins, these ancient monuments revealed certain anomalies and deficiencies. As earthworks, they lacked that delicate balance between the artificial and the organic, the architectural and the natural, that was a defining characteristic of a ruin. Equally problematic was the absence of any accompanying legends or histories. Without having been "hallowed" by the "footsteps and immortal verse" of a Milton or Petrarch, Cole conceded, these "most venerable remains of American antiquity" can only evoke the "sublimity of a shoreless ocean un-islanded by the recorded deeds of man" ("American Scenery," 11). Nor could one resort to the oral traditions of local Indian tribes; in Clinton's view, "they were generally as ignorant as the inquirer."[86] To defer to those tribes, moreover, would be to lend credence to the idea that their forefathers built them, and thus to acknowledge their current rights to the land. Before these mounds could be celebrated as legitimate antiquities, then, they had to be stripped of all associations with Indians, and invested with substitute legends. Alluding to the nomadism of Indians, the impermanence of their settlements, and the simplicity of their artifacts (which Jefferson had refused in 1782 to "honour" with the name of "monument"), archaeologists concurred that the mounds must have been the work of some other people, an assumption endorsed even by French travelers sympathetic to their plight, such as Chateaubriand and Tocqueville.[87] To confer an aura of European antiquity on them—analogous to the gothicizing of trees and rock formations—several identified the Mound Builders as originating from the Old World, whether as an errant band of Carthaginians, Phoenicians, Tyreans, Greeks, Romans, Welshmen, or even (in the religious vision of Joseph Smith, at Palmyra, New York) as a lost tribe of Israelites. To distinguish them from Indians, they characterized these nations or tribes as having progressed beyond the nomadic state to the point of developing a settled pastoral economy and even founding cities. And to circumvent European insinuations that the climate or ecology of North America may be inhospitable to the progress of civilization, they attributed the Mound Builders' untimely demise not to natural causes but to the "barbarian" invasions of Indians from the west. But even as they invoked its residual vocabulary of "social stages" and "barbarian" hordes, these speculative theories stretched the discourse of cyclicality to breaking point. Such accounts of other nations settling the New World centuries before the appointed time, succumbing to ruin while still only "partially civilized," and failing to leave behind any written trace or cultural legacy, contradicted three of the central pillars of universal history.[88]

Precocious Cities, Proliferating Ruins: The Untimely Landscapes of the Erie Canal

If the Enlightenment framework of history struggled to account for the rural remains of some ancient mound-building empire, it was undermined still further by the urban landscapes that an emerging capitalist empire was now building in the same western regions of New York. For Northern Tourists taking the Erie Canal out to the mounds and Niagara (or back to New York City), the windows of their packet boats offered views of an equally startling spectacle, one that this "artificial river" had itself helped to create: namely the growth, seemingly overnight, of brand-new cities. Their assumptions about history and temporality were confounded by the rapidity with which this waterway appeared to be transforming a thinly settled, underdeveloped part of the state into a hive of commercial, industrial, and architectural activity. Not even the "virgin forest" surrounding Lake Oneida, which Tocqueville and Beaumont had visited while following the route of the canal (albeit by horse), was impervious to these forces of economic transformation ("Journey," 322). Far from being a site of the "remotest solitude," that lake lay within ten miles of the canal and the booming town of Syracuse (*Democracy*, 283). The "column of smoke" Tocqueville identified as the distant backdrop to the ruins of Frenchman's Island (283–84)—a blemish tellingly erased from his longer account, "Journey to Lake Oneida," in which "no smoke was seen to rise over the forest" (323)—betrays the imminent encroachment of urban-industrial civilization upon their cherished scene of romantic ruin.

In his original 1816 proposal for a "Grand Canal," Clinton had signaled his break with Jeffersonian republicanism by promising state legislators that "villages, towns, *and cities*" would rise up from Lake Erie to the mouth of the Hudson.[89] The opening of the first sections in 1819–20 did mark the inception of a forty-year phase of urbanization that was unprecedented in the nation's history, and remains unmatched ever since. Although the United States did not become predominantly urban until 1920, it was a century earlier, in the 1820s, that the rate of population growth in cities and large towns began consistently to outpace that in rural locations.[90] The chief beneficiary was the city of New York, which witnessed a 64 percent population surge during that decade. But the prodigious growth of existing metropolises was not the most significant demographic development; of the total urban population, metropolitan Americans still constituted only 22 percent in 1830. A more revealing index was the number of cities and towns, which increased sevenfold between 1820 and 1860.[91] The vast majority were relatively recent or entirely new, and located not on the eastern seaboard but in the continental interior. Those "inland cities" lining the banks of "Clinton's Ditch"—from Troy, Utica, Rome, Syracuse, and Palmyra, to Rochester, Lockport, and Buffalo—decisively shifted the state's demographic balance to the counties north and west of Albany.[92] In the canal's first decade, the nation's fastest-growing urban area was neither an established seaport nor factory town, but the flour-trading town of Rochester. Following the canal's routing through its central district, its population grew exponentially, from 1,502 in 1820 to 10,863 by 1830, an increase of over 600 percent.[93] Visiting in 1829, Cole declared this incipient city "one of the wonders of the world," insofar as it had "risen in the midst of a wilderness almost with the rapidity of thought."[94] The transformative energy of American urbanization was likely experienced with even greater intensity in Rochester than in Manhattan.

However solemnly their founders appealed to the *translatio* through their choice of Roman and Greek town names, the sheer velocity of urbanization belied such claims of continuity.[95] In defiance of eighteenth-century notions that cities emerged through an orderly progression of stages, Rochester was described—with satisfaction by its promoters and most American visitors, but with varying degrees of ambivalence by Europeans—as undergoing an abnormally accelerated growth. What Cole found startling was Rochester's attainment in a short time of a state of consummation that is usually "the work of ages."[96] The lapse of centuries presumably separating his *Course of Empire* canvases was here condensed into a mere decade. Indeed, by midcentury, Cole's successors, most famously Asher Durand, collapsed those five canvases into a single one, presenting the *Progress* of empire as synchronous rather than serial.[97] Claims about the rapidity of American urban growth typically functioned as repudiations of other patterns of development, whether those of Native Americans (included in the foreground of Durand's painting as a counterpoint to Anglo-Saxon progress), or of Europeans (whose cities were mischaracterized as static). By contrast, the blossoming of new American cities seemed to transform the very meaning of time. "Ten years in America," declared both the German legal and political philosopher Francis Lieber and the English novelist Frederick Marryat, were equivalent to an entire "century" in Europe.[98] Contrary to the earlier hopes of Jeffersonian Republicans, America's expansion across space appeared to be hastening its development through time.

Such temporal compression posed a particular problem for Charles Lyell, who employed the analogy of the piecemeal rise and fall of "great nations" to convey his Uniformitarian theory of the imperceptibly slow evolution — or ruination — of the earth. To believe, as his Catastrophist opponents did, that the earth was formed in a short space of time seemed as absurd as to condense the course of an empire into decades rather than millennia: "A crowd of incidents would follow each other in thick succession. Armies and fleets would appear to be assembled only to be destroyed, and cities built merely to fall in ruins."[99] But while traveling along the Erie Canal in search of ancient geological formations and fossils to substantiate his evolutionary model, he witnessed a landscape undergoing an "extraordinary revolution." Sounding more like a Catastrophist, he recorded the "brief moment of time" in which the buildings of towns like Rochester had "ris[en]" out of forests only recently "own[ed]" by the Oneida Indians. Such was the temporal flux in this rapidly developing region that maps became useless within months of being published.[100] Time on the urban frontier seemed anything but deep.

The phenomenal quality of American urban expansion thus demanded new metaphors and analogies. Some urban boosters continued to pay lip service to traditional stage theory by troping these burgeoning cities as the legitimate offspring of American agrarianism, the natural fruits of democratic development, or the estuarial outlets to which the rivers of commerce flowed.[101] But the only organic metaphors that seemed appropriate to a town like Rochester were those indicating an abnormal or excessive growth. Rather than through long cultivation, this town had "sprung up like a mushroom" all by itself, Hawthorne wrote after an 1830 visit, as if "fertiliz[ed]" by the very water of the canal; while for Trollope, it exemplified the "Jack and Bean–stalk principle" of overnight growth. The New York writer and editor Col. William Leete Stone also deployed images of preternatural growth in his comparison of Rochester's sprouting to that of "Jonah's gourd."[102] Such tropes conferred seemingly magical, fairy-tale, or biblical qualities on the processes of American urbanization, while also implying that they might be as short-lived as those mythical beanstalks and gourds, neither of which lasted more than a day, the former "toppl[ed]" by an ax, the latter "smote" and "withered" by a worm. Clinton, in Hawthorne's account, was not merely the leading advocate of internal improvements but nothing less than "an enchanter, who had waved his magic wand" over the region, making cities materialize out of thin air (398). Even the less impressive growth of Canandaigua was likened in Henry Gilpin's guide-book, *The Northern Tour*, to the "effect of magic!" (122).

The acceleration of urban growth did not merely compress the stages of empire; it challenged the very idea. Well into the nineteenth century, travelers and political economists attempted to reconcile economic and urban expansion with the Enlightenment model of empires unfolding steadily in time, in particular by reenacting it spatially—whether through actual travel or the vicarious travel afforded by print or visual media such as panoramas—as a journey from the western territories to Atlantic cities. As late as 1824, Jefferson described that eastward itinerary as recapitulating the "gradual shades of improving man," from primitive hunter-gatherers, through the "semi-barbarous citizens" of the frontier, to the fully developed "seaport towns." Even those who reversed the direction and observed the temporal regression of "inverted history" were still reinscribing the notion of discrete stages.[103] With the advent of the Erie Canal, however, there emerged a chaotic patchwork of landscapes that called into question such spatializations of temporal succession. Between the streets of towns like Rochester and the surrounding fields, there were no gradual transitions (as in Durand's *Progress*), only jarring contrasts. One moment the traveler is in a "busy" town, observed the Scottish naval officer Basil Hall. But "at the next crack of the whip—hocus pocus!—all is changed. He looks out of the window—rubs his eyes, and discovers that he is again in the depths of the wood at the other extremity of civilized society."[104] Tocqueville himself experienced this kind of spatio-temporal rift when, straying barely ten miles from the canal and the bustling town of Syracuse, he found himself in the dense forest surrounding Lake Oneida. As he traveled west and encountered further "abrupt and unexpected" oscillations between "extreme civilization" and "nature . . . run . . . riot," he eventually abandoned his original assumption that "one could follow step by step all the transformations which social conditions have brought about for man" merely by covering a "few degrees of longitude." On the contrary, it was "without transition" that one passes "from the wilds into the street of a city."[105]

Missing from such landscapes were pastoral scenes. The nascent canal towns appeared to have bypassed that stage altogether, exhibiting signs of urbanity within a few months or years of their founding. One could already find merchants in the upstart city of Buffalo, Tocqueville observed, who were just as "well stocked" with French luxuries as their counterparts in Manhattan ("Fortnight," 333). Similarly, in his 1835 sketch of the seemingly "instantaneous city" of Rochester, Hawthorne enumerated an inventory of metropolitan phenomena—from lottery offices, courthouses, and taverns to the pedestrians and vehicles that crowded its pavements—that belied how recently "the forest-leaves have been swept away" (408, 407). At the canal-opening festivities of 1825, Rochester's leapfrog from "hamlet" to "full grown . . . city"—"disdaining, as it were, the intermediate grade of a village"—had been a cause for Colonel Stone to celebrate.[106] But those who clung to traditional conceptions of urban growth tended to characterize such metropolitan ambitions as premature or artificial. Jefferson denounced the canal (as late as 1822) because he believed that it was causing the state of New York to "anticipat[e] by a full century, the normal process of improvement."[107] In *Home as Found*, Cooper similarly re-pudiated those "precocious cit[ies]" that had eagerly exploited some "peculiar advantages in the way of trade" instead of "advanc[ing] steadily *pari passu* [at an equal pace] with the surrounding country," as had the "sober country town" of "Templeton," or its model, Cooperstown (126). Rather than evolving or-ganically out of local agriculture or craft, or waiting for the timely granting of a city charter, Rochester seemed to Basil Hall a "ready-made" affair, as if "a great boxful of new houses had been sent by steam from New-York, and tumbled out on the half-cleared land." One could not even distinguish older districts from newer ones; all was a jumble of streets in varying degrees of completion, some "nearly finished" but not yet named, and others "named, but not com-menced," denoted only by "lines of stakes" (1:160–61).[108] Whereas Rochester and Buffalo were at least founded prior to Clinton's survey of 1810–11, other boomtowns owed their existence entirely to the Erie Canal (which differed from English canals insofar as it preceded the very industrial and urban centers it would link together). In these newer towns, often denominated by the suffix "-port," the standard sequence of stages and priorities was inverted still further. As the Marquis de Lafayette's secretary, Auguste Levasseur, observed on the general's 1824 tour, Lockport boasted an "immense hotel" before building "any other habitation," a printing press before securing the "necessaries of life," and "luxur[ious]" vehicles before clearing its streets.[109] Such "odd spectacle[s]," Tocqueville confirmed in Cincinnati, were indicative of cities that "see[m] to want to get built too quickly to have things done in order."[110]

   If such scenes of consummation could appear out of sequence, so too could "scenes of desolation." Among the several kinds of untimely ruins precipitated by American urbanism were those of the few Native Americans still inhab-iting the region. America's ruins go unsung, suggested the humanitarian au-thor John Neal in his 1829 short story about an Oneida chief, because they do not assume the "pillared" or "turret[ed]" forms of the Old World. Instead, they take the bodily form of these "last" remaining Indians: this "live wreck of a prodigious empire that has departed before our face within the memory of man."[111] It was along the Erie Canal—at Oneida Castle, then Buffalo—that Tocqueville first witnessed these living ruins. Unlike the noble savages in

Rousseau, Montesquieu, and Chateaubriand, the Oneida Indians turned out
to be in a state of moral, physical, and pecuniary decay—"too feeble," added
Beaumont, to resist the "brilliant cities" that white settlers were erecting on
their "ruins." Their only consolation was that these indigenous "ruins" por-
tended the usurpers' own ruin, that "day when other peoples make them undergo the same destiny."[112] It seemed unlikely to Tocqueville that the Indians would inflict this retribution; despite their superficial similarities to the
Germanic tribes "described by Tacitus," they had not been elevated through
contact with civilization, but rather reduced to an even more "barbarous condition" (*Democracy*, 330–35). Clinton had speculated that they would be
avenged by their kinsmen, the "barbarous nations of Asia," who would descend on America in "some remote period of time" and usher in a "new, a
long, and a gloomy night of gothic darkness," in the aftermath of which the
"ruins . . . of our magnificent cities" would become as fruitful a "subject of
curious research and elaborate investigation" as the mounds were in his own
time.[113] Alternatively, in the apocalyptic predictions of Cole's kindred spirit,
Bryant, Americans would bring ruin on themselves by sabotaging their own
environment. The Indian who returns to the burial place of his fathers, in Bryant's eponymous poem of 1824, observes how white settlers have been deplet-
ing its soils and rivers, and infers that their race may "vanish hence, like mine, /
And leave no trace behind, / Save ruins o'er the region spread." Such premonitions were rare, however, voiced mainly by aristocratic French travelers and by
American literati such as Bryant, Neal, and Gilpin. More often, descriptions
of Native Americans as ruins effectively denied them a future by consigning
them to a safe and nostalgic past, or else presented them as helpless victims requiring white paternalism. Even Bryant, in another poem of the period, could
lament the successive civilizations who have left "columns strown / On the
waste sands," yet conclude with the encomium: "thou, my country, thou shalt
never fall."[114]

Another kind of ruin produced by the sheer rapidity of urbanization in
northwestern New York were the tree stumps that stood in busy streets, in the
cellars of houses, or even alongside imposing warehouses, factories, and civic
structures. For Cooper, Hall, Lyell, Marryat, and Trollope, the incongruous
juxtaposition of rising buildings with rotting stumps was the very hallmark
of rampant urban growth.[115] Not necessarily indicating the rapid march of
progress, these stubborn remnants of the forest testified to the overreliance
on private capital rather than civic spirit, and to a general disregard for traditional notions of orderly succession (Hall, 1:162).[116] Furthermore, they
exposed the pretensions of urbanity. In Trollope's imagination, these decidedly unpicturesque stumps were not receding compliantly into the past, but

rather "contest[ing] the ground with pillars" as if in militant defiance of the new urban order being erected around them. This urbanizing landscape resembled a "battle-ground" on which stumps and columns waged a struggle for "mastery" (293).[117]

But as remnants of larger, absent wholes, there was also a certain affinity between stumps and columns. In mid-nineteenth-century funerary art, tree stumps shared with broken columns the symbolic function of memorializing premature or "untimely" deaths.[118] Familiarized with this iconographical linkage, viewers of Cole's *Course of Empire* may well have read the stump in *Pastoral State*'s foreground as anticipating or heralding the broken columns in *Desolation*'s background. That stump thus functions as a kind of *amorce* (bait) or *pierre d'attente* (toothing-stone), terms introduced by the literary theorist Gérard Genette to refer to those brief and indirect allusions to future events that will be consummated later in the narrative. By hinting at or foreshadowing the eventual outcome in a kind of hallucinatory flash-forward, such heterodiegetic devices undermine any unidirectional sense of narrative time, whether cyclical or linear.[119] Thus, the tree stump, both in Cole's *Course of Empire* and in the townscapes of western New York, provoked an experience of temporality that was disjunctive and discordant. Within a single picture-frame or canal-boat window, one could observe multiple, overlapping stages of historical development.

Canal-boat passengers registered similar conflations of arboreal and architectural remains—or ruin-effects—on these embryonic towns' outskirts, where forests were falling victim not only to the ax but also to the indirect and unintended consequences of draining swamps to fill the Great Ditch. The sight of giant trees lying "prostrate before civilization" along the stretch of canal between Rome and Syracuse (that is, in the vicinity of Lake Oneida) triggered Marryat's memory of the fallen columns that littered the ground of such "dismembered empires" as Carthage and Rome. Although the circumstances were quite different—the former scene representing "Nature . . . deposed [by] . . . Art" (107), the latter, Art deposed by Nature—the general "feelings . . . conjured up" in his mind were otherwise the "same."[120] Hawthorne, passing through this very region and viewing its "prostrate" trees in the phantasmagorical light of the boat's lanterns, also drew an analogy to Old World ruins. There, Decay, the queen of ruins, "sits among fallen palaces; but here, her home is in the forests." Even in this site of exile and "solitude," she cannot end her reign in peace, but remains at the mercy of the "encroachments of civilized man," not least that "vulgar . . . throng" of canal-boat passengers such as himself (403). So rapid and inexorable was American urban and economic development that even trees that were still standing could evoke ruins.

Tocqueville likened the virgin forest bordering the "city to be" of Saginaw, Michigan, to the Greek city-in-ruins of Himera, Sicily (which he had visited four years earlier), for its capacity to project one's "imagination" through vast expanses of time—except that it does not plunge the imagination "backwards . . . into the past" but rather sends it "rushing on ahead" into the chasm of an "immense future" when the forest "will have fallen" to make way for the roads and buildings of an emergent empire ("Fortnight," 364, 371–72). Americans may remain unmoved by such melancholic associations, failing even to notice these forests "until they begin to fall beneath the ax" (*Democracy*, 185). But in this era of "quick and inevitable change," and in the "arrière-pensée" of a romantic European mind, trees could be perceived as ruins even before they have been felled ("Fortnight," 372).

Such forlorn-looking trees—capitulating (or about to capitulate) to the lumbermen or canal diggers, and persisting only as rotten stumps, ghostly snags, or prostrate logs—were hardly the "Sylva Americana" warranting celebration as the world's noblest antiquities. Indeed, tree stumps suffered from the same aesthetic problem that Simmel detected in marble columns broken off too short: "The stumps of the pillars of the Forum Romanum are simply ugly and nothing else, while a pillar crumbled—say, halfway down—can generate a maximum of charm."[121] Even when lined with healthy trees, canals were believed by William Gilpin to "disfigur[e]" the countryside, their "lineal, and angular course" contrasting unfavorably with sinuous rivers.[122] There were hopes, however, that the built landscapes along the canal would become more enduring monuments than the natural landscapes—and indigenous nations—they were supplanting. Travel guides such as Henry Gilpin's (a distant relative of William's) included in their itineraries not only rural and historical sights but also the new engineering structures spawned by the canal. On his visit to Rochester, even Cole—a supposed opponent of American materialism—marveled at its newly constructed bridges, warehouses, flour mills, and above all its grand aqueduct that miraculously carried the canal over the Genesee River. He confided in his diary that these commercial structures (rather than religious or civic ones) were the "Castles of the United States" that "in future ages shall tell the story of the enterprise and industry of the present generation."[123] Indeed, only through such a vast passage of time could the recent political controversies surrounding their construction safely recede from memory. From the distant perspective of "future history," wrote Henry Gilpin, "the views of partial policy shall be forgotten and the objects of temporary aggrandizement [shall] have become insignificant," permitting the canal to be remembered as one of the "noblest works of art" (144–45). With its Romanesque arches, Rochester's aqueduct, which even Basil Hall conceded was "noble" (1:153), evoked those Cole subsequently painted in the Roman Campagna.

An anonymous American traveler, writing in the *New-England Magazine* in 1835, agreed with Cole and Gilpin that such technological artifacts could eventually ripen into genuine antiquities. While acknowledging that the absence of feudalism and religious warfare precluded the kinds of clustered and crenellated ruins that beautify European landscapes, the author refused to concede that American capitalist "commerce" was incapable of producing ruins: "Our ruins if we ever have any, must be the ruins of factories and warehouses." Against the complaints of pedants, he denied that such utilitarian structures would make bad ruins; after all, numerous classical ruins, most notably the ruined aqueducts of the "campagna di Roma," were "in their original purpose, of anything but a romantic character." Moreover, all structures—even functional ones—inevitably acquire "some degree of romance and interest" as they disintegrate over time, becoming unintentional monuments. "We smile at the notion of a manufactory in ruins; yet, invest it with all the charms which a ruin in England or Scotland gathers around it, and it becomes at once romantic and beautiful." But above all it is the size and durability of modern American structures that would render them equal or even superior to the ruins of classical antiquity. The author imagined a traveler undertaking the Northern Tour some two thousand years in the future, and rediscovering with the aid of a guide the remains of edifices so large as to overawe him with the "power, energy and wealth of the ancients": the "stupendous ruin" of an industrial mill (now "crumbling and vine-covered" but of vaster proportions than any "feudal castle"), the "dried and half-choked beds of canals" extending into the interior, and "that superb piece of masonry, which time itself can hardly destroy, the stone bridge by which the Erie canal crosses the Genesee, at Rochester." In the author's view, no region in the United States was "more likely to realize" such a fantasy of ruin than the northwestern region of New York State through which that canal passed.[124]

It was this very conceit—that the scale and intensity of modern American development would ultimately supply ruins surpassing those of the ancients—that Tocqueville disputed in a brief chapter on monuments in *Democracy in America*. Americans, he wrote, tend on the one hand to throw up a large number of "trivial" buildings (exemplified perhaps by the humble and ephemeral log cabin), and on the other to erect a very small number of "grand" ones. The "magnificent palace" housing the U.S. Congress and the "prodigious" internal improvements undertaken by individual states are physical expressions of the tendency of individual citizens in a democracy to subordinate themselves to the supreme power of the state. But these larger monuments are not necessarily more capable of memorializing the civilization as a whole. On the contrary, a "few scattered remains of enormous buildings" would disclose "nothing about the social conditions and institutions of the people who put them up . . . [or] about their greatness, civilization, and real prosperity" (469). All they would reveal to future historians is the power of that state to "concentrate" vast labor power on a "single undertaking." Moreover, far from confirming technological accomplishment, larger ruins may well manifest incompetence to future generations, as ruined aqueducts "bear massive testimony" to the Romans' "ignorance" of "the laws of hydraulic engineering." Conversely and paradoxically, it was the more banal, unembellished artifacts of modern American civilization that would, as ruins, most effectively attest to its genius, above all in bridging greater distances with more economical means. "A people who left nothing but a few lead pipes in the ground and some iron rails on top of it might have mastered nature better than the Romans" (470). Yet even these more prosaic, unobtrusive ruins would presumably shed little historical light on the everyday lives of the workers who had labored on them.

These doubts about the potential of grand monuments as ruins were borne out by the fate of the canal's infrastructure. The Rochester aqueduct barely lasted a decade, let alone the centuries or millennia that Cole and the *New-England Magazine* had imagined. In 1833, the canal commissioners found it reduced to a "state of rapid dilapidation" by the regular spring floods of the Genesee (fig. 1.10). Nor did its ruined arches—left standing for another thirty years, even after a new aqueduct was completed alongside it—convey the superior "enterprise" of those ancient Americans. As it continued to disintegrate, its limestone was revealed to be a veneer concealing a cheaper and more porous local sandstone, proof of the builders' disregard for materials.[125] Other bridges in the region proved equally impermanent. The Genesee Bridge, upstream from Rochester, was supposed to be "one of the great Archimidean [*sic*] undertakings of the modern age," but by 1832 all that remained of this jerry-built structure were two "rickety" wooden frames "perched" on each river bluff.[126] Even in this state of decay, such "day-old ruins" were unlikely to provoke pleasure. The emergent category of age-value, Riegl noted, was not yet applied "indiscriminately" to "older and more recent monuments" alike (42). Rather than enchanted, "we are . . . disturbed at the sight of decay in newly made artifacts," or what he called "premature aging" (32). Nevertheless, it was the commercial triumph rather than failure of the Erie Canal that had condemned its physical infrastructure to premature ruin. Even while intact, the Rochester aqueduct—and soon the original canal as a whole—had been rendered obsolete by the sheer quantity of shipping and by the demand for wider, steam-driven canal boats.[127] Far from serving as a melancholy emblem

ERIE CANAL AQUEDUCT, ROCHESTER, N. Y.

Fig. 1.10. [Edmund N.?] Tarbell (engraver), [Samuel S.?] Kilburn (artist), *Erie Canal Aqueduct, Rochester, N.Y.*, 1855. Engraving. From *Ballou's Pictorial Drawing-Room Companion* (Boston) 9, no. 24 (1855): 376.

of the futility of man's works or of economic decline, the aqueduct appeared a victim of its own success.

The influence of the Erie Canal on local economies likewise proved capricious. Clinton had originally assured the legislature that the "blessings" of such a canal would be distributed evenly across space and became "as durable as time."[128] But this was hardly the experience of towns located some distance from its route. On "flourishing" towns like Batavia, twenty miles to the south, the canal "has not had a favourable effect," observed Gilpin's guidebook (129); on the contrary, the rise of the canal towns spelled its decline. Farther south, newspaper editors viewed the canal as a force that would reduce the cities of Pittsburgh and Philadelphia to "deserted villages," unless Pennsylvanians responded with their own internal improvements.[129] There were also temporal as well as spatial limits to the economic benefits of the canal. Palmyra experienced a rapid growth as its initial terminus when it opened in 1823, but declined just as rapidly once the western section was opened two years later. Similarly, the fate of Buffalo and its neighboring rival, Black Rock, entirely hinged upon which town the commissioners would select in 1822 as the ultimate terminus; the harbor that Black Rock's promoters were prematurely constructing would end up, Clinton warned, as enduring "ruins" testifying to their overweening ambitions.[130] Even Rochester soon found the canal's "blessings" to be decidedly mixed. By the late 1820s, settlers were increasingly continuing their journeys beyond Rochester to newer towns farther west, taking many Rochesterians with them. Thus downgraded from the status of "boom town" to "way station," wrote its leading historian, its "days as the leading western market town" were over. The arrival of the railroad in the 1830s only hastened the dilapidation of the town's original central district. The opening of three railroad lines in 1837 drew business away from the Four Corners—the commercial blocks fronting the canal—causing property values to plunge, and turning the finest hotel into a "derelict" shelter for indigents.[131]

If certain towns (or districts of towns) witnessed scenes of desolation after only a few years of consummation, there were others in the region that by-passed all the prior stages of empire, suffering ruin without any of the preceding glories. Just weeks before the canal's opening in 1825, a City of Refuge for the Jewish people was founded by Mordecai Noah, the Democratic newspaper editor, playwright, diplomat, and author of the phrase about the "golden column" cited above.[132] Partly inspired by Zionist dreams of an eventual return to Palestine, for which this colony would serve the preparatory role of retraining ghetto-born Jews in the skills of industry and agriculture, Noah was also motivated by the financial profits to be derived from such speculative town ventures. With the aim of founding a town that would become "the greatest trading and commercial depot" in America, he selected a site on Grand Island in the Niagara River, directly opposite the canal's mouth.[133] Setting out to conscript both the capital of private investors and the migration of Jews of all nations—including Native Americans, whom he, like Joseph Smith, considered "descendants of the lost tribes of Israel"—Noah inaugurated his aptly named city of Ararat with an extravagant cornerstone-laying ceremony that September. Despite the grandiosity of that ceremony (which, due to a shortage of boats, was performed on the mainland, in an Episcopal Church in Buffalo), Noah's project failed to get off the ground.[134] The hostile reaction of European rabbis to his self-designation as "Governer [sic] and Judge of Israel," along with the indifference of local speculators, resulted in the city's abandonment by January 1826, without the arrival of a single settler.[135] For the subsequent two decades, steamboat passengers passing Grand Island en route to Niagara Falls paid sardonic homage to the ruins of Ararat. Although no buildings were ever constructed, one tourist imagined that "numerous spires and turrets" lay concealed behind the dense forest; while another, Noah's Whig adversary, William Leete Stone, issued a mock lamentation for the grand metropolis that once stood there.

> Like Thebes and Palmyra, Troy and Babylon, . . . not a vestige of this ancient capital now remains. Its palaces have disappeared, its towers and battlements

have tumbled into ruins; tall trees now choke up its beautiful streets and avenues, and even the corner-stone, once consecrated by a great Rabbin, now lies in the cellar of a distinguished Gentile in Black Rock. Historians have neglected all notice of this great city and its illustrious founder.[136]

In 1834, the cornerstone was rescued from that Black Rock cellar, relocated to Grand Island, and enshrined as a monument to the "great city" that never was, if only for the benefit of artistic tourists who disembarked to sketch the solitary ruin and record its faded inscription.[137]

The canal's unpredictable and fluctuating effects upon the fortunes of settlers, boosters, and town founders may finally account for Lake Oneida's ruins, too. For all Tocqueville's and Beaumont's romantic fantasies about the afflictions of exile, the dangers of the New World wilderness, and the virtues of rustic simplicity, the reality behind the Frenchman's mysterious disappearance might have been somewhat more prosaic. In 1792, the year des Watines arrived on the island, the Western Inland Lock Navigation Company was incorporated, with the aim of linking Lake Oneida via the Oneida River to Lake Ontario, and via the Mohawk River to the Hudson. Although underfunded and overambitious, the project immediately stimulated investment and settlement along the anticipated route. According to a later historian, the shores of Lake Oneida became a booming region, one that settlers considered, well into the nineteenth century, "one of the most desirable portions of our state." But once construction on the Erie Canal began, the state acquired and abandoned the infrastructure of the Western Company, with "ruinous" consequences for the inhabitants of Lake Oneida. Land values plummeted, prosperity evaporated, and the population dwindled, as outgoers outnumbered incomers. Those who remained repeatedly petitioned the state legislature to construct a feeder linking Lake Oneida to the Erie Canal. Although the legislature eventually incorporated an Oneida Lake Canal company in 1832, at the time of Tocqueville's visit the previous year there were "few signs of recovery."[138] Indeed, the local fisherman's wife who informed Tocqueville and Beaumont about the ruins on Lake Oneida advised them not to settle on that island themselves. That would be a "losing speculation" (*une mauvaise speculation*) she warned them, "on account of it still being very far from the market."[139]

"Even Eden, you know, ain't all built"

Paper Cities, British Investors, and the Ruins of Cairo, Illinois, 1837–1844

"Let not the traveller," warned the Englishman William Oliver in his 1842 guide, *Eight Months in Illinois*, "when he looks at his map, and sees the name of some city hallowed by antiquity, be confident that he will find a place realizing his ideas of the original."[1] Oliver addressed his caveat about the disjuncture between metropolitan pretensions and objective realities to potential emigrants among the English lower classes. But in the eyes of a more eminent Englishman visiting the United States that year, the disjuncture revealed a more deep-seated flaw within the nation. It was at Cairo, Illinois, a speculative town site promoted as the future "Metropolis of the West" in broadsides, maps, and lithographs of the late 1830s, that Charles Dickens abandoned whatever hopes he still had for the American democratic project. Although already cognizant of this would-be city that failed to live up to its great expectations, Dickens was apparently unsettled by the landscape of ruin he viewed from the deck of his steamboat on April 9, 1842. A devastating flood had recently breached the jerry-built levees and engulfed the unfinished town, destroying property and infrastructure and prompting all but a hundred of its citizens to flee. All that remained, he recalled in his travelogue *American Notes*, was a "dismal swamp" of mud, debris, and the "rot[ting]" remains of "half-built houses."[2] A project that less than two years earlier had been "vaunted in England as a mine of Golden Hope, and speculated in, on the faith of monstrous representations," was now little more than a "hotbed of disease, an ugly sepulchre, a grave uncheered by any gleam of promise" (190). As another British traveler cautioned that same year, there was little chance of this blighted town "ever resembling the Cairo of the Nile, in any thing but its name."[3]

If travelers on the Erie Canal in the 1820s found sporadic ruins of tree-stumps, canal bridges, and cornerstones, those who ventured farther west in the 1830s and 1840s discovered scenes of total ruin. Cairo provides a case study of a town whose decline was even more precipitous than Rochester's rise was meteoric. Historians of western urbanization have tended to overlook such cases, focusing instead on the speculative cities that succeeded, most famously Chicago.[4] Unwisely located at the confluence of two regularly overflowing rivers, the Ohio and the Mississippi, Cairo's failure could easily be written off to the natural forces of flooding. For contemporaries, however, the untimely ruins of such "paper cities" raised crucial questions about the larger social and economic forces shaping the American urban frontier. By excavating the various interpretations of Cairo's ruin we can expose the contingencies and contradictions that appeared to mark the process of urban growth throughout the nation.

One issue raised by Dickens's juxtaposition of grand urban imagery and desolate town sites was the booster's role in American urban history. Geographer and historian William Cronon has recently portrayed these promoters of speculative cities not simply as loquacious publicists but as amateur theorists of urban growth. Rereading their books, speeches, and pamphlets alongside the works of geographers, he claims that they shrewdly perceived the codependency of city and country (34)—that crucial symbiosis between an embryonic metropolis and its agricultural hinterland that even Frederick Jackson Turner subsequently overlooked (34, 46–54). Cronon also emphasizes the power of their predictions of "urban and regional growth" to become "self-fulfilling prophec[ies]" (34–35, see also 46, 52). Such a reading, however, is colored by the context Cronon is exploring, namely the spectacular success of the speculative town of Chicago in becoming the metropolis of the "Great West." Resituated instead within a context of speculative *failure*, the limits of boosterism as an instrument of urbanization come into view. But rather than simply attribute Cairo's failure to unscrupulous boosters, as Dickens did, we need to restore the ambivalence of contemporaries' views toward them. Despite Cronon's claims, nineteenth-century consumers of commercial prospectuses, pseudo-geographical treatises, and promotional lithographs did *not* necessarily share the boosters' beliefs in ineluctable growth, nor were they always persuaded by the latter's "seemingly rational arguments" and "visionary faith" (46). Rather, viewers and readers understood them as a kind of fictional subgenre demanding a certain suspension of disbelief.

Taking place in the midst of a panic, Cairo's failure also raised the issue of the financial vulnerability of American speculative cities. Like so many other town sites mapped out during and immediately after the Jacksonian land boom, Cairo was founded not merely on the representations of boosters, but on countless other baseless fabrications, including government securities, state bonds, mortgage certificates, corporate stocks, bank notes, and the state charters that established those corporations and banks. The entanglement of cities within larger processes of capital accumulation was nothing new; the metropolis, as Georg Simmel later acknowledged, had "always been the seat of the money economy" as well as that of government and culture, and became increasingly dominated by money during the nineteenth century.[5] Yet these new prospective metropolises appeared to consist of little more than monetary fictions. Cities had perished from wars, disasters, and religious conflicts, but rarely if ever from financial panics.

Cairo's rapid rise and fall, moreover, highlighted the international as well as national economic forces that governed the fortunes of speculative cities in general. Far from limiting their operations to local markets, Cairo's promoters and boosters became involved in an intricate web of commercial operations extending from the neighboring bank in Kaskaskia, through Nicholas Biddle's bank in Philadelphia, to the exchange rooms and brokerage houses four thousand miles away in London. Cairo's history thus needs to be plotted not only on local maps of rivers, canals, and railroads—that regional geography of capital charted by Cronon—but also on a much more expansive terrain of transnational capital. Its ruins were particularly sensational insofar as they threatened to expose the extent to which America's embryonic cities lay at the mercy of the whims and priorities of distant British bankers and investors.

Finally, just as Cairo's ruins cannot be written off to its peculiar vulnerability to river flooding, neither can Dickens's preoccupation with its ruins be dismissed as a displaced expression of some other concern. Rejecting the earlier claim that Dickens had himself invested in Cairo, literary historians have typically explained the anti-American tone of such passages in *American Notes*—and his subsequent novel *Martin Chuzzlewit*—in terms of his personal circumstances, experiences, and preconceptions.[6] Some have attributed the scenes of desolation that recur in these writings to his aesthetic bias toward the English tradition of the picturesque, as if those principles could not be reconciled with the newness and blankness of many American landscapes.[7] Others have emphasized his political reappraisal of his earlier faith in

American democracy, his physical revulsion to social practices such as spitting in public and keeping pigs in city streets, or his psychical disgust with the cult of celebrity surrounding him.[8] But above all Dickens's anti-Americanism has been attributed to his grievances toward American publishers pirating his novels and thus defrauding him of royalties.[9] Although each of these concerns is evident both in the published texts and in personal letters he wrote en route, Dickens's denunciation of the speculative funding of American urban growth was a significant critique in its own right. The full title, *American Notes for General Circulation*—usually read as insinuating that disregard for copyright allowed such travel notes to be reprinted and sold in America at will—might be reread literally as an intervention in a much broader and even more contentious debate about the role of bank notes, and their general circulation, in both subsidizing and bankrupting cities on the western frontier.[10]

Prospective Views, or Founding Myths

The vast majority of cityscapes produced by nineteenth-century American lithographers were "substantially accurate" representations, according to their leading historian John Reps, and thus "Reliable Records of the Urban Past," to cite a chapter subtitle from his definitive *Views and Viewmakers*.[11] By this standard, an 1838 lithograph of Cairo appears a notable exception (fig. 2.1). Its title announces it as a "prospective" rather than actual view of a thriving city. These buildings, streets, and crowds do not yet exist, but are forthcoming. The one detail that might have legitimated this fantasy is the name of William Strickland, inscribed in the lower left corner. The distinguished (but then struggling) Philadelphia architect and engineer had been sent to southern Illinois to determine the suitability of "Township 17" for a speculative town. It was on the authoritative evidence of his measurements and surveys (carried out with his colleague, engineer and geologist Richard Taylor) that the promise of this visionary city apparently rested.[12]

Strickland's lithograph does serve, however, as a reliable record of one aspect of the urban past, namely the confidence of nineteenth-century boosters, land jobbers, and geographers in certain natural laws of development. Its depiction of congested commercial traffic converging on a wharf expresses the basic geographical precept that unrestricted access to a navigable river would assure the growth of any town or city. Situated alongside not one but *two* rivers, the Ohio and the Mississippi, and at the uppermost point on the latter that remains navigable year round, Cairo was expected to become the vital hub within a triangular trading route linking the Gulf states, the Great Lakes, and the Ohio Valley (fig. 2.2).[13] The site's natural advantages did not end there.

Fig. 2.1. William Strickland, *Prospective View of the City of Cairo, at the Junction of the Ohio with the Mississippi River, Illinois* (lithographed by Alfred Hoffy, printed by P. S. Duval of Philadelphia, 1838), 10 9/16 x 19 7/16 inches. Chicago History Museum.

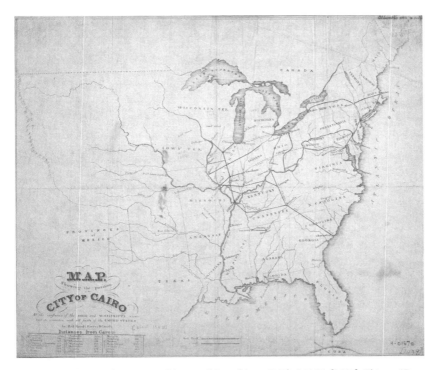

Fig. 2.2. Map showing the position of the city of Cairo (about 1838). 4-0167e [1839], Chicago History Museum.

Another providential sign apparently lay in the acute angle at which the rivers intersected; that narrow peninsula would guarantee a scarcity of land and rapid appreciation of real estate.[14] Strickland also touted its proximity to abundant natural resources. Situated at the "threshold of the most fertile regions of the west," and with unrivaled access to local timber, bituminous coal, iron, and stone, it would inevitably grow into a "great city." And if all this were not sufficient proof of future greatness, Strickland cited Cairo's geopolitical centrality. As the southernmost point of the North (at the tip of free-soil Illinois), and the westernmost point of the East (at the mouth of the Ohio), it was "nearly in the center of the United States." Viewed topographically, cartographically, and lithographically, Cairo was thus set to become *the* "central city" that mid-nineteenth-century western boosters envisaged as the heir to the urban centers of the Eastern seaboard, and perhaps even the future capital of the nation. Naming another metropolis flanked by two rivers, its promoters concluded that Cairo "must become to the west what New York is to the north" (Cairo prospectus, n.p.).[15]

While declaring that "no human opposition can prevent this city [from] becoming the '*Great Central Commercial and Manufacturing Emporium of Western America*'" (Cairo prospectus, n.p.), Cairo's promoters did recognize the limits of relying wholly on nature. Numerous speculative towns in the Ohio Valley that claimed "unrivaled advantages," conceded one western booster, ended up like Tyre and Nineveh (albeit on a "smaller" scale), "rising to splendor and falling to decay."[16] The junction of the Ohio and the Mississippi was itself the site of an earlier speculative collapse, that of the original Cairo. Founded in January 1818 by the Baltimore businessman John G. Comegys, the project failed to attract the backing of investors, and after a year the land reverted to the government and the city-to-be became a "wood-yard" (fig. 2.3).[17] This time around, the directors of the new Cairo City and Canal Company (CCCC), led by their founding president Darius B. Holbrook, intended to supplement its natural advantages with the "second nature" of canal, road, and railroad networks. These modes of transportation would ideally complement rather than challenge the primacy of river traffic. As depicted in the foreground of Strickland's lithograph (see fig. 2.1), the road runs *to* the river rather than alongside it as a rival route. Also projected to terminate at this peninsula was the Illinois Central Railroad, approved only days earlier by the state legislature. And to cater to the anticipated influx of freight and migrants, the lithograph imagined various other man-made improvements: commercial depots to rival any in the "city of London," factories to produce steamboat parts, a turreted armory and church to mitigate frontier lawlessness, and levees to protect the future city from flooding. This last feature of the plan was especially critical. Cairo's situation at the confluence of these rivers clearly exposed it to flooding.[18] For this reason Strickland reoriented the city toward the Ohio, the less turbulent of the two rivers. Determining that the "Mississippi side of this peninsula [cannot] well be made eligible as a landing place for this front of the contemplated city," Strickland relegated it to the lithograph's background, selecting the Ohio shore for his envisaged wharf (Cairo prospectus, n.p.). His town plan confirms this move by modifying Comegys's original 1818 plan, skewing the grid off its north–south axis, and aligning it with the Ohio (fig. 2.4). Nature and topography were thus brought into line with artifice and enterprise, and "in due time . . . a large commercial city [will] no doubt exist" (S. A. Mitchell, in *Report*, 10). Indeed, he had already designed the obelisk that was to have adorned the tip of the peninsula—a monument inscribed to the memory of Robert Fulton, whose invention of the steamboat had secured such "Great benefits."[19]

Scenes of Deception, Visions of Ruin

As yet existing primarily in the words of its promoters and lines of its lithographers and surveyors, Cairo was one of many town speculations of the 1830s commonly known as "paper cities." If the rapid growth of Erie Canal towns a decade earlier had compressed the normal stages of development (from pastoral village to commercial hub), the launching of paper cities in the new states and territories of the west now disrupted the cyclical framework of history still further. By 1830 Rochester had become a way station for settlers gambling on brand-new cities mapped out entirely from scratch. Prior models and metaphors of urban growth were invalidated by the "magic" of cities that were literally conjured out of thin air, or speculated into existence, some even claiming the status of metropolis before acquiring any infrastructure or population.[20] In the absence of those conventional criteria, such cities-to-be articulated their urban status through an impressive array of paper documents, including the survey that subdivided the township into sections and subsections, the plat that laid out and even named its streets (Cairo's containing as many as 142 blocks), and the charter submitted to the state legislature, followed by freshly minted real estate certificates and local bank notes, and the lithographs and prospectuses that promoted them.[21]

The very term *paper city* did not merely evoke the torrent of paper documents issued in its name, but was understood by critics as a blatant contradiction in terms. For British travelers such as Anthony Trollope, these instant cities, with their "intention" of future metropolitanism, deviated from the great cities of the past, whose "first founders" could hardly have had such "aspiring ambition[s]." For more radical domestic critics, such as the abolitionists

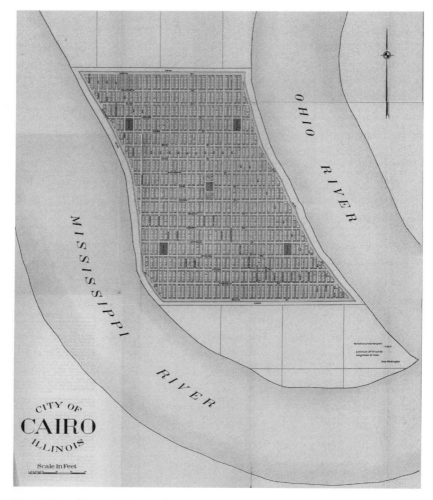

Fig. 2.3. Map of Cairo, 1818. From John McMurray Lansden, *A History of the City of Cairo, Illinois* (Chicago: R. R. Donnelley, 1910), opposite p. 30.

of William Garrison's *Liberator*, "cities on paper" constituted a "great felony attempted on an unborn posterity." But perhaps the most outspoken of all American critics was the novelist James Fenimore Cooper. In *Home as Found* (1838), a novel revolving around a land title dispute, Cooper identifies the paper city with certain undesirable characters: the lawyer (Aristabulus Bragg) who supplements his income by moonlighting in the "town-trade," the various proprietors who use maps and surveys to peddle vacant fields as city lots, and the real estate auctioneer (the aptly named Mr. Hammer) who plies these fic-

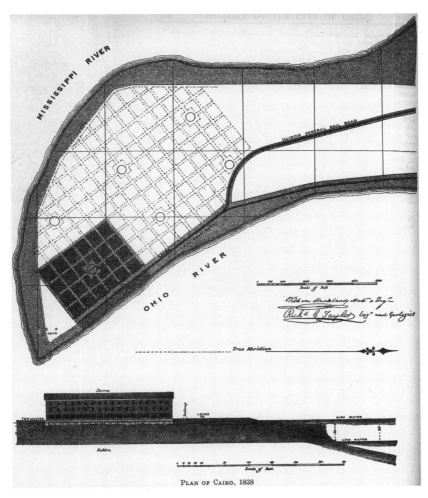

Fig. 2.4. William Strickland and Richard Taylor's "Plan of Cairo," 1838. From John McMurray Lansden, *A History of the City of Cairo, Illinois* (Chicago: R. R. Donnelley, 1910), opposite p. 111.

tions on Wall Street. But Cooper also blames this "traffic in cities" on a whole nation—the elderly, lower classes, women, and clergymen included—that has succumbed to the "western fever." New York's Great Fire of 1835, the novel subsequently suggests, serves as divine retribution for such excesses, above all in its instantaneous transformation of the Merchants' Exchange from a "bustling temple of Mammon" (and epicenter of the "town trade") into a "dark and sheeted ruin" (fig. 2.5). Invoking the traditional meaning of ruins as emblems of *vanitas*, Cooper presented the desolation of the city as a "rebuke . . . [to] the rapacious longing for wealth"—and perhaps even a harbinger of the

Fig. 2.5. Nathaniel Currier, "Ruins of the Merchant's Exchange N.Y. After the Destructive Conflagration of December 16 & 17 1835," 1835. Lithograph. 9 x 11 inches. © American Antiquarian Society. Seventeen years before hiring James Merritt Ives, Currier rose to popularity as a producer of disaster lithographs such as this one, which appeared in the *New York Sun* only four days after the fire. Whereas the characters of Cooper's novel, *Home as Found*, read the ruins of the fire as "fearful admonition[s] for those who set their hearts on riches" (107), other witnesses such as the ex-mayor Philip Hone found solace in the way that it had turned this already "splendid edifice" into what looked like an "ancient temple" (*Diary of Philip Hone*, 1:181).

1837 Panic.[22] Indeed, the periodic collapses of nineteenth-century speculative bubbles were often allegorized in terms of the ruins of natural cataclysms such as earthquakes (fig. 2.6).[23]

The visual exaggerations of these town traders, in the view of both British and American critics, were as insidious and deceptive as their verbal excesses, if not more so. Travelogues and emigrants' guides frequently warned of what power maps and lithographs could exert over the innocent eye. Buildings and infrastructure "all appeared on paper," wrote the British traveler Frederick Marryat, "as if actually in existence." American settlers such as Caroline Kirkland also testified to these images' capacity to seduce the "ordinary observer" with promises of future attractions, "splendidly emblazoned on a sheet of super-royal size" and "portrayed with bewitching minuteness." As depicted

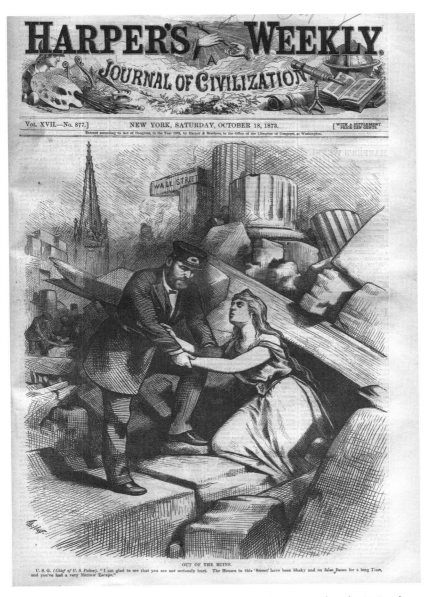

Fig. 2.6. Thomas Nast, "Out of the Ruins." From *Harper's Weekly* 17, no. 877 (1873): 913. President Ulysses S. Grant rescuing Columbia from the ruins of Wall Street in the aftermath of the 1873 Panic: "I am glad to see that you are not seriously hurt. The Houses in this 'Street' have been Shaky and on flase Bases for a long time, and you've had a very Narrow Escape."

in *The Paper City*, an 1838 sketch by the genre painter (and ambivalent Wall Street banker) Francis Edmonds, land agents typically drew on visual aids such as town plans to coax customers into buying lots (fig. 2.7). Accounts of Cairo included similar scenes of viewing, in which a prospective settler, investor, or traveler was ensnared by such representations as Strickland's. The New Hampshire reformer Thomas L. Nichols recalled a map of Cairo that would have tricked a purely "utilitarian eye" into seeing "at the confluence of these great rivers a favorable point for a great city." The "lithographed plans of the city" were especially beguiling: "There were domes, spires, and cupolas, hotels, warehouses, and lines of steamboats along both rivers. How fair—how magnificent it all looked on the India paper!" Clearly referring to the Strickland lithograph, Nichols was also playing on the pervasive trope of the paper city—the promise of grand urbanity imprinted on the thin, delicate surface of India paper.[24]

Fig. 2.7. Francis Edmonds, *The Paper City*, 1838. Wash on paper. 8 1/4 x 7 inches. Negative #45129a. Acc. #1944.386. Collection of The New-York Historical Society.

The counterpart to this ecstatic scene of mediated viewing was the bathetic moment of direct observation. In Nichols's case, Cairo's failure was blatantly apparent when he arrived to find it largely submerged: "You should see the result as I saw it in the misty miasma, by the pale moonlight. Cairo is a swamp, overflowed by every rise of either river" (168). Contrasting cities on paper with their actual appearance was a common trope in the critical discourse on urban speculation. Even the sight of prospective cities that had not (yet) suffered such physical and financial devastation could still conjure visions of ruin. Arriving as a settler in 1837 in the Michigan village whose glorious potential had been "emblazoned" on paper, Kirkland was immediately reminded of the ruined city of Palmyra. This strange daydream, or *ruin-effect*, was sparked by a shock of temporal contrast: not in this case between the present scene of "desolation" and "the retrospect of departed grandeur"—that backward glance tradition-ally associated with ruins—but between present desolation (the "dead silence, the utter loneliness, the impenetrable shade" of the town site) and the "antici-pation of *future* life and splendor" (49; emphasis added). It was a similar sense of temporal disjuncture in the virgin forests of Michigan, combined with an "arrière-pensée" about their imminent replacement by urban structures, that had stirred up Alexis de Tocqueville's memories of the ruined city of Himera in Sicily (see chapter 1). Simmel, too, detects a secret affinity between the states of decay and becoming. The sight of a disintegrating building "is, as it were, the counterpart of that 'fruitful moment' for which those riches which the ruin has in retrospect are still in prospect."[25]

In describing actual or imagined ruins, eyewitness accounts tended to be as exaggerated as the original speculative imagery of the boosters. They even vied to outdo one another in negative superlatives. For some, such as the Austrian travel writer Ernst von Hesse-Wartegg, Cairo was simply "more miserable, more desolate, more wretched" than any other place "on the Mississippi."[26] Others, especially British travelers, did not limit themselves to regional com-parisons. Anthony Trollope, passing through in 1862, judged it to be "the most desolate" "of all towns in America" (2:154), while the following year, his com-patriot Edward Dicey, not content with national rankings, wondered whether "*anything* more dismal than the prospect from the windows of the St. Charles Hotel, out of which I looked over the whole city . . . [could] be conceived." Dicey even cited a Yankee legend that Cairo was not of this world at all: that it "owes its terrestrial existence" to a "topographical error" that took place "when the universe was allotted out between heaven, earth, and hell."[27]

Such a polarity between promised grandeur and perceived devastation structures Dickens's account of Cairo in *American Notes*. It was Dickens's recurrent "dream" (even before he embarked for America) of "cities growing up, like palaces in fairy tales, among the wilds and forests" that had lured him westward (141).[28] And it was the nightmarish sight of a waterlogged, largely abandoned Cairo that conversely distilled all his disappointments about the United States. Similarly, Dickens characterized Cairo's initial representations as not merely exaggerated but utterly "monstrous." And without even disembarking from his steamboat he pronounced it "more desolate" than anything else he had seen en route; even "the forlornest places we had passed were, in comparison with it, full of interest" (190). Passing by it a second time on his return from St. Louis, he hoped never again to set eyes on the Mississippi, "saving in troubled dreams and nightmares" (207).

As it turned out, Dickens did revisit Cairo only two years later, if not in person then through the eyes of his fictional character, Martin Chuzzlewit. In the eponymous novel of 1843–44, this apprentice architect, disinherited by his grandfather and expelled by his master, crosses the Atlantic in the hope of making his name and fortune, and soon hears about the profits to be made as an architect and businessman in the "thriving city of Eden," a thinly fictionalized version of Cairo.[29] On his passage out from New York, he is repeatedly frustrated in his attempts to get an objective, impartial assessment of Eden's prospects. Ostensibly disinterested Americans encountered on the railroad, such as General Choke—a character derived from the passengers who had pestered Dickens with unsolicited advice about some "clever town in a smart lo-ca-tion" to be found "some three miles from the next station" (*American Notes*, 73)—turn out to be investors in the Eden Land Corporation themselves. Affecting an air of neutrality, Choke encourages Chuzzlewit to "*see* the maps, and plans, sir" and use them to resolve whether "to go or stay," to buy or not buy (334; emphasis added). Chuzzlewit finds such a plan in the office of Zephaniah Scadder, agent for the Eden Land Corporation, but it is so spellbinding in its verisimilitude, and comprehensive in its depiction of "banks, churches, cathedrals, market-places, factories, hotels, stores, mansions, wharves; an exchange, a theatre; public buildings of all kinds" that it overwhelms his powers of judgment. Scadder has to reassure him that building opportunities still remain for an architect and investor—that Eden "ain't all built . . . not quite" (340, 341). The abominable duplicity of such misrepresentations and understatements is echoed not only in the doubleness of the agent's name, the coarse-sounding surname contrasting with the biblical forename, but also in the doubleness of his face: one side is deformed by a sightless, motionless, yet apparently cautious eye that made it so "monstrously unlike [the] other" (338, 343).

When Chuzzlewit and his former (unpaid) manservant, now business partner, Mark Tapley, finally reach the valley of Eden to claim the fifty-acre lot purchased from Scadder, they find only "a few log-houses" and little sign of "the wharves, the market-place, the public buildings" he promised (360). In the novel as in the travel accounts, the extreme negativity prompted by the eyewitness view merely inverts the fantastic embellishments of the prospective bird's eye one. Externalizing their disappointment, the failed colonists perceive ruins all around them. Even through the eyes of the upbeat Tapley the cabins appear "rotten and decayed" and many "untenanted," the trees misshapen "like cripples," the domestic animals "wasted and vexed with hunger," and the few inhabitants "wan, and forlorn" (363). Further evidence of failed intentions is found in the ruins-in-reverse of fences left unfinished and logs left to "moulde[r] away" (363).[30] "The most tottering, abject, and forlorn" of all Eden's decaying structures, though, is the cabin named, "with great propriety, the Bank, and National Credit Office," a ruin now "past all recovery" (363). It is precisely because their expectations were so dangerously inflated—or "poetically heightened" (484)—by American promotional imagery that the travelers now construe the primitive condition of the town as a site of utter ruination: ruin that is simultaneously architectural, vegetative, and corporeal. But more catastrophic to the spirit than any physical ruin is the dissolution of the chimerical city fabricated in Scadder's office. Not even those who could survive the ordeal of seeing their "home dismantled," Dickens wrote, could endure the "razing of an air-built castle" (361).

If Dickens considered this disparity between advertised and observed town site fundamental to American urban speculation, the illustrated serial was perhaps an ideal vehicle for conveying that belief. Like so many of his novels, *Martin Chuzzlewit* first appeared in monthly installments, each illustrated with two engravings by Hablot Knight Browne, a.k.a. "Phiz." Browne typically used this format to draw parallels or contrasts between two events in the text. In the ninth installment, this doubling effect is announced in the very titles of the illustrations: *The thriving City of Eden, as it appeared on paper* (fig 2.8) and *The thriving City of Eden, as it appeared in fact* (fig. 2.9). Viewed side by side, they initially appear to mirror each other: one takes place inside, the other outside; in one, Chuzzlewit is confident and Tapley doubtful, in the other the roles are reversed. Nevertheless, signs of impending doom are already evident in the first illustration. Among the details Browne himself contrived are a mouse trap looming ominously over the unsuspecting travelers in Scadder's office, a cobweb ensnaring them in a web of deceit, and a town plan itself resembling a dense cobweb rather than the transparent grid of Strickland's plan.[31] Misrepresentations even spill over into the scene of Eden's ruin, further binding the paired images together. The "great placard" bearing the name of the firm, "CHUZZLEWIT ~ CO., ARCHITECTS AND SURVEYORS," is as pathetically fictional as the sign on the neighboring ruin, "BANK ~ NATIONAL CREDIT

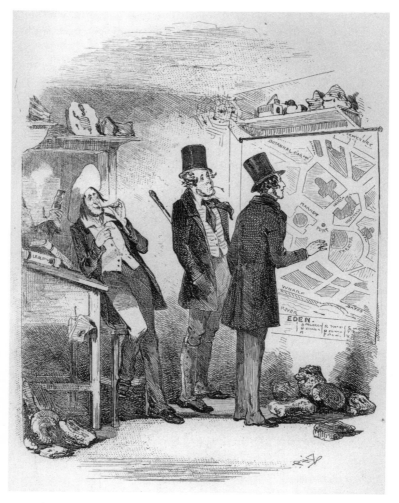

Fig. 2.8. Hablot Knight Browne, *The Thriving City of Eden, as It Appeared on Paper*. Illustration for the ninth installment of Charles Dickens, *The Life and Adventures of Martin Chuzzlewit*, September 1843. Reprinted in the first book edition (London: Chapman and Hall, 1844) as plate 17.

OFFICE" (see 363–64). Tapley also perpetuates the charade of urban booster-ism. Desperate to distract his master from melancholy thoughts, he maintains the pretense by arranging various architectural instruments on a tree stump and undertaking to "perfor[m] some [architectural] impossibilities" with the aid of nothing more than a hatchet (364). Ultimately, though, in Chuzzlewit's depressed and malaria-ridden mind, the tree stump cannot pass for a drafting

Fig. 2.9. Hablot Knight Browne, *The Thriving City of Eden, as It Appeared in Fact.* Illustration for the ninth installment of Charles Dickens, *The Life and Adventures of Martin Chuzzlewit*, September 1843. Reprinted in the 1844 edition as plate 18.

table. It instead represents the decimation of all his selfish fantasies and aspirations. The only apparent escape from his shattered illusions is to follow the frogs (another of Browne's innovations) and throw himself headlong into the river.[32] Chuzzlewit finds himself on the very verge of death, led astray not only by his own overweening acquisitiveness but also by the base, or rather baseless, representations of American hucksters.

Beyond Cairo: Ruins of the North and South

For all the negative superlatives, Cairo was just one of several sites of untimely ruin Dickens identified on his American tour and described in his travelogue. The dangers of boosting the growth of cities, rather than allowing them to emerge steadily and organically, were evident to him all across the nation. Even before his steamboat reached Cairo, he noticed how every "small town or village" on the Ohio seemed to call itself "a city" (*American Notes*, 177). And those towns that *had* grown into cities already betrayed signs of decay. In Louisville he found buildings prematurely blackened by the smoke of bituminous coal, along with the ruins-in-reverse of "unfinished buildings and improvements" indicating it had been "overbuilt in the ardour of 'going a-head,' and was suffering under the re-action consequent upon such feverish forcing of its powers" (186).[33] Even well-funded projects were vulnerable to the hazards of overreaching. The marble Greek temple designed for Girard College in Philadelphia with money bequeathed by arguably the wealthiest man in the country might claim to be the "richest edifice of modern times" if only legal difficulties had not caused its construction to be suspended. "Like many other great undertakings in America, even this is rather *going* to be done one of these days, than doing *now*" (111; emphases added).[34]

The most extensive ruins-in-reverse, however, were those of the nation's capital. Forty years after the French architect Pierre L'Enfant laid out that "city of magnificent vistas," Dickens rechristened it a "City of Magnificent Intentions" (129). Gazing out from the top of the Capitol, he observed further examples of "great undertakings" left undone.

> Spacious avenues, that begin in nothing, and lead nowhere; streets, mile-long, that only want houses, roads, and inhabitants; public buildings that need but a public to be complete; and ornaments of great thoroughfares, which only lack great thoroughfares to ornament are its leading features. . . . To the admirers of cities it is a Barmecide Feast [a mouthwatering meal that fails to live up to expectations] . . . (129–30)

The reasons for Washington's unfinished appearance were manifold: the reluctance of Congress to raise national taxes for local improvements; the transience of the population, much of which left town during summer recess; and the disadvantages of its site, located like that other border city, Cairo, on a malarial swamp.[35] There were also flaws in L'Enfant's plan. Even more optimistically than Strickland's in Cairo, it far exceeded the existing demographic and economic conditions. The vast distances between its nodal points—notably the White House and the Capitol—thus impeded the coherent and contiguous development of the city.[36] But above all the capital's shortcomings derived from its speculative character. In their attempt to transform (in L'Enfant's words) a "Wilderness into a City," its commissioners—anticipating the western boosters of the 1830s—encouraged real estate speculators to gamble on the supposed advantages of its location on the Potomac, and on the trade and commerce that would hopefully follow. They had resisted L'Enfant's call to complete the roads, bridges, and public structures first, insisting instead on an immediate auction of lots as the means to subsidize those improvements.[37] Underwritten by speculative (and even foreign) investment capital, Washington was thus rendered vulnerable to repeated bankruptcies and bank failures, as well as periodic campaigns to remove the capital to another location.[38] The outcome of all this, in Dickens's eyes, was a city resembling "a monument raised to a deceased project, with not even a legible inscription to record its departed greatness" (130).

It was not only jaundiced English travelers like Dickens who pronounced Washington a monumental ruin. Americans who lived and worked there repeatedly complained about the eyesores of abandoned canal projects, ruined bridges, unpaved streets, and primitive facilities. One congressman who arrived in 1800 considered it "both melancholy and ludicrous . . . a city in ruins."[39] Even more critical was the architect Benjamin Henry Latrobe, who served as Surveyor of the Public Buildings from 1803 to 1811 (and Strickland's teacher from 1803 to 1805). As a result of the malarial conditions but also the "capricious manner" in which public construction funds were granted, workmen who were "ruined in circumstances and health" could be found squatting in the "half-finished houses, now tumbling to ruins, which the madness of speculation has erected."[40] But of all the ruins-in-reverse in Washington, none was as grand as the Capitol itself, whose construction Latrobe supervised. In 1813, a year before the British reduced it to literal ruins, a local newspaper editor likened the unfinished edifice—as yet lacking its central portion and making do with a covered walkway connecting the two wings housing each chamber of Congress—to the Roman ruins described in the Comte de Volney's celebrated treatise, *Les Ruines*.[41]

The Capitol was repaired and completed by 1826, but the decision to rebuild the dome in 1855—a project that took another eleven years—prompted further visions of ruin. During the tour of 1861–62 that included Cairo, Anthony Trollope described how the sight of that still "unfinished dome" (whose construction was by then suspended due to the war) could deceive one into thinking one was "approach[ing] the ruins of some western Palmyra" (2:3) (fig. 2.10). This *ruin-effect,* or "idea of Palmyra" (2:12), was generated in large

Fig. 2.10. [Inauguration of President Lincoln at U.S. Capitol, March 4, 1861], 1861.
Photograph print. LC-USZ62-48564. Library of Congress. Anthony Trollope, visiting at this time,
compared the U.S. Capitol's "unfinished dome" to the "ruins of some western Palmyra."

part by the vast open spaces of the "uninhabited, and desolate" city. It was the
disparity between the grand, "full-blown" boulevards indicated on the map
and the inhospitable, undrained bogs that existed on the ground, that created a
feeling of melancholy and disorientation similar to that of a traveler lost in the
"deserts of the Holy Land, between Emmaus and Arimathea," which in turn
induced the mirage of the Capitol in ruins (2:3). Henry Adams later recalled
a similar experience as a child visiting Washington for the first time in 1850.
From the incongruous perspective of the "earth-road, or village street" that
connected them, the neoclassical columns of the Treasury, Post Office, and
Patent Office buildings all resembled the remains of "white Greek temples in
the abandoned gravel-pits of a deserted Syrian city."[42] Crowning this desert
ruinscape, according to both the English traveler and the Boston Brahmin,
was the Washington Monument. As a memorial intended to be the tallest and
grandest in the world when its cornerstone was laid in 1848, but condemned

(by lack of funds) to remain for years a "useless, shapeless, graceless pile of stones" (Trollope, 2:22) or a broken or "unfinished square marble shaft" (Adams, 47), the unfinished obelisk perfectly encapsulated the abortive qualities of the capital city (fig. 2.11).[43]

Dickens gravitated not only toward the ruins of overambitious and underfunded structures, but also toward those that exposed the more serious social problems afflicting the nation. The unexpected poverty of many Americans was manifested in the ruins he passed along the way, from the cabins with "broken windows" viewed from his canal boat in the swamps of the Alleghenies (171) to the "ruinous and filthy" huts viewed from his stagecoach in the Catskills (235)—any of which could have inspired the "rotten and decayed"

Fig. 2.11. "Beef Depot Monument," in *Leslie's Illustrated Newspaper* 13, no. 323 (1862): 173. The stump of the incomplete Washington Monument, surrounded by cattle requisitioned to supply the troops. *Leslie's* commended its readers "to ponder over the strange contrast presented by the unfinished monument to the founder of our republic, and the assembled beasts to sustain those who are laboring to save [his] work" (167).

log cabins of Eden. Such ruins appear unsuitable for picturesque appreciation, not only because they are "patched" up with recycled "fragments" of cloth, board, and paper (171), or "propped up by stakes and poles" (235), but also because they are still inhabited by settlers living in conditions of dire poverty and insalubrity. Dickens would have found the Catskills shantytown particularly indefensible insofar as it housed Irish immigrants working on a nearby railroad. As he commented elsewhere in his travelogue, the American landscape was constructed on the backs of the Irish: after all, "who else would dig, and delve, and drudge, and do domestic work, and make canals and roads, and execute great lines of Internal Improvement!" (91).

Dickens's social and moral conscience was also troubled by the ruins he encountered on a walking tour—guided by two policemen—of New York's notorious slum, Five Points. Only steps from the bright lights and fashions of Broadway (97–98) were gloomy scenes of "poverty, wretchedness, and vice" (99). Dickens displaces his bourgeois fear of, and fascination with, the destitute, diseased, and dissipated African American and Irish slum dwellers onto the tenements they inhabited. Assuming the guise of tour guide himself, and adopting the sensationalist mode of the urban exposé, he invites his genteel reader to "see how the rotten beams are tumbling down, and how the patched and broken windows seem to scowl dimly, like eyes that have been hurt in drunken frays" (99). He seems concerned primarily with the state of the buildings themselves, blaming "debauchery" for having "made the very houses prematurely old" rather than the overcrowded, unsanitary buildings for engendering the debauchery (99), and complaining how one can see into these "ruined houses" from the street, and indeed through them to "other ruins" beyond (101). Those ruins not fostered by vice and misery were forged by the almost daily fires that ravaged these neighborhoods. But even these "charred and blackened walls" were unnatural ruins: the products of financially motivated acts of arson, indicating that "speculation and enterprise found a field of exertion, even in flames" (103). Dickens's account of the ruins of Five Points had material repercussions for that neighborhood, not only in the increased numbers of middle-class slummers wanting to take similar tours, but also in the energized efforts of evangelical urban reformers. His words were quoted verbatim by the Ladies Home Missionary Society, which founded a Mission House there and eventually demolished the most notorious ruin of all, the "rickety and dilapidated" tenement known as The Old Brewery.[44] It was not that New York lacked ruins, Trollope subsequently observed, just that its ruins were not the sort that "travellers admire"—they "disgrac[e] rather than decorat[e]" (1:302).

If Dickens was disgusted by New York's ruins, he was "glad to the heart" to witness the ruins of the South (150). In rural Virginia, between Fredericksburg and Richmond, his railway window provided glimpses of "barns and outhouses . . . mouldering away; . . . sheds . . . patched and half roofless;" and "squalid" cabins inhabited by "negro children" living in bestial conditions (151). The "air of ruin" pervading this "once productive" region, he was told, resulted from tobacco monoculture (150).[45] Much as Louisville was suffering the consequences of "forcing" its urban growth (186), these vast slave plantations had "exhausted" the soil by "forcing crops, without strengthening the land" (150). But he also imagined these ruins as a kind of moral retribution, as if the "curses of this horrible institution" of slavery had condemned the land itself to "withe[r]" (150). The great "pleasure" he takes in these ruins arguably works to expunge his feelings of guilt regarding slavery (150). He had allowed himself in Baltimore to be served by slave waiters, an experience that induced feelings of "shame and self-reproach" (127). And although he devoted a whole chapter of the travelogue to denouncing slavery, at no point in his tour did he meet with abolitionists or deliver public speeches endorsing their cause.[46]

Even before General Sherman's campaign left whole cities in rubble, these scattered ruins of the slave South were hotly debated. For abolitionists, they served as proof that slavery was both economically and morally unsustainable. In a slave narrative that was popular in the mid-nineteenth century (but is now largely overlooked), the freedman Charles Ball expounded (through his abolitionist amanuensis) on the ruins he saw in that same region of Virginia: planters' mansions that had become "weather-beaten and neglected," fences that had "rotted away," "out houses, stables, gardens, and offices . . . fallen to decay," and most poignantly a "deserted and forsaken" church, where he "sat musing upon the desolation that surrounded me."[47] Ball's meditations among these ruins were colored—and made all the more remarkable—by the fact that he was suffering from the traumas of being separated from his wife and children (36), chained in iron collars and handcuffs (37), and transported hundreds of miles by foot (38–122), rather than traveling in the comfort of a railway carriage. Yet he echoed Dickens in attributing the ruins of this once "rich and populous country" (47) to overcultivation of tobacco and to the "folly and wickedness of slavery" (48).

For the leading proslavery advocate George Fitzhugh, the ruins of the South stemmed not from its "peculiar institution" but from the economic hegemony of the North. The "melancholy" scenes of desolation and ruin bordering the Mississippi downriver from Cairo brought home the destructiveness of capitalist speculation.[48] Whatever is "spared" by that "all-devouring and resistless river" that engulfs houses, fences, animals, trees, and the land itself, is swept away by the artificial "current of trade"—a force of *second* nature that "inflict[s] far wider and more cruel devastations, and leave[s] [behind] naught but misery, wrecks, and ruin" (160, 159, 162). The Mississippi furnishes Fitzhugh with a metaphor for the larger national and transnational capital flows that drain the whole of the South of its "wealth, . . . skill, refinement, education, and population" (160). Like a river in flood, capitalism may appear most ruinous during panics. But just as the work of erosion and deposit continues while the Mississippi is "confined within its banks," so is the economy "continually" removing and transferring wealth during periods of normalcy (162). Thus it was free trade, not slavery, that had reduced the South to an agrarian backwater of a rapidly urbanizing and industrializing North. Appearing in popular southern magazines such as *De Bow's Review*, such complaints about the unevenness of capitalist development contributed to sectional tensions during the antebellum years.[49]

By engorging themselves on the extracted agricultural resources of their Southern hinterland, however, Northern cities had become vulnerable to ruin themselves, in the eyes of Southern leaders and intellectuals. In another issue of *De Bow's*, Fitzhugh recalled visiting the "fine towns and cities" of New England, and realizing that its "mighty factories," "palatial private residences," and "stores and warehouses filled with rich merchandise," could prove short-lived. "Changes in the course of trade are things of ordinary and continual occurrence, as the crumbling ruins of Asia and Africa, and hundreds of dilapidated cities in Europe abundantly prove."[50] But the wealth of the North was particularly fragile, he believed, because it was founded upon the "fugitive and cosmopolitan" capital of manufacturing and commerce rather than rooted in the stable soil of agriculture, and was thus dangerously dependent upon trade with the South. If the Union were to be dissolved, "capital will quit the Northeast, and nothing will remain to her but poor lands, tenantless houses, harbors without shipping, valueless stocks, [and] exploded humbugs" (589).

The ruins that Fitzhugh predicted would result from secession were delineated in more sensational detail in an 1860 novel by Edmund Ruffin, another champion of slavery, contributor to *De Bow's*, and native of Virginia. Narrated by an English journalist as a series of dispatches to the London *Times*, *Anticipations of the Future* follows the train of events triggered by the 1864 election of the presumptive Republican candidate William H. Seward as President.[51] The introduction of antislavery policies eventually forces the South to secede (33–44, 86–93). Yet, as Fitzhugh predicted, secession and the ensuing civil war prove more detrimental to the North's economy than to the South's. Given the latter's agrarian self-sufficiency, the naval blockade of its ports does not prove disastrous; on the contrary, it causes grain, tobacco, and cotton shortages in the northern states (282). Without the additional revenues those states used to receive from southern taxpayers and debtors, and the profits from handling southern imports and exports, they begin to suffer economic distress, above all in their industrial and commercial cities (283–84). Rising food prices and declining employment eventually spark riots in Boston, Philadelphia, and worst of all New York, where a mob of 40,000 plunders churches, banks, mansions, armories and the government subtreasury; murders its property owners; then sets fire to the remainder of the city—partly out of class resentment and partly "to gratify their appetites and cupidity" (285–98; quotation on 295). Even after the cessation of hostilities, those northeastern cities never fully recover. As a result of the drain of capital, industry, and labor to the victorious South, and the strain of taxes and tariffs now enacted against them, "many northern residents predict and believe that grass will grow in the streets of Boston, and that the site of New York will remain, as now, overspread by the ruins left by the conflagration" (324). Washington, too, might have fallen to ruins—the "dissolution of the Union," Fitzhugh believed, would surely sound "the death-knell of its Metropolis"—had it not been granted a second life as capital of the southern confederacy (299).[52]

Such lurid intimations of ruin, while certainly derived from an agrarian theory of value, were not necessarily antiurban or antimodern. Despite the persistent myth of southern ruralism, Fitzhugh, Ruffin, and other contributors to *De Bow's* were advocates—indeed *boosters*—of the diversification of their economy and the redevelopment of their cities.[53] Dickens himself remarked how such towns as Richmond, Virginia, with its "deplorable tenements, fences unrepaired, walls crumbling into ruinous heaps," exhibited the "same decay and gloom" as that found in the neighboring countryside (153). If southerners were to become economically independent from the North, Fitzhugh believed, they would have to promote the growth of industrial and commercial cities (for example, through road construction) so as to supply a local manufacturing base and local markets for their agricultural products. Extending the aquatic metaphor, he conceived these cities as "breaks" that would prevent the erosion of the region's resources.[54]

Even when voiced in the rhetoric of "the revolutions of time," such calls to revive the ruined cities of the South necessitated further modifications to the discourse of *translatio imperii*. In a *De Bow's* article resolving that the "commercial phoenix shall arise from its ashes and fulfil its predicted destinies" in Charleston, Col. James Gadsden defied assumptions that the course of empire was irreversible (precluding the rebirth of decaying cities), and northward (bypassing the tropical and subtropical latitudes).[55] He also challenged

Enlightenment conceptions of the ruin as an emblem of vanity, tyranny, or folly, in presenting the ruined cities of Palmyra, Tyre, Sidon, Carthage, and Alexandria as proof of what the southern "spirit of enterprise" could achieve (127). Indeed, it was those cities' "very natural advantages, improved condition and prosperity" that "caused their ruin," by arousing barbarians from the "frozen regions" of the north to invade and pillage—acts of appropriation that the North now continues through policies that are less violent but all the more "insinuating and effectual" (128). It was also significant that those— and other—celebrated ruins were built by slaves. "The ruins of Thebes, of Nineveh, and of Balbec, the obelisks and pyramids of Egypt, the lovely and time-defying relics of Roman and Grecian art, the Doric column and the Gothic spire," extolled Fitzhugh in *Sociology of the South*, all "attest the taste, the genius and the energy of society where slavery existed" (243). It was perhaps because Washington—including the Capitol—was in part slave built that Fitzhugh celebrated its ruin value: "The day will arrive when the citizen, or the visitor, of Washington will be inspired with this elevating influence by the lovely specimens of art around him. Already many of her public buildings . . . send him speculating on that distant future when the immortal marble alone shall remain to tell of the past."[56] By contrast, the "sordid spirit" of capitalism that prevails in the North would fail to produce any "monuments" or "vestige[s] of art" (*Sociology*, 243–44). In the meantime, as an antidote to that materialistic ethos, Fitzhugh elsewhere recommended visiting the "grand and beautiful" ruins of antiquity: "The silence now reigning around them, and the long line of historical associations connected with them, combine to lift the soul above the groveling aims, the busy hum, and low ephemeral enjoyments of modern marts and cities."[57]

If Americans began to conceive ruins in sectional terms—northerners casting southern ruins as signs of the economic or moral weakness of slavery, while southerners recast them as signs of the destructiveness of capitalism, and each section claiming the legacy of antiquity for itself while invoking ruin as a threat confronting the other—Dickens continued to view them in resolutely national terms. He found little to distinguish the ruined cabins in Cairo from those in the Alleghenies, Catskills, or Tidewater Virginia, or from the decaying tenements of New York or the abortive buildings of Louisville, Philadelphia, or Washington. And he found nothing redeeming about any of these ruins. Their abjectness became even more pronounced when compared with the Roman ruins he celebrated in his subsequent *Pictures from Italy* (1846), especially when the two travelogues were merged into a single edition a decade later. Despite his consciousness of the bloody crimes haunting Roman ruins, he considered the panoramic view from the top of the Coliseum "the most impressive . . . sight, conceivable."[58] Dickens's aversion to American ruins, however, cannot be characterized as displaced bitterness over copyright.[59] Although American reviewers accused him of writing the book (and taking the tour) out of "mercenary motives," and of fixating obsessively on certain negative features at the expense of the more positive aspects of their society (such as the culture and manners of the elite), Dickens considered those ruins meaningful in their own right.[60] "Hinting gloomily at things below the surface," he wrote in the passage on Richmond's ruins, such scenes "force themselves upon the notice, and are remembered with depressing influence, when livelier features are forgotten" (153). They belie not only the youthful appearance of the American landscape—as in the pristine bricks and stones of Boston, the flimsy walls of Lowell, or the "cardboard colonnades" of Worcester (34, 75, 81)—but also the supposed innocence of the nation itself.

Boosters, Banks, and Banknotes: Dickens's Economic Geography of America

Although Dickens did not explicitly map these various sites of ruin—except to say that Cairo was the most "desolate . . . yet beheld" (190)—he did provide a clue as to how one might do so. In the very commercial heart of the city of Philadelphia, from the bedroom window of his hotel on Chestnut and 4th Street, he noticed yet another abandoned building: a "handsome building of white marble."

> [It] had a mournful ghost-like aspect, dreary to behold. I attributed this to the sombre influence of the night, and on rising in the morning looked out again, expecting to see its steps and portico thronged with groups of people passing in and out. The door was still tight shut, however; the same cold cheerless air prevailed; and the building looked as if the marble statue of Don Guzman could alone have any business to transact within its gloomy walls. I hastened to enquire its name and purpose, and then my surprise vanished. It was the Tomb of many fortunes; the Great Catacomb of investment; the memorable United States Bank. (109–10)

One connection between the literal ruin of Cairo and the figurative ruin of the Second National Bank of the United States (once the largest bank in the world) is the coincidence—unmentioned either by Dickens or by subsequent critics—that Strickland was involved in both projects (fig. 2.12). He had designed the bank in 1818, following Latrobe's example in modeling it on the ruins of the Parthenon (as reconstructed in Stuart and Revett's influential

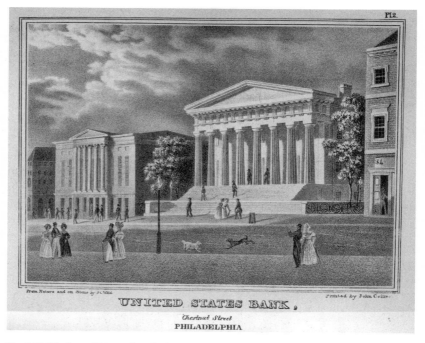

PL2.

From Nature and on Stone by J. C. Wild   Printed by John Collin

UNITED STATES BANK,

Chestnut Street
PHILADELPHIA

Fig. 2.12. The Second National Bank of the United States (architect, William Strickland; completed 1824); Plate II from J. C. Wild, *Panorama and Views of Philadelphia, and Its Vicinity* . . . (Philadelphia: [J. T. Bowen], 1838).

survey, *The Antiquities of Athens*), while updating it with modern materials to "safeguard [it] against the ravages of the incendiary, and the no less fatal but inevitable attacks of time."[61] But it was financial forces that caused the premature ruin of this bank at 3:00 p.m. on February 4, 1841, when it closed its doors for the last time. The "ruinous consequences" of the panic were still evident to Dickens twelve months later, in the "gloom" it seemed to "cast" on the whole city (110). The ruin-in-reverse or "modern Parthenon in ruins" of Girard College, another commentator observed, was in fact the result of financial losses from the bank's failure, to which it would serve as an "emblematic" monument, or "mausoleum."[62] Many of the ruins Dickens witnessed across the country, from Washington to Louisville, could be traced back—at least indirectly—to the failure of this bank. Like Chuzzlewit, Dickens happened to visit America during "a season of great commercial depression" (*Chuzzlewit*, 261).

In drawing attention to the financial ruin of the Bank of the United States alongside the physical ruins found elsewhere in the country, Dickens was not holding its directors solely responsible. The problem was not any single bank, but the American banking system as a whole, including that ruined "Bank, and National Credit Office" of Eden (363). In the novel as well as the travelogue, Dickens consistently gives the impression that a paper currency and a decentralized, unstable banking system were monstrous American contrivances alien to English minds. Even before embarking for America, Chuzzlewit had learned of its economic perils as well as prospects from the story of an immigrant, Ned, who allegedly "landed there without a penny to bless himself with," quickly "made his fortune," and then lost it all "the day after, in six-and-twenty banks as broke." Misunderstanding the meaning of a "paper fortune," Chuzzlewit's informant assumed that Ned could have safeguarded it "so very easy, by folding it up in a small parcel" (214). Throughout their pursuit of wealth in America, Chuzzlewit and Tapley keep their—or rather Tapley's—savings in sterling rather than exchanging them for U.S. dollars, perhaps as a precaution against the "commercial depression" currently afflicting the country, the volatile currency of such an "elastic country," or the instability of local banks (261–62). Such fiscal caution was entirely necessary, Dickens wrote in a letter to his editor John Forster the previous year, given the "strange state of things in this country." As "bank paper won't pass," he kept his travel money in foreign specie: at first "English sovereigns" and later "French gold; 20-franc pieces; with which I am travelling as if I were in Paris!"[63]

By comparison with America's financial precariousness, British banking institutions represented for Dickens—or at least his characters—the epitome of soundness and dependability. Tapley has such "unbounded confidence in the wisdom and arithmetic" of Savings Banks (mutual societies catering to workingmen) that when withdrawing his fortune of "thirty-seven pound ten and sixpence" for the trip to America, he had trusted the clerk to count the money on his behalf (336). Other characters share this faith in British financial institutions. Cast adrift in the alien city of London, Chuzzlewit's naive confidant Tom Pinch is wary of all strangers except those he would find in those "concern[s]" of "perfect respectability," the Mint and the Bank of England (545). Moreover, it was a Bank of England note for twenty pounds Chuzzlewit received in an anonymous envelope (later revealed to be from his grandfather) that in part made his American expedition possible (222). Dickens expounded on the dependability of the Bank of England in an account of a visit there six years later.[64] Founded in 1694, that "Old Lady of Threadneedle Street" (unlike those recent upstarts in the United States) embodied "stable antiquity" (124). The privileged position granted it by the state allowed it to function as the "mighty heart of active capital, through whose arteries and veins flows the entire circulating medium of this great country" (126).[65] Consequently, almost all the notes that it discharged ultimately flow back to its shelves, where they are inspected for signs of wear or counterfeiting, before being recirculated. (If only the circulation of Dickens's own issues was as well regulated, and protected by the deterrent of capital punishment [128].) It was the lack of such a "mighty heart" in America that rendered its circulation of money unreliable and its economy shaky—another reason why Chuzzlewit, Tapley, and Dickens adhere to the soundness of British currency rather than put their faith in the "monstrous" fiction of the dollar.

That deserted and melancholy edifice outside Dickens's window in Philadelphia thus designates a limit within his political economy. As an advocate of free trade, he would have been in favor of "general circulation," in the financial if not literary realm.[66] But the ruins of the American banking system reveal what happens when circulation becomes too general, and trade too free.[67] Thus, whereas the Bank of England had largely refrained from issuing notes of denominations lower than £5, thereby maintaining paper money for merchants and coins for everyday consumption, American banks had followed the Scottish example in liberally issuing "small" notes, sometimes for fractions of a dollar.[68] With so many kinds of paper bills (or "shinplasters" as they were called) in circulation, they were subject to forgery, alteration, and uncertainty about their true value.[69] Some were so worthless as to be priceless. Dickens's compatriot Marryat narrated the "adventures" of "one of the glorious Cairo Bank twenty-dollar notes" that allowed its possessor "to eat, sleep, and drink, free of cost" all across the West, because proprietors would rather waive the price of their rooms and meals than give up their "good change for bad money."[70]

American frontier investments appeared treacherous not only because they were underwritten by worthless paper bills and unreliable banks, but also because they circulated beyond their national boundaries. Although American banknotes would not have been accepted as legal tender in Britain, where the pound now reigned as its "territorial currency," various money substitutes did cross the Atlantic.[71] Bank securities, bills of exchange, real estate certificates, and above all the stocks and bonds floated by states and corporations to fund internal improvements, all swamped the London markets.[72] Darius Holbrook traveled to London twice, in 1838 and 1839, to arrange for his Cairo City bonds to be sold to British investors by the joint-stock bank, John Wright and Company of Covent Garden.[73] While some welcomed the influx of American securities as a kind of "cash remittance" providing a timely relief from economic difficulties, others feared it would jeopardize the value of real money.[74] These complaints increased with the subsequent failure of that bank in Philadelphia, which had led the way in encouraging foreign investments in American urban and infrastructural projects. The "fortunes" entombed within that "Great Catacomb" on Chestnut Street are thus implicitly those of British shareholders. Overseas investors, principally from Britain, had held more than half the bank's shares and thus suffered the most from its bankruptcy, apparently prompting "all classes" in England to call for war.[75]

The transatlantic circulation of American securities was all the more alarming because of the advertising materials accompanying them. Taking advantage of the inconvenience for British investors of traveling as far as southern Illinois to inspect town sites at first hand and thereby appraising their real value as speculative ventures, American town promoters disseminated promotional pamphlets and maps. On his fund-raising trips to Britain, Holbrook reportedly brought copies of Strickland's *Prospective View* (see fig. 2.1) along with the various Cairo Company broadsides that bore the latter's written testimony. "Flaming" or "florid lithographs portraying a metropolis at the junction of the Ohio and Mississippi" reportedly turned up in the "pubs, halls, and squares of London."[76] Lithographic views were commonly produced not as illustrations in books but as larger, loose-leaf prints to be distributed and displayed in public spaces such as hotels, banks, and offices.[77] Even if he did not invest himself, Dickens may thus have seen the Strickland lithograph in London, and may have been alluding to it in his account of Scadder's "great plan" of Eden, and in that ambiguous phrase "monstrous representations." Such representations were monstrous not only in their fictitiousness but also in the promiscuity of their circulation across national borders.

In offering the "mournful ghost-like" Bank of the United States as a potential clue to the ruin of western speculative towns and the American economy as a whole, Dickens also raised another crucial financial issue, that of "repudiation" or "states' debts." British investors in that bank, and in the state bonds it promoted, came to associate it with the subsequent repudiation of those obligations by several states. By February 1843 nine states (including Pennsylvania) had reneged on their loans, while Illinois had defaulted on its annual interest payments.[78] To Dickens, borrowing money with no apparent intention of repaying was no different from promoting a speculative town with little prospect of growth, or offering a bank note not backed by specie: all were abominable crimes. Such practices are identified in the novel with the Pennsylvanian merchant Major Pawkins, one of the first Americans Chuzzlewit and Tapley meet after disembarking in New York. Besides being able to "start a bank, or negociate [*sic*] a loan, or form a land-jobbing company (entailing ruin, pestilence, and death on hundreds of families), with any gifted creature in the Union," he also upheld certain political principles, such as his country's right to "run a moist pen slick through everything, and start fresh" (261). En route to Eden, Tapley further voices the frustrated demands of London bankers and investors, insisting that "the defaulting part of this here country" has to realize that "not paying 'em won't do in a commercial point of view"; even if they were to pay, they would be intolerably arrogant, "mak[ing] such bragging speeches, that a man might suppose no borrowed money had ever been paid afore, since the world was first begun" (357).[79] On their homeward journey, they continue to admonish their fellow passengers for the "Dishonor" and "Fraud" of repudiation (506–8).

Dickens is at least reassured that this national proclivity for fraudulent schemes is "not . . . without its retributive operation" (*American Notes*, 267), as is clear from the recent ruin of Cairo, and of the nation's economy as a whole—which, like the ruins of the Merchants' Exchange described by Cooper, might serve as some kind of "rebuke" or *vanitas*. But whereas Chuzzlewit's failure as a speculator arguably enables him to realize the futility of such schemes, the selfishness of his own ways, and the need to return to England (497), Americans tend to "gil[d] over" these failed speculations and thus seem unlikely to ever learn the lessons of their ruins (*American Notes*, 267).[80] The problem is not merely the acts of fraud, but that they are unanimously extolled—even when they fail—as testimony to the perpetrator's expertise, or in the local euphemism, "smartness" (*Chuzzlewit*, 258, 494). Thus, Major Pawkins's exploits as a land speculator who caused widespread "ruin" has apparently earned him respect as an "admirable man of business" (261). Even an American settler who has been reduced to physical and financial "ruin" in Eden can find comic relief in how that "smart" land shark Scadder "had drawd [*sic*] a lot of British capital" (494). In the "Concluding Remarks" to *American Notes*, Dickens returns to the ruins of Cairo as exemplary of this fundamental trait in the American character, the "love of 'smart' dealing" (267).

> I recollect, on both occasions of our passing that ill-fated Cairo on the Mississippi, remarking on the bad effect such gross deceits must have when they exploded, in generating a want of confidence abroad, and discouraging foreign investment: but I was given to understand that this was a very smart scheme by which a deal of money had been made: and that its smartest feature was, that they forgot these things abroad, in a very short time, and speculated again, as freely as ever. (268)

In Dickens's view, it is this legitimation by all Americans of such "gross deceits"—along with their "national love" of moneymaking (268)—that links the most duplicitous boosters in Cairo to ostensibly respectable merchants in Pennsylvania.[81] The directors of that bank in Philadelphia—which after all goes by the name of "United States"—might be considered equally remiss in failing to bail out their bankrupt countrymen, or to accept responsibility for their foreign debts.

The Other Side of the Coin: American Whig Rereadings

Dickens's indictment of all Americans elided their internal differences over urban speculation and its associated institutions and practices. No issue, arguably not even slavery, dominated party politics in this period more than banking. Since 1832, the country had been consumed by the "Bank War," Andrew Jackson's bitter campaign against that very edifice Dickens later surveyed from his Philadelphia hotel, Nicholas Biddle's Bank of the United States. Even into the 1840s, well after the expiration of the Bank's federal charter and the Whigs' recapture of the presidency, politicians and the press continued to argue over what kind of banking system would take its place. President Van Buren's Democrats, who remembered Biddle's institution as a "Monster Bank" that deserved to be reduced to "stupendous but melancholy ruins" by Jackson (fig. 2.13), now called for a decentralized system of independent subtreasuries, while those Whigs who recalled the adverse effects of a denationalized banking system advocated an even stronger, central bank.[82] Appearing at this juncture, Dickens's allusions to controversial fiscal issues added fuel to the

Fig. 2.13. E. W. Clay, *The Downfall of Mother Bank: Draw'd off from Natur* [sic] *by Zek Downing, Neffu* [nephew] *to Major Jack Downing*, 1833. Cartoon. © American Antiquarian Society. The fictional New Englander Major Jack Downing (left) cheers Andrew Jackson's "Order for the Removal of the Public money deposited in the United States Bank" (the scroll in his right hand), which has toppled the Bank's columns, burying its behorned president Nicholas Biddle, along with its Whig advocates (including Henry Clay and Daniel Webster).

fire, stirring up responses from Whigs and Democrats in the form of literary reviews.

Reviews of Dickens's travelogue and novel, published in venues affiliated with one or the other party, were thus largely dictated by internal, partisan affiliations. Typical of Whig reviews of *American Notes* was an 1843 pamphlet titled "A Letter to a Lady in France . . . With Answers to Enquiries Concerning the Books of Capt. Marryat and Mr. Dickens," written anonymously by the Massachusetts businessman and state senator Thomas Greaves Cary.[83] Cary's response to insinuations about the "reputation and . . . character of the United States" was typical of the Whigs: he laid the blame for the current troubles largely on Jackson's veto of the Bank's recharter a decade earlier, on July 10, 1832 (2). This veto unwittingly prompted the individual states to "exercis[e] their sovereign powers . . . in borrowing money" and creating new banks whose failure ultimately "contributed" to a "ruinous" decline in property values (16, 14). The redistribution of the Bank's federal deposits to numerous state or "pet" banks and subtreasury offices did indeed spell the loss of a crucial mechanism for regulating the issue of paper money. State-chartered banks could now print bills at will, as there was no longer any national bank that might demand their redemption for specie.[84] Known as "wildcat banks" (after the wildcats that supposedly haunted such remote outposts), they issued notes that were themselves "monstrous" in that they appeared—like Strickland's lithograph— to have no basis in reality, and thus signs without referents, or empty signifiers. Cairo's bank—located, *pace* Dickens's account and Browne's illustration, in the neighboring town of Kaskaskia—issued notes that were doubly fictional, in that they depicted vignettes of nonexisting warehouses and factories (fig. 2.14). Thus, although Jackson distrusted all banks and especially loathed paper money, his veto had the unintended consequence of stimulating a rapid, chaotic growth of state banks across the country (in Cary's calculation 268 alone in the space of two years [14]) and a simultaneous expansion of suspect paper money that ultimately, in the Whig analysis, caused the devastation of western speculative towns.[85]

This reckless expansion of credit was perceived by Cary, among other Whigs, as having led in turn to overinvestment in construction projects that were unlikely to be profitable because they were "too mighty," "ill conceived," and badly financed (17, 16). Turning rags into money, Caroline Kirkland observed, was viewed as a kind of sorcery that could "transmute these acres of wood and meadow into splendid metropolitan residences" (*New Home*, 204–5). Moreover, infrastructural improvements such as canals and railroads were motivated at least in part by the desire to drive up the property values of neighboring towns. The intimate relationship among new towns, banks,

Fig. 2.14. Five-dollar bill issued by the Bank of Cairo at Kaskaskia, 1839. From John McMurray Lansden, *A History of the City of Cairo, Illinois* (Chicago: R. R. Donnelley, 1910), opposite p. 231.

and transportation routes on the western frontier could be gleaned from the timing of legislative decisions. Only two days prior to granting Cairo's city charter, the Illinois legislature approved the Illinois Central Railroad, whose route was to terminate at that very city.[86] To generate the $10 million for such transportation projects, that same state legislature passed a supplemental act increasing the stock of the Second Bank of Illinois (chartered two years earlier) and issuing $8 million in bonds.[87] This simultaneous boom in real estate and internal improvements, in the Whig analysis, was thus artificially stimulated by the expansion of credit Jackson had unleashed.[88] This process was particularly visible in Illinois. Cairo was just one of more than five hundred new towns established in that state between 1835 and 1837, making it arguably the epicenter of the Jacksonian land boom. Many of those towns were sited not in areas of prior settlement and agricultural development, but rather along, or at the end of, imaginary lines marked out by internal improvement acts.[89]

If, in the Whig account, Jackson's opposition to the National Bank had initiated this dangerous bubble of bank credit, state debts, speculative towns, and internal improvements, his equally bitter hatred of paper money subsequently punctured it. Seeking to reverse the rampant inflation he had caused, Jackson finally issued a "Specie Circular" in July 1836, an executive order requiring public lands now be paid for with hard currency. This overreaction, Whigs argued, only exacerbated the problem. Within weeks, banks ran out of specie reserves and suspended payments, many not resuming until well into the 1840s. Meanwhile, the general population began to avoid paper bills and hoard specie, causing an unprecedented contraction in the money supply.[90] Dickens's visit thus took place during a period in which the circulation of American notes was anything but general. Indeed, he confided in a letter to his editor written from Cincinnati that "this country . . . has *no money*; really no money," its gold is "scarce," its paper money "won't pass," and "the newspapers are full of advertisements from tradesmen who sell by barter."[91]

Surveying the economic legacy of the 1830s, Cary concluded that the pioneers of the "newly settled states like Indiana and Illinois," which subsequently repudiated or defaulted on their debts to British investors, were not intentionally dishonest, but rather the victims of "premature" canal and railroad schemes and a depreciated dollar (21). Furthermore, Cary assured his "Lady in France" that other states had been prompt in paying their debts (disproving the charge that "we are all swindlers, and knaves"), and that the delinquent states should—and would—pay theirs in due course (18). In the meantime, Biddle's bank could not be held liable for those outstanding debts. Dickens and his compatriots were misguided in calling for such reimbursement, not least because the National Bank was no longer national. Strickland's marble edifice continued as a bank after the expiration of its federal charter in 1836, but under a very different guise. Rechartered as a state bank, it retained "Second National Bank of the United States" as its title, appending the suffix, "of Pennsylvania." The British belief—or *feigned* belief—that it was a national bank, "a renewal of that which had just been closed," was in Cary's view unfortunate (13). It was "merely a creature of one of the states," yet another of those precarious financial institutions chartered by state legislatures during Jackson's second term of office (15). Foreign investors needed to understand—or admit they had understood all along (24)—that many businesses, taverns, and even "omnibus coach[es]" appropriated the name "United States" as their prefix or suffix without assuming the authority or accountability of a "*national establishment*" (13). Dickens must have been aware of such customs of nomenclature from his stay at the United States Hotel, just across the street from the "gloomy walls" of that ruined bank.

A Tale of Two Nations: Jacksonian Counterreadings

If Whigs exonerated that defunct bank from Dickens's allegations about American financial practices by displacing the blame onto wildcat banks out west, their opponents were less forgiving of Biddle's enterprise. Democrats may have been divided over the money question—their entrepreneurial faction favoring state-chartered banks, bank notes, and commercial credit, while their radical wing of "Loco Focos" denounced soft money and wildcat banks (or "Cairo swindling shops")—but they remained united in their opposition to that marbled edifice in Philadelphia. Just as they had earlier joined forces to defeat Biddle in the Bank War, they now rediscovered a common cause in denouncing his latest venture, and its role in precipitating the collapse of the recent land speculations.[92]

In the Democratic version of events, the appearance Biddle's state bank gave of being a "national bank" was not inadvertent but rather a deliberate act of deception, or to borrow Dickens's phrase, a monstrous representation. Rather than curtailing its activities in the aftermath of the withdrawal of federal deposits by 1836 and the Panic of 1837, Biddle had launched even greater speculations to restore American credit abroad and reassert his personal influence at home.[93] Although this enabled town speculators like Holbrook to sell their bonds in London in 1838–39, in the long run it deferred (and worsened) the effects of the Panic, while saddling the states with even greater debts to foreign investors. Town speculations on the western frontier were rendered more vulnerable than ever to the vicissitudes of international finance. The ruins of paper cities such as Cairo were thus attributable less to local conditions such as the level of the Mississippi than to distant factors such as the state of stock and bond markets in London. This new interdependency became immediately apparent when the failure of the 1838 harvest in Britain triggered a train of events leading to the suspension of payments by Biddle's bank in October 1839, and ultimately the bankruptcy of several states.[94] Similarly, the disastrous run on Cairo's bank (in Kaskaskia) in December 1840 could be traced back to the bankruptcy of its London agents, Wright and Company, several days earlier, on November 23. This transatlantic domino effect finally accounted the following year for the failure of Biddle's own bank, victim of tightening credit in London.[95] These later crises of 1839–41 were arguably more devastating and far-reaching than the often-cited Panic of 1837. Biddle's agents in London, wrote the *Democratic Review*, had merely "postponed the day of reckoning for a period, but at the expense of greatly enhancing its severity" ("Currency Reform," 170; see also 168). In the opinion of Democrats, then, the ruin of western speculative projects and the repudiation of states' debts was the fault not of Jackson's policies or boosters' fabrications but of the very institution he had tried to destroy, that deceptively "handsome building of white marble" on Chestnut Street.

Democrats thus went beyond both Dickens and the Whigs—who faulted America's national character and monetary policy respectively—to foreground the deleterious impact of British economic hegemony. The financial ruin of Holbrook's bank in Illinois and Biddle's bank in Pennsylvania could only be explained by attending to the dealings of a third bank, the Bank of England. The latter's decision to raise its interest rates, and its refusal to discount the bills of banks and merchants speculating in American commodities, had compounded the effects of the poor harvest and ultimately precipitated the bankruptcy of several American states in 1839.[96] In reviews of Dickens's books (among other writings) published by their party's magazines and presses, Democrats offered impassioned arguments against the "Old Lady of Threadneedle Street," all of which countered the novelist's estimation of her restraint and responsibility.

Despite the naïveté of Dickens's characters when confronted with the phenomenon of American bank notes, it was in fact the Bank of England that had pioneered the dangerous experiments in paper currency. That bank was responsible, wrote the *Democratic Review*, for introducing a system of credit that replaced "actual money" with "promises to pay," an act of extortion against the people ("Currency Reform," 183). Nor did Democrats view the Bank of England as an effective or reliable force for maintaining the stability of that nation's currency and economy, let alone as a model on which to base the American system. It did not become the sole issuer of paper money, that unrivaled "heart" of the nation's circulation Dickens later celebrated, until the Bank Charter Act of 1844; up to then, provincial or "country" banks could freely issue notes. The dangers of this "heterogeneous circulation" became clear during the 1820s when the country banks "eagerly availed themselves of the restoration of public confidence" to issue notes far in excess of their specie reserves, and to "forc[e]" this bad paper "into . . . general circulation" ("Currency Reform," 187). The Bank of England was thus powerless to prevent the subsequent contractions of 1825 (and again of 1836 and 1839), when those notes rapidly became "worthless" and the nation came close to "a state of barter" (187, 188). This "continuous succession of ruinous revulsions" not only revealed that a paper currency pumped through "the veins and arteries of circulation" would "excite the [economy] to the verge of insanity," wrote another American Democrat; it also disproved that a national "paper-issuing authority . . . [could] regulate with steadiness and wisdom the paper issues of other institutions."[97] The Bank even failed to fulfill its other role as the Lender of Last Resort that would bail out smaller banks in times of crisis. On the contrary, merchant houses and joint-stock banks, such as Wright and Company, were encouraged by the Bank of England's generous rediscount policies of the 1830s to venture ever deeper into American securities, only to be left high and dry when the Bank cut credit, raised interest rates, or refused to discount their bills of exchange.[98]

The bitterest complaint Democrats leveled against the Bank of England was that, despite all these crises and challenges, it dominated the world economy in the 1840s. With growing specie reserves that enabled it effectively to adopt the first gold standard by 1821, and with its notes—declared legal tender by Act of Parliament in 1833—rapidly becoming the world's first reserve currency, the Bank of England was in a position to regulate not only domestic but also global trade.[99] By interfering with free trade (as in its support of the Corn Laws), it "exerts a despotic control over the currency and banks of the United States," the *Democratic Review* complained ("Currency Reform," 183). Indeed, it was thanks to the Bank's success in maintaining a dominant and stable currency and a favorable balance of trade that even those cash-strapped British travelers, Chuzzlewit and Tapley, are able to purchase their lot in Eden for an "astoundingly small sum total of purchase-money . . . [of only] one-hundred and fifty dollars," which, at the prevailing exchange rates, amounted to little more than thirty pounds (343).

Given such an economic imbalance between the two countries, Democrats argued, debt repudiation must be considered a purely defensive reaction, an act of desperation forced on the powerless by the powerful. Any transaction negotiated in London between the American states and British investors was likely to be an unequal one. As the *Democratic Review* complained, the original terms of those loans and their rates of interest were decidedly usurious, and therefore the blame for their subsequent repudiation lies ultimately with the moneylenders in London.[100] The people of Cairo, in other words, were ultimately as vulnerable to the flow of capital back and forth across the Atlantic as their embankments were to the Mississippi. Moreover, in failing to pay their debts, wrote the anonymous author of a pamphlet against Dickens titled "Change for American Notes: In Letters from London to New York, by an American lady," the inhabitants of those states were merely "following the precedent" of the Bank of England, which had itself "'repudiated' cash payments" in the past.[101] These authors thus echoed Colonel Diver's response to Chuzzlewit's insinuations about repudiation: "we got it all [the arts of deception] from the old country, and the old country's to blame for it, and not the new 'un" (258). Literary reviews of Dickens's American writings thus participated in this political dispute over the ethics of repudiation.

This financial imbalance between lender and borrower was precisely what Dickens concealed by narrating Eden's ruin not from the perspective of a London-based speculator in American bonds but through the eyes of an apprentice architect and an innkeeper's assistant who actually traveled there to exercise their productive skills (226, 499). There was no logistical need for Dickens to send Chuzzlewit to the United States to "push his fortune" (211); he might easily and more effectively have invested in the Eden Land Corporation from the comfort of London. Indeed, many readers—both British and American—judged the American episodes a gratuitous digression, an

"unaccountable excrescence."[102] But as a means of concealing the unequal
terms of British capital investment in American frontier towns, the move was
necessary, as it allowed Dickens to conflate the pecuniary setbacks of wealthy
speculators with the more serious misfortunes of impoverished immigrants.
Seeking to dismantle this conflation, Democratic critics reminded readers
of the remoteness of British investors, who having never visited America remained unaware of its real potential. The anonymous author of "Change for
the American Notes," apparently a Democratic sympathizer, complained of
this "English Ignorance." They "know nothing," she wrote, of America's "vast
resources . . . [of] the nature of her laws and institutions, of *her cities rising
amid primeval forests*, of the capabilities of her rivers and bays" (17; emphasis added).[103] Even those like Dickens who did experience the country first
hand failed to perceive its future promise. "In the Mississippi he [Dickens]
beholds but a muddy stream flowing through a woody wilderness; his mind's
eye catches no prescient glimpse of the cities that in the fulness of time will
adorn its banks; he alludes not to the 'all hail, hereafter!'" (6). Nor did British investors appear to understand the speculative logic of American town
building. The Cincinnati publisher George Conclin blamed Cairo's problems
in large part on the decision of the "English company" to "monopolize" the
land, construct the buildings themselves, and offer only long-term leases to
settlers, rather than to adopt the American practice of allowing the free sale
of lots.[104] It was in the uncertain hands of such foreign investors that the destiny of America's future cities lay. The dramatic failure of towns like Cairo
thus revealed to contemporaries—or at least to Democrats—the extent to
which American urban development remained dependent on transnational
capital.

Given the close involvement of English financiers in American town speculations (particular that of Cairo), Dickens's complaints that his countrymen
had been the innocent dupes of "monstrous representations" by American
boosters would appear, at least from a Democratic perspective, somewhat dis-
ingenuous. From their position of financial strength, they had entered into
those transactions fully aware that they would benefit from injecting funds
into American securities and thereby prolonging the American land bubble
beyond the initial bank failures of 1837 and 1839. British absentee investors
would also have understood well enough the risks involved in many of these
schemes; they would have been able to "read" a lithograph like Strickland's
precisely as the speculation it was, to weigh it up against the advice of ana-
lysts, and to invest accordingly.[105] In that respect, they would have been far
more wary than Chuzzlewit, who repeatedly failed to heed the bad omens.[106]
A Jacksonian reinterpretation of the real estate scene in that novel, and its il-

lustration by Phiz, would perhaps focus more on Tapley (see fig. 2.8). Whereas Chuzzlewit appears mesmerized by Scadder and his fictitious plan, Tapley appears perfectly conversant in the verbal and visual language of boosterism. Approaching the town plan with the skepticism or "stolid[ity]" it called for (according to the advice in contemporaneous emigrants' guides to not trust such promotional materials), Tapley maintains a critical distance, while prudently keeping an "ey[e]" on the agent himself (341)—not unlike the aloof, standing figure in Edmonds's sketch, who refuses to be lured too close to the image (see fig. 2.7). In a knowing parody (through hyperbolic extension) of the standard booster rhetoric about future cities' miraculous natural advantages, Tapley slyly remarks that for such "public buildings [to] grow spontaneous," without the apparent intervention of architects, the "soil" must indeed be "very fruitful" (341). Instead of presuming (with Chuzzlewit, and arguably Dickens himself) that the depiction must correspond exactly to some empirical "city" actually existing out there, Tapley knows how to read it semiotically, as an arrangement of signs shaped more by the conventions of boosterism than any empirical survey. And yet it is he who proceeds to offer his remaining savings to invest in the city's future.[107] This decision—while perhaps attributed by Dickens to his excessive optimism or naive faith in Chuzzlewit—in fact echoes the tendency of so many British investors to see through such coded representations and lay down their money anyway. The risks of such overpromoted town projects did not discourage British backers; on the contrary, their rapidly expanding economy thrived on those highly speculative investments known as "fancy stocks." Indeed, Strickland's lithograph—that "monstrous representation" of Cairo's prospects—had been commissioned not by the American booster Holbrook, but directly by his London agents, Wright and Company.[108] British investors in American town sites were thus fully implicated in the machinations of land speculation. "As men of intelligence," the Democratic governor of Illinois retorted, those "original creditors were open to the same reproach" of recklessness as the citizens of his own state.[109]

Salvaging the Ruins

Dickens and his readers thus came to widely varying conclusions about what or who caused the untimely ruin of America's nascent cities. Depending on their national and party allegiances, they blamed topographical disadvantages (most notably Cairo's exposure to flooding rivers) or overambitious architectural designs; the National Bank of Pennsylvania or the wildcat banks of western states; the fraudulence of American businessmen or the fickleness of English investors. Still others rejected all of these causes, claiming that the success or failure of paper cities was essentially unfathomable. The western booster James Hall concluded in 1848 that the rise of any city "requires the united influence of *many* individuals and various interests, and the concurrence of a *diversity* of circumstances," a conjuncture "almost impossible to forsee [*sic*]." Alluding to the famous case of a city "at the junction of two noble rivers"—almost certainly Cairo—Hall conceded that "town making" was ultimately a crapshoot. All the signs had indicated a successful outcome. Its location appeared "to combine every advantage," its viability had been endorsed by an "engineer of high reputation," its plats had been "beautifully executed" and "circulated industriously," and its promoters had secured "immense sums of money . . . abroad." It thus remained a mystery why it became "the residence only of frogs and mosquitoes [*sic*]," while far less promising sites had thrived.[110]

But the failure of paper cities also raised larger ethical questions about the proper task of representation. Should a representation necessarily correspond in a one-to-one relation with an actual referent, or can it also anticipate some future, not-yet-existing referent? While British visitors and speculators wanted promotional lithographs and prospectuses to represent what had already been realized, American apologists for the western states countered that such representations were implicitly understood by both purveyor and potential purchaser as standing for some future outcome. The bankruptcy of speculative cities prompted further debates between—and within—the two countries over the monetary representations that had underwritten them. Whig national bankers (along with their Currency School counterparts in England) insisted that paper money should function as a certificate of deposit representing an original consignment of specie in a bank, and thus redeemable at any date. Soft-money Democrats (echoing the English Banking School) countered that banknotes—by virtue of their general circulation—had mutated into legitimate tokens of credit whose value remains yet to be determined. Meanwhile, hard-money Democrats or Loco Focos (following the English radical, William Cobbett) proposed a third alternative: doing away with paper substitutes altogether and dealing only in the metallic thing-in-itself, freed from all representations and temporal constraints.[111] One's position in these debates thus hinged upon one's attitude toward representations that remained fluid and undecidable. To Dickens (and some American Whigs) American representations—whether advertisements circulated by urban boosters, long-term bonds offered by debtor states, or notes issued by unreliable banks—were all "monstrous" precisely because their true value could be redeemed only in some distant and unknowable future. But to many Jacksonian Democrat readers America's "elastic" and future orientation was what guaranteed its greatness.

These epistemological differences extended to the meaning of America's ruins. Dickens read the melancholy remains of new buildings, from the Greek temples of Philadelphia to the log cabins and wildcat banks of the urban frontier, as emblems of recent failures, specifically the moral failings of cupidity, duplicity, and (in the case of slave and tenement ruins), inhumanity. While some Americans, most notably James Fenimore Cooper, endorsed this *vanitas* interpretation of ruins as "rebuke[s]" to excessive materialism, others insisted on reinterpreting them as signs of future potential. The ruins of failed town speculations were not to be lamented but rather celebrated as evidence of western states' ability to attract vast quantities of capital from eastern and European markets. They were also recuperated as sites of precious scrap materials for new land schemes. Americans regard an "old building," observed the French political economist Michel Chevalier in 1836, as "a quarry of bricks and stones" to be plundered "without the least remorse"—a process facilitated by the absence of, and uncertainty about, its owners.[112] Claiming to disdain the "value which [the English] set upon ruins," one Ohioan woman told the English traveler Isabella Bird that Americans prefer to "chaw them up . . . make roads or bridges of them, unless Barnum transported them to his museum: we would never keep on our own hook as you do."[113] Even the sites of ruined cities could be recycled into opportunities for fresh investments. Holbrook himself subscribed to this understanding of American urban ruins as redeemable and reversible. Within five years of Cairo's bankruptcy, he had relaunched it under the guise of a new company, the "Cairo City Property Trust," and rededicated himself to the task of securing it as the terminus of a state-funded railroad. Just as it had risen from the ruins of 1819, so would it rise again from those of 1841.[114] Indeed, as the ruins of paper cities were largely (if not entirely) on paper they could be instantaneously erased. Projected city lots that were never sold were redrawn and sold off as farm land, and projected courthouses or capitols never approved by the county or state were simply dropped.[115]

It was this epistemology of the American ruin that Charles Dickens and Martin Chuzzlewit were deemed incapable of grasping. Confronted with the sight of the "dreary waste of Eden," complained an American critic later in the century, Chuzzlewit on the one hand "saw only the ignominious contrast between the prospectus and the present reality." Tapley on the other hand was commended for his ability to read through Eden's ruins, as he had Scadder's plan. Indeed, Tapley's embrace of the ruins as an occasion for optimism, humor, and action—albeit with nothing more than a hatchet—was considered quintessentially American. He embodies the spirit of those Americans who can admit with a "smil[e]" that "Eden ain't all built yet," yet "se[e]" into the future" and imagine "what Eden *will be* when it is all built!"[116] This embrace of Tapley as an honorary American would be endorsed by none other than Theodore Roosevelt. In a speech at Cairo in 1907, Roosevelt recommended rereading the novel, not to learn from Chuzzlewit's lessons but to emulate Tapley's faith that in the swampy desolation of Eden lay the fertile seeds of progress.[117]

The Petrified City

Antiquity and Modernity in Melville's New York,
1835–1865

He hath no speech, save in the ruins round

WILLIAM GILMORE SIMMS, "Caius Marius"

Among the ranks of unemployed young men who migrated to Illinois in 1840 to make their fortunes in speculative cities was a twenty-one-year-old teacher, sailor, and trained surveyor from New York. Herman Melville's expedition, although a financial failure, proved fruitful as a literary source. Not only did his return journey by steamboat—allegedly passing through Cairo just weeks before it collapsed—eventually inspire the account of the Mississippi (including that "swampy and squalid," indeed "villainous" town site) in *The Confidence-Man* (1857); but his traveling companion also purportedly served as the model for one of his most famous literary characters. Soon after their return that fall, Eli Fly, a law student with neat handwriting, secured a position as a scrivener in a New York law office, a job that involved "incessant writing from morning to Eve[nin]g." Thirteen years later, by which time Fly had become a "confirmed invalid," Melville created his fictional scrivener, "Bartleby."[1]

Although Melville's eponymous short story of 1853 takes place in the rising metropolis of New York, it includes brief allusions to the ruined cities of the Mediterranean. Entering his chambers on a Sunday morning, when "Wall-street is deserted as Petra," the lawyer-narrator is startled to find Bartleby living there among the scattered legal papers—a discovery that conjures a vision of the exiled Roman general, Caius Marius, "brooding among the ruins of Carthage!" (65). The subsequent efforts of the lawyer to dispose of his stubborn clerk benevolently—to simultaneously dismiss, evict, and patronize him—make no impression: he remains "standing mute and solitary," "like the last column of some ruined temple" (78).[2] These classical allusions remain unexplicated in the text. The lawyer-narrator reveals no more about Petra and Carthage, or their connection with New York, nor why precisely a stubborn employee should remind him of an exiled Roman general or a ruined temple. This ambiguity is part of the larger mystery Melville weaves around the inscrutable figure of Bartleby, who shows up without "telling who he was, or whence he came" (67) and leaves behind no "materials" and few "sources" from which to reconstruct anything like a "full and satisfactory biography" (31–32). Not even the posthumous information disclosed in the penultimate paragraph regarding Bartleby's prior job at the Dead Letter Office in Washington, DC, can dispel the mystery (106–7). It only multiplies the conjectures and speculations.

It is the very mystery of this story, and of its eponymous scrivener in particular, that has generated so much critical scrutiny. A rich body of interpretation has developed out of the effort to demystify Bartleby, to identify him variously as a melancholic or agoraphobic; a nihilist or proto-existentialist; an object of the older lawyer's disavowed homosexual desires or a prototype of the exploited and alienated wage laborer; or even Christ incarnate.[3] A typical move has been to posit Bartleby as a double for Melville. Some critics have read Bartleby's preference not to copy documents for the lawyer as standing for Melville's preference not to write according to the commercial dictates of the literary market, which construed novelists as glorified clerks and had spurned the metaphysics of *Moby-Dick* and morbidity of *Pierre*; while others read Bartleby's fate as indicating Melville's self-critical realization that he had erected "walls" imprisoning himself from his fellow men through his very preference for the metaphysical and the morbid.[4] Still others have viewed Bartleby's intransigence as embodying Melville's supposed antiurbanism. For these critics, the story marks the culmination of his life-long critique of the alienating effect of all cities—above all Liverpool and New York—detected in allusions in his other works to those biblical symbols of evil, polyglotism, and decadence: the apocalyptic cities of Sodom, Gomorrah, and Babylon—all of which ended in ruins. From that perspective, the conflation of New York with those other con-

demned cities, Petra and Carthage, appears an equally uncompromising statement of the author's renunciation of all things urban, his refusal to construe
the "city as an arena of possibility."[5]

Resisting the allegorical reading of "Bartleby" as a veiled indictment of dominant values (economic, sexual, or urban), we will read it phenomenologically
for what it reveals about the changing nature of urban experience. We will turn
our focus from the figure of Bartleby, and the personal circumstances and views
Melville supposedly projected onto him, to way the story bears the imprint of
the new structures and phenomena of New York life. In the middle years of
the nineteenth century New York was radically transformed from a close-knit,
"walking city" of merchants and artisans to an industrialized, class-stratified
metropolis. With its subtitle, "A Story of Wall Street," and its specific references to neighboring streets (Broadway, Canal Street), institutions (churches,
courts, prisons), and landlords (Astor), "Bartleby" offers indirect glimpses of a
city in transition, and above all of the epicenter of that transition: an emerging
business district.[6]

This process of urban restructuring generated ruins and visions of ruin. The
redevelopment of mixed-use neighborhoods into financial and retail districts;
the relocation of churches to new, middle-class enclaves; and the widening and
extension of streets through densely populated slums, all involved the razing
of mansions and counting-houses, churches and cemeteries, taverns and tenements, each of which briefly resembled ruins in their half-demolished state.
Even structures that narrowly evaded the pickax, surviving as "holdouts" from
an earlier era of the city, reminded residents and visitors of intact temples rear-
ing up over a classical ruinscape. Meanwhile, given the pace of urban and architectural transformation, the Greek Revival banks, exchanges, and offices
now under construction appeared no more permanent than the buildings they
replaced; indeed, in their half-finished state, they too invited comparisons to
ruins. As products of an unpredictable and ongoing speculative economy,
these various ruins departed from those of the Mediterranean in both appearance and significance. If New York, like Baalbek and Palmyra, was a city of
ruins, it was—in the influential phrase of one newspaper editor—a "city of
modern ruins."[7]

But it was not just through acts of construction and demolition that the
city came to resemble a field of ruins. Urban restructuring also generated visions of Petra (and indeed Palmyra, Pompeii, and Herculaneum) in more
subtle ways, for example by segmenting New York (like other American cities)
into distinct zones defined by function, class, and ethnicity. A downtown district filled with crowds, traffic, and noise during business hours could at other
times of day become as desolate and depopulated as the deserted cities of the

Mediterranean. This capacity of modern cities to transport—or in the words of one commentator, "Aladdiniz[e]"—their inhabitants and visitors to those of other epochs or continents—was what Walter Benjamin called their *"vertu évocatrice*, their evocative power." Through the power of street names, especially those referring to "long-vanished" features (as indeed "Wall Street" did, with respect to the Dutch stockade long-since removed), or through the eyes of the infant, the inebriated, or the insane, a city could generate a phantasmagorical "interpenetration of images" (or what the surrealists called a "profane illumination"), morphing a row of run-down tenements into a landscape in the Moroccan desert.[8] For Melville and his contemporaries, such phantasmagoria of Petra and Carthage (among other ruined cities of the Mediterranean and the Middle East)—or what I term *ruin-effects*—in turn generated insights into the destructive and disjunctive effects of capital upon their own built landscapes. The contrast between sensory intensity and uncanny silence was one of several conflicting tendencies that accompanied the growth of their city. New York was also becoming a site of social propinquity *and* emotional distance, a booming speculative marketplace in housing *and* a breeding ground of homelessness, a sphere in which landlords possessed new powers *and* renters or even squatters exercised new rights.

Unmemorable Ruins: Petra, Carthage, and New York

The mere mention of Petra and Carthage in the same paragraph provides us with the first clues as to the meaning of Melville's classical allusions. Those versed either in ancient history or modern travelogues would have recognized the commonalities between those two cities. Besides the impregnability of their sites—the former literally carved out of the red rock-face that lent the city its name, the latter built atop equally imposing cliffs—they shared the status of leading commercial entrepôts of their respective eras. Petra was founded by the Edomites in the fourth century BC and developed by the Nabateans from the third century BC as an inland trading post at the intersection of crucial caravan routes, midway between the Arabian peninsula and the Mediterranean, in what is now southwest Jordan; while Carthage was a Phoenician port in present-day Tunisia that briefly threatened Rome's commercial dominance over the Mediterranean by the second century BC. Both cities experienced a precipitous decline, albeit in different circumstances. After its capture by the Romans in AD 106, Petra's fortunes diminished as maritime trade superseded the caravan routes and earthquakes struck the region. Carthage's ruin was even more rapid, the result of a deliberate and systematic act of destruction by Rome in 146 BC that was intended to remove any challenge to her commercial supremacy by literally razing it to the ground and symbolically plowing it into the earth. The fall of both cities was absolute and irrevocable; neither recovered. Indeed, the very location of Petra was lost to the West for several centuries until its rediscovery by Johann Burckhardt in 1812, while Carthage (also rediscovered by nineteenth-century archaeologists) was said to remain under a curse that stymied future attempts to re-found it as a Roman colony. In this respect, their ruins diverged from those of Athens or Rome, which continued to be inhabited and visited after the fall of the civilization that had founded them.[9]

The association of Petra and Carthage with opulence and materialism—and their subsequent decline, destruction, and oblivion—might imply that the lawyer-narrator's allusion to their ruins was a memento mori for New York, and thus an indication of Melville's own antiurban sentiments. But the precedents of Petra and Carthage were rarely invoked, even by Melville's more millenarian contemporaries, as straightforward declarations of the futility of city building. More often they served as reminders of the need for New Yorkers to rededicate their commendable energies to cultural as well as commercial endeavors. In an 1855 lecture at the New York Geographical Society, the professor and clergyman Henry P. Tappan reminded the civic elite of the Carthaginians' notable failure—so utterly absorbed were they by commerce and luxuries, and lacking in any common bond other than the nexus of money—to have "left to mankind one work of literature, or one precious remain of art."[10] Thus, while Athens endures as the "resort of pilgrims, who sit among the ruins of the Parthenon" and appreciate its lasting contributions to literature and sculpture, Carthage is nothing more than a "desolate plain" bearing few traces of its former greatness—except, as others pointed out, for its sewers (10).[11] The lessons for New Yorkers were clear. They too had come from far and wide to "congregate here only for one purpose—to make money" (34). Their restless desire (noted by Alexis de Tocqueville) to uproot themselves in search of new cities and frontiers similarly militated against any deep-seated fidelity to New York's genius loci (34). But most troubling was their disregard for posterity.

> Were New York now to experience the fate of Athens, or Rome, or Venice, she would leave to the world no memorials whatever. There would be no massive and beautiful remains of architecture to strew the ground, or to stand here and there in pillared and imperishable magnificence; no statues, no frescoes, no epics, and no old and sacred institutions of learning to be resorted to by pilgrims and scholars, when her harbor should no more be crowded by the commerce of the world. What would she be but a mere mass of bricks and clay and sunken sewers! (32)

Tappan's warning about the oblivion of Carthage, and ultimately New York, was not an expression of antiurban sentiment. On the contrary, he envisioned the consummation of New York's commercial greatness in the form of enduring cultural monuments and institutions such as parks, universities, museums, libraries, and other modern-day "obelisks and pyramids" (33, 35, 37). Cities were thus "scene[s] of conflicting elements": they may be "hotbed[s]" breeding the worst evils, but they also favor the "highest development of humanity" (28, 27, 15). Nor did Tappan, despite his religious and classical teaching, consider ancient cities superior to modern ones. He retained a faith in the "natural development" of cities into ever more refined and enlightened entities as they gradually transcended their military and mercenary origins, those origins most clearly seen in the "impregnable" city of Petra (5, 3).[12]

The rediscovery of Petra and Carthage after several centuries of oblivion was also a source of fascination for nineteenth-century Americans. Edgar Allan Poe—who had earlier recounted Petra's "utter loss, for more than a thousand years, to the eyes of the civilized world," in a review of John Lloyd Stephens's pioneering travelogue about *Arabia Petraea* (a book read and admired by Melville)—imagined Manhattan emerging from a similar period of obscurity in his proto–science fiction narrative, "Mellonta Tauta" (1850).[13] For centuries after its destruction (like Petra) by a massive earthquake, antiquarians failed to recover "any sufficient data (in the shape of coins, medals or inscriptions) wherewith to build up even the ghost of a theory concerning the manners, customs, &c., &c., &c., of the original inhabitants"—except that they were a "portion of the Knickerbocker tribe of savages" who suffered from a "monomania" for erecting temples to their two idols, "Wealth and Fashion"—until the fortuitous unearthing in 2848 of a cornerstone in the middle of that island (882–83). But the lack of any other stones in the vicinity testifies to the failure of those Knickerbockers—as Tappan warned—to complete any lasting monuments. The future antiquarian deduces that they had filled this cornerstone with "Amriccan" coins and newspapers, engraved it "to the memory of GEORGE WASHINGTON," and deposited it as a "mere indication of the design to erect a monument at some future time" (883, 884). Poe may have been referring here to an actual cornerstone, bearing precisely the same inscription and contents, that was laid in 1847 in the presence of 30,000 militiamen, officials, and civilians, on what is now the Upper East Side of Manhattan. This Washington monument, like the one in the nation's capital (see fig. 2.11), remained unfinished due to lack of funds and disagreement over designs.[14]

Along with general concerns about materialism and cultural oblivion, contemporaries would also have associated Carthage with the specific historical figure of Caius Marius, and thus recognized Melville's allusion to a history painting by John Vanderlyn depicting that Roman general meditating among its ruins (65) (fig. 3.1). Earlier American artists (including Washington Allston and Samuel Morse), and subsequent writers (Lydia Maria Child, William Gilmore Simms) had tackled various episodes in Marius's life, from his rise out of obscurity to the consulship, his subsequent defeat by his rival Sylla and flight to Carthage as a proscribed enemy of the state, to his final triumphant return to Rome a year later at the head of a new army.[15] But Vanderlyn's painting of

Fig. 3.1. John Vanderlyn, *Caius Marius Amid the Ruins of Carthage*, 1807. Oil on canvas. 87 x 68 1/2 inches. Fine Arts Museums of San Francisco, Gift of M. H. de Young, 49835.

1807 was the best known, having been awarded Napoleon's gold medal for "best original picture" in Paris in 1808, exhibited at his Rotunda in New York on his return, and widely reproduced as engravings and painted replicas.[16] The scene he chose to depict was not one of his political and military successes but rather the moment that marked the nadir of his career, when shortly after arriving in Carthage in 87 BC (fifty-nine years after its destruction) he received a message from the Praetor of what was now a Roman province, forbidding him from seeking asylum there. Unmoved, iron-jawed, and clenching his scabbard, Vanderlyn's hero has just issued his defiant reply, "Go tell him that you have seen Caius Marius sitting in exile among the ruins of Carthage."[17]

Vanderlyn appears to have intended the painting as a conventional *vanitas*, an attempt to convey, in his own words, "the instability of human grandeur." Indeed, he found here not one but "two great instances" of the mutability of earthly glory—a "city in ruins and a fallen general"—combining them in what might be called a *double vanitas* directed at the Praetor.[18] Vanderlyn universalizes these sentiments further by supplementing Carthage's uninspiring ruins—its sewers—with what appear to be the classic ruins of Hadrian's Villa in the foreground, the Parthenon in the middle ground, and the aqueducts of the Campagna in the background; indeed, in a letter he acknowledged "avail[ing]" himself of the abundant "classical ruins" to be found in Rome, where he executed the painting. By generalizing his ruinscape, as Thomas Cole would in *Course of Empire* (another painting Melville knew well), Vanderlyn allowed its lessons to resonate through time and space. He may even have had in mind, one art historian has suggested, the contemporaneous case of his former patron Vice President Aaron Burr. Exiled from New York in 1805, Burr had fled to the western territories and plotted, like Marius, his revenge at the head of a new army.[19]

It is far from certain, however, that Melville, writing a half-century later, shared Vanderlyn's classical assumptions regarding ruins as expressions of the vanity of human strivings. As a writer whose career was in decline by midcentury, Melville may well have been moved by this romantic image of a great but maligned man brooding over the ruins of his ambitions, and indeed by stories of the painter's own failures. (After some early successes, Vanderlyn had struggled against the declining popularity of history painting, the rise of genre and landscape painting, and the erosion of aristocratic patronage, dying in poverty in 1852). It is this theme of "personal and artistic as well as political ruin," one critic has suggested, that Melville identified in the conflated figures of Marius, Vanderlyn, Bartleby, and himself.[20] But this elevation of Bartleby into a figure of romantic failure is belied by the disparity between that "poor, pale, passive" legal copyist who apparently never rose higher than "subordinate clerk" in Washington (90, 107) and the imposing, muscular figure of a general who had once been Consul of Rome. Melville's allusion seems more ironic and comic than tragic. The Marius simile, far from being proof of classical erudition, was becoming a staple of the mainstream press, employed to ridicule the foibles and pretensions of financiers and politicians (fig. 3.2). To grasp the full meaning of the Marius analogy, we therefore need to turn to the broader economic, social, and political transformations taking place in New York at this time, and to the new kinds of ruins (and meanings of ruin) that accompanied these transformations.

The Stranger in the City

Despite the comic mismatch between the heroic general and the "pitiably respectable" office clerk (45), what they do share is the status of outsider to the cities they inhabited. Plutarch reveals that Marius "was born of parents altogether obscure and indigent," and was well into adulthood before he ever set eyes on Rome.[21] And while less is known of Bartleby's parentage and childhood, the narrator's postscript reveals he too was a stranger in the city, having arrived in New York from Washington. Like Marius, Bartleby suffers the ignominies of exile, being deprived of the resources (social, material, or psychological) that would allow him to make his home there. The two figures merge not so much as emblems of romantic or artistic failure, but of displacement, alienation, and the exilic condition. Such inhospitality could invite divine retribution; indeed, Petra's ruin was often attributed to the Edomites' alleged refusal to provide refuge to the Jews on their exodus from Egypt.[22]

The mystery Melville makes of Bartleby's origins is thus more than just a stock device of nineteenth-century Gothic fiction designed to entice the reader into the diegesis. The trope of the stranger in the metropolis is fundamental to the story. In characterizing Bartleby as an isolated outcast or alien, as "solitary" as "the last column of some ruined temple" (78), Melville articulates an emerging feature of modernity, one increasingly considered a social problem, namely the displacement of individuals from intimate and organic communities into anonymous cities. "The town makes much of the country cousin just now," confirmed another article in *Putnam's*. "He is everybody, and he is everywhere, mistaking the Bowery for Broadway, and Bond-street for the Fifth-avenue."[23]

The phenomenon of the stranger was in part a product of sheer demographics. The so-called market revolution emphasized by recent social historians, along with the transportation revolution described by an earlier generation, dislodged rural families from subsistence or semisubsistence economies, luring

Fig. 3.2. Thomas Nast, cartoon in *Harper's Weekly* 15, no. 778 (1871): 1097. Caption reads: "What are you laughing at? To the Victor Belong the Spoils." This was one of several satirical allusions to "Marius Amid the Ruins of Carthage" in the popular press. While William "Boss" Tweed was reelected state senator in 1871, the election marked the downfall of the corrupt Tammany Ring (in part due to Nast's cartoons).

many to cities like New York.[24] Their influx coincided with that of even greater numbers of immigrants, especially in the aftermath of the Irish potato famine and the failed European revolutions of the 1840s. The combined effect was a dramatic increase between 1820 and 1860, both in the population of New York (from 124,000 to 814,000), and in the overall rate of urbanization in the country as a whole (from thirteen cities to ninety-three; and from an urban population of 693,000 or 7 percent to 6,200,000 or 20 percent). These statistics testify to an acceleration of urban growth that far exceeded that of any earlier period, or any period since, allowing us to speak of a third revolution, an *urban* revolution.[25] Returning to New York in 1844 after a decade in Baltimore and Philadelphia, Poe found it "thronged with strangers."[26] While many could count on support from relatives, compatriots, and co-religionists within their immediate neighborhood, or on informal networks across the city, others (such as Bartleby) found themselves cast adrift without the traditional anchors of church and community.[27]

These demographic and migratory patterns precipitated a cultural crisis even for established residents of the city. Within this new urban setting, recent cultural historians and urban theorists have argued, it was no longer easy to read the stranger—to identify his or her origins, class status, or potential criminal intent. In the smaller towns of the colonial period, where strangers were the exception, their disruptive threat could be absorbed through traditional protocols such as the reporting of their names by ship captains and innkeepers to local officials.[28] Such practices could serve, in the words of urban sociologist Lyn Lofland, as rites that transformed or "coded" strangers into "personally known others." Even in colonial cities strangers could still be ordered on the basis of their visual appearance, their clothing, hair, or adornment—all examples of what she terms "appearential ordering."[29] By the mid-nineteenth century, however, the dramatic inflation and ethnic diversification of the urban population, combined with the democratization of fashion, had undermined such attempts to assimilate the stranger. Alternative strategies for negotiating this "world of strangers" did emerge, to be sure, such as the technique that Lofland terms "spatial ordering" whereby the stranger could be identified by his/her location in an increasingly stratified and balkanized city, or the rules and rituals of emotional and bodily performance that cultural historians Karen Halttunen and John Kasson claim stabilized social identities both in bourgeois parlors and out on the streets. However, such strategies proved tentative at best; as we shall see, the spatial stratification of American cities remained partial through the antebellum period, and the performance of class threatened to degenerate into a farce of deceit.[30] Thus, although Bartleby's "neat" and "respectable" appearance marks him as a newcomer to New York, neither his clothing, his comportment, nor his location in the city enable the lawyer to decipher his social identity (45).

The problem of the stranger, however, was more than just that of an alien population arriving from the country, from another country, or in Bartleby's case, from another city, and remaining somehow unassimilable or illegible in the view of the resident population. It was also an immanent phenomenon, a product of new forms of interaction and social life emerging from within the city. In a 1908 essay, Georg Simmel investigated "The Stranger" as a social type (comparable to his other types: the miser, spendthrift, cynic, adventurer) who has undergone a revealing transformation.[31] Originally understood as a "wanderer who comes today and goes tomorrow" (402)—as in the traders (often Jewish) who entered and left preindustrial towns, remaining in a position of exteriority to those communities (403–4)—the stranger, while remaining outside any social group, has become "fixed within a particular spatial group" (402). In Melville's New York, boardinghouses constituted just such a space, serving not merely to accommodate recent arrivals such as himself in 1840, but to produce its residents, sometimes even long-term ones, as strangers. Whole neighborhoods of transients or "floating populations" were then emerging, most infamously Five Points, where Bartleby meets his end, imprisoned in the "Tombs" on the charge of vagrancy (99).[32] Lacking the mobility of his premodern counterpart, Simmel writes, the modern stranger is only a *"potential wanderer"* (402). The lawyer-narrator acknowledges this oxymoron of the permanent stranger, the purely nominal itinerant, in his reservations about having the immovable Bartleby arrested and jailed: "What! he a vagrant, a wanderer, who refuses to budge? It is because he will *not* be a vagrant, then, that you seek to count him *as* a vagrant" (91).

While the lawyer seemingly penetrates the mystifications of city life to grasp the contradictoriness of the resident alien, the story also reads as an account of his failure to come to terms with Bartleby's alienness. Interpreted through Simmel, the strangeness of the scrivener ("the strangest I ever saw, or heard of" [31]) owes not simply to his recent arrival in the city but to a more essential and intractable condition of modern life. Because of the increasingly *"abstract nature"* of social relations, Simmel writes, one may feel a stranger even to someone one sees daily (405). Paradoxically, the "trace of strangeness" emerges out of a realization of the commonness of one's relationship with another city dweller, compatriot, or even "love[r]"—the sense that such relationships have become so generalized throughout a city or nation that there is nothing special about this specific one, or that one's commonalities are so common that they "connect a great many people" and thus connect no one (406, 407). In 1840s and 1850s New York, the paternalistic, particularistic worlds of rentier and freeholder, artisan and apprentice, patrician and servant, were radically reorganized into the abstract, contractual relationships of landlord and tenant, industrialist and wage laborer, employer and employee.[33] Melville's lawyer, as a remnant of that earlier cultural formation having until recently held the ancient office of Chancery (33), struggles to come to terms with the fact that his relations with those close at hand are now mediated externally, and thus appear remote. Moreover, there is the added threat that the stranger who enters into such relationships—arriving, like Bartleby, from another city and job—will see them for what they are. "Bound by no commitments" and freed from "habit, piety, and precedent," Simmel writes, the stranger is able to "experience and treat even his close relationships as though from a bird's eye view" (405). It is precisely this detached, Olympian perspective—articulated in Bartleby's matter-of-fact "I would prefer not to" (48, passim)—that appears so threatening. Such "objectivity," Simmel concludes, "contains many dangerous possibilities," not least that of provoking "uprisings of all sorts" (405).

"Bartleby," then, is in part the story of a lawyer's vain efforts to overcome this simultaneous nearness and distance of the stranger. First he asks biographical questions about "who he was, or whence he came, or whether he had any relatives in the world"—only to have such questions politely "declined" (67, see also 70–71). Next he adopts a spatial strategy of reasserting the closeness and intimacy of an earlier, more paternalistic relation by bringing Bartleby's desk into his own office, albeit behind a green screen (46)—only to find that in the inverted world of modern urban relations described by Simmel "he, who is close by, is far" (402).[34] Subsequent acts of philanthropy prove equally incapable of bridging this distance; even if Bartleby had accepted the extra twenty dollars, such monetary transactions, as Simmel elsewhere reminds us, only "erect a barrier between persons."[35] And the mysterious final sentence of the story, "Ah, Bartleby! Ah, humanity!" represents a last, desperate attempt to overcome this estrangement through a rhetorical gesture of commonness—not of workplace, city, or even nation, but of mankind itself (107); or what he earlier called the "bond of a common humanity" (65). Such a category, warns Simmel, is so "general" and "common" to all that it only exacerbates the condition of strangeness (406).

The City of Modern Ruins, the Spirit of Improvement, and the Demon of Dilapidation

The lack of entanglements that enabled strangers to observe social relations with detachment also granted them insight, in the view of Melville and others, into the modern city. Urban commentators regularly scrutinized the dramatic

physical, social, and experiential metamorphosis of New York through the
sensitive eyes of some newcomer (real or imagined), or else the resensitized
eyes of a former resident returning after a period of absence. Even Melville
experienced his native New York as a stranger of sorts between 1850 and 1863,
when he lived in the Berkshires.[36] Whereas habituation to the *quotidia* of city
life renders one oblivious to them, the alienation of the stranger (or returnee)
provided a standpoint from which to see them afresh, the standpoint of someone in but not fully of the city. Through this estrangement effect, the mundane
could be reenvisioned as the extraordinary, the permanent as the transitory,
and ultimately the modern as the archaic.

The outlook of the stranger or returnee was most often invoked to dra-
matize the extent to which the city, especially its emerging downtown, was
being radically transformed through tumultuous processes of real estate
speculation, construction, and demolition. In the two decades after the 1835
fire, New York witnessed two distinct real estate booms. The first began in
the immediate aftermath of the disaster, stimulated partly by the need to rebuild fire-damaged structures and the desire to keep pace with the newest
architectural styles and materials, but also by that expansion of credit that
(as we have seen) generated a land fever throughout the nation.[37] After the
downturn of 1839–41, a second boom began that lasted until 1857. The
length and intensity of this latter boom also reflected macroeconomic developments—most notably, railroad networks and transatlantic steamship lines
converging, like the earlier Erie Canal, upon the port of New York—and at
the same time local conditions and institutions within that city: the demand
of merchants for increased warehouse and retail space, the rapid growth of
an immigrant tenant class, the infrastructural improvements of sanitation
and water supply, the resumption of real estate auctions in the rebuilt Merchants' Exchange, and of course the preexistence of an ambitious city plan
that had already conceived the entire island as a uniform grid of purchasable
plots.[38] But above all the boom was driven by an emergent class of landlords
who developed radical new strategies for extracting capital from the land they
leased (under a tiered system) from an older, more conservative rentier class.
Not content with the steady income of rent, these new entrepreneurial (and
nonresident) landlords gambled on rising land values, constructed speculative buildings to rent out to the burgeoning middle classes, or else sublet to
smaller landlords who would do so. They thus resembled their counterparts
in contemporary Paris who, as Marxist geographer David Harvey writes, were
reconceptualizing landed property as a "pure financial asset, as a form of fictitious capital" prized more for its exchange than its use value.[39] In both cit-

ies the outcome of these concurrent trends was an upsurge in construction and demolition.

While few residents could fail to notice the omnipresent crews of builders and wreckers, the experience of a visitor or returnee could register the upheaval more fully. In 1860 retired cartman Isaac Lyon invoked the imaginary example of someone revisiting the city for the first time since 1834, when the "spirit of improvement" was only just materializing; such a person "would no more know where he was than he would if he were suddenly dropped from a balloon down in the midst of London for the first time."[40] Even a brief absence could reveal the rapidity with which the city was changing. After a trip upstate in August 1839, ex-mayor Philip Hone returned to discover Trinity Church, his place of worship for almost four decades, already half-demolished. The sight of Trinity's "dark mass of ruins still overlooking the magnificent temples of mammon in Wall street" prompted "melancholy reflections" in his diary concerning not only his own mortality and impending demise, but also "the changes which have occurred there during the time the venerable spire which is now removed has thrown its shadow over the place 'where merchants most do congregate.'"[41]

Such critiques of ruptures in the physical fabric of the city cannot be divorced from critiques of ruptures in its social fabric. For Lyon, obliterated old theaters and Dutch houses represented more than just lost memories. The earlier city was one in which native-born cartmen like himself—and like Gingernut's father in "Bartleby" (43)—were among the most highly respected artisans. Crucial to the efficient circulation of goods and furniture (especially on May 1, or "Moving Day"), they were considered the virtual custodians of the secrets of the city ("an encyclopaedia and an intelligence office combined"), not least regarding its real estate market (5). But by midcentury, with the decline of artisanship, the growing influence of Irish Democratic voters, and Tammany's abolition of a 180-year-old licensing act that had granted a monopoly to native-born cartmen, Lyon had become a living relic of that earlier period, much as the lawyer of "Bartleby" was to become a relic of an age of Chancery privileges.[42] For Hone too, the demolition of cherished buildings resonated with the abrogation of privilege and prestige, except for him it was the lost privileges and prestige of a declining patrician class. While Lyon's Whig allegiances were of a nativist workingman, Hone's were of a German-born, elitist merchant. Since his brief stint as Whig mayor in 1825–26, the latter had bemoaned the Democrats' growing control of over City Hall, not least because they encouraged the speculative construction. Hone would have blamed them for the condemnation in May 1839 of his "poor, dear house" at

235 Broadway, which was about to be "incontinently swept from the earth"
to make way for so-called improvements (1:359). Hone thus concurred with
Lyon in viewing spatial restructuring through the refracting prism of a changing social structure.[43]

Where Hone and Lyon departed was over the question of whether such
dramatic changes would actually yield ruins. In Lyon's view, the "onward
march of the spirit of gain" was annihilating "all the ancient and time-honored
landmarks of the city," indeed "everything that bears the impress of age and
antiquity" (9). A number of Whigs shared this view of midcentury New York
as a cauldron of construction, in which (to adapt Marx and Engels's famous
phrase) all that is *old* melts into air. Writing in the *Whig Review*, Walt Whitman decried how the "pull-down-and-build-over-again spirit" seemed to sacrifice any house "not built within the last ten years" to the hammer, ax, and pick.
Whereas the *Democratic Review* derided the notion that "houses, like wine, improve with age," Whitman denounced the blind impulse to replace "noble old
building[s]" with "modern 'improvements.'"[44] In the 1855 lecture cited above,
Tappan similarly argued that New York confronted a fate of historical oblivion
equivalent to that of Carthage not only because of its absorption in money
making and its failure to erect cultural and architectural monuments, but also
paradoxically because of its overbuilding. While embracing these improvements as the necessary precondition for reaching the higher stages of urbanity,
Tappan regretted that "the old and abrogated are ever prone to be forgotten
in the new," and that merchant's "palaces" never have time to age before being
"turned into boarding-houses, then pulled down and replaced by warehouses"
(31–32). Such defilement of the city's architectural patrimony diminished its
aesthetic and spiritual qualities. In the view of *Harper's* editor George William
Curtis, this "constant demolition and erection" militated against "picturesque-
ness," prevented buildings from "becoming hallowed and interesting from association," and betrayed a general disregard for the "household gods"—those
Roman deities (or *Lares*) that embodied the spirits of ancestors and protected
the home. Even if Britain were to "bombard New York to-morrow" and reduce
its "banks, warehouses, churches and dwellings" to "nameless confusion," he
wrote two years later, no "pilgrim" would "sit and wonderingly muse" upon its
ruins, because, after all the years of "eternal demolition," its buildings had not
stood long enough to accrue any affections or associations. No trace of antiquity could survive in such a landscape of perpetual newness.[45]

Writers like Hone, while no less critical of the razing of old landmarks, experienced ruin-effects almost everywhere they looked. Observing the "pulling
down" of shops and houses throughout lower Manhattan, and of large banks on
Wall Street—while dodging the debris "showering down in every direction"—

Hone was reminded of nothing less than "the ruins occasioned by an earth-quake" (1:359). The artist whose paintings Hone collected, Thomas Cole, compared his persistent alterations of architectural details in *The Course of Empire* to those he must have observed on regular visits to the city. "I have had to tear down [i.e., overpaint] some of the buildings that were nearly finished," he wrote to his patron regarding the temples and edifices of *Consummation*, "in order to make improvements, à la mode New York."[46] The scenes of desolation accompanying those of renewal led other Whigs to invoke specific ancient cities, even as they remarked upon the striking modernity of New York's own ruins. For C. F. Daniels, editor of the Whig-leaning *New-York Gazette*, the city that came to mind was Baalbek. But in contrast to those time-worn Roman temples of the Bekaa Valley (in modern Lebanon), Manhattan was a "city of modern ruins—a perfect Balbeck [*sic*] of a day's growth and a day's dilapidation," much like those "ruines d'un jour" Tocqueville found upstate. As in the region of the Erie Canal a decade earlier, the pace of construction in New York was so rapid by 1839, the final year of the first construction boom, that it appeared to compress or even invert the temporal stages of rise and fall. A specter of untimely ruin haunted not only buildings that were being demolished but also those being erected. Given the abbreviated rate of architectural obsolescence—estimated at seven years by Hone—even buildings as grand as Isaiah Rogers's new Merchants' Exchange were likely, Daniels suspected, to "share the fate of their 'illustrious predecessors.'" With that building's protracted construction (due to budget overruns that had devastated lenders like Hone and had necessitated new loans from British bankers), it is not surprising that Daniels feared it would be demolished even "before" it was "half finished," thus creating what the artist Robert Smithson would call "ruins in reverse." Like that temporarily suspended highway construction site Smithson viewed on his 1967 tour of Passaic, New Jersey, the fragments of the Exchange's current unfinished (or "transitional") state appeared to prefigure its eventual ruin. Temporal compressions and inversions such as these ultimately distorted the traditional meanings of the ruin. There was little indication that New York's untimely ruins conveyed the kinds of moral lessons about decline and fall embodied by their Mediterranean archetypes. On the contrary, while "stones are falling" on Wall Street, "stocks may rise" on the exchange.[47]

Sometimes commentators discerned in such scenes of construction and demolition the mirror image of more than one ancient civilization, as if all the ruins of the world had magically materialized in the modern cosmopolis of Manhattan. Such a ruin-effect was described in an anonymous 1849 article in *Literary World*. As a "Manhattaner" returning from the country, the author experiences the city's sounds and sights with renewed intensity and emotion, and discerns "what changes have taken place in the accustomed contour of build-ings" (309). In addition to pleasure and pride in Broadway's renovation (the lo-cation of *Literary World*'s editorial offices), these changes provoke a multilay-ered vision of antiquity. Stretching all the way up Broadway are certain strange monuments consisting of "truncated cones of brick-work." These "ponderous piles" would "puzzl[e]" even "traveler[s]" and "antiquaries." Some might iden-tify them as "artificial ruins" designed to lend Broadway an aura of "reverend antiquity" reminiscent of Babylon or Nineveh. Others would identify them as "pyramids," built to entomb not pharaohs but "our sovereigns, viz. the people." Challenging these various antiquarian attributions on the evidence of their architectural design—or lack thereof—the narrator wonders whether they are the proliferating symptoms of an incurable disease afflicting the street itself, a physiological "infirmity" resulting in a funguslike "over-secretion of brickwork," especially in the summer months. These mysterious structures, it is by now clear, are in fact piles of bricks, temporarily stacked on the curb and waiting to be assembled into buildings. Through this deliberate misreading of construction materials as ancient monuments, New York's ruination appears to precede the completion of its buildings, or indeed the very commencement of their construction. The sheer force of construction is prematurely petrify-ing the city. Were it not for the saving grace of some art galleries on upper Broadway, the whole street would "congeal into brickwork" and "our citizens . . . degenerate into a race of mere builders."[48]

Such articles were well received in the New York press, eliciting approving citations and generating further commentary on the phenomenon of modern ruins.[49] Another anonymous author even appropriated Daniels's earlier phrase, "city of modern ruins," as the theme and title of an 1840 article in the *New-York Mirror*. Echoing Daniels's observations about the temporal idiosyncrasies of these ruins—their instantaneous quality and their sequential inversion—the *Mirror* also remarked upon their spatial peculiarities. The uneven redevelop-ment of lower Manhattan meant that a "wayfarer" could find one street (cur-rently John Street) in a state of total ruin, and a neighboring one completely untouched. One could even find sharp spatial discontinuities within a single street. Thus, "while one block in Broadway exhibits all the grandeur of splen-did architecture, complete in its proportions and fresh in its finish, the next square exhibits all the baldness of Balbec" (fig. 3.3). Such jarring discontinui-ties did not necessarily undermine the impression of antiquity. On the con-trary, an unscathed building juxtaposed alongside a demolished one evoked those unbroken columns and enduring monuments that embellished a classical ruinscape—as in the intact shaft crowning the final canvas of Cole's *Course of Empire*. Thus, an "isolated church stand[ing] . . . amidst the fragments" of

Liberty-street, in process of re-building, 1852.

Fig. 3.3. J. W. Orr, "Liberty-street, in process of re-building, 1852." Engraving from "New-York Da-guerreotyped," *Putnam's* 1, no. 2 (1853): 127. While the right side of the street remained intact, the left was a confusion of scaffolding, cranes, ladders, and building materials, as domestic residences made way for dry goods stores and warehouses.

a street-in-transition could resemble a "half-spared temple in Palmyra of the desert." Such accounts, while remaining critical of the costs and excesses of urban improvements, implied that they had perversely reenchanted the city, spiritually and aesthetically. Whereas *Harper's* decried New Yorkers' disregard for the "household gods," the *Mirror* blamed the very "worship [of] false dei-ties," such as the "demon of dilapidation," to whom architectural sacrifices are offered in the name of "civic adoration." And whereas the former might assume one had to travel to European cities to find the urban picturesque, the latter remarked that "admirers of the city picturesque" could at long last, thanks to the "restless . . . tastes and habitudes of the city," find enchanting ruins here in America.[50]

The Street Where No One Lives:
The Differentiation and Depopulation of Downtown

Whether measured in buildings erected and demolished, or gleaned from the sight of bricks stockpiled in the streets and falling from above, transience appeared to define antebellum New York. But alongside that architectural flux, the city seemed to be acquiring certain fixed forms, to be ossifying or petrifying into something more solid. In the 1840s and '50s the labyrinthine, close-knit "walking city" was rapidly—although not entirely—supplanted by a distinctly stratified city of clearly defined regions and spaces.[51]

Class divisions were forming one set of strata within the urban topography as elite residential enclaves coalesced on the West Side around a succession of squares (Hudson, Washington, Union), while immigrant slums and native-born working-class neighborhoods congealed toward the east around Five Points and the Bowery respectively. Although still limited, residential segregation was well under way in antebellum New York.[52] The class of certain neighborhoods was already distinguished by housing type and the presence (or absence) of amenities such as gas lighting; denoted by ward numbers, landmarks, parks, streets, and nicknames; and taxonomized by urban exposés, reformers, guidebooks, and brothel directories.[53] According to the editor of the *Mirror* Nathaniel Parker Willis, even Broadway, that so-called dividing line between the "fashionable" West and "dangerous" East, was demarcated internally, with leisurely bourgeois pedestrians claiming the "golden-side" of the street, and lower classes the "shilling side," thus exemplifying how the everyday practice of walking constituted a territorial act during this nascent spatial differentiation. And as the residential landscape became polarized between rich and poor, the growing clerical workforce (to which scriveners belonged) struggled to preserve a diminishing middle ground.[54]

Overlapping this class differentiation of urban space was a growing differentiation by function, as patterns of property investment, industrial production, and consumption combined to allocate land for specific uses. Rapid growth of the manufacturing sector—combined with Manhattan's constraints, its high land values, congested streets and docks, and lack of water power and direct rail connections—yielded a bifurcated economic geography. While larger industries moved out of the cramped lower wards into specialized industrial districts on the periphery (along both waterfronts, to the north, and increasingly across the Hudson), small-scale trades that were more location-sensitive and labor-intensive remained.[55] A similar segmentation between retailing and wholesaling emerged, with the formation of a specialized shopping district on Broadway above City Hall Park, spearheaded by A. T. Stewart's "marble palace" of 1846. Unlike their precursors—the dry goods stores interspersed on lower Broadway among warehouses and offices, occupying the ground floor of those buildings or converted private residences such as Hone's former house (1:203)—the new department stores filled entire, custom-built edifices and were deliberately located at a "safe" distance from the overcrowded wholesale and financial districts. This demarcation became more pronounced as they advanced rapidly northward in subsequent decades.[56]

This solidifying north–south divide was part of a larger process of vertical stratification between downtown and uptown now materializing through the separation of those most basic of functions, work and rest. The modern and distinctly American usage of the terms *downtown* and *uptown*—as nouns or adjectives designating that part of the city dedicated to commerce or residence, rather than directional adverbs referring simply to the lower or upper part of town—was itself a product of this spatial segregation and northward expansion of land use in midcentury New York. Thus, Hone (born in 1780) and the old lawyer of "Bartleby" continued to use the phrase "down town" in its original, geographic sense as late as the 1850s (80), just as the younger diarist George Templeton Strong (born 1820) and the new magazine *Harper's* were beginning to use it in its modern, functional sense.[57]

While Strong's generation grew up habituated to the notion of a bifurcated city, Hone's would have remembered (not always nostalgically) the lower Manhattan of their childhood as a largely undifferentiated whole, a place encompassing both residences and workplaces, and both elite and working populations. As late as the 1790s Wall Street still had large, brick merchant houses scattered among its coffee shops (which served as makeshift exchanges), countinghouses, banks, insurance companies, and law offices. A mansion there provided a merchant with convenient access not only to these sites of financial transaction, but also to the warehouses, wharves, and workshops on neighboring streets. Even a merchant's own home was integrated. Apprentices, indentured servants, and slaves (or "found labor") were all subsumed, along with family members, within an extended "household." Tied to the paternalist head of the house through bonds of mutual dependency and reciprocal social obligations, they often lived and worked within the same building, which functioned as a "consolidated workplace" incorporating craft workshops, kitchens, and stores.[58] The newly incorporated banks and insurance companies that moved into existing houses similarly cohabited with the domestic residents.[59]

Not until the 1820s did Wall Street become the heart of a business district, the first of any American city.[60] After losing their paternalist authority over apprenticed, indentured, and found labor—most dramatically by the state's abolition of slavery in 1824, but also by the gradual rise of a wage labor market—the merchant class soon relinquished their downtown residences too, as the post–Erie Canal real estate boom increased the value of and demand for land on Wall Street. At the same time, an emerging "cult of domesticity" prompted them to purchase newer, single-family houses to the west, and later uptown, in entirely residential neighborhoods spatially isolated from the realm of work. Acting now as nonresident landlords, they could even impose this work-home separation upon their former artisanal dependents, by renting them subdivided properties that had no room for workshops.[61] Meanwhile, their old homes on Wall Street were demolished to make way for new, purpose-built banks and a stock exchange, a process accelerated by the cholera outbreak of 1832 and the fire of 1835. These financial structures contained no residential quarters, and tended to be built from marble and granite rather than brick, and in Greek Revival style rather than Georgian or Anglo-Palladian. Thus, by the 1840s, the city's functional specialization could be traced through distinctions in architectural style, building material, and height (fig. 3.4).[62] This process of segmentation was also marked by the relocation of those anchors of civic community, its churches. Grace Church and the First Presbyterian were among those that vacated Wall Street in the 1840s for new premises uptown.[63]

This functional specialization of urban space resulted in a demographic anomaly. Between 1840 and 1855, while the total population exploded, that of lower Manhattan declined. This decline reflects not only the voluntary relocation of merchants from Wall Street, but also the forced removal of residents throughout the lower wards, as housing was gradually eliminated from retail, financial, and warehousing districts. By 1843, the Whig businessman Caleb Woodhull observed the remarkable development—for a city that until recently had no "uninhabited" buildings—of "whole quarters . . . devoted to stores alone in which no one dwells." There may even be a time, he imagined, when the "whole island" will be dedicated to commerce, and its population rehoused in outlying areas. Although this phenomenon was evident in smaller cities such as Rochester, it was particularly pronounced in New York.[64]

That uncanny depopulation of Wall Street and its environs in the evenings and on Sundays was what summoned visions of an abandoned city, a place as "deserted as Petra." The strange phenomenon of office space that "hums with industry and life" during the week, yet by "nightfall echoes with sheer vacancy,

NEW-YORK

WALL STREET

Fig. 3.4. Augustus Köllner (artist) and Isadore Laurent Deroy (lithographer), *Wall Street*, 1850. Tinted lithograph. Emmet Collection, Miriam and Ira D. Wallach Division of Art, Prints and Photographs, The New York Public Library, Astor, Lenox and Tilden Foundations.

and all through Sunday is forlorn" ("Bartleby," 65), recurs in other writings of the period. When Wall Street had been the "Broadway of New-York" and the "oldest families inhabited the oldest mansions there," the *Mirror* recalled in 1840, "gay belles and beaux" would have been seen promenading there, especially on Sundays. With their subsequent departure, the street became in the daytime a male homosocial space where the sight of a woman is "extraordinary," and at night a "deserted," shadowy landscape inhabited only by a "watchman" and his "faithful dog" who "howls at the distant approach of a footstep"—or, as a contemporary engraving illustrates, by an African American sweeper who clears away the detritus of the day (fig. 3.5).[65] This nocturnal and sabbatical desolation was especially perceptible to the ear. On Sundays, wrote the journalist George Foster, the usually "nois[y]" Wall Street became as "silent and lonely as a city of the olden time deserted centuries ago by its inhabitants, and left to the winds and sands of the desert"—a ruin-effect, added a writer for *Harper's*, only heightened by the sound of Trinity's church bells reverberating through "those deserted precincts."[66] The abandonment of the business district was not merely temporary but also local; while Wall Street was deserted in the evenings, neighboring Broadway remained busy. Nevertheless, by the early hours

CLOSE OF BUSINESS AT WALL-STREET, NEW YORK.

Fig. 3.5. "Close of Business at Wall-Street, New York," 1856. Engraving. 4 1/4 x 3 1/4 inches. From "Sketches in the Free States and Slave States of America," in *The Illustrated London News* 29, no. 822 (1856): 314. The accompanying article describes a "solitary negro . . . sweeping away the dust" after the markets had closed (313).

of the morning the latter too became so quiet and empty as to induce a sensation of having been "Aladdinized" to some "solemn and deserted" street in Palmyra, while on Sundays it was as "hushed as Herculaneum and Pompeii."[67] Thus, it was in the city's circadian and circaseptan rhythms that its functional subdivision was rendered most visible and audible. If New York resembled the ruined cities of the Mediterranean, it did so only in certain quarters and at certain times.

Few experienced as powerful a ruin-effect on Wall Street as an anonymous visitor writing in the *Southern Literary Messenger* in 1851. This southerner recalled an "incident" in that "court of Mammon"—where "worshippers" make their devotions at the temples or "shrines of *Diva Pecunia*"—that induced a "feelin[g] . . . [of] shocking discordance." The incident was not a financial panic (although at the time of his visit one had just taken place) but simply a funeral. An everyday event in most cities, this funeral was "strange" because it took place on Wall Street, a street where by now "no one *lives*."

> Seven hours in the day is its only period of vitality, after which it is *as silent as that petrified city in the story of Scheherazade*; men tarry there for a short time, but do not dwell or abide there; a *home* in such a quarter is simply an impossibility, the Lares [Roman household gods] would fly the spot (first emphasis added).

Certainly, the author acknowledged, people have been known to die on Wall Street—from "apoplexy," sun stroke, or even from a "falling block of stone from the scaffolding of a new edifice"—but they are all carted off elsewhere. To conduct a funeral on Wall Street was to contravene its newly commercial character. His intense curiosity about how that man came to die and be buried here amid "the daily din of business" reminded him of the "feelings . . . inspired by the tomb of Cecilia Metella." That half-ruined, cylindrical burial structure erected circa 50 BC may have come to his mind because of its location just off the Via Appia, the busiest of all roads leading to ancient Rome. This southern "loiterer" presumably found in Rome the same "striking antitheses" he witnessed on Wall Street: between "Death" and "Life," the affairs of the heart and the "empty occupations and concerns" of business.[68]

Holdouts

The reconfiguration of the mercantile walking city of Melville's youth into a commercial-industrial metropolis spatially (and temporally) segmented along the lines of class, ethnicity, and function, remained a work in progress through the antebellum period. The modern capitalist city developed unevenly and haphazardly rather than uniformly and predictably.[69] Thus, to counterbalance historians' emphasis on a collective "Mov[e] Uptown" and an ineluctable "Rise" of "Downtown"—to cite the titles of two histories—we must now attend to the exceptions: those relics of an older city that stubbornly persisted within the emerging cityscape.[70]

That "isolated church" on a transitional street that the *Mirror* compared to a "half-spared temple" in a ruined city (the very phrase Melville applied to the lone figure of Bartleby) would now be termed a "holdout." Defined by urban critics as a structure that has become a surviving remnant of an earlier era, encircled and overshadowed by new structures of a very different function and scale, the holdout can serve as a rallying point from which to make "one last stand" against the forces of redevelopment.[71] Some view holdouts nostalgically, as small islands of relative permanence within a rapidly flowing river of commerce and construction, often safely located in its backwaters, namely its alleys and side streets. But within a city undergoing such rapid yet uneven redevelopment as Manhattan, holdouts were to be found in the very heart of its business district. The old Jauncey stables on Wall Street stood until as late as 1849 as a veritable "relic of antiquity," while Walton House, a pre-Revolutionary mansion on neighboring Pearl Street, survived as a "venerable" monument into the 1880s, having been converted into a lodging house.[72] In America, wrote James Fenimore Cooper in his unfinished manuscript, *The Towns of Manhattan*, "[a] dwelling that has stood half a century is regarded as a sort of specimen of antiquity, and one that has seen twice that number of years . . . [is revered as though it were] the tomb of Cecilia Metella."[73] Deconsecrated churches were similarly adapted to new uses, briefly becoming soup houses, emigrant information offices, seed stores, stables, or tenant houses for the poor. Even a relatively new building in a prominent location such as Trinity Church—rebuilt in 1846, climbed by Melville in 1848, and frequented by the lawyer of "Bartleby" that Sunday morning (62)—could qualify as a holdout. By midcentury, the northward migration of the congregants of downtown churches resulted in dwindling attendance at their "Sunday Schools, prayer-meetings and lectures."[74] While some of these holdouts were beginning to be celebrated as monuments of historical or even age value, others tentatively lingered on as stubborn specters of the past haunting the newly renovated spaces of the city.[75]

If certain buildings held out against the spatial logic of neighborhood formation, like "half-spared temple[s] in Palmyra," so did occasional human holdouts. Even as financial institutions consolidated their hold over Wall Street, some New Yorkers defied the injunction to move uptown, such as the family that lived above a bank until as late as 1841 or the old man Hone eulogized for "adher[ing] pertinaciously to his old domicile" for half a century, "resisting the encroachment of banks and insurance offices."[76] While they became self-imposed exiles—"isolatoes" as Melville's Ishmael might have called them—from the members of their own class, by remaining in place and putting up with higher rents and increased congestion, other holdouts had less choice in the matter.[77] Many African Americans found themselves unable to relocate to new neighborhoods, their continued presence delaying the Hibernianization of Five Points (as Dickens observed) or the gentrification of West Broadway (as Willis complained).[78] Such holdouts expose the limits of the capitalist real estate market as a tool for demarcating space. The market apportions land to the highest bidder rather than rigidly on the basis of social conceptions of class, ethnic, or racial identity.[79]

It was out of these overlaps and time lags between the vanishing mercantile city and the emerging commercial-industrial city—out of the cracks and crevices between the old and the new—that specters of ruin emanated. The propensity of this unevenness or nonsimultaneity of modern urban development to produce such ruin-effects lies at the heart of another Melville short story set in New York, "Jimmy Rose" (1855). Read through an urbanist lens, its central protagonist is neither the eponymous merchant who lost his entire fortune yet continued to frequent the spaces of his former social triumphs, nor the ambivalent narrator William Ford, but the "great old house in a narrow street of one of the lower wards" in which the story begins and ends. Once belonging to Jimmy but bequeathed "unexpected[ly]" and inexplicably to the narrator, this house was not the sole surviving "monument of departed days." Ford reminds us that even at this late date the street's "transmutation" from a place of elite residence to one of trade remained incomplete; the influx of "counting-rooms and warehouses" have not entirely erased the vestiges of its earlier status as a "haunt of style and fashion." Some other houses still stand, and some old-timers are occasionally sighted "linger[ing]" among the warehouses. Whether those elderly residents stayed in the neighborhood because they "would not, could not, might not quit it," whether their immobility was thus recalcitrant, inadvertent, or hesitant, their effect is to remind the narrator of "those old English friars and nuns, long haunting the ruins of their retreats after they had been despoiled."[80]

Jimmy's house itself, for all the protectiveness of its new owner, cannot escape the aura of ruin either, not so much because of the physical decay so evident in the "wilted resplendence" of its ancien régime peacock wallpaper (253), but because of its anachronistic location in a street now full of "bales and boxes . . . ; day-books and ledgers" (241). This sense of displacement, however, was not a recent development. Even in the much earlier period when Jimmy enjoyed and lost his fortune, such a house had already become a holdout on "C—— Street" (245, 247)—possibly Courtlandt Street, the site of Melville's early childhood home.[81]

> Few or no people were in the street; for even at that period the fashion of the street had departed from it, while trade had *not as yet* occupied what its rival had renounced (emphasis added).

The house's "dreary, deserted air" might thus be attributed to the transitional condition of the street, which languishes between the passing of an old order and the coming of a new one (247). Attempts by intervening owners to refurbish its ancient exterior only exacerbated the problem, lending it "an incongruous aspect, as if the graft of modernness had not taken in its ancient stock" (242). It thus lies suspended uneasily between past and present, neither stable in its antiquity nor reconcilable with modernity.

This theme of the holdout, occupying an interstitial space or intervening moment within the urban, is central to "Bartleby" itself. We have already seen how the lawyer is a holdover from the age of paternalist social relations and Chancery privileges. Given Wall Street's spatial transformation, his chambers may also be considered a relic; as the *Times* reported in the 1850s, such offices were gradually yet inexorably being expelled beyond "the boundaries of Wall-street" to make way for the larger banks.[82] But it is Bartleby who most powerfully embodies the holdout. Bartleby does so not merely because he refuses to resign his office as scrivener, but also because he insists on occupying the office as tenant—or rather, we shall see, as squatter.

> I surmised that for an indefinite period Bartleby must have ate, dressed, and slept in my office, and that, too without plate, mirror, or bed. The cushioned seat of a ricketty old sofa in one corner bore the faint impress of a lean, reclining form. Rolled away under his desk, I found a blanket; under the empty grate, a blacking box and brush; on a chair, a tin basin, with soap and a ragged towel; in a newspaper a few crumbs of ginger-nuts and a morsel of cheese. Yes, thought I, it is evident enough that Bartleby has been making his home here, keeping bachelor's hall all by himself. (64–65)

Bartleby, along with a nameless cleaning woman "residing in the attic" (62), thus defies the separation of working and living spaces, that new but already critical distinction between a financial and a residential district.[83] Such a living arrangement has its risks. Being holed up in a room so lacking in furniture that it resembles a deserted ruinscape might well drive one to murder (78, 92), as it did in the case of the notorious John C. Colt, who had been confined to a "solitary office" in a "building entirely unhallowed by humanizing domestic associations" (84–85). Or, if one actually lived there on a Sunday, when Wall Street morphs into Petra, it could induce melancholia—if not in Bartleby then in the narrator (65). Bartleby's eventual imprisonment and death might be read, then, as punishment for having disregarded the city's emerging spatial order—just as Jimmy Rose's tragic decline and death ensues from his reversion to a street that was no longer residential. These New York characters thus resemble those of Balzac's Paris who "mov[e] into the wrong place at the wrong time" and end up (in David Harvey's reading) "pay[ing] the price." But for an "indefinite period" Bartleby, like some other characters in Balzac's work, could at least "command and produce space" and "subvert the spatial pattern and the moral order" of the city. This "power," Harvey claims, can be exercised by "even the lowliest of people in society."[84]

Vagrants and Ghosts in the Ruins:
Slum Clearance and Cemetery Removal

In 1857 the *National Magazine* published a description of Petra that almost read, in places, as a portrait of lower Manhattan. Of the few avenues into the city, explorers had found that the one leading to the "northern extremity of the town" was particularly "narrow" and impractical for vehicles. The main commercial street, however, was the one running east–west through the "old city" toward the central Treasury building. The vast traffic of commerce "to and from . . . [this] immense dépôt and exchange" was so great that merchants' vehicles had worn away ruts in its stone-paved surface. Lined with "gray, perpendicular walls" and "imposing façades," this "long shady chasm" limited one's vista to small "glimpses." Indeed, the cavernous "chambers" overlooking the street were so constricted that a traveler might well wonder whether they were "tombs for the dead" rather than "dwellings for the living."[85]

This account of a compact and labyrinthine city could well apply to lower Manhattan, among other American downtowns undergoing rapid modernization at midcentury. Even as the residential population of the lower wards declined between 1840 and 1855, their spatial congestion dramatically increased. In a number of respects, these years mark the moment of greatest urban density in U.S. history. Rising land values on Wall Street had prompted speculative builders to fill any available space (inner courtyards, back gardens, side alleys) with rental properties—while building regulations remained limited. Similarly, the old omnibus system had exacerbated congestion by bringing more commuters and shoppers downtown, while proposals for new forms of mass transit (elevated railroads or extended horse-car lines) that would open up outlying suburbs were as yet unapproved.[86] Lower Manhattan was also becoming increasingly overburdened with commercial freight from the rapidly expanding waterfronts, which had to navigate a labyrinth of narrow and convoluted streets largely unaltered since Dutch rule. Courtlandt street, site of Melville's first house and possibly Jimmy Rose's last, was especially notorious for being "so blockaded by carts, and . . . barricaded by packing-boxes" as to be virtually impassable. The outcome of all this spatial compression was that quintessentially modern urban problem: the traffic jam.[87]

This spatial compactness of lower Manhattan at midcentury is registered in "Bartleby's" claustrophobic mise-en-scène. Located in one of those "densely populated law buildings," the office has just three windows, all of which look

out over some kind of wall and thus admit only varying degrees of indirect light
(62). The window in front of Bartleby's desk is particularly impeded; it once
had a view of "certain grimy back-yards and bricks, but . . . owing to subsequent
erections, commanded at present no view at all"—except that of a "dead wall"
three feet away (46). Such confinement was typical of antebellum Wall Street,
whose office buildings were often likened to "mole-hills" and "anthills."[88] The
previous year a visiting Seminole chief who was shown "the labyrinths of its
hundred or two of brick and granite buildings; and their whole courts and
corridors of varied offices, vaults and cuddie [sic] holes," purportedly inquired,
"How in the world do all these folks live in so small a compass?"[89]

Only a sustained program of public works projects could solve the problem
of urban density, open up the constricted canyons to light and air, and create
an infrastructure for the efficient circulation of goods and people through the
lower wards. Such a program was already under way, initiated as early as 1829
and gathering pace in the 1830s and '40s, with plans to widen, straighten, extend, regrade, or resurface a number of streets, including Wall Street.[90] Instead
of promising benefits to the public or "commonweal" (as earlier ordinances had
done), these new projects were justified on the postrepublican grounds that
they would benefit a specific class: property-owning citizens. Improved streets,
whether in residential or commercial districts, would increase the value of real
estate; and propertied wealth in turn underwrote the morality of middle-class
home life. These kinds of appeals conscripted a range of property-holding
citizens, from landlords, real estate investors, and city officials to respectable
house owners and moral reformers, into a new cross-party coalition for the
reshaping of their city.[91]

Whereas in the fashionable districts street improvement projects could
safeguard or even boost real estate investments (for example by converting
certain intersections into squares or "places," and by installing utilities such as
gas, water, and sewerage), in poorer neighborhoods they served another purpose: that of displacing unwanted populations.[92] Concerns about the threat
to nearby middle-class residences posed by Five Points, with its ethnically and
racially mixed populations and its brothels and gambling dens, led to repeated
efforts after 1829 to demolish deteriorating buildings, construct a new city
jail, and widen its streets, all in the name of enabling respectable citizens to
pass through safely en route to work or home.[93] Street-widening proposals had
considerably more traction in these poorer neighborhoods, where there were
fewer conflicts of commercial interest and little recourse for the propertyless
who lay in their path. For some, there was the temporary compensation of employment in these public works. But most found themselves shunted to even
more overcrowded "model tenements" farther east.[94]

Such spatial solutions to the economic and social threat of "disreputable" neighborhoods intensified another problem, that of homelessness. Not all residents of "improved" streets found their way to new tenant houses elsewhere. With the decline of real wages and the emergence of a full-scale housing crisis in the 1840s, many were forced to take to the streets as vagrants. Traditionally defined as those lacking shelter and employment, and thus differentiated from slaves, servants, and the working (or "virtuous") poor, vagrants had been especially common during economic downturns. But once street and slum clearances gathered pace, genteel New Yorkers feared they were becoming a permanent presence in the city. New York's homeless population reached 50,000 by the early 1840s, many of whom congregated in Battery Park or found shelter in police stations.[95]

As once-impenetrable neighborhoods were opened up with the pickax and lit up with gas lights, previously hidden levels of vagrancy became visible to a horrified yet fascinated bourgeois gaze, giving birth to a new genre, urban sensationalism.[96] Conversely, the same widening of streets invited the poor to explore the bourgeois territories of the city. Just as Baron Haussmann's grand boulevards unwittingly released Parisians from their sealed-off slums, so too were New York's most "wretched" now enticed, according to Willis, to leave their "haunt" of "poverty and crime" and "come to . . . Broadway . . . and watch the happy."[97] Both in Second Empire Paris and antebellum New York, such spatial transformations were accompanied by new relations of visibility. For Baudelaire, on the one hand, the "eyes of the poor," gazing through the window of a "dazzling" new café on a half-completed boulevard, could estrange a liberal bourgeois from his conservative lover.[98] In Willis's observation of Broadway, on the other hand, it is the poor who are more "consciou[s]" of being seen." Urbane New Yorkers may have a reputation for walking through the streets with "an eye wholly at ease" and a "countenance free of any sense of observation or any dread of [their] neighbor," but the poor remain "painfully sensitive" to the gaze of those who do not even notice them. In fact, in Willis's view, the degree of sensitivity to the gaze of the other is inversely proportional to one's actual social visibility.[99]

The bourgeois fear of vagrants, however, was more than simply a function of their greater mobility and visibility within the city's unblocked streets. It was also the simultaneous attempt to draw new boundaries between rich and poor neighborhoods, and between private and public, that raised the prospect of their being transgressed. Like Haussmann, bourgeois New Yorkers wished to displace the poor and to keep them in place, to fracture space and to solidify it. At stake here was nothing less than the ownership of the streets: whether they were the responsibility of enlightened private citizens or the common

property of the "people." Even the semipublic spaces of the city—its offices
and churches—were in dispute. Within this politically charged context, an
unkempt man who strays into the bell tower of one of those "splendid, new-
fashioned" Gothic churches, in Melville's "Two Temples," finds himself hauled
before the Halls of Justice ("The Tombs") as a "lawless violator"—although he
ultimately gets off with a fine.[100] Bartleby's encroachment upon the law office,
however, ultimately incurs a full prison sentence, perhaps because his appropriation of private space was defiant, raising the specter of a more radical form
of homelessness.[101]

While the plight of homeless indigents—or even homeless clerks—did
not elicit sufficient sympathy to halt the progress of the pickax, the posthumous rights of corpses buried in downtown graveyards apparently did. Like
the people of ancient Petra who "beheld the habitations of their dead engir-
dling them round," the residents of lower Manhattan in the early nineteenth
century were surrounded on almost every street by cemeteries.[102] Beginning
in 1834 with the razing of part of the First Presbyterian's churchyard on Wall
Street, an impassioned debate erupted over whether cemeteries could be removed northward, tomb by tomb, to make way for widened streets and commercial buildings.[103] The debate reached its apogee in 1853–54 over the case
of Trinity's churchyard, to the rear of Wall Street. Those in favor of extending
Albany Street through the yard to connect up with Broadway appealed once
again to the rights of property, specifically the right of the living to "enjoy the
legitimate and equitable use of their property," unencumbered by "some dead
people [who] were once buried in the wrong place."[104] But this same rhetoric
of property was also employed by opponents of the plan, a disparate group
of citizens, led by Trinity Corporation, and supported by the *Times*, *Courier*,
and *Evening Post*. In addition to arguments about hallowed ground and civic
memories, one opponent claimed that the fees New Yorkers paid to have their
relatives and friends buried there amounted to a kind of title on the land. The
elasticity of arguments about property threatened to sunder the already fragile
coalition for civic improvements.[105]

Melville could have learned firsthand of these cemetery controversies during visits to his brother Allan's law office at 14 Wall Street.[106] Indeed, number
14 was the "somber-looking brick building" that had recently replaced the
First Presbyterian Church and cemetery, provoking a similar outcry over the
migration of churches and violation of sacred ground (fig. 3.6).[107] The *Knickerbocker* magazine had urged its readers to go there to view "the vaults of the
dead," some "almost demolished, and others slowly yielding to the crow-bar
and pick-axe." That scene of desolation—of "bones, large and small" being
"deposited, in a promiscuous heap"—should prompt one to "meditate" about

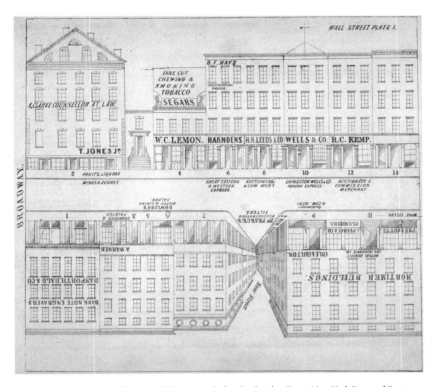

Fig. 3.6. Panoramic view of 1–14 Wall Street, including both sides. From *New-York Pictorial Business Directory of Wall-St. 1850* (New York: C. Lowenstrom, 1849). Lithograph. Rare Books Division, The New York Public Library, Astor, Lenox and Tilden Foundations. Plate I. The list of occupants includes Allan Melville at no. 14.

the vanity of worldly endeavors in these "busy thoroughfares of the metropolis."[108] Indeed, it led the *Knickerbocker* in its very next issue to reflect on the theology of resurrection and even a "theory of ghosts." "While standing by a newly opened vault of the dead in Wall-street, the other day, as mentioned in . . . our last number, . . . we could not help asking ourselves . . . 'Will the "material body" rise again from the grave . . . on the last great day?'" The decayed condition of these corpses prompted the author to endorse a heterodox, rationalist version of the resurrection, in which only the spiritual body will rise again.[109] Nevertheless, it was the continued belief in the ultimate resurrection of the spirit that paradoxically permitted corpses to be disinterred; only when doubts emerged about the very notions of the soul and the resurrection, Michel Foucault suggests, did there emerge a new belief in the utter inviolability of the corpse—its "right," as our only surviving "trace," to inhabit a "little box" in perpetuity.[110]

If 14 Wall Street *was* Melville's source, the troubled history of that site explains the ghostly appearance of Bartleby. Allusions to the impending abolition of the Chancery courts suggest the scrivener turned up at the law chambers around 1843–44—precisely when the Presbyterian cemetery was demolished and the new offices constructed.[111] There are numerous intimations in the text, picked up by contemporaneous reviewers, that the scrivener may not in fact be a living being.[112] He is described as an "apparition" who materializes "like a very ghost" when summoned and stubbornly "persists in haunting the building generally" (62, 59, 95)—until he is finally reentombed in the Tombs (105–6). There is also something physically deathly about Bartleby, evident in his "pallid" countenance (66) and "cadaverous" demeanor (63, 72, 82). Melville was not the only one to invoke the specter of disinterred bodies lingering in the commercial spaces of Wall Street. An earlier critic of the desecration of a downtown cemetery—for the sake of "erect[ing] a building which shall yield ten per cent per annum" or "run[ning] a street through the middle" of it—claimed to glimpse a long-deceased girl he had known in his youth. Such sightings suggested that the future erections of commerce might end up haunted by the victims of such gross acts of "cupidity."[113]

Moreover, the spectral presence of Bartleby (along with other ghosts sighted in the ruins of Wall Street during the period in which "grave-yards bec[a]me hives of business") offered a perspective—analogous to that of the stranger or returnee—from which to apprehend the upheavals (literal and spatial) of lower Manhattan.[114] Such a perspective could serve celebratory as well as critical purposes. The president of Columbia College, Charles King, lecturing in 1851 on the *Progress of the City of New York, during the Last Fifty Years*, surveyed the transformation of Wall Street through the eyes of corpses. The "unconscious dead" roused by the emptying of the Presbyterian's tombs could hardly have "dreamed" of the "offices of the California Expresses and Lightning Telegraphs" that now stand on the site—one door down from Melville's brother.[115]

Squatting and the Limits of Urban Capital

Melville's story leaves the ontological status of Bartleby's body unresolved, perhaps because it is more preoccupied with the lawyer-narrator's various responses, the most remarkable of which is his ultimate decision not to have the scrivener physically or legally removed from his chambers, but to find new chambers himself. Reasoning that "since he will not quit me, I must quit him," he takes the drastic step of moving office—while making the plausible excuses of wanting closer proximity to City Hall and fresher air (91).

However sympathetic the lawyer is to Bartleby's plight, and however prevalent the practice of moving during that period, his recourse to "carts and [cart]men" rather than "constable" and "common jail" seems out of character (91–92). He is after all a man of the law, indeed a specialist in real estate law. Conveyancing and resolving title disputes were among the tasks he would have performed as Master of Chancery (45)—the officer reporting to that court of equity, in which Melville's brothers Gansevoort and Allan also held posts.[116] And even after that "good old office" was abolished by the state in 1846, the lawyer continues to cash in on the property transactions of his wealthy clients (32). He is particularly proud to have acted for that paragon of real estate men, John Jacob Astor, whose very name resonates with the jangle of gold, and whose suburb of Astoria he now visits while agonizing how to rid himself of Bartleby (33, 90, 99). After his death in 1848, Astor was remembered not only as the fur trader celebrated by Washington Irving, and the land speculator who shrewdly gambled on New York's northward advance—using the chancery court to acquire land through foreclosed mortgages, especially during the crises of 1837–41—but also as a ruthless landlord who during the last decade of his life collected more than $1.25 million in rents on both downtown and uptown properties.[117] According to critics ranging from Mike Walsh's radical *Subterranean* to James Gordon Bennett's sensationalist *New York Herald*, Astor wrote onerous stipulations into his leases, forced tenants to renew them at higher rents, and took "appropriate legal remedies" when they defaulted.[118] Melville's lawyer aligns himself with Astor when he invokes the rights of those who own the building (a "portly" landlord) and the land beneath it (conceivably Astor himself, or more likely Trinity Corporation), and also of those who dutifully "pay [their] rent" and "taxes" (84). The question thus remains: why, if he admired Astor, would the lawyer allow Bartleby to remain on the premises? Or, put differently, to what extent could the working and nonworking poor of antebellum New York obstruct the interests of property, and by extension those urban processes of real estate speculation, neighborhood formation, street improvement, and building demolition?

Bartleby's continued "tenanting" of the Wall Street office (even after the lawyer's departure) appears all the more inexplicable given the powers and privileges of property-owning New Yorkers by the antebellum years (63). Those trespassing on private property could be instantly arrested and imprisoned in the Tombs as common "vagrants," or at least given a "round fine" and a "stinging reprimand"—as the narrator of Melville's "Two Temples" discovered.[119] Even legitimate tenants remained legally vulnerable. If they fell behind on rent payments, their personal property could be confiscated and liquidated by their landlord under the common law doctrine of "distress and distraint." And when abolishing that doctrine in 1846, New York State's constitutional convention bestowed new powers upon landlords, enabling them to sue tenants for back rent and if necessary evict them. The transformation of tenure relations from the paternalist model of the mercantile era to a liberal model structured around supposedly neutral contracts and impersonal market forces paradoxically led to further asymmetries and biases. The doctrine of freedom of contract effectively left tenants at the mercy of their landlord, who was free to set the rent, establish the duration of the lease, and decide whether to offer a renewal of it—just as that of caveat emptor left them without recourse when the property was found to be substandard. No longer able to claim reciprocal obligations or maintain proprietorship through long-term leases, New York's laborers were reduced to a class of propertyless wage-earning tenants who struggled to keep pace with rising rents. Rents reached a peak in 1853, the year "Bartleby" was published, leading to numerous evictions and a *Times* campaign against this "species of speculation."[120]

Yet, on closer inspection, Bartleby's persistent presence on Wall Street, far from being legally and historically implausible, exposes certain structural limits to the powers landlords could exercise. Their ability to enforce their rights was restricted in practice by their tenants' lack of property worth seizing and ability to abscond and find cheaper housing; by the expense and difficulty of repossessing a property through the courts; and by the diminished deference toward landowners and proprietors.[121] These practical limits enabled wage-earning tenants to forge various strategies of resistance. To be sure, urban tenants rarely took the kinds of direct political or legal action witnessed in the Anti–Rent War upstate.[122] Such tenant militancy would easily have been neutralized by the tiered system of land tenure in New York City, which rendered the large landlords such as Astor anonymous to the lowest rung of sublandlords and subtenants.[123] Instead, urban tenants' resistance typically assumed more implicit, everyday forms. They could gain a measure of control through various foot-dragging tactics—deployed either individually or collectively—such as the deliberate delay of rent payments or irregularization of the payment schedule, the obstruction of prospective tenants from visiting the property, and the refusal to give up the keys.[124] It is the latter that Bartleby adopts, when he disregards the lawyer's demand to vacate the premises, lock the door behind him, and "if you please, slip [the] key underneath the mat, so that I may have it in the morning" (78). But the ultimate tactic employed by New York tenants to redress grievances against their landlords was mob action, either against the person or property of the landlord.[125] Such violence is precisely what the landlord of the building fears, not from Bartleby but from his increasingly irate tenants, who are now threatening to form a "mob" (95).

Unlike those tenants, however, Bartleby occupies Wall Street as a mere squatter, having set up residence in the office—and later the entryway—without lease, title, or even color of title. But more than anyone else it was squatters who exposed the limits of landowners' and landlords' power by the 1850s. They had gained legal recognition (first from various states and then from the federal government) as homesteaders with certain settlement and preemption rights, and a public reputation for being militant and unmanageable.[126] In California, propertied elites were alarmed to find that squatters were well organized, backed by a sympathetic public, versed in Jeffersonian and Jacksonian political philosophies, and prepared to defend themselves legally in the courts or violently in the streets—as in the squatter uprisings of Sacramento in 1850 and San Francisco in 1854.[127] If squatters posed a threat to property out west, they also did so in cities back east, where their settlements were deemed detrimental rather than beneficial to land values. Bourgeois New Yorkers seeking to establish a "central park" in the 1850s came up against over ten thousand Irish, German, and African American squatters who had settled on that rocky and swampy ground. For the *Times*, those uptown squatters were as much a "terror and a scourge" as the insurgent squatters of California, and equally difficult to eject: "they will submit to none" and "are banded together to support each other in their mutual defence," paying a kind of community tax to provide legal aid "when suits of ejectment are brought."[128] Nor were those squatters afraid to venture southward, where "they haunt the crossings; . . . swarm about our doors; [and] creep shiveringly through the City."[129] Indeed, Bartleby's occupation raises the specter of squatter insurgency in the very heart of downtown.

The lawyer's protracted deliberations over the appropriate legal procedures for ejecting Bartleby from the Wall Street office attest not simply to some deeper moral crisis or ambivalent attachment on his part, but rather to the numerous rights and protections granted squatters under the laws of the state and nation. If a squatter remains settled in the premises (becoming a "fixture") and retains visible means of support (and "indubitably [Bartleby] *does* support himself"), he cannot be treated as a vagrant (76, 91). Nor can Bartleby, as long as he remains an employee or dependent of the lawyer, be classified as a "common trespasser" (91). Squatting, unlike vagrancy and trespass, was not even punishable as a misdemeanor in New York until the passage of an antisquatting law in 1857.[130] Meanwhile, under the common law, those seeking to evict squatters had to observe strict protocols. A formal written request, or "writ in ejectment," had to be submitted to the squatter, allowing a certain number of days' notice to quit. And even when that deadline expired, the owner still could not use unreasonable or violent force to repossess his property.[131] The lawyer-narrator correctly observes each of these requirements when he "*assume[s]* the ground that depart he must," gives notice that "in six days time

he must unconditionally leave the office," and refrains from any "vulgar bul-
lying" (79, 77, 79). But squatters were above all empowered by the common
law doctrine of "adverse possession," which eventually grants them title if they
occupy the site, and "the owner sleeps upon his rights," for a certain number of
years—varying by state, but then codified by New York's statute of limitations
at twenty years.[132] Bartleby may have arrived only recently, but as he continues
to stand his ground like "the last column of some ruined temple," the lawyer
begins to contemplate the disturbing possibility that he might "in the end perhaps outlive me, and claim possession of my office by right of his perpetual
occupancy" (89).

Ultimately, the lawyer's fears of being usurped are of course misplaced.
Bartleby has no intention of asserting his rights to the chambers through adverse possession—and according to the legal doctrine, without such clear (i.e.,
public) "intention" to take sole possession of the property, and without any
formal "claim of 'right' or 'title,'" de facto occupation can never become de
jure occupation.[133] To make such a claim would be to accept the very notions
of property to which the lawyer subscribes, conform to the legal statutes of
the state, and thus compromise the absolute negativity of his dissent. After
all, adverse possession was established not so much to reward squatters for
their productive labor as to clear title disputes, and thus lubricate the circulation of property.[134] Instead, Bartleby's act of squatting resists recuperation into
the logic of urban capital. He implicitly rejects the very terms through which
property disputes are adjudicated, and under which tenants and even squatters
are protected. To his ejectment and imprisonment as a vagrant he "offer[s] not
the slightest obstacle" (100).

This stoic impassivity in the face of his eviction and incarceration, this refusal to consent actively to the laws of the land, is what ultimately links the
modern Bartleby to the classical figure of "Marius amid the ruins of Carthage."
Uninterested in the local customs of the place in which they find themselves,
neither Bartleby nor Marius want anything more than the right to remain in
situ. If anything, they are demanding what Marxist philosopher Henri Lefebvre termed "the right to the city," a right to inhabitation that goes beyond
the narrowly defined and privately owned rights to property sanctioned by
existing laws.[135] But where Marius is sitting amid the literal ruins of a city deliberately destroyed by a foreign army, Bartleby stands amid ruins inadvertently
created out of the self-generating processes of capitalist urbanization. The various ruins alluded to in the text—the provisional ruins of demolished and half-
constructed buildings; the nocturnal and sabbatical ruins of deserted neighborhoods and offices; the figurative ruins of churches and mansions that survived
as architectural holdouts; and ultimately the physical ruin of that ghostly

holdout, Bartleby himself—all perform a double function. They express the destructiveness of capitalist development as it carves its relentless path through the urban landscape and also the stubbornness of various obstacles that lie in its path—those persistent individuals, communities, and structures that appear to defy the forces of progress yet are themselves the products of those very forces.

Relapsing into Barbarism

Labor, Ethnicity, and Ruin in Prospective Histories of
Urban America, 1865–1906

A recurrent motif in the aesthetics and poetics of the ruin is the seated human figure, typically conveying architectural scale, temporal distance, or vicarious experience. Thomas Cole's arcadian ruinscapes feature goatherds and troubadours, Vanderlyn's history painting of Carthage a defeated general, while more picturesque renderings might include an artist, poet, tourist, or band of local peasants. But of all these figures, the most prominent is arguably the historian. Dating back at least to Edward Gibbon's claim to have conceived his *History of the Decline and Fall of the Roman Empire* in 1764 as he "sat musing amidst the ruins of the Capitol, while the barefooted fryars were singing Vespers in the temple of Jupiter," the power of the ruin to stimulate epiphanic visions of the past became a key trope of modern historiography.[1]

This image of Gibbon sitting in the ruins of Rome in turn inspired late nineteenth-century Americans to imagine the future historian who would investigate the decline and fall of their own republic. The last three decades of the nineteenth century and the first of the twentieth witnessed the publication of at least twenty-four prospective histories (as I will call them), many of which recast American cities—including San Francisco, Chicago, and Washington, as well as New York—as mysterious archaeological sites arousing historians' curiosity about the civilization that had built them and the causes of its downfall.[2] The historian-narrators of these fictions typically draw on the expertise of other scholars of the past. They enlist archaeologists to salvage, excavate, and identify its extant monuments and everyday artifacts; numismatists to decipher inscriptions on its coins and medals; and geographers and explorers to locate its cities, often concealed by impenetrable forests or buried in sand. But as apparent inheritors of nineteenth-century standards of evidence, these future historians are not content with material and architectural traces alone; they also seek out textual fragments of American culture that have survived the intervening centuries, either in some kind of unintended repository or in a purpose-built vault—what was later termed a *time capsule*. Librarians and archivists procure and preserve the dusty volumes and manuscripts, linguists translate them, and philologists and etymologists study the grammar and roots of the ancient language in which they were written. Indeed, some prospective histories consist of the recovered manuscript itself, with the future historian's editorial commentary relegated to the preface and/or footnotes.

Once accumulated and interpreted, such evidence yields a variety of hypotheses for the downfall of the American republic, ranging from the spread of neurasthenia to the rise of Christian Science. But by far the most commonly cited cause is the conflict that erupted in the late nineteenth century between an industrial working class that had grown politically militant and ethnically heterogeneous, and a capitalist class that had begun to use force to suppress it. In the preceding chapters, we have seen how antebellum American cities came to appear vulnerable not only to the physical destructiveness of fires and floods, but also to the systemic disorders generated by rampant and uneven growth, overextended credit and overzealous boosters, and excessive construction and demolition. In the decades after the Civil War, those perceived vulnerabilities were compounded, and to some extent supplanted, by the singular apocalyptic scenario of ethno-class conflict.

These futurological texts were thus firmly preoccupied with contemporary questions, above all that of *labor* versus *capital*. Less interested in furnishing the exhaustive descriptions of future social, economic, and political arrangements found in that other popular genre of the period, the utopian novel, prospective historians instead dedicated themselves to reconstructing the lost civilization. As a vehicle of contemporary critique, prospective historiography offered certain advantages. Where antebellum critics (as we have seen) invoked the *spatial* externality of a stranger or returnee, their postbellum counterparts found in the *temporal* distance of the postapocalyptic historian an even more powerful perspective from which to reassess the economic and social (dis)order of the nineteenth-century city, whether from radical or reactionary standpoints.[3] Political or economic events that newspapers reported as random and disconnected could be endowed with epochal meaning and coherence when viewed through a historian's hindsight.[4] Writing well after the fall of the American republic, the latter could finally impose pattern and structure upon the flux of late nineteenth-century capitalist urbanism. He—and these historians were with just one exception male—could perform the critical work of sifting those events that were significant (sometimes ones deemed insignificant when they occurred), determining the motives and factors underlying them, tracing their causal connections with other events, and ultimately grasping them as decisive moments of transition. Authors bestowed those events with a further sense of historical directionality by appropriating the implicitly finitist narrative model of "decline and fall" from Gibbon. They could measure the injustices and mistakes of the present not so much in terms of their deviation from an ideal beginning (the founding of the republic) but insofar as they had led to a catastrophic ending.[5] Moreover, by speaking in the detached, "scientific" voice of a professional historian, they could do so "rationally" and "objectively," circumventing the charge of sensationalism leveled at contemporary muckrakers, millenarians, or populist demagogues. Even the more celebrated signs of progress and cooperation could be recast subtly as the first stages of decline and fall, and the most apparently enduring institutions as utterly ephemeral. The growing subgenre of prospective historiography thus presented the tantalizing possibility of historicizing the present.

These prospective histories were not entirely presentist, however. They also offered readers the prospect of momentarily transcending their present and contemplating the enigma of time. Reading these future historians, especially those adopting the guise of philosopher of history, contemporaries could reflect upon the significance—if any—of the failed experiment of the American republic within the larger scheme of human history. Would its ruins disclose any broader patterns (linear or cyclical) in the passage of time? Do those patterns unfold steadily or fitfully? Is history determined by fixed laws or open to the indeterminacy of accident? Can it be divided into distinct periods (golden and dark ages, civilization and barbarism) and to what extent are they discernable to those actually living in them? These kinds of questions necessitated a radical detachment from the political disputes of the day, a will to view the present merely as the prelude to—or prehistory of—larger, even more momentous phases of history, and a willingness to contemplate a future that might be something other than the extrapolated progress of the present. Moreover, it was the recurrence of such questions from the field of the philosophy of history that led late nineteenth-century Americans back to Gibbon. The *Decline and*

Fall, among other "classic" works of history, the theorist of historical narrative Hayden White has argued, "continue[s] to appeal . . . long after its scholarship has been superseded and its arguments exploded as prejudices of the cultural moment of its production"—and indeed, many American readers objected to its alleged anti-Christian prejudices—because it is essentially an "allegory of temporality." It thus appeals to the "need to reflect on the insoluble mystery of time." While White considers this a "universal human" need, it was one that became particularly pronounced amid the social, temporal, and experiential flux of late nineteenth-century urban modernity.[6]

Yet, even as American novelists and critics invoked the eighteenth-century philosopher-historian seated meditatively among the ruins of the past, they subtly but crucially altered the circumstances and contexts in which the future Gibbons would appear. Authors intimated that historians visiting ruined American cities might not find them populated (as Gibbon did Rome) with "barefooted fryars"; might not write their histories as sympathetic beneficiaries of that former civilization; and, most disturbingly, might not even be Caucasian—as in Baron Macaulay's famous allusion to "some traveller from New Zealand" in the ruins of London, an implicitly aboriginal figure that was repeatedly appropriated and transplanted into various American ruinscapes.[7] Such modifications indicate a further breakdown in Enlightenment philosophies of history. Confronted with the seemingly intractable ethnic and class conflicts of modern American cities, critics collectively questioned the applicability of various tenets of that earlier discourse. Was America necessarily at an earlier, more virtuous "stage" in its "course of empire," relative to the fully urbanized Old World? Are modern nation-states better insulated against the agents of "barbarism"?[8] And if American cities did fall to ruin, would the "course of empire" necessarily continue westward onto new regions, as the *translatio imperii* proclaimed? Or might their destruction be so catastrophic, given the modern ingredients of dynamite and class conflict, as to annihilate the republican idea altogether and precipitate a reversion to monarchy, autocracy, plutocracy, theocracy, or even a socialist or agrarian utopia? Such questions exposed further cracks in the Enlightenment construction of the ruin.

Although jeremiads about civilizational decline now appear the intellectual property of reactionary critics, at the turn of the twentieth century they freely circulated within the public domain, and could be articulated to a wide variety of political views, from agrarian populist to revolutionary socialist. They even permitted politically unaffiliated writers such as Mark Twain and Ambrose Bierce to speculate about the outcome of the mounting conflicts between labor and capital without ostensibly aligning themselves with either side. Thus, while the general tropological structure of the metanarrative remained constant across the political spectrum, there were considerable differences over the particulars. Future historians effectively engaged in an extended debate over the precise etiology of ruination. Was it the fault of labor or capital, immigrants or nativists (or the combined effect of all parties)? Was it inevitable or avoidable, anticipated or unforeseen, precipitous or protracted, imminent or remote, nationwide or regional? But they also differed over the question of ruins. Have the mansions, tenements, statues, bridges, and stockyards of nineteenth-century American cities survived intact as ruins or disappeared without trace? And if ruins persist, do they serve as intelligible or even eloquent evidence of the cultural and technological deeds of American urban dwellers, or do they remain mute, impenetrable, or even misleading?

Seeds of Ruin: Gibbon and Macaulay

In the decades after the Civil War, as in those during and after the Revolution, Americans contemplating their destiny as a nation undergoing rapid economic and demographic expansion regularly looked to the historical example of Ancient Rome. But whereas the founding generation (as we have seen) evoked the original virtue of the Roman republic as well as the subsequent demise of the empire in their speeches and sermons, a century later their descendants were more likely to evoke only the latter. The rhetorical value of the *declinatio imperii*—like that of its counterpart, *translatio imperii*—derived from both its familiarity and versatility. For centuries it had accommodated an array of historical arguments (focusing variously on causes such as paganism, territorial overexpansion, slavery, or luxury) and temporal metanarratives (linear, cyclical, apocalyptic). Rome could be imagined as falling instantaneously as the Goths invaded in AD 410, or declining gradually over the preceding four centuries of imperial rule (or since its very inception). This latter emphasis on the gradual decline of Roman virtue—present even in the classical histories of Polybius, Gracchi, and Tacitus, and elaborated by the Florentine republican historians, Bruni, Biondi, and Machiavelli—was ultimately inherited by Edward Gibbon.[9]

This republican notion of gradual decay through internal contradiction would permit American critics of the Gilded Age to speak of a seed of ruin germinating in a nation apparently rising in commercial and military strength. That seed—or in Gibbon's metaphor, "slow and secret poison" released into the "vitals of the empire"—could only be fully detected retroactively. "It was scarcely possible," he wrote of the glorious age of the Antonines with which his first volume begins, "that the eyes of contemporaries should discover in the public felicity the latent causes of decay and corruption" (1:71). Despite the persistent misconception dating back to his first ecclesiastical critics that Gibbon's "poison" was Christianity, his argument about its deleterious effects on Roman virtue (in chapters 15 and 16 of that first volume) was in fact ancillary to the larger theme that *imperium* is doomed by the loss of the very thing that had created it, namely *libertas*. That Gibbon shared the Enlightenment view of Rome's decline as a systemic and immanent process is evident in his discussions of those Montesquieuian "general causes"—the atrophy of military discipline, the resort to a mercenary army, the spread of luxury—that arose from the need to expand (1:68–74).[10] The most famous statement of this argument came in a later volume.

> The decline of Rome was the natural and inevitable effect of immoderate greatness. Prosperity ripened the principle of decay; the causes of destruction multiplied with the extent of conquest; and, as soon as time or accident had removed the artificial supports, the stupendous fabric yielded to the pressure of its own weight. (6:289)

The slow erosion of the architectural ruin until it collapses from within serves here as a metaphor for the cumulative, internal process of imperial decline, of which the ruin itself was product.

Yet the *declinatio*—as reformulated by Gibbon—presented as many problems as possibilities for American critics of the Gilded Age. If republican virtues are so vulnerable to the corruptions of territorial conquest and commercial prosperity, how did the Roman Empire remain intact for another four centuries? "Instead of inquiring why [it] . . . was destroyed," Gibbon wondered how "it had subsisted so long" (6:289)—which led him to recognize the role of laws and *moeurs* (customs), including religious tolerance, in creating a self-perpetuating civil society even under an absolute military dictatorship.[11] In the process, he betrayed an admiration for the late Roman Empire that distinguished him from other Enlightenment historians. And in the subsequent volumes, he further countered the reassuring "Enlightened narrative" of the eventual emergence of liberty out of the ruins of empire by documenting the more gloomy "triumph of Barbarism and religion" (12:191).[12]

Gibbon's general optimism about the future of the West, more typical of the Enlightenment, posed an even greater complication for those who would invoke him as a prophet of the impending cataclysm of American civilization.[13] While he conveyed the terminal decay of Rome (albeit qualifying it by attending to the complexity of causes and effects, the indeterminacy of origins, and the contingency of history), he doubted whether European civilization faced a "repetition of those calamities" (6:292). Without discounting ongoing fluctuations in the balance of power and wealth of nations, he was struck rather by the significant differences between past and present. The colonization of the North had by now removed the threat of marauding barbarians from those parts; while Europe's division into multiple kingdoms and states provided a check against the "abuses of tyranny" that arise from a single emperor, at the same time multiplying the armies with which to defend against any "savage conqueror [that] should issue from the deserts of Tartary" (6:292–95; quotations on 294–95). And with new scientific inventions such as gunpowder, those armies could now raise an "impregnable barrier against the Tartar horse" (6:295–96). But above all it was the broad diffusion of civilization that rendered its "benefits" so "solid and permanent." Arts, sciences, trades, and laws, once confined to the initiated, were now embedded in the population at large, and thus "strike an everlasting root" (6:297, 298). Even if "the victorious Barbarians [should] carry slavery and desolation as far as the Atlantic Ocean," the "American world" would serve as a kind of lifeboat for Western civilization, and a fertile terrain in which to transplant its fruits (6:295). Surveying these differences, Gibbon confidently concluded that "no people, unless the face of nature is changed, will relapse into their original barbarism" (6:297).

During the course of the nineteenth century, first in Britain and subsequently in the United States, Gibbon's guarded faith in the impossibility of a second Dark Age came under increasing doubt. Some of the earliest and most memorable challenges were ironically issued by the leading "Whig historian" Thomas Babington Macaulay. Although Macaulay's *History of England* embodied that confident, Whiggish teleology toward the glorious constitutional monarchy and economic power of his own age, his essays for the *Edinburgh Review* and speeches in Parliament occasionally disclosed a darker vision of history. A moderate advocate of limited electoral reform in the late 1820s, he vented his concerns about James Mill's more radical suffrage proposals through lurid predictions of future ruin. While accepting Gibbon's premise that the "civilised part of the world has now nothing to fear from the hostility of savage nations," he warned that Mill's utilitarian principles would "engende[r]" an even greater "malady" within the "bosom of civilisation itself," one that "may undo the work of so many ages of wisdom and glory, and gradually sweep away taste, literature, science, commerce, manufactures," until ". . . [after] two or three hundred years, a few lean and half-naked fishermen may divide with owls and foxes the ruins of the greatest European cities—may wash their nets amidst the relics of her gigantic docks, and build their huts out of the capitals of her stately cathedrals."[14] The revolutions of 1848 instilled further lingering "doubt[s]" as to "the progress of society," which he voiced in Parliament four years later.

I remembered that Adam Smith and Gibbon had told us that the dark ages
were gone, never more to return, that modern Europe was in no danger of the
fate which had befallen the Roman Empire. . . . It had not occurred to them
that civilisation itself might engender the barbarians who should destroy it.
It had not occurred to them that in the very heart of great capitals, in the
neighbourhood of splendid palaces, and churches, and theatres, and libraries,
and museums, vice and ignorance might produce a race of Huns fiercer than
those who marched under Attila, and of Vandals more bent on destruction
than those who followed Genseric.[15]

But by far the most cited of all Macaulay's scenes of future barbarism was that
of "some traveller from New Zealand" stationed "on a broken arch of London
Bridge to sketch the ruins of St. Paul's." Although the point of this brief aside
from an 1840 review of a history of the papacy was to convey not the fragility of his own city, but the longevity of the Roman Catholic Church—which
would perhaps "still exist in undiminished vigour" even in this deep future—
this powerful literary image was ripped out of its original context, illustrated
by Gustave Doré (fig. 4.1), and ultimately inserted into very different American contexts.[16]

Henry George and the Gathering Hordes

Macaulay's vision of a skyline reduced by barbarians to broken arches and
ruined domes, and ultimately rediscovered by another race of pilgrims, appealed especially to Americans confronting the dire conflict between rich and
poor, or capital and labor, in the Gilded Age. One of the first American authors to take up the Gibbon-Macaulay debate within this new context was the
radical political economist Henry George. In the final "book" of *Progress and
Poverty*—his 1879 treatise against the injustice of rent that sold more than 2
million copies by 1905—George clearly sided with Macaulay.[17] Gibbon was
misguided in asserting that "modern civilization could never be destroyed because there remained no barbarians to overrun it" (528). There are already
"indications that we are actually turning back again toward barbarism" (535).
One need only visit "the squalid quarters of great cities"—which had witnessed
violent confrontations during the Great Railroad Strike two years earlier—to
see the "gathering hordes" of "new barbarians," precisely those "more hideous
Huns and fiercer Vandals of whom Macaulay prophesied" (538, 7). Although
it was conceived by an English historian and rendered by a French illustrator, George appropriated the "picture of the New Zealander" as an allegory
that should "appea[l] to the imagination of even those who see cities rising

Fig. 4.1. Gustave Doré, "The New Zealander." From Blanchard Jerrold and Gustave Doré, *London: A Pilgrimage* (London: Grant, 1872), opposite p. 188.

in the wilderness and help to lay the foundations of new empire," that is, to urban Americans (486). Already his contemporaries seemed to acknowledge the prospect of their own ruin. In sealing away "some mementos of our day" in the cornerstones of new buildings, we anticipate "the time when our works shall be ruins and ourselves forgot" (486).

Yet, unlike the later authors we will examine (for whom he arguably paved the way), George invoked the specter of barbarism as a warning and a call for action. His response to the emerging conflict between capital and labor was to point to a deeper conflict between landowners and renters. Taking land rather than capital as the "initial point" of his political economy (163), he explained how a growing monopoly of that crucial asset could fatally erode a nation's wealth, hinder its social development, and ultimately reduce it to ruins. Macaulay's grim predictions, however, could be avoided if the appropriate solution were adopted. That solution would not come from the agrarian populists, whose slogans about the "mystique" of the land he echoed but whose calls for the "confiscation and forced redistribution of land" he opposed.[18] Nor would it come from socialists or labor unions: he endorsed the socialists' "ideal" but disdained their methods (320–21), and although a union member, he denounced their organizations as "tyrannical" and their strikes as "destructive of the very things which workmen seek to gain" (315–16). Nor could society simply be left to its own devices, as Malthusian, Darwinian, and Spencerian social theorists urged (91–150, 478, 485).[19] Only one thing could avert the coming catastrophe: the Single Tax. This levy on all profits landowners make from ground rent was what he called his "simple yet sovereign remedy" (405)—and what Karl Marx derided as his reactionary "panacea"—for *all* the evils of society.[20] The appropriation and redistribution of that unearned income would "raise wages, increase the earnings of capital, extirpate pauperism, abolish poverty, give remunerative employment to whoever wishes it, afford free scope to human powers, lessen crime, elevate morals, and taste, and intelligence, purify government and carry civilization to yet nobler heights" (405–6)—all without further recourse to strikes or strikebreakers.

In some respects, George still inhabited a residual eighteenth-century Enlightenment worldview of rising and falling empires. Perhaps conscious of the quixotic hopes he invested in his Single Tax, he supplemented his arguments for its fiscal and social benefits with a lengthy historical excursus into patterns of progress and decline over preceding millennia (431–552). According to his "law of human progress," civilizations progressed as they forged and strengthened various bonds of sociability or "association"—for example, through market exchange, religious rituals, or cooperative institutions—and preserved a fundamental "equality" of wealth (527, 508). And they "retrogress[ed]" as that spirit of association and equality was gradually negated by growing distinctions between the free and the enslaved; skilled and unskilled; salaried and wage-earning; or most fatally, landlords and tenants (506, 525–26, 513–14, 516–17). In insisting that this law cuts across national borders and historical epochs, he was aligning himself with the kind of metahistory practiced by English Whigs, French *philosophes*, American revolutionaries, and the more recent "universal historians," whose works he had closely studied.[21] And in arguing that "every civilization that has been overwhelmed by barbarians has really perished from internal decay"—and that it is "extremely difficult" for contemporaries to "recognize" the first stages of that decay, such as afflicted Rome even amid the "wealth" and "magnificence" of Augustus—he echoed those crucial early chapters from Gibbon's *Decline and Fall* (487, 539, 528).

George's relationship to those earlier philosophies of history, however, remained ambivalent. He questioned the universalist faith that each cycle in the course of empire would elevate civilization to ever greater heights in a kind of upward spiral. Mankind was instead condemned to a Sisyphean nightmare of eternal cyclicality in which barbarism develops into civilization only to be replaced by a "fresh race" of barbarians (486). If meaningful improvement were possible, it would come about only through a dramatic leap into the posthistorical world of social harmony conjured by the Single Tax. Thus George borrowed his language of corruption from the classical republicans and his dream of an ultimate "City of God" (552) from the postmillennialists, but without conforming to either's conception of historical time.[22] There could be no faith in a larger course of empire or progress; the simple choice facing Americans was adoption of the Single Tax or retrogression into barbarism, millennial glory or cultural oblivion.

Furthermore, George undermined dominant beliefs that America would represent the culmination of history, whether as the secular endpoint of the westward course of civilization or the spiritual fulfillment of the millennium. The only thing exceptional about America was the degree to which its unprecedented economic and social development had rendered it vulnerable to those forces of "retrogression." Its rate of territorial expansion, far exceeding that of Roman imperialism, had prevented it from absorbing and assimilating its indigenous people; even Rome had been able to absorb its barbarians (501). The timetable was compressed still further by the discovery of new technologies. "With steam and electricity, and the new powers born of progress, forces have entered the world that will either compel us to a higher plane or overwhelm us" (551). The Enlightenment signs of imminent decline—the corruptions of luxury, the loss of virtue, the standing armies—have thus been replaced by such symptoms or "marks" as tramps, almshouses, and prisons (7)—to which he added brothels and tenements (339). "Over and again have nations and civilizations been confronted with problems which, like the riddle of the Sphinx, not to answer was to be destroyed," George subsequently wrote, "but *never* before have problems so vast and intricate been presented."[23]

It was no coincidence that all these symptoms existed in urban settings. Since his first published treatise, the short pamphlet titled *Our Land and Land Policy* (1871), George had maintained that the nation's fatal defects emanated from "the heart of [its] great cities," where, he wrote, quoting Macaulay, "poverty and ignorance might produce a race of Huns fiercer than any who followed Attila, and of Vandals more destructive than those led by Genseric."[24] *Progress and Poverty* expanded on the significance of the "great city" as the locus of "the greatest wealth and the deepest poverty," the breakdown of "popular government," and political corruption to rival that of "declining Rome" (533–34). But it was in his 1883 sequel, *Social Problems*, that he explicitly spelled out his nightmare of urban apocalypse—a nightmare of cities "sacked and burned" by "terror-stricken mob[s]" and "arm[ies] of thieves"; armed conflict not between "armies" but between social "classes;" and bombs of "nitroglycerin" detonated under "railroad bridges and tunnels" so as to "bring famine quicker than the wall of circumvallation that Titus drew around Jerusalem" (5). Despite this lurid fantasy, George was not an antiurbanist; a Philadelphia native who began his career in San Francisco before moving to New York, he dreamed of an urban utopia of libraries and opera theaters open to the public, and single-family homes equipped with modern conveniences (239). Rather, he invoked ruins to draw attention to the present contradictions of capitalist urbanization. The peculiar vulnerability of American cities stemmed from the "intricate interdependence" of their citizens, who relied more than ever on a hidden complex of machinery and labor for such necessities as water, lighting, and transportation. The slightest disruption to the social order of cities— overpopulated as they are with atomistic and anomic individuals who remain "utter strangers" even to the "tenants of adjoining rooms"—could unleash the apocalypse. "Let jar or shock dislocate the complex and delicate organization, let the policeman's club be thrown down or wrested from him, and the fountains of the great deep are opened, and quicker than ever before chaos comes again" (5–6).

From the size and fragility of industrial cities, and the incendiary potential of "petroleum, nitro-glycerine, and dynamite" (*Progress*, 538), George concluded that the war precipitating the downfall of modern civilization would be unprecedented (*Social Problems*, 5). He thus directly challenged Gibbon's faith in the immunity of modern civilization to barbarian assault, and in the imperishability of the arts and sciences in the event of such an assault. Moreover, while technologies of warfare have increased the power to destroy, technologies of inscription and construction have diminished the power to preserve.

> It is startling to think how slight the traces that would be left of our civilization did it pass through the throes which have accompanied the decline of every previous civilization. Paper will not last like parchment, nor are our most massive buildings and monuments to be compared in solidity with the rock-hewn temples and titanic edifices of the old civilizations. (*Progress*, 538)

Even "[our] religious and funereal monuments," he added, would give an "inadequate and utterly misleading" picture of "our civilization" to future historians, presumably because of their eclectic borrowings from other nations (538 n.). There is thus no indication that the aftermath of American civilization would be any different from earlier dark ages, when the "remnant of squalid barbarians, who had lost even the memory of what their ancestors had done," came to "regar[d] the surviving fragments of their grandeur as the work of genii, or of the mighty race before the flood" (485). No improvements in building and writing materials, archival preservation techniques, or monument designs could avert that future. Ultimately, the persistence of this civilization could only be ensured by the passage of the Single Tax.

Labor Unrest and the New Rome

Progress and Poverty, according to one historian, "defined social criticism for an entire era."[25] Even while advancing other solutions to the current crisis — a socialist commonwealth, Christian brotherhood, or "new aristocracy" of wealth — critics found themselves echoing George's words and formulas. Lawrence Gronlund's socialist tract *Coöperative Commonwealth* (1884) offered a typical Georgian warning of an imminent reversion to barbarism, in pointing to the "striking parallels" between the Augustan golden age and the American Gilded Age: the "same destructive forces," the "same mad chase after wealth," the "same deadening scepticism in regard to high ideals," the same degree of political "corruption."[26] Although he faulted George for privileging the "land question" over the social relations of production (86), Gronlund still "hope[d]" his readers had all consulted *Progress and Poverty*, especially those passages exposing the "utter absurdity of the Malthusian philosophy" (86, 131). And in place of George's "Utopian" vision of society under the Single Tax (92), Gronlund substituted his Coöperative Commonwealth, based on the nationalization of industry and transportation as well as land, as the only alternative to "barbarism" (7).

But not until the late 1880s, when armed force was increasingly used to suppress strikes, did George's jeremiad acquire a heightened topicality. In just three days in May 1886, an incipient national strike for an eight-hour day was met with a wave of violent repression: first outside McCormick's Reaper factory in southwest Chicago, where policemen killed four picketing workers; then at Haymarket Square (west Chicago), where police responded to a bomb allegedly thrown by anarchists by firing indiscriminately into the crowd, killing at least seven; and then in Milwaukee, where state militia shot into a crowd of Polish workers, killing another seven.[27] George subsequently found himself alternately lionized and vilified. Responding to the shootings, the wave of arrests that ensued, and the death sentence of the Haymarket "martyrs," the Central Labor Union of New York successfully persuaded him to enter politics as their mayoral candidate, and to campaign not only for the land tax but also for the innocence of the "martyrs" and the right of workers to strike and boycott.[28] Capitalist apologists also considered George an ally of organized labor, despite his criticisms of unions in *Progress and Poverty*. The narrator of Anna Bowman Dodd's 1887 dystopia, *The Republic of the Future*, looks back from 2050 to the "reign of blood," a war that had erupted out of the Single Tax movement in 1900 and resulted in the dynamiting of New York by foreign radicals and the building of a lifeless "Socialist City" on its ruins. To commemorate George's decisive role as the "founder," they had erected a "colossal statue" in the "Temple of the Liberators," enshrined *Progress and Poverty*, and dedicated one day of the year to a public reading of it.[29] Among the bourgeois traditions the socialists repudiated was the aesthetic cult of the ruin. The ruins of merchant's mansions from the nineteenth century are freely plundered for treasures, old churches razed, and the Ruskinian notion of ruins as a "necessary element" in the landscape dismissed as obsolete (22, 81, 82).

In the years following these initial skirmishes, many members and sympathizers of the labor movement began to ascribe them less to the recklessness of the police or provocations of anarchists than to the underlying cause of economic inequality. A typical strategy was to present statistics demonstrating the uneven diffusion of wealth in American society, and to compare them with those of ancient civilizations at their downfall. "When Egypt went down 2 per cent. of her population owned 97 per cent. of her wealth," warned the Boston newspaper *The Progress* in 1889, citing equally precise figures for Babylon and Rome.[30] Reverend E. D. M'Creary, writing in the *Christian Advocate* two years later, claimed that America, with "two-thousandth" of its population owning "more than one-half" of its wealth, had in fact exceeded all prior nations in its "concentration of wealth." Some critics, M'Creary among them, viewed this maldistribution, which had been "the ruin" of former states such as Rome, as an unfortunate by-product of economic growth. Ignoring the modes of production specific to industrial capitalism, they assumed that a simple redistribution of that wealth would suffice to "insure [*sic*] competence, comfort, and prosperity for every household in the land" and to end the "fierce strife . . . between capital and labor."[31] Others, such as the agrarian populist leader Herman Taubeneck, perceived those inequalities—which now threatened to "destroy this nation" as they had "every nation of antiquity," albeit "ten times more rapidly" because of the greater forces unleashed by modern technologies—as the intended and unnatural outcome of specific banking acts of the 1860s and

'70s by which Congress had legislated wealth *"out of the pockets of the masses and into the pockets of the* [upper] *classes."*[32]

Counterarguments against such indictments of American economic inequality were similarly embellished with allusions to antiquity. Commenting on the turbulent "events" of recent years, Harry Thurston Peck, the classical scholar and editor of the recently launched conservative New York review *The Bookman*, deployed his knowledge of Roman life and literature to reject the charge that the growth of fortunes augured the decline of nations. Those "pessimist[s]" had essentially "misread history." Slavery and provincial particularism were the true causes of Rome's decline. "Concentration of wealth," by contrast, was what made Rome—and by extension America—so "great," by mobilizing resources, instilling a "sense of civic responsibility" in its leaders, and stimulating "supreme achievement in every sphere."[33]

Critics and champions of capitalism also disagreed with one another—and among themselves—over whether unionization was advisable and justifiable. As national chairman of the People's Party, Taubeneck was adamant that the condition of wage laborers had in fact worsened under the Knights of Labor and other unions, and that they could save themselves and "our republic" only by uniting at the ballot box.[34] Writing in the same progressive magazine, *The Arena*, the New York psychic and spiritualist Dr. Joseph Rodes Buchanan was even more critical of organized labor. In "The Coming Cataclysm of America and Europe" (1890), he predicted the outbreak of a full-blown "civil war" between capital and labor as a result not only of the "aggressive power" and "corruption" of the former but also the unionization of the latter. The laboring masses, now conscripted into "hostile camps," where "angry passions are fanned by leaders . . . and by social agitators," could easily be "electrified" into a "national convulsion" by "disturbances" that might otherwise have been "local and temporary."[35] Drawing on his "scientific" studies in the "periodicity" of historical calamities and the psychometric detection of "coming events" through the "shadows" and "reflection[s]" they cast on the present, this latter-day Nostradamus predicted that the violent settlement of that "old feud between capital and labor" would begin in 1909 and would lead not to "social redress" but to "universal ruin" (298–300, 293). It would usher in a period of destruction that *"will surpass anything . . .* [in] *history,"* involving a racial struggle, the downfall of Christianity, and natural disasters ranging from earthquakes, floods, cyclones, and meteorites to arctic winters and tropical summers, until finally in 1913 or 1914 a giant tidal wave destroys "every seaboard city south of New England" (299, 303, 306–7, 309–12). The one consolation would be the destruction of capitalist monopolies in the process, clearing the way for a reinvigorated democracy founded upon public ownership of industry (310). Buchanan evidently subscribed to the goals of George and the utopian novelist Edward Bellamy, yet considered them attainable only by a national apocalypse.[36]

Those who upheld the strategies of unionizing and striking therefore had to disprove they were radically new or inherently inflammatory. G. A. Danziger, writing in the new "family magazine," *Cosmopolitan*, refuted that unions and strikes were modern phenomena by tracing their noble lineage back to ancient Rome, specifically to the mechanics' guilds and musicians' strikes of the fourth century BC, while also denying that such class struggle brought down the Roman Empire, crediting it instead to the "gentle yet powerful hand" of Christianity. The *un*-Christian contempt (especially of "small traders") for those ancient mechanics and musicians, and their right to organize, provided modern Americans with a historical lesson of how the tendency to "undervalue the employee's work, to ill-treat and to oppress him" could prompt him to "reac[h] . . . for . . . the strike."[37]

Rather than the workers, these apologists argued, it was the industrialists—with their inclination to use armed force—who were imperiling the republic. Not content with the assistance of police and state militia in breaking strikes (as in 1886), they now increasingly enlisted their own private agents, culminating by the summer of 1892 in deadly firefights between strikers and Pinkerton detectives at Carnegie and Frick's steel factories in Homestead, near Pittsburgh.[38] Later that year, the progressive owner of *Cosmopolitan*, John Brisben Walker, explicated the incident as a further "Object Lesson" for the public. Like Danziger, he affirmed that the "steadily" growing labor movement stood for wholly legitimate ideals, above all that of a republic "where all men shall be equal."[39] That republic was instead jeopardized, as Homestead demonstrated, by the wealthy, who were not merely increasing the gap between "luxury" and "poverty," and buying off judges and senators to do so, but even "hiring private armies" as dangerous as the "bands of fighting bullies" recruited by Romans patricians. The American plutocrat, telegraphing "orders [to] his army" from the safety of his "secret office," was even more contemptible than his ancient forebear, who at least had the courage to "parade the streets" in person (572). Whereas George, for all his sympathy for labor, had discerned Macaulay's "barbarians" gathering in American tenement districts (*Progress*, 538), and whereas Bellamy's future utopians used the term to refer to *all* Americans of the nineteenth century, those identifying more closely with the labor movement redirected the epithet against the capitalists.[40] "If our civilization is destroyed, as Macaulay predicted," wrote the Chicago journalist and antimonopolist Henry Demarest Lloyd two years later—and just two months after President Cleveland had sent in the army to break up the Pullman strike in south Chicago — "it will not be by his barbarians from below. Our barbarians come from above."[41]

Wonder Cities and Labyrinths of Ruin: Jack London's Prospective History

As industrial violence spread in the late 1890s and early 1900s to the coal towns of Illinois and Pennsylvania and the boomtowns of the Colorado gold and silver belt, many became convinced that civilization could not be safeguarded from barbarism by such panaceas as George's Single Tax, nor would it necessarily evolve peacefully into the kinds of classless and cooperative societies imagined by Gronlund or Bellamy.[42] Some even began to invoke barbarism not as something to be avoided through the administering of a social, moral, or legislative tonic, but as an inevitable and necessary stage in the eventual emergence of some utopian society. That indeed was the conclusion to which the novelist Jack London had arrived by the summer of 1906 when he began to write his prospective history, *The Iron Heel*.[43]

The Iron Heel was in some respects the culmination of over two decades of apocalyptic warnings issued across the left, from socialists to Social Gospellers, and from labor leaders to agrarian populists. Like many of them, London considered American capitalist society as riddled with internal contradictions as Gibbon deemed Antonine Rome.[44] But he doubted that the capitalist class would simply give way at the appointed time to the redistribution of wealth or nationalization of industry, at least not without a protracted and bloody struggle. His book thus narrates the outcome of that coming counterrevolution: the suppression of radicals and their writings, the literal enslavement of industrial labor, the accession of a cruel plutocratic dictatorship called "The Oligarchy," or the "Iron Heel" (98), and ultimately the destruction of Chicago. In exposing capitalists' inner brutishness, London was also targeting many on the left: socialists who maintained faith in gradualism, antimonopolists who longed to restore some golden age of independent proprietorship, and populists and Grangers who clung to an outmoded agrarian ideal of American yeomanry, oblivious to how it would be vanquished even more rapidly than the yeoman class of ancient Rome (78–90, 80–81, 131 n.). As a supporter of the radical Syndicalist movement, Industrial Workers of the World (founded in Chicago in 1905), London even targeted the moderate unions for failing to realize the power of the general strike to reduce Americans to scavenging "savages" in the "ruins" of their own cities.[45] The intensity of the oligarchic reaction would demand nothing less than an underground cadre of armed socialist revolutionaries acting as the advance guard of the revolution, as Lenin theorized four years earlier.[46]

These developments, however, are presented to the reader neither as the predictions of a millenarian prophet or scientific forecaster, nor as the direct testimony of a contemporary protagonist transported into the future, but through the device of a historical manuscript written two decades after the events by Avis Everhard, widow of the socialist hero, Ernest. Temporal distance is further extended by the manuscript's disappearance for another seven hundred years. Not until the twenty-ninth century, by which time that eventual utopian socialist state had been attained, was it rediscovered by archaeologists in the ruins of California (3–4, 173 n.) and finally published, with preface and annotations by Anthony Meredith, a prospective historian of ancient America—one of several in London's fiction.[47]

Although Darwinian racial prejudices are less evident here than in London's other novels, this temporal distance allows him to employ a social-evolutionary model to illuminate the patterns of history.[48] In Avis's retrospection, the early twentieth century can be comprehended as a period of "transition," from the "flux" of which "new institutions were forming" (189). Drawing on his historical knowledge of the time after Avis's death, Meredith shed further light on that transition. Just as Buchanan detected future events from the "shadows" they project upon the present ("Coming Cataclysm," 300), Meredith's footnotes to the manuscript show how the violence of the oligarchic reaction was foreshadowed in the phenomena of the Gilded Age, above all those involving labor and capital. Thus, the "political machines" that controlled American cities evolved into governmental apparatuses of the capitalists, while the commercial trusts merged into the five bodies of the Oligarchy (54 n., 101 n.). Late nineteenth-century strikebreaking techniques underwent similar modifications. The industrialists' Pinkerton detectives evolved into the "Mercenaries of the Oligarchy"; their industrial spies into the "Black Hundreds" who "in turn . . . became . . . the agents-provocateurs"; and their "favoured unions" of moderate, skilled workers into the hereditary "labour castes" (54 n., 110–11 n., 142 n.). Even the 1886 trial of the Haymarket martyrs and the 1904 prosecution of the Colorado miners are presented as mere precursors to later plots to frame innocent radicals (164–65 n.). The corollary of this "slow social evolution" was the devolution or extinction of those unable to adapt (142). William Randolph Hearst, whose newspapers "appealed to the perishing middle class and to the proletariat," briefly "managed to take possession of the empty shell of the old Democratic Party" before himself disappearing into the dustbin of history (129 n.). And as the caste system emerged, unskilled laborers descended into such a "brutish" condition that they became known as the "people of the abyss," after the term coined by that "sociological seer," H. G. Wells (192, 159 n.).[49] Although most visible in hindsight, these processes are also perceptible at the time, if only to those like Ernest Everhard (and Wells) trained in historical materialism to deduce from the underlying "changes in our industrial" base, "the shadow" of impending "changes in our religious, political, and social [super-]structures" (67)—or to distinguish "out of this flux" that which "is about to crystallize" (107).[50]

The precondition for tracing those oligarchic and utopian futures out of the urban-industrial present is the assumed survival of written records and artifacts—and in making this uncharacteristically optimistic assumption, London again breaks with George's work. In spite of George's fears of the perishability of modern civilization, Meredith is largely able to fill the various lacunae in the historical record and to interpolate the facts omitted from the manuscript (162 n.). As it breaks off mid-sentence, and was intended to be "read in her own day," some details remain obscure, such as those concerning the author and the circumstance of her husband's death (162 n., 4, 224)—a historiographical problem exacerbated by the apparent suppression of certain texts (such as censuses) by the Oligarchy (56 n.; see also 118, 185 n.). But as an objective historian, Meredith remains committed to bridging the hermeneutic gap between present and past, and entering "the minds of the actors in that long-ago world-drama" (2).[51] He thus avails himself of the advantages of linguistic continuity (few words have become archaic, and even their original meanings are known [53 n., 145–46 n.]); material and cultural survivals such as inventions, songs, and stories (173 n., 175 n., 180–81 n., 184 n.); and above all books. A new National Library contains not only official ancient documents such as the *Congressional Record* but also the oppositional writings of socialists, while even the works of "one Ambrose Bierce, an avowed and confirmed misanthrope of the period," have survived (20 n., 90 n., 68 n., 159 n., 63 n.). This depiction of the wealth of sources available to the future historian echoed London's earlier essay, "The Shrinkage of the Planet," which in turn echoed Gibbon in arguing that modern technologies of transportation and communication, besides "annihilat[ing] space and time," have disseminated knowledge so widely as to preclude the kind of intellectual "relapse" that occurred after the destruction of the Library of Alexandria. "Civilizations may wax and wane, but the totality of knowledge cannot decrease. . . . Arts and sciences may be discarded, but they can never be lost."[52]

Just as *The Iron Heel* repudiates George's notion of cultural erasure, so too does it break with Bellamy in the way it figures that eventual utopia. Unlike the latter's fully fleshed-out utopia, whose social and economic features are related by the narrator in exhaustive expository detail, London's can be glimpsed only by reading between the lines of the historian's marginal annotations. Meredith's footnotes, moreover, articulate that utopia negatively, in terms of what no longer exists. All we know is that it lacks the capitalist monopolies, labor exploitation, and union "troubles" of the early twentieth century (23 n., 34 n., 92 n.), along with other "peculiar institutions" and practices such as nativism, domestic violence, insurance companies, cluttered bourgeois interiors, bankruptcy legislation, and political lobbyists (19 n., 23 n., 39 n., 49 n., 81 n., 102 n.). Even the advent of that utopia is left unexplained, suspended in the vast temporal chasm signified by the typographic gap between body-text and footnotes. Through the device of prospective historiography, London thus conceives what the Marxist theorist Ernst Bloch later called a "concrete utopia" (as against the merely compensatory and wish-fulfilling "abstract utopia") — a future so radical in its otherness that it can only be apprehended indirectly through its fragmentary traces.[53]

Piecing together these utopian fragments, one can in fact retrace the outline of London's vision of the afterlife of American cities. The rise of the Oligarchy appears to have marked a rupture in American urban history, when nineteenth-century cities of contiguous, albeit increasingly specialized, neighborhoods, splintered off into entirely separate cities: "great squalid labour-ghettos" for the "people of the abyss," "delightful cities" of "comfortable homes" for "members of the great labour castes," "practically self-govern[ing]" cities for the "Mercenaries," and entirely new "wonder cities" for the oligarchs themselves (192, 189, 143). Eschewing the piecemeal process of speculative urban construction, which had left Melville's New York in that perpetually "half finished" state, these "wonder cities" would be built, indeed "completed," in just a few years by a permanent army of slave laborers (192, 193 n.). And unlike the rapid decay of their predecessors, they would "endure" undiminished in beauty for three centuries until finally inherited by the citizens of the socialist utopia (142–43, 143 n.), who would build further "wonder cities" albeit with free, unalienated labor. Again, we can perceive the utopian conditions of those cities only through their absences: the lack of "ruined and dilapidated" tenements, extortionist landlords, or fortresslike architecture (31 n.). These urban utopias are predicated, however, upon the destruction of earlier cities, above all Chicago. Not coincidentally, the oligarchs had selected that "storm-centre of the conflict between labour and capital"—the scene of so many "bitter strikes" and "street-battles," the veritable "industrial inferno of the nineteenth century A.D." (196–97, 196 n.)—as the battleground on which to incite and suppress a proletarian uprising. A new kind of urban warfare, consisting of "street-fighting and sky-scraper fighting," had culminated in the incineration of Chicago—stockyards, immigrant "ghetto," and Pullman included. All that remained was a "labyrinth of ruin" (212, 216, 221–22).

Efflux of Capital, Influx of Barbarians

In prospective histories, the labor-capital conflict rarely destroyed American cities single-handedly; the latter were already vulnerable to the variable flow of capital and population. Even in London's apocalypse, the oligarchic reaction was a symptom of the larger capitalist struggle to avert crises of overproduction, or in Everhard's Marxist phraseology, to "dispose" of "unconsumed surplus[es]" (94). London elaborated the following year that, just as Rome's "unwise distribution" of wealth allowed it to be conquered by "Teutons" and to lose its control of world "commerce," so conversely could loss of control over trade routes lead to domestic ruin, as exemplified by the plowed ruins of Carthage ("Shrinkage," 148–49). The notion that American cities could succumb to the vagaries of trade—raised a generation earlier by the proslavery ideologues, Fitzhugh and Ruffin—became more widespread.

The trade routes now threatening New York's commercial ruin were its waterways. If that metropolis owed its rapid rise to the coupling of its natural advantages of a deep harbor and wide rivers with its access to a new "artificial river," then any disruption to those channels could spell an equally rapid decline. By midcentury, the Erie Canal had been undermined by the construction of railroads and newer canals, the suspension of plans for its extension and widening, and the deterioration of its existing infrastructure. The *Times* was so troubled by its neglect that it warned in 1857 that "the day is not far distant when the commercial greatness of New-York, having passed its zenith, shall decline and fall rapidly into decay."[54] Two decades later, it was clear that the city's commercial hegemony could only be preserved by "abandon[ing]" it and building a new one wide enough for steam-driven boats—a remedy that would at least yield some picturesque "ruins of aqueducts" for "the New Zealander of Macaulay" to "sketch" on his return from London.[55] The wharves and piers of Manhattan's riverfronts were also of concern. Jerry-built during the boom of the 1850s, and with no public body responsible for their upkeep, they were so "dilapidated" by 1870 as to be unusable and irreparable, prompting the mercantile elite to campaign for new docks to ensure their city's future.[56] Given the overdependence of New York, among other American cities, on commercial traffic—contrasting with those European metropolises that also served as seats of government—any of these infrastructural flaws could be considered potentially fatal.

The concerns of leading merchants in the East were heightened by the competing claims voiced by the boosters of rising cities in the West. Logan Uriah Reavis was one of those who challenged the conceit that New York, or any other city on the Atlantic coast, would inherit the title of "future great city of the world" from London, maintaining that the honor would belong—"within one hundred years from our date," that is, by 1970—to his own adopted city of St. Louis.[57] In support of this counterclaim, he cited the conventional factors of his city's climate and location (within the "isothermal belt or zodiac . . . of empires") and its natural resources, along with the "lessons of magnitude and durability" conveyed by the "ruins" of ancient civilizations, and the power of accident—"a kind of happening so!"—to "impoverish" one city and "give vitality and strength to the other" (11, 56–57, 9, 24–25). But Reavis emphasized above all that the recent ascendancy of railroad networks over ocean routes had altered that age-old assumption of the *translatio*, namely that great cities need to be located near coastlines. The steam engine, as applied both to production and transportation, was one of those "new agencies and influences that tend in modern times with such irresistible force to concentrate mankind in the great interior cities of the Continents" (25). Although those railroad networks and industrial factories were increasingly converging on the rival city of Chicago, he felt confident they would ultimately transform St. Louis into the global metropole to which even New York would serve as peripheral "outpor[t]" (29).[58] The book was poorly received back east, with one Bostonian denouncing its claims as "sheer nonsense . . . unequaled in American literature."[59]

Nevertheless, in an apparent effort to hasten the fulfillment of his "prophecy" that St. Louis would become that final "Apocalyptic City—'The New Jerusalem'" (215), Reavis launched a campaign to remove the nation's capital to the banks of the Mississippi—if not to St. Louis then to its neighbor, Alton, Illinois. Reviving arguments first made in 1814, he argued in no less than four books published between 1867 and 1883, and in numerous petitions, pamphlets, lectures, and articles, that its current location on the Potomac was atmospherically unhealthy, militarily indefensible, and above all demographically unrepresentative, as the majority of the nation's population now resided "west of the Alleghenies."[60] Urbane easterners may still despise those unrefined westerners—as "Rome despised the barbarians"—but the westward course of empire would have the final say. By the time the cities of the Mississippi valley and the Pacific coast become thriving metropolises, their predecessors on the Atlantic will have long since been abandoned.

> Civilization, like the ostrich in its flight, throws sand upon everything behind her; and before many cycles shall have completed their rounds sentimental

pilgrims from the humming cities of the Pacific coast will be seen where Boston, Philadelphia, and New York now stand, viewing in moonlight contemplation, with the melancholy owl, traces of the Athens, the Carthage, and the Babel of the Western hemisphere.[61]

Reavis did not specify the fate of Washington's buildings after the transference of federal government to the Mississippi (others did predict their ruins would be sufficiently grand to impress that "tiresome New Zealander" of the "former existence there of a noble edifice, the expression in architecture of a very high civilization").[62] Yet, in predicting that ruin would extend only partially over the United States, rather than uniformly as it did over the Roman Empire, Reavis again departed from the model of the *translatio*, even as he echoed Gibbon's observation that the pilgrims and friars in the ruins of Rome were the offspring of former barbarians.

While urban boosters like Reavis warned easterners of the sand-engulfed ruins the westering "star of empire" would leave in its wake (*St. Louis*, 31), an emerging group of agrarian politicians warned of the vulnerability of all American cities, given their dependency on agricultural resources. Neither great fires, earthquakes, nor even financial panics were needed to reduce urban America to ruin; all it would take is a disruption in the production or distribution of grains. Voiced first by the Grangers in the late 1860s and the Greenbackers in the 1870s, the theme of imminent ruin through the parasitism of urban plutocrats upon agricultural producers was taken up by the Populist or People's Party in the early 1890s, whose founding platform hinted at the "terrible social convulsions, the destruction of civilization, or the establishment of an absolute despotism" looming on the horizon. The author of that platform, Ignatius Donnelly, a former U.S. congressman from Minnesota and a failed town speculator, had explored such a scenario in his recently published, best-selling, cataclysmic novel *Caesar's Column* (1889). During the late twentieth-century insurgency that destroyed New York, and ultimately capitalist civilization, the revolutionary mobs disregarded the warnings that their "vast city, of ten million inhabitants, had been fed by thousands of carloads of food which were brought in, every day," and that with the rupture of that supply chain, they would begin to starve.[63] This third-party rhetoric about urban indebtedness to the rural entered the political mainstream at the Democratic Convention of 1896. There, William Jennings Bryan, co-opting the rhetoric of his Populist endorsers, famously reminded the gold bugs in the cities to heed the bimetallist demands of farmers: "[Your] great cities rest upon our broad and fertile prairies. Burn down your cities and leave our farms, and your cities will spring up again as if by magic;

but destroy our farms and the grass will grow in the streets of every city in the country."[64]

American cities appeared destructible by class warfare not merely because of their dependence on external provisions. Various social critics—radical and reactionary, rural and urban—believed they were undermined internally by their own demographic and social conditions.[65] For the immigrant progressive Jacob Riis, it was the urban "blight" of the tenement that imperiled the republic. In addition to exposing—and almost igniting—those poorly ventilated, overcrowded, and underregulated multifamily dwellings with his magnesium-flash camera, Riis condemned them in magazine and newspaper articles at the turn of the century. He argued that their rapid proliferation over the previous few decades was eating away at the "corner stone" upon which American civilization was constructed, namely the sanctity of the home. Without such a cornerstone, that civilization would go the way of its "dead and forgotten" predecessors whose only remains are some inscrutable stone-carved antiquities in the British Museum.[66] While attributing the phenomenon in part to demographic pressures of nineteenth-century urbanization, Riis elsewhere asserted that it was not entirely "new to mankind." The "teeming multitudes" of Ancient Rome, he learned from Juvenal, were also "pent up" in tenements erected by "rapacious" and negligent slumlords, and tolerated by complacent—and thus complicit—citizens at large. And it was those slums, "more destructive than wars," that ultimately "killed Rome." Riis's reminders of the historical lessons conveyed by the residential ruins of ancient civilizations may have contributed to the passage in 1901 of a new Tenement House Act, designed to outlaw the so-called dumbbell tenements that had emerged in the wake of an earlier housing act, and to ensure proper inspection and enforcement of regulations.[67]

Those concerned less by the physical environment of cities than the ethnic origin of their populations also raised the specter of Roman ruins. Nativists increasingly invoked the *declinatio* in their efforts to stem the "invasion" of immigrants from Asia and eastern and southeastern Europe, and to denounce the rule of Irish demagogues in the cities. In his 1895 poem, "Unguarded Gates," the New England writer Thomas Bailey Aldrich lamented the barbarian hordes flooding through the "portals" of the New World and threatening to rip the "clustered stars" from Lady Liberty's "brow," just as the "thronging Goth and Vandal trampled Rome"—violent words that were quoted in the Senate the following year by the leading restrictionist Henry Cabot Lodge in support of a literacy requirement that would exclude those immigrants "who remain for the most part in congested masses in our great cities."[68] Such rhetoric was not confined to conservatives and nativists. Advocates of social reform such as the pastor and Social Gospeller, Lyman Abbott, also complained that the immigration of those without "capital," "education," and "culture" was exacerbating current labor disputes, although he remained confident (writing just prior to Haymarket) that Protestant Christianity's cooperative spirit would safeguard America from "revolutions such as destroyed Rome."[69] Even an immigrant could write of the "heterogeneous hordes" descending upon the country, bringing with them corruption, socialism, and other "alienism[s] in thought and conduct." Congregated in "our cities," wrote the Norwegian American novelist and literature professor Hjalmar Boyesen in 1887, those hordes were now "clamoring for *panem et circenses*, as in the days of ancient Rome, and threatening the existence of the republic." Without a new law to restrict the further influx of unskilled immigrants, he argued, these cities would continue to "accumulat[e]" that "inflammable material" until they erupt in "inevitable conflagration."[70] While allowing some to disavow the economic contradictions that fostered labor unrest by displacing them onto the external threat of barbarians at the gates, classical allusions could also be reconciled with Gibbon's idea of a slow dissolution from within. In Boyesen's version of the decline and fall, the ethnic working class played two roles simultaneously: that of barbarian horde *and* plebeian rabble.

Turkish Archaeologists, Chinese Historians, and the Ruins of the Polyglot City

The identification of ethnic populations with future ruins lay at the heart of several prospective histories. In *The Last American* (1889), a novel written and illustrated by the founder of the original *Life* magazine, John Ames Mitchell, archaeologists exploring the long-forgotten ruins of "Nhû-Yok" in 2951 discover a clue to its downfall in the form of coins dated 1937, bearing the head of "Dennis, the last of the Hy-Burnyan dictators."[71] The demagoguery of Irish "Caesars" had not been the sole cause of its downfall. The Gibbonesque historian among them, a professor from "Imperial College at Ispahan," recounts how immigrants "from all parts of Europe came here in vast numbers" (18, 33). As a result of this dilution of Anglo-Saxon blood, the "Mehrikans" suffered various degenerative disorders, including "flat-chested" physiques, "fragile teeth," and "weak digestions," along with "nervous diseases" that rendered them unable to withstand the worsening climate (33). Alongside these xenophobic allusions Mitchell also offered—both here and in *Life*—gentler satires of the contemporary fashions and foibles of his urbane middle-class readers, as viewed through the eyes of postapocalyptic explorers (figs. 4.2 and 4.3).[72]

THE RUINS OF NEW YORK, A.D., 2500.

First Scientist : THEY MUST HAVE BEEN A REMARKABLE PEOPLE. THEIR WOMEN
WERE APPARENTLY AMAZONS, AND THEIR MEN FIERCE AND WARLIKE.

Fig. 4.2. "The Ruins of New York, A.D., 2500." Cartoon from *Life* 18, no. 459 (1891): 209. Future visitors to New York, discovering theater advertisements among the fallen columns, read them literally: "They must have been a remarkable people. Their women were apparently Amazons, and their men fierce and warlike."

A STREET SCENE IN ANCIENT NHU-YOK.

[The costumes and manner of riding are taken from metal plates now in the museum at Teheran.]

Fig. 4.3. John Ames Mitchell, "A Street Scene in Ancient Nhu-Yok. (The costumes and manner of riding are taken from metal plates now in the museum at Teheran.)" Illustration from Mitchell, *The Last American: A Fragment from the Journal of Khan-li* (New York: Frederick A. Stokes and Brother, 1889), 57. Printing blocks for late nineteenth-century advertisements, discovered by Turkish archaeologists in AD 2951, are again taken as literal evidence of "the manners and customs of this ludicrous people" (54).

The explorers' origins in *The Last American* are as significant as their discoveries. Unlike Gibbon in the ruins of Rome, Macaulay's New Zealander in London, or even Reavis's Californian pilgrims in Boston, Philadelphia, and New York, these archaeologists have traveled from the *east*—from Persia—to rediscover the civilizations of the past. The fall of the American republic appears to have terminated both the westward trajectory of republics and the technological progress of humanity. The "Oriental" civilization of the thirtieth-century explorers remains as backward as it was assumed to be in archaeological and anthropological discourses of the nineteenth. They are thus mystified by the architectural and technological achievements of modern American civilization: the sublimity of cities that had been illuminated at night, the velocity of interurban travel, the instantaneity of remote communications (23–24). Even the ruins of the Brooklyn Bridge (six years old when Mitchell was writing) prove unintelligible; they fail to "divine [the] meaning" or purpose of the two massive structures rising up from the East River, their iron cables dangling (36) (fig. 4.4). Hopes of shedding light on these and other sights are briefly raised when they encounter three surviving Mehrikans in the ruins of the Capitol in Washington (64–65). But in contrast to the friars Gibbon encountered in the Roman Capitol, they find that these "barbarian[s]" are ignorant, degenerate, and violent; and in an ensuing skirmish, they inadvertently kill these last remnants of the race (65, 73–76) (fig. 4.5). The notion of American barbarians as irredeemable was subsequently developed by one of Mitchell's most promising illustrators, Winsor McCay, in a 1904 cartoon in *Life* depicting scavengers in the ruins of Wall Street. Even when their city has fallen into desuetude, New Yorkers would remain "Busy to the End," their acquisitive impulses unabated (fig. 4.6).

The prospect of non-European historians and archaeologists dwelling in and upon the ruins of American cities was reiterated a year later by the retired Brooklyn lawyer, Arthur Dudley Vinton, in his critical sequel to Bellamy's *Looking Backward*, titled *Looking Further Backward* (1890). Where Mitchell's novel consists of the diary entries of a Turkish archaeologist, Vinton's is a series of fourteen history lectures by the Chinese professor Won Lung Li, delivered (in English) to a class of freshmen students in 2023, and subsequently "collected, edited, and condensed."[73] The same "Historical Section" of Boston's Shawmut College that had published Julian West's original memoir in 2000 (erroneously attributed to one "Edward Bellamy"), and subsequently appointed him professor in the "philosophy of history," has since hired this new Chinese scholar (10 n., 53). Drawing on such primary sources as the diaries of West and his son, along with various anonymous manuscripts, Professor Won lectures on the recent fall of the "Nationalist" utopia (15). He narrates

THE TWO MONUMENTS IN THE RIVER.

Fig. 4.4. John Ames Mitchell, "The Two Monuments in the River." From Mitchell, *The Last American: A Fragment from the Journal of Khan-li* (New York: Frederick A. Stokes and Brother, 1889), 37.

the events of its rapid capitulation, beginning with the landing of the Chinese fleet in October 2020, the immediate surrender of the coastal and inland cities, and the eruption of a "great riot in New York" that forced the invaders to reduce it to ruins, and culminating in the country's incorporation as a province of China (77–78, 101, 77, 83, 97). But he also urges his students to attend to the larger underlying "causes that led in the past to those social changes which have marked the rise or decadence of nations" (17–18). Among those Gibbonesque "general causes" are the very features that the Nationalists had

THE LAST OF THE MEHRIKANS.

Fig. 4.5. John Ames Mitchell, "The Last of the Mehrikans." From Mitchell, *The Last American: A Fragment from the Journal of Khan-li* (New York: Frederick A. Stokes and Brother, 1889), 77.

considered utopian: the atrophy of individualism, the introduction of credit cards, and above all the renunciation of military defense (94, 119, 30). But Won traces the decline even further back, to the nineteenth century, when "emigrants from the slums of other nations" were allowed to "over-run" the country, acquire "equal rights," and "intermarr[y] with your native stock . . ." (31). Those European immigrants were merely the forerunners of the millions

BUSY TO THE END.

Fig. 4.6. Winsor McCay, "Busy to the End." Cartoon from *Life* 44, no. 1141 (1904): 241.

of Chinese who entered the country after 2020 as part of a "Chinafication" policy—subjugation not by force of arms but by sheer "numbers" (179, 176). As in Mitchell's novel, America's downfall gave rise not to the rebirth of any new republic farther west, but to certain reversions and inversions. The utopian experiment has been replaced by a more authoritarian imperialist government and women have returned to the "proper state of subordination" (180). Even the very binary of civilization and barbarism has been inverted; Professor Won refers to his students as "American Barbarians," on whom the "glorious civilization of China" is to be bestowed (9, 11).

Vinton's novel belongs not only to the resurgent genre of utopian fiction (albeit as an anti-utopian offshoot) but also to an emergent genre of invasion fiction. Narratives of national surrender to foreign armies and navies had been published in Britain as early as the 1870s as interventions in political debates over military rearmament and diplomatic realignment. The ur-text of invasion fiction, Sir George Tomkyns Chesney's *Battle of Dorking* (1871), may also have been the first to present the imagined battles in the form of a prospective history, recounted fifty years afterward by a survivor to his grandchildren.[74] Although the United States' relative isolation from those military and diplomatic rivalries has led some to assume its immunity to this literary trend, as many as sixteen invasion narratives were published between 1880 and 1916, by leading American publishers such as Harper and Lippincott, and mass-circulation magazines such as *McClure's*.[75] These American adaptations spoke less to anxieties about naval building and alliance formation than to perceived ethnic threats. Their imagined aggressors were almost as likely to be Mexicans, Italians, and Chinese, as the industrialized "Great Powers" of Europe or the hemispheric rival of Spain.[76] But above all it was the ethnic heterogeneity of American cities, especially New York, that allowed those foreign navies to subjugate them. In Park Benjamin's "The End of New York" (1881), the destructiveness of the Spanish artillery shells was compounded by the railroad accidents caused by a transportation system ill-equipped for a mass evacuation, and by the violent riots of Irish and German populations in the "great tenement districts." In the process of reducing half of the "proudest city of the Great Republic" to "ruins," the Spanish navy conveniently demolished an "entire block" of those tenements.[77]

The explosive combination of naval power and urban disorder was the subject of the 1908 novel *The War in the Air*, by the English author, socialist, and (in London's words) "sociological seer," H. G. Wells.[78] Wells's narrator, a historian writing in a utopian future that is "orderly, scientific, and secured," explains that the destruction of the cities of the "Scientific Commercial Age," beginning with New York, was the "necessary and inevitable consequence" of the "clash" of tradition with modernity—the "tradition of a crude, romantic patriotism" with the modernity both of military technology, in the form of bomb-dropping Zeppelin airships that had replaced the infantry divisions of old, and of capitalist urbanism with its attendant "social conditions" (351, 179, 193, 184–85). Even before the German zeppelins had arrived New York was already "the modern Babylon." It resembled that "apocalyptic cit[y]" not only in its control of world commerce and extreme contrasts between "palaces of marble" and neighborhoods of "indescribable congestion," but also in its "black and sinister polyglot population" (179). In fact, the balkanization of modern New York into an "ethnic whirlpool" of neighborhoods eluding the control and surveillance of the city government and police force was like "no previous state" in history (180–81). After observing the immigrants of Ellis Island and lower Manhattan on his 1905 trip, and warning in his 1906 travelogue that "this huge dilution of the American people with profoundly ignorant foreign peasants" casts a "dark shadow of disastrous possibility" over America's future, Wells now predicted that this "vast and varied population" would fail to heed the warning shots that reduced designated targets such as City Hall to "exemplary ruins," instead erupting in a citywide insurrection (192, 201, 206).[79] It was this insurrection that overdetermined the total obliteration of the city. The German airships—unable either to maintain a truce with a municipal government that could not control its own insurgent population, or to occupy

the city as conventional ground forces would have done—were forced to raze
the remainder of the city and slaughter its population "as though they had been
no more than Moors, or Zulus, or Chinese" (205–6, 211).

In *The War in the Air*—and elsewhere—Wells reveals a certain ambivalence
toward Gibbon's historiographical legacy. His familiarity and fascination with
that historian is evident not only from his narrator's allusions to the "slow decline and fall" of the Roman Empire (355), and from the claim of his fictional
persona in *Tono-Bungay* to have read all "twelve volumes" of that book—albeit "in a muzzy sort of way" and "with some reference now and then to the
Atlas"—but also from his retracing of Gibbon's steps through the ruins of the
Capitol in an 1898 trip to Rome.[80] And he directly echoed Gibbon both in his
ironic delineation of modern civilization on the eve of the "War in the Air" as
basking in an apparent golden age of technological and social progress eclips-
ing that of the Roman Empire "under the Antonines"; and in his tragic emplot-
ment of the series of complex, overlapping "phase[s]" of descent into religious
superstition and barbarism—a decline "as great as that between the age of the
Antonines and the Europe of the ninth century" (352–53, 360, 363).[81]

But Wells otherwise distanced himself from the Enlightenment historian.
As a socialist, he criticized Gibbon for neglecting class divisions—in ancient
Rome and also in his own eighteenth-century London, where he only had to
take an "easy walk" to witness the emergence of a "new barbarism."[82] Wells's
prospective history also departs from *The Decline and Fall* in its characteriza-
tion of the collapse of modern civilization triggered by the fall of New York and
its stock market (249, 357–58). That collapse was more rapid than Rome's, as
it imploded in just five years rather than decaying over centuries, and more far-
reaching in its "disintegrat[ion]," as it encompassed America and ultimately
Asia as well as Europe, thereby precluding the *translatio* of Western civilization
(355, 358–60). Moreover, whereas Gibbon became absorbed by the decline
and fall not just of a city but an empire, Wells's historian insisted on the specifically urban nature of the catastrophe, describing how the "great capitals"
were deserted once money, industry, and communications disappeared, while
rural areas remained populated (366), thus echoing Bryan's populist predictions. But above all he repudiated Gibbon's faith in the resilience of modern
civilization in the face of such a catastrophe. Like George, whose *Progress and
Poverty* he had read as an adolescent, Wells imagined a posturban dark age
even more barren than that of medieval Europe.[83] Future historians would have
only a few "surviving fragments of literature" and "scraps of political oratory"
at their disposal (351). Not even agricultural techniques would endure. An
"urban population sunken back to the state of a barbaric peasantry" would
lack even those "simple arts a barbaric peasantry would possess" (379). Thus,

in the prospective historiography of future ruin, cities functioned not simply as some neutral stage on which labor and capital, or citizens and barbarians, act out their apocalyptic struggle. The social and structural conditions of modern urbanism, Wells and others suggested, would incubate and compound the political contradictions of the age.

Encapsulating the Present

Not all American readers would have accepted the premise underlying Wells's and Mitchell's prospective histories, namely that modern civilization's material and cultural accomplishments would be forgotten. Many acknowledged the catastrophic potential of labor and ethnic conflicts, yet rededicated themselves to the task of ensuring—or at least assuring themselves—that the memory of American urban civilization would endure such a catastrophe, and that future historians would have more than a few literary fragments or an occasional coin and inscription with which to interpret its significance. American cities, they believed, would follow not Babylon and Carthage, which disappeared almost without trace, but Rome, whose buildings (as Gibbon observed) survived the barbarian incursions largely intact, only later suffering from the vandalism of Catholics, stonemasons, and warring factions (12:191–92, 193, 194, 198).

Those who maintained that the legacies of American civilization would endure in its aftermath denied that they need do so in the form of architectural monuments. Printed paper, rather than stone and mortar, was the medium that would transmit American urban culture across the ages. The argument that the Gutenberg revolution had effectively immunized modern civilization against Macaulay's "malady" was most broadly popularized by the famous abolitionist and reformer Wendell Phillips in "The Lost Arts," a lecture delivered extemporaneously "nearly two thousand times" across the country between 1838–39 and his death in 1884. A number of ancient civilizations, he speculated, had discovered technologies ranging from lightning rods to steam engines, only to vanish along with their discoveries, thereby disproving "Gibbon['s]" conceit that "knowledge of 'iron and fire'" guarantees a civilization against destruction. But the technology of printing, by disseminating and democratizing that knowledge, now provides just such a guarantee.[84] Although invented in medieval Germany, it was in modern America that the printing press apparently developed into an indemnity against cultural oblivion. Because the slave-owning "ancients" lacked "our modern system of [wage] labor," claimed a writer for *Harper's* in 1868, they failed, despite all their other innovations, to discover the art of printing and thus the potential to "endur[e]."[85] And because of the proliferation of print media such as newspapers and journals in

America, claimed another writer for *Harper's*, a "future historian" research-ing nineteenth-century New York a hundred years hence would have vastly more materials and sources than Gibbon had to "complete his great work," enabling him to surpass even Macaulay in accuracy and artistry.[86] The only danger was that the sheer accumulation of printed sources and media outlets might by then have "outgrown the reach of individual acquisition or even knowledge." *Harper's* thus offered itself as precisely that central archive collat-ing and "preserv[ing]" the "thousand fugitive traits" of the present age for the convenience of the "future historian."[87] Affirming that when it comes to the "most valuable" books and artworks of a civilization Time is indeed a "pre-server" rather than "inexorable destroyer," the Boston Unitarian clergyman and historian Alexander Young repudiated the "gloomy sentimentalism" that nourishes itself on the "ruins of ancient monuments"—and in particular on the ruins that those imaginary "Maori reporters" of Macaulay endlessly report for antipodean "Land gazettes"—as inappropriate for Christian Americans.[88]

Those texts would endure, however, only as long as the buildings housing them. If libraries were to crumble—and some scientists and engineers advised that modern public edifices were more corrodible than ancient ones, due to the declining quality of construction, materials, and the urban-industrial atmo-sphere—then their contents would be exposed to the elements.[89] Compared with those ancient media of stone, brass, papyrus, or parchment, warned the *North American Review* in 1884, the leather-bound paper on which we have "impressed" our "written memorials" would hardly withstand the effects of "fire and water"—yet another reason, along with the current misunderstand-ings "between capital and labor," to believe that "our civilization is perish-able."[90] Even before concerns arose in the 1910s about the fragility of "wood pulp" (used since the 1870s) and newspapers considered printing archival cop-ies on cloth, it was clear that paper lacked the durability of older media.[91]

It was out of these concerns, as well as an intensified sense of historical consciousness and a growing investment in the "objectivity" of historical and archaeological evidence, that the phenomenon of the time capsule emerged.[92] Although other technologies of verbal inscription and archival storage were proposed—*Harper's* even advocated reviving the ancient custom of imprint-ing the year and city on bricks so that even as ruins they would allow "future chroniclers and historians" to reconstruct the country's urban history—it was the idea of sealing a selection of texts and/or artifacts for a later generation to reopen that attracted most attention.[93] Usually dated to 1939–40, when the two most famous time capsules were launched and the term coined, its geneal-ogy reaches back to two exhibits at the Philadelphia Centennial Exposition of 1876.[94] Mrs. Charles Deihm's "Century Safe" and Charles D. Mosher's "Memorial Time Vault"—the former containing mainly autographs of distinguished figures and paying customers (inscribed on parchment), the latter photographs of Chicago's civic elite (preserved in charcoal)—were to be sealed until the Bicentennial in fire, damp, and rust-proof iron vaults (fig. 4.7).[95] Limited in range of materials and time span compared with their twentieth-century successors, and criticized at the time for their commercial orientation or male bias, they nevertheless qualify as time capsules avant la lettre in that they were to be opened at a predetermined future date. They thus departed from older deposit practices such as Mesopotamian and ancient Egyptian burial rites and Freemason cornerstone ceremonies.[96]

Insofar as they presumed the recipients would be citizens of the same American republic and included ceremonial rather than documentary objects, Deihm and Mosher affirmed their confidence in the business class's ability

Fig. 4.7. Mrs. Charles F. Deihm's "Century Safe." From C. F. Deihm, ed., *President James A. Garfield's Memorial Journal . . .* (New York: Deihm, 1882), 194.

to maintain the status quo and continuity of knowledge; the former solicited endorsements from leading businessmen, and the latter appealed to the
philanthropic duty of Chicago's mercantile elite.[97] Such expressions of confidence were undermined, however, by the subsequent class unrest. In Colorado
Springs, fifteen miles from the Cripple Creek gold mines where armed battles
broke out in 1894, the time capsule acquired a very different form and function. The Century Chest, a steel box sealed at Colorado College in 1901, was
the product of a more pessimistic outlook on the current troubles. In one of
over a hundred letters written in India ink on bond paper, addressed to the
citizens of 2001, and sealed within large linen envelopes, its creator, the Jewish financier Louis Ehrich, articulated his sense that a piecemeal and peaceful
solution was no longer viable. A "great national calamity" was now not only
unavoidable but in fact desirable—the only thing that could "purify" America
and avert it from the "downward path of the nations that have disappeared."[98]
Conceiving the chest as an essential depository of information about a social
order threatened with extinction, Ehrich solicited letters by men and women
on almost every aspect of the life of the city, from its political, financial, and
religious institutions to its leisure activities, slang words, and clothing fashions.
The texture of its everyday life was also preserved through nontextual media,
such as artifacts of material culture (including fabric samples, hairpins, and
badges), wax phonographic recordings, and photographs—not just of individuals, but also of street traffic, commercial spaces, domestic interiors, and even
plumbing fixtures.[99] The sealing of documents *unread*—that is, for future eyes
only—emboldened citizens to express strong opinions on contemporary political issues. While certain businessmen denounced unions as "tyrann[ical]"
and "aggressive," a labor leader justified them as a defensive reaction against
the tactics of capitalists, and urged the workingmen of 2001 to "carr[y] on the
struggle."[100]

Nor were these isolated projects. Various dignitaries, including an enthusi-
astic Theodore Roosevelt, deposited at least twelve capsules between 1876 and
1903—several of which would suffer from the problem endemic to time capsules, that of preserving a record of their very existence and location. That such
early projects ultimately failed to enshrine the memory of urban-industrial
America for distant futures—whether by going missing, getting prematurely
opened, or addressing future officials who failed to materialize—should not
obscure their meaningfulness to contemporaneous audiences.[101] Through
public ceremonies and newspaper coverage, they articulated their convic-
tion that American civilization was a unique and complex whole that could
be grasped hermeneutically through its fragments, even by temporally remote
others; that it was defined as much by the urban as the rural, and by the com-

mon as by the illustrious; and that it was something worth celebrating and preserving. But they also betrayed, through the very extremity of their efforts to ensure historical continuity, a latent fear that history would be marked by some kind of rupture. In the attempt to celebrate and perpetuate the accomplishments of American culture, they exposed doubts about its capacity to endure.

Historical Catachresis

Such schemes of cultural entombment were most harshly deconstructed by two of the period's leading ironists, Ambrose Bierce and Mark Twain. Taking stock of the acute contradictions plaguing American society, they expressed their radical skepticism about the possibility of embalming even the most celebrated phenomena of the present, let alone in a form intelligible to future historians. This chapter concludes with their experiments in prospective historiography, a series of fragmentary sketches written between 1888 and 1906. While they did not expand these sketches into the kinds of fully fleshed-out, book-length versions authored by London, Wells, Mitchell, and Vinton—and in Twain's case did not even publish them—they took prospective history to its most nihilistic and apocalyptic extremes. From the detached perspective of the future historian, Bierce and Twain momentarily transcended their own political inclinations—elitist and egalitarian respectively—and launched a multifaceted critique of all social groups, capital and labor, plutocrats and socialists, nativists and immigrants included. The critical potency of their prospective histories derived from the addition of that active ingredient for which they were famous, that of satirical humor. If Gibbon narrated Rome's decline and fall as tragedy, Bierce and Twain narrated America's repetition of that history as farce.[102]

It was in 1888, as the resident "curmudgeon philosopher" at the *Examiner*, the San Francisco newspaper recently acquired by William Randolph Hearst—and again in 1905–06 at *Cosmopolitan*, the magazine Hearst acquired from John Brisben Walker—that Bierce drafted his postapocalyptic histories of "ancient America."[103] His prospective historians (fig. 4.8), lacking the kinds of textual sources available to those of London and Vinton—the archives of late nineteenth-century America having apparently been lost—have to depend on secondary works: classic histories with such Gibbonesque titles as "Mancher's *Decline and Fall of the American Republics*, . . . and . . . Staley's immortal work, *The Rise, Progress and Extinction of the United States*."[104] A number of errors have consequently crept into the historical record. The names of statesmen (Gufferson, Jaxon, and Lincon) and cities (Sanf Rachisco, Kikago) have become distorted. So too has the significance of various practices

Fig. 4.8. Illustration from Ambrose Bierce, "Ashes of the Beacon: An Historical Monograph Written in 3940," *The San Francisco Examiner*, February 26, 1905, 44.

and monuments. Insurance is assumed to have been a sport like gambling but with questionable odds. And the ruined obelisk recently rediscovered in the "wilderness" along the "ancient Potomac" is assumed to have been religious: a "temple erected to the glory" of that chief deity of American antiquity, "Woshington."[105] The misattribution of the Washington Monument may be read as a critique of the protracted controversies surrounding its construction; for decades, it had remained an abortive "stump," or ruin-in-reverse, in the middle of the nation's capital, until completed and opened in 1888, the year Bierce was writing. As for the inability of explorers to decipher its ruins, as they are "curiously inscribed in many tongues," he appears to be ridiculing the multilingual tributes by foreign governments engraved on various blocks.[106] He elsewhere complained about the defacement of that monument by people "pencil[ing]" their own names on it, in defiance of the traditional notion of the lapidary inscription as a privilege for "illustrious person[s]." There were also doubts, at least among Bierce's contemporaries, regarding the suitability of an obelisk — given its Egyptian origins — as an architectural source for a modern republican memorial.[107] The imported obelisk in Central Park led a Turkish explorer in *The Last American* to wonder, "When did the Egyptians invade Mehrika?" (51). Commenting on the Place de la Concorde's obelisk, Walter Benjamin later relished the irony of a modern city "bear[ing] at its centre the memorial" to a pharaoh who had died four millennia earlier. Forged in the desert, he wrote (citing Chateaubriand), this obelisk may yet find its new surroundings one day echoing the "silence and solitude of Luxor."[108]

The various historiographical, philological, and archaeological inaccuracies in Bierce's satires thus functioned not merely as a source of humor, but also as a kind of cover of fallibility behind which he could criticize some of the most sacred precepts of his day. He aimed those criticisms, moreover, at the entire spectrum of American society and politics, thus stepping out of his usual guise as a reactionary contemptuous of idealism, whether utopian, feminist, reformist, socialist, or unionist.[109] His various targets encompassed both the irrational cult of true womanhood ("Gyneolatry") and the equally misguided resolution of women to enter the masculine domains of office and factory; both the "monstrous process" of extortion through tariffs justified as "Protection to American Industries" and the provocation of foreign powers through colonialist ventures.[110] Even those American constitutional shibboleths, "freedom of speech," "rule of the majority," "government of the people, for the people, by the people," and "trial by jury," proved to be dangerous fictions.[111] As far as the historian can determine from the "meager record," these follies and contradictions precipitated a succession of violent struggles or revolutions. The "smoldering resentment" toward the insurance industry led to the incineration of all insurance buildings in America; the provocation of foreign powers led to the destruction of all American seaport cities by the Emperor of China; and a series of intertribal wars led to the relegation of womankind to "her old state of benign subjection."[112] Unlike the singular class apocalypse of London and Donnelly, or the ethno-racial apocalypse of Vinton and Mitchell, the ruin of Bierce's republic appears to have been radically overdetermined by multiple developments, as it fell to barbarians within and without.

But of all these terminal struggles, "by far the most important" was that between capital and labor. The multitude of workingmen made redundant by women entering the workforce added fuel to the "fires of sedition, anarchy, and insurrection" ignited by foreign-born anarchists and their socialist and reformist fellow travelers, setting cities across the country ablaze. Originating in St. Louis in 1920, where "half the city [was] destroyed," this urban insurrection spread with "frightful rapidity," consuming New York then Washington, along "with all its public buildings and archives" (24, 9, 24–25).[113] Meanwhile, the trade unions had evolved into "great tyrannies" or "leagues" that were "reasonless in their demands" and "unscrupulous in their methods." Refusing to learn from the fate of labor unions in ancient Rome, Greece, Egypt, and Assyria, they launched a general strike in 1931, resulting in industrial "paralysis," "famine," and "armed conflicts" (27). This verdict on the labor movement was consistent with Bierce's political commentary for Hearst's otherwise labor-sympathizing *Examiner*, where he generally denounced unions as a scourge, and accepted trusts as natural developments.[114] But in masquerading as a future historian,

Bierce could momentarily transcend partisan journalism to denounce capitalists, too. Judged from this temporal distance, they could be held accountable for treating labor on the basis of "supply and demand" rather than with "humanity" (26). Even trusts could become agents of ruin. Merged into "gigantic corporations," they fell into the hands of "bold and unscrupulous men" inclined to bribe judges, newspapers, and legislators, and sell "'watered' stocks" to naive shareholders (28–29). It was the merger of unions and trusts into a single monopolistic body intent on extorting the public that precipitated the final conflict that toppled the republic (30–31).

Bierce's fallen republic exceeded those of other authors not only in the sheer multiplicity of its problems but also in the absoluteness of its destruction. After centuries of warfare and "hideous barbarities," all that remained of its cities were some "fallen columns and scattered stones" inhabited by a dwindling number of anarchists, who were themselves "succeeded by hordes of skin-clad savages." Bierce's prospective history thus denies the possibility of the democratic tradition eventually being restored by its survivors (as in London's), or inherited by a new civilization to the west; instead, it remains irredeemable, extinguished in a "darkness impenetrable to conjecture" (30–31). That extinction is not to be lamented, however. Eschewing Gibbon's tragic tone, Bierce's historian considers the fall of the American republic an entirely fortunate one, in that it cleared the way for a conservative utopia to be constructed upon the sounder foundations of monarchical and aristocratic principles ("Fall of the Republic," 102).

Despite their divergent political views and mutual animosity, Bierce's prospective histories accorded most closely with those of Mark Twain.[115] In as many as six future-historical fragments written (but not published) between 1901 and 1905, Twain exhibited an equally Gibbonesque capacity to marshal the disparate causes (trivial and general, intentional and accidental) that accumulate and overdetermine the downfall of a state. The longest of those fragments, "The Secret History of Eddypus" (1901–02), although discounted by critics as a paranoid diatribe against Mary Baker Eddy's Christian Science movement or a displaced "vent[ing]" of his own recent financial and personal losses, represents a sustained engagement with multiple social and political issues of the period.[116] The rise of Eddyism to the status of "World-Empire" is merely a pretext to identify other contributing factors to the downfall of the republic: the strain of scientific, material, and intellectual advances; the pressures of overpopulation; the corruption of domestic politics; and the hypocrisy of imperialist exploits—which Twain denounced in other speeches and writings even more vigorously than did Bierce (215, 224, 188–89, 183, 185).[117] And in a kind of postscript to "Eddypus," published in the *North American Review* in

1903, Twain's future historian elaborated in AD 2902 (technically AM 1082, or "year of Our Mother") on the additional role of corporations and unions. The former merged into "one prodigious Trust" and the latter formed a giant "Labor Trust" of their own, resulting in a succession of dictatorships that paved the way for a third trust, the "Christian Science Trust," to rise to power on the ruins of the republic.[118] Both accounts present the "eclipse" or "extinction" of civilization not as the chance outcome of some Eddyist plot, but as simultaneously inevitable ("there was no power that could stop its march"), immanent (the outcome of the "resistless forces which itself had created"), and yet imperceptible to any contemporary ("each stage a circumstance whose part in a vast revolution was unforeseen") ("Eddypus," 188, 190, 225).

Twain further echoed Bierce's prospective histories in the devices he employed to convey the radical otherness of that Eddyist future. The reign of Christian Science is marked not only by the irretrievable ruination of cities such as New York and Washington (and transference of the capital to Boston, renamed "Eddyflats") and by the reversion to prior political institutions and economic conditions (slavery, theocracy, and pastoralism)—reversions that Twain, unlike Bierce, clearly deplores; it is also evident in the comic muddling of words and events (176, 189, 196, 187, 203–5, 196). In a catachrestic (or what Twain termed "drunk[en]") confusion of names outdoing even Bierce, his future historian refers to Columbus arriving in the Mayflower, and to yellow journalism being "invented by Ralph Waldo Edison" during the glorious reign of the "Black Prince," son of George III (177, 183).[119] Unlike Bierce, however, Twain attributes such historical distortions not merely to the "lapse of time" or the acts of vandals (185). It was the Eddymanian papacy that had deliberately suppressed all unofficial knowledge of the past, both by destroying libraries and books, and by prohibiting ancient documents from being translated and buried cities from being excavated (180, 184, 189). Even the misattribution of monuments, such as the "colossal copper statue" recovered from the entrance to New York Harbor and identified as of Mary Baker Eddy, stemmed from this official suppression of history (189).

In presenting a second dark age of religion and barbarism, Twain also implicitly challenged time-capsule advocates, whose preoccupation with the susceptibility of books and other paper documents to gradual decay blinded them to the possibility of their succumbing to intentional destruction. Further overlooked by those advocates, Twain suggested, was the hermeneutic question of their intelligibility to future generations. A time capsule did succeed in preserving one document of ancient times, an autobiographical manuscript by one "Mark Twain," titled "Old Comradeships." Intended for the "distant posterity" of five hundred years rather than the readership of his own age, and typed on vellum rather than handwritten on pulp, it had been carefully "sealed" in a purpose-built "vault," whose location was even recorded in the "public archives" (195–96). "Twain" failed to plan, however, for the contingency that his time capsule would overshoot its target date. By the time it was accidentally rediscovered by shepherds "after an interment of ten centuries," the language in which it was written was dead (181, 196). Its value as a pristine document "undoctored by meddling scholars of later days"—a primary source that might have enabled the dissident historian-narrator to fashion a "secret history" (inclusive of "all grades" of society and of the role of "*circumstance and environment*") that could counter the official history promulgated by the Eddymanian popes—is diminished by the fact that few "philologists" could "spell out its meanings" (190, 194, 196).[120] The illicit hermeneutic recovery of the text is further impeded by ignorance of its context—such as the fact that Bishop Twain was in fact a novelist (190–91). But it is above all the culturally specific phenomenon of humor that reveals the limits of the time capsule.

Fig. 4.9. Cartoon from *Life* 67, no. 1752 (1916): 997. "*First New Zealander:* Well, sir, I never really expected to be 'talking on a broken arch of London Bridge—' 'And you aren't. This is the Brooklyn Bridge.'"

Oblivious to Twain's comic reputation, the future historian mistakes his absurd burlesques for literal insights (189, 195–96). The effect is to undercut the tragic narrative of that Gibbonesque historian by presenting him as the unwitting victim of a millennial hoax.

This unrecuperability of the manuscript ultimately precludes any redemptive outcome. Whereas Wells, London, Donnelly, and even Bierce's cataclysmic histories were at least narrated or edited from the standpoint of an eventual utopia (whether socialist, agrarian, or monarchical), Twain's historian offers little hope of a second renaissance of any kind. Unable to remember the past, civilization appears—in Santayana's contemporaneous phrase—"condemned to repeat it."[121] In the words of another of his prospective historians, transcribed as a "Passage from a Lecture," Twain elaborated on his conception of history as nothing but cyclical repetition, as each civilization "perishes" and is "forgotten" only to be duplicated centuries later, right down to the "*names* of things." Such a "Law of Periodical Repetition" represented the utter repudiation of that long-standing historiographical belief in a larger progression of civilization, as it spreads gradually westward with the rise and fall of every republic.[122]

A *Life* cartoon of May 1916 conveys the full extent to which Americans had, over the previous half-century, appropriated Macaulay's New Zealander as an emblem of their own future ruin (fig. 4.9). The New Zealander, here depicted in tribal dress, has migrated from a "broken arch of London Bridge" to the crumbling deck of the Brooklyn Bridge. Instead of the shattered dome of St. Paul's, the backdrop now consists of the tottering ruins of lower Manhattan and the dilapidated docks of the East River. As in so many of the prospective histories of the period, however, these ruins remain inscrutable, providing no reliable information about the civilization that built them. Indeed, without his companion, the New Zealander would not even know what continent he was on.

"Plagued by Their Own Inventions"

Reframing the Technological Ruins of San Francisco, 1906–1909

The ruins of the bourgeoisie will be an ignoble detritus of pasteboard, plaster, and coloring
HONORÉ DE BALZAC, quoted in Walter Benjamin, *The Arcades Project*, 87 [C2a,8]

In "The Ruins of San Francisco," a now-forgotten prospective history published in 1873, the California poet Bret Harte anticipated the destruction of that city by an earthquake, erring only in the dating of the event. According to Tulu Krish, the Maori philosopher renowned for his "admirable speculations on the ruins of St. Paul," San Francisco fell to ruin in AD 1880, a date challenged by some historians. The archaeological rediscovery of that lost city—administrated by the Hawaiian government several centuries later—yielded some important discoveries: that women wore steel cages resembling parachutes and men "remarkable cylindrical headcoverings"; that their rulers were drawn largely from an aristocratic class of "idlers" and their pursuit of gold blinded them to all other matters, including seismic hazards. These archaeological discoveries owed to the abruptness of the tidal wave immediately following the earthquake, which instantaneously engulfed the city and "embedded" its buildings and citizens in mud. Just as Vesuvius's eruption embalmed the everyday life of Pompeii and Herculaneum, this disaster "arrested" the "busy life of this restless microcosm." San Francisco was frozen in a single moment of time, or—in a photographic neologism of the period— captured like a snapshot.[1]

The birth of photography thirty-four years earlier had immediate and long-lasting repercussions for the representation of both cities and ruins. By the end of 1839, Louis Daguerre had already turned his own camera on the Boulevard du Temple to produce the first urban photograph, while his compatriot Frédéric Goupil-Fesquet had deployed his to document the ruins of the Middle East. But for several decades thereafter, both in Europe and the United States, it remained debatable whether this mechanical invention could truly express the poetics of ruins. Charles Baudelaire conceded in 1859 that it could excel at scientific tasks, not least archaeologically rescuing "crumbling ruins from oblivion," but warned against its encroachment upon the terrain of art—a verdict shared by English aestheticians such as John Ruskin.[2] There were some notable attempts to produce artistic photographs of ruins, such as the views of the Acropolis published in 1870 by William James Stillman, a former member of the Hudson River School and founding editor of the Ruskinian art journal, *The Crayon*.[3] But the dominant aesthetic of the ruin continued to privilege canvas, sketchbook, and engraving, or poem, travelogue, and treatise, over glass plates and silver paper.

If the camera's potential for artistic renderings of ruins remained debatable, its prolific capacity to reproduce ruins in large quantities—especially those of modern wars and disasters—was beyond dispute. The torching of Columbia, South Carolina, in 1865, the assault on the Paris Commune in 1871, and the Great Fire of Chicago five months later each led to an outpouring of photographic depictions of architectural remains. The Charleston earthquake of 1886, the Johnstown flood of 1889, and the Galveston hurricane of 1900 occasioned further images of ruins.[4] But it was the San Francisco earthquake and fire of April 1906 that exceeded all previous disasters in the degree to which its ruins were reproduced, circulated, and consumed through the medium of photography. While the city remained paralyzed, news agencies and photographic companies based in neighboring towns turned out "several thousand" pictures, with one firm generating thirty a minute and selling them on "six continents."[5]

Those larger photographic and news outlets certainly had superior facilities for producing and disseminating images of the disaster, but they did not monopolize its representation. Neither did the leading art photographer Arnold Genthe, however much his images have come to define the event. Whereas the visual representation of Chicago's ruins was dominated by commercial photographers, San Francisco's streets teemed with photographers of all kinds: engineers, geologists, and seismologists preserving photographic data for their research, insurance adjustors collecting visual evidence to contest claims, film crews shooting actualities for East Coast studios, serious amateurs composing artistic impressions, and most numerous of all, casual "snapshooters" using their new Kodak handheld cameras. "Never since cameras were first invented," enthused one amateur photographer, "has there been such a large number in use at any one place as there has been in San Francisco since the 18th of last April. Everyone who either possessed, could buy, or borrow one, and was then fortunate enough to secure supplies for it, made more or less good use of his knowledge of photography. This has been the case not only with residents of the city but also with those of the surrounding towns. People have brought their cameras from all over California and . . . [even] from other states."[6] Although these photographers attended to diverse aspects of the disaster—from fire crews to refugee camps—their main subjects were the ruins themselves, of which the most popular were those of City Hall.

Such widespread preoccupation with San Francisco's ruins would appear to contradict historians' emphasis on American optimism in the face of disaster. In the aftermath of the Great Fire, most Chicagoans supposedly repressed the memory of their ruins, preferring to focus their attention on the construction derricks rising like phoenixes from the ashes.[7] Similarly, San Francisco's commercial elite allegedly played down their disaster, underreporting the number of mortalities and the dangers of seismic vulnerability so as to reassure outside investors.[8] Yet many of them confessed that their first impulse was to reach for their cameras and record the destruction. For "all its horrors and dangers," one amateur admitted he "could not help viewing it with the eyes of an artist and photographer," while Genthe was more concerned with rescuing his camera than any other "possessions," so eager was he to "make photographs" of these scenes.[9] How, then, do we reconcile the alleged disavowal of the disaster with the apparent mania to photograph—and to view and collect photographs of—its ruins?

Recent psychoanalytic theories of trauma and the media might prompt us to read this mass compulsion as a kind of "protective action" or "shield" against the disaster. Filtered voyeuristically through the camera's mediating lens, the violent destruction could be distanced or contained, or better, reconfigured into an aestheticized or commercialized form. Taking multiple photographs— sometimes of the very same ruin—would allow survivors to work through their trauma over time, via a "repetition of it in a mitigated form," which defuses or masters the threat by transforming it into habit.[10] Ruins might appear to provide the perfect subject matter for such photographic therapy, insofar

as they invoke in the beholder a sense of pleasurable relief at having survived
that which caused their destruction. To focus on the ruins, moreover, would
be to consign the "late unpleasantness" (as the *San Francisco Chronicle* called
it) to the realm of ancient history. With the heat of the fire and the shroud
of ash having forged the impression of a "ruin of a thousand years," witnesses
could pretend that they were surveying an ancient city like Pompeii that was
only now being "dug out of its lava."[11] This line of argument may account for
the conspicuous lack of dead or maimed bodies in photographic archives of
the disaster.

It is far from certain, however, that photographs of San Francisco's ruins
provided such relief or reassurance. The remains of structures and machines
they depicted bore little resemblance to those of classical temples or gothic abbeys. Rather than eroding gracefully over centuries and becoming enveloped
in foliage, these ruins were instantaneous and barren. They had been constructed, furthermore, with modern techniques and materials that precluded
their disintegration into the irregular forms favored by picturesque travelers.
The flimsy facades of some tall buildings had cracked or disintegrated during the earthquake and fire, exposing unsightly steel skeletons. And the fire
had similarly consumed all combustible materials in the streets, leaving behind the residua of infrangible metal: trolley poles, tangled electrical and telephone wires, and the chassis of automobiles and streetcars (fig. 5.1). Where
the earthquake and fire did alter the shape of steel objects, they did so in a
decidedly unaesthetic fashion. "Girders two feet wide" had been "tortured
into strange curves," lamp posts impaled upside down like some "grotesque
statuary," telegraph poles "blackened" and "charred," their wires hanging loose
and "rattling dismally," and cable-car tracks buckled, resembling "gigantic
inch-worms." Whereas Pompeii's excavations had unearthed precious classical statuary, San Francisco's cellars contained only "indestructible . . . viscera":
"stoves, grates, bath-tubs, boilers, window-weights, safes, sewing machines,
and kitchen utensils were overlaid with a wild confusion of pipes and wires,
mixed with hundreds of springs from box mattresses."[12] Contemporaries
who trained their cameras on these disturbing relics of steel and iron were
neither evading nor repressing but rather confronting the impact of disaster
on a modern, technologized city. They fixated upon these ruins precisely because they seemed to reveal how their everyday lives had been transformed
by the recent introduction of technologies of transportation, communication,
and construction, and by the provision of gas, electricity, water, and sewerage. In the wreckage of an extraordinary event, they found opportunities
to reflect on how those new technologies had altered ordinary conditions
in the city.

Fig. 5.1. Untitled, 1906. Stereograph. Keystone-Mast Collection. 1996.0009.WX8726. UCR/California Museum of Photography, University of California, Riverside. Caption on reverse: "Call Building (centre) U.S. Savings Bank[,] trolley cought [*sic*] in wreck, Third street, San Francisco, disaster."

Responses to these technological ruins, as we shall see, varied widely. Photographers (and observers more generally) disagreed over whether the relics should be viewed as ignoble or ennobling, objects of shame or pride. Did photographic evidence of twisted girders point to engineers' and architects' failings? Or did the mere fact that these immense ruins remained standing through the earthquake vindicate their methods and expertise? Similarly, was the wreckage of City Hall a "disgraceful ruin" that served as a fitting rebuke to the corrupt politicians who had profited from its construction, and that therefore deserved to be demolished immediately? Or had it acquired through ruination a "noble . . . beauty" worthy of the canvas and camera, and perhaps even preservation?[13] There were even sharper disagreements over the implications of these ruins for San Francisco's future. Would they indicate—as ancient ruins traditionally do—the terminal decline of a decadent city (and the ascendancy of other cities in the region), or would they be temporary, merely ushering in fresh opportunities for financial investments and construction jobs? Even those who agreed that they augured the city's triumphant rebuilding, diverged over how it should be rebuilt, whether along old lines or new. Read pragmatically as designating lost income through rent and commerce, the ruins justified restoring the city rapidly to its prior status. But reframed as aesthetic objects, they gestured to the possibility of constructing a "New San Francisco," one beautified by urban planning and purged of civic corruption, ethnic neighborhoods, and technological eyesores. Given these stakes, the diverse photographic practices of amateurs and professionals were critical. The ways in which they depicted ruins—above all those of City Hall—affected the resolution of these larger urban questions.

Technological Breakdown and the Urban Lifeworld

"Looking up Market street from the Ferry Building, through a blaze of fire, the eye rested upon what seemed to be a huge wall of fire in the sky. The great dome of the City Hall was ablaze." But if San Francisco's commercial district "seemed to be on fire," it was merely the illusory effect of a decorative girdle of electric lights strung up in 1902 and switched on for the first time that summer in honor of a visiting fraternal order. Recently completed—$3.5 million over budget and almost three decades overdue—City Hall was the centerpiece of this sublime technological spectacle, its dome and columns bejeweled with 6,016 incandescent lamps (fig. 5.2).[14]

Despite its lack of local energy resources, San Francisco had acquired a reputation by the turn of the century not only for "electrical displays" that outshone all "other cit[ies] in the world, except Paris," but also for leading the way in introducing new technologies into the more mundane spheres of everyday life.[15] In 1874 it was the first city in the nation to deploy electricity for street lighting, and five years later the first to set up a commercial power station, distributing electricity to hotels, businesses, and wealthy homes. The growth of mining industries in the region further stimulated development of new technologies and energy sources (including hydroelectric power by 1901–02) that were promptly converted for manufacturing and urban uses.[16] As in other emerging *networked cities*, San Francisco's technologies were most visible in its streets, which were perpetually being resurfaced with tarmac, grooved with cable car and streetcar tracks, overhung with power and telegraph wires, and underlaid with sewerage and water pipes.[17] But its networks also extended outward beyond the city limits. In 1903 alone, San Franciscans witnessed the departure of the first transcontinental journeys by automobile and motorcycle; the completion of the transpacific telegraph cable connecting the United States with China via the Philippines; and the inception of a wireless station for sending radio messages to Hawaii. And while the telephonic connection of San Francisco to New York remained more than a decade away, its telephone lines already extended as far as Boise, Idaho.[18] All these technologies were invested with utopian dreams of urban comfort and safety. The electrification of lighting and heating would liberate city dwellers from the dangers of gas leaks and coal pollution, and from the domestic drudgery of manual labor, while the electrification of communications would forge an urban and interurban network for rapid response to emergencies. Although largely limited to bourgeois

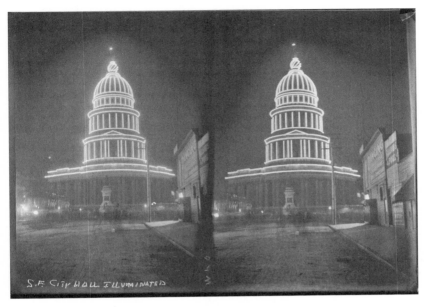

S.F. CITY HALL ILLUMINATED

Fig. 5.2. [William Letts Oliver?], "S.F. City Hall Illuminated," 1902. 5 x 7 inches, glass stereograph. Electric display in honor of the Knights of Pythias' convention in San Francisco. Oliver Family Photograph Collections, BANC PIC 1960.010 ser. 2 :1115—NEG, Bancroft Library, University of California, Berkeley. William Letts Oliver was an amateur photographer and member of the Pacific Coast Amateur Photographic Association.

homes before the First World War, such improvements were even deemed capable of suturing the class rifts that divided American cities, thereby ushering in a new era of social and political harmony.[19]

The wiring of cities, however, hardly shielded them from natural disasters. The 1906 earthquake served as a reminder to San Franciscans (and urban Americans in general) that despite these scientific and technical innovations they remained at the mercy of the vagaries of nature. "All the cunning adjustments of a twentieth-century city," Jack London observed in his eyewitness report for the weekly muckraking magazine *Collier's*, "all the shrewd contrivances and safeguards of man had been thrown out of gear by thirty seconds' twitching of the earth-crust." Writing in the same issue, Frederick Palmer perceived the earthquake as "prov[ing]" how even a "modern city" could be rendered "helpless."[20] It was soon evident that the city had been destroyed not despite but because of those very technological "adjustments" and "contrivances." Even those invested in technological progress, such as the leading San Francisco–based engineering magazine *Mining and Scientific Press*, conceded that the earthquake merely triggered a chain reaction of mechanical failures that followed its own inexorable course of destruction. The bursting of pipes and stoves released inflammable gas into the air, which was then ignited by sparks from severed electrical wires, setting off fires that could not be extinguished due to the simultaneous rupture of the underground water mains. This Rube Goldberg–like domino effect continued with the collapse of transportation and communications, which left the city with inadequate supplies, and the disruption of the sewerage system, which exposed it to disease (36). Nor could the ruins themselves be ascribed entirely to natural forces. The most serious damage was sustained by buildings knowingly constructed on landfill. The expansion of the city during the Gold Rush had led to the reclaiming of the Yerba Buena Cove and the Mission Bay Swamp (which became part of the business district and a slum district, respectively), and those areas of "made land" were "liquefied" by the earthquake. Raising the city's sidewalks "to secure greater depths for sewers," *Mining and Scientific Press* added, had similarly undermined the integrity of the structures above them (80, 26).[21] San Francisco's infrastructure thus experienced a total, systemic breakdown. The very technologies that were to safeguard it from common hazards (epidemics, overcrowding, smoke pollution) ironically combined to precipitate a greater catastrophe.

Taking stock of this overdetermination of the earthquake by new technologies, a number of commentators concluded that modern urban civilization was not equally but altogether *more* vulnerable to seismic disturbances than premodern ones. The same writer for *Mining and Scientific Press* asserted that earthquakes could hardly have wreaked such devastation upon nomadic settlements: "Those who live in tents and know no illuminant save the camp fire, would have remembered an earthquake such as that of April 18 only as a dizzy moment when trees rocked and the tent-poles shook." Even through the era of Spanish and Mexican rule, major earthquakes (like that of 1838) had caused comparatively little damage. Thus, far from providing greater security, "the complexity of civilization add[s] new terrors" (79).[22] Urbanization, moreover, had rendered earthquakes even more hazardous by concentrating populations in built-up areas, such as the dense slum neighborhoods of the Mission. Contemporaries thus reflected on the instantaneity of San Francisco's collapse. The spectacle of this city of steel, iron, concrete, and mortar reduced to ruin "in a day"—or rather four days—led one photographer to wonder "why it took so long for Rome to fall."[23]

Recent scholars have sought to illuminate this paradoxical vulnerability of modern technologies (and cities). Technology critic Edward Tenner has coined the term *revenge effect* to describe how machines, once organized into complex systems or networks, generate unforeseeable and unintended problems.[24] Moreover, the introduction of technologies that harnessed and concentrated nature—as in the channeling of fire into electrical illumination, or gas into pipes and stoves—exponentially increased the explosive potential of any earthquake. Writing about nineteenth-century railroad accidents but with relevance to earthquakes, German cultural historian Wolfgang Schivelbusch posits "an exact ratio between the level of the technology with which nature is controlled, and the degree of severity of its accidents." As steam engines converted ever greater energies into forward momentum, and as construction materials became stronger (and thus less elastic), railroad accidents became correspondingly more violent. The very notion of an "accident" (as in a mishap causing injury or death) is entirely modern.

> The pre-industrial era did not know any technological accidents in that sense. In Diderot's *Encyclopédie*, "Accident" is dealt with as a grammatical and philosophical concept, more or less synonymous with coincidence. The pre-industrial catastrophes were natural events, natural accidents. They attacked the objects they destroyed from the outside, as storms, floods, thunderbolts, and hailstones. After the Industrial Revolution, destruction by technological accident came from the inside. The technical apparatuses destroyed themselves by means of their own power.[25]

Thus, the 1906 earthquake may have been a naturally occurring event, but it was the propensity of interlinked machines to turn against themselves that rendered it catastrophic. Although a few reporters still spoke of the ruins as Mother Nature's revenge upon civilization, or the gods punishing the moral sins and Promethean ambitions of mankind, many suspected they were the result of an in-built logic of self-destruction.[26]

For early to mid-twentieth-century German theorists, this perilous subjugation of nature to technology was most pronounced in the burgeoning American metropolis. Within the discourse of German critiques of modernity (from Weber, Sombart, and Simmel, to Benjamin, Kracauer, and Heidegger), "Amerikanismus" served as a shorthand for the hypermechanized existence already evident in American cities, and now emerging in European cities such as Berlin. In "The Anxiety of the Engineer" (1929), the Marxist philosopher Ernst Bloch specified New York as the archetype of a city so "detach[ed] and distance[d]" from nature that it is "increasingly threatened by accidents to the same extent that it has rooted itself in midair—that is, the city is built upon roots that have grown more and more synthetic. This grandly suspended, inorganic metropolis must defend itself daily, hourly, against the elements as though against an enemy invasion."[27] Bloch, however, is not referring to the natural elements. Insofar as nature has been supplanted by the abstract (or second) nature of advanced "machines" and rational "calculations," the threat to cities now derives from "the complexities of mechanized existence itself" (307). American cities are thus the antithesis of older, "southern" cities such as Naples, where the organic and inorganic are permitted to remain in "equilibrium," even under the menacing shadow of Vesuvius. Bloch cites the example of a hill overlooking Naples where a broken water pipe and abandoned railroad track have been left in place for years, as rainwater leaking from the pipe flows along the tracks into a district where it was needed (306–7). Thus, whereas the breakdown of infrastructure can have catastrophic implications for the "Americanized big city," whose "technology has achieved an apparent victory over the limits of nature" (304), for older (and poorer) cities—where nature is allowed (literally) to take its course—it may have unintended benefits. If given the chance, "new . . . life" can "blossom out of that which is defective and ruined" (307).

Even before the 1906 earthquake, many Americans were conscious of life's growing precariousness in their industrializing cities. By the 1890s, newspapers regularly reported electrical accidents and depicted the urban environment—with its tangle of live wires and preponderance of steel structures—as presenting a heightened risk of electrocution.[28] Electric streetcars were even greater objects of fear (and fascination), causing death less through electrocution than collision. The San Francisco & San Mateo Railway Company, which introduced the city's first electric streetcars in 1892, had an especially poor safety record, with numerous incidents involving runaway cars that struck pedestrians or collided with other vehicles, sometimes head-on (fig. 5.3).[29] Commuters who escaped injury or death remained subject to the everyday sensory shocks and physiological assaults of the city, with its jostling crowds, jarring noises, lurching elevators, and garish advertisements—now mounted on electric billboards and (as Walter Benjamin later observed) "all but hit[ting] us between the eyes."[30] In his *Education* (published the year of the earthquake), Henry Adams attributed the escalation of "so-called accidents" to a general "Law of Acceleration," whereby the scientific extraction of ever greater "force" from the universe outpaced society's ability to control or even comprehend it. As the daily "destruction of property and life" wrought by "railways" and "automobiles" verged on the "carnage of war," man "helplessly groaned and shrieked and shuddered, but never for a single instant could stop." For an age traumatized by such technological destruction, a natural catastrophe such as "an earthquake became almost a nervous relaxation." Indeed, there were reports of neurasthenic patients being miraculously "cured" by the San Francisco earthquake.[31]

Fig. 5.3. Rube Goldberg, "Things ain't what they used to be," *San Francisco Chronicle*, October 7, 1904, 9. Goldberg's first strip cartoon to be published, commenting on both landfill and streetcar accidents.

Fears of technology run amok prompted some antimodernists to portray even the earthquake as, at least in part, the work of man. Disregarding geological science, they blamed these new technologies not merely for igniting fires but for precipitating the very movement of tectonic plates. One paper, by the naturalist and spiritualist Charles Hallock, attributed the seismic tremors in part to "men's dabbling with electricity." By "gridironing nearly the entire globe with wire conductors, overhead and underground, in the atmosphere and through the oceans, and in practically every house in town and country, and keeping them constantly charged by powerful dynamoes [*sic*]," they had fatally overloaded the earth's natural electrical charge. The disaster, he reportedly concluded, thus accorded with Isaiah's prophecy that "men shall be plagued by their own inventions."[32] The idea that disasters could be triggered by the surcharging of the earth—especially in cities, where there was much leakage from electrical, telegraphic, and telephonic wires—had become popular among millenarians in the late nineteenth century, with one African Methodist reportedly preaching that it would "cause whole cities to be blown away at a time, and floods unlike any save Noah's."[33] Similar conjectures were made about the skyscrapers recently constructed in San Francisco. Those "heavy" structures of "iron, steel, stone and brick," an anonymous Oaklander claimed, were the final straw that broke the fragile crust beneath.[34] And if Americans had disturbed the earth's "equilibrium" by placing excessive weight upon it, they had also done so by removing excessive weight from it through mining. In a meandering meditation on the earthquake's material and spiritual implications, an

Ohio author suggested it might have been "stimulated appreciably by the . . . strenuous mining operation[s]" conducted in the region, just as the great Lisbon earthquake of 1755 might have had something to do with the "celebrated aqueduct" completed there six years earlier.[35] For these writers, San Francisco's ruins presented concrete proof of technology's transgression against nature—although if earthquakes were man made, they could no longer be viewed in traditional religious terms, as God's revenge against that transgression.

Such apocalyptic beliefs, however, were confined to a small minority. (Failing to sell his manuscript for two million pounds, the Ohioan published it privately.)[36] By 1906 most urban Americans were reconciled to urban technologies. After more than a decade of electrical wires, streetcars, and skyscrapers, they had trained themselves to disavow the omnipresent threat to their bodies and senses, learning to read or sleep while in transit, or to affect nonchalance among crowds, noises, and advertisements. But it was this very repression of technological fears—through the routinization of habit and timetables—that rendered the occasional accidents so traumatic. According to Bloch (the son of a railroad engineer), those periodic collisions and explosions—accidents that have "no civilized timetable"—precipitate the violent return of repressed fears, and thus rekindle the earliest associations of trains with "demonic" forces. One newspaper account of an 1895 trolley-car accident in Chicago described how the live electric wires leaped around in the street like "demons spitting fire."[37]

The 1906 disaster similarly brought home to middle-class San Franciscans their dependency upon technological systems they had come to ignore in their everyday urban routines. Almost as traumatic as the initial destruction was the subsequent difficulty of subsisting in a city stripped of mechanical conveniences that were taken for granted. As a precaution, gas and electric utilities that withstood the disaster were shut down until further notice, by proclamation of Mayor Eugene Schmitz. Survivors recounted their horror at the "absolute" or "almost stygian" darkness into which their city was plunged at nightfall, and their relief at the "very sight" of "ordinary electric lights" on arriving in Oakland.[38] Underlying this horror of darkness was a bourgeois fear of the social "demons" it could unleash in the form of vandals and looters. Interruptions in electrical power—later termed blackouts—provoked this same response from city dwellers. For a city like Baltimore that had come to rely on the "policing" effect of continuous electrical lighting, regardless of the natural cycles of the moon, the sudden "total darkness" of May 1900 raised concerns of an outbreak of "thieving."[39] And in the 1912 science fiction novel *Sign at Six*, a nameless villain induces widespread panic, stampeding mobs, and mass looting, merely by depriving New York of its electrical supply.[40]

If the absence of electrical lights rendered the 1906 disaster palpable by night, so did the absence of mechanical (and nonmechanical) sounds during the day. *Mining and Scientific Press* contemplated how the usual "full-toned voice of a big town, intensified by traffic over the cobbles of Market street and the confused shouts of hotel runners, the strident cries of newsboys and the clanging of car bells"—a relentless chorus to which one had become "accustomed"—was now "silent" (78). Habituated to the multisensorial flux of the modern city, witnesses were thus struck as much by the silence of technological ruins, such as abandoned streetcars and automobiles, as by their immobility. Perhaps most alarming was the "still[ing]" of the "busy click of the [telegraph] instruments." Cut off from the "ceaseles[s]" flow of information from the outside world, San Franciscans allegedly swallowed rumors that an array of catastrophes—floods, tidal waves, and fires, as well as earthquakes—had ruined cities across the continent, from Los Angeles to Washington.[41] Such examples contradict the claim (made by historian Michael Barkun) that the modern industrial city, as an effective "bulwark against disaster," contributed to the waning of the millenarian imagination.[42] On the contrary, a new discourse of apocalypse was evident in San Francisco, one concerned less with the revelation of religious truth than with what technological ruins revealed about the secular mysteries of modern urbanism, not least its peculiar ineffectualness as a bulwark against disaster. Nor was this a softer mode of apocalypse. These technological anxieties, Bloch writes, may well "prove equal to all the death anxieties of late antiquity and all the medieval anxieties about hell" ("Anxiety of the Engineer," 308).

This revelation of ordinarily imperceptible structures through technological breakdown was illuminated in 1927 by Bloch's intellectual opponent, Martin Heidegger. In Division One of *Being and Time*, Heidegger provides a detailed phenomenology of the broken tool, drawing on the low-tech example of a hammer in a workshop, and treating it as something "ready-to-hand" rather than "present-at-hand," used rather than conceptualized.[43] In such everyday usage, the hammer "withdraw[s]" from itself; it becomes invisible and inconspicuous—as does the larger support network or "totality of equipment" (in this case, the manufacture and supply of nails) in which it is necessarily embedded—in favor of the "work" for which it is intended (97–99). Only through some kind of disturbance in the smooth functioning of things (which is to say, not through some kind of intellectual inspection in isolation or out of context) is their "being" fully illuminated. But what precisely gets "lit up" in the moment when a hammer gets broken—or otherwise disrupts the "work-world," by going missing or getting in the way—is not simply the hammer but also that larger equipmental totality (102, 101, 103). Thus, it is paradoxically in the rupture of the tool from its worldly context that the "worldhood of the world" presents itself—where the world (or what Edmund Husserl called the "lifeworld") refers not simply to the sum total of things on earth, but to that horizon of complex interconnections that structures human perception and action (91, 106). As a meditation on the simple tools of the artisanal work-shop, Heidegger's phenomenology of the broken hammer cannot be mapped directly onto his later critique of technology. But he does assert here its ap-plicability to the larger *"public world"* of the built environment: what we might call the *urban* lifeworld. A "covered railway platform" or an "installa-tion for public lighting" are also tools deployed to deal with rain or darkness (100–101). Through such tools, or indeed the breaking of them, nature itself is revealed—not as a resource to be exploited (in this case) but as an entity that threatens to get in the way, to interfere.

It is not only the "equipmental totality" of the urban lifeworld but also its social totality that infrastructural failure renders conspicuous. Henry George earlier described a web of "intricate interdependence" binding city dwellers together, such that they rely on anonymous others not only for "the water they drink, and the artificial light they use" but also for their safety in transit; a "broken rail, a drunken [railroad] engineer, a careless switchman" is all it takes to "hurl them to eternity." And when left stranded without the specialized skills of others and "thrown [back] upon nature," "highly civilized man" finds himself "helpless."[44] The disconnection of electricity in Baltimore in 1900 and Paris in 1907 similarly revealed the interconnectivity of technologies—insofar as it caused, along with the suspension of public lighting, the "paralysis" of mass transit, theaters, department stores, and newspapers—and also the inter-dependency of city dwellers themselves, or more specifically their dependence upon the electrical workers who went on strike in those cities.[45] The evolution of capitalist industry into a finely balanced "system of interlocking mechanical processes," the economist Thorstein Veblen wrote during the labor unrest of 1919, has rendered it vulnerable to the smallest disturbance in any of its parts; a single act of "sabotage" (including a strike) could paralyze the whole system, jeopardizing the "material welfare of all the civilized peoples."[46] But (as Veblen recognized) systems could also be sabotaged by capitalists. With the transi-tion from the competitive era of public utilities (the "battle of the systems") to an era of monopoly, a gas or electric corporation could hold an entire city at ransom by breaking off contract negotiations with the local government—as occurred in Chicago in 1897.[47] It was the similar monopolization of energy in San Francisco on the eve of the earthquake that exacerbated that disaster. Given the intense opposition to the Spring Valley Water Company's virtual monopoly and the controversial merger creating the Pacific Gas and Electric

Company, the ruins of their pipes and wires served as powerful object lessons of the dangers technologies posed to all when consolidated in the hands of the few.[48] It was not the technologies that were the problem, but the way in which an urbanized society organized them, allowing them to be operated by underpaid workers and predatory capitalists.

The dependency most glaringly disclosed by the San Francisco disaster, however, was that of urban Americans upon the expertise of engineers. Electrical engineers appeared to be responsible for the fires resulting from poorly insulated wires.[49] And civil engineers were likewise believed to have compromised the durability of water and sewerage pipes. Indeed, among the engineers who had worked on the water system prior to the earthquake was none other than the future illustrator Rube Goldberg; though only recently graduated from engineering school at the time, he later claimed sole responsibility for the fire.[50] But above all, the ruins seemed to betray the negligence of structural engineers. "Like a relentless inspector," the earthquake uncovered numerous poorly designed structures. The most egregious was City Hall (fig. 5.4). Augustus Laver's 1871 design had included earthquake- and fire-proofing and a state-of-the-art reinforcement system, but the architects and engineers who succeeded him apparently cut corners.[51] Combing through its ruins, the U.S. geological survey found brick walls inadequately tied to the steelwork, "poor quality" mortar, and "top-heavy" neoclassical ornaments.[52] Particularly ill advised was the replacement of Laver's mansard roof with a massive domed tower, too tall and heavy for the foundations and too poorly fastened to the base.[53] Where modern bracing materials were used, they further undermined the building's structural integrity. The iron trusses that engineers inserted

Fig. 5.4. "City Hall—Photographer in foreground—tall brick chimneys left standing in foreground," 1906. Stereograph. Griffith & Griffith. Author's collection.

into the dome for additional support had the opposite effect during the earthquake of thrusting the cornices and columns outward. And in another classic
instance of a "revenge effect," the corrugated iron they used to reinforce the
arches only weakened them when they melted in the fire.[54] By contrast, neighboring buildings of simpler construction and materials proved much stronger.
Thus, to the extent that the damage was self-inflicted, City Hall's ruins could
not be ascribed to natural or divine forces, nor could they readily be enjoyed
on an aesthetic level. Encircled by concrete and iron debris, and crowned by a
skeleton denuded of its exterior cladding, it was the city's most visible emblem
of modern technological failure—an ironic "monument," one member of the
geological survey concluded, to the laxity of technical experts. A building that
"should have been an example of architectural skill and artistic taste," *Mining
and Scientific Press* concurred, ended up a "disgraceful ruin" (82).[55]

The Will to Mastery: Reasserting Technological Expertise

Engineers responded ambivalently to such monuments of technological failure.
Some held them up as sobering rebukes to their negligent colleagues. *Mining
and Scientific Press* lapsed into a secularized rhetoric of apocalypse, interpreting
them as some kind of "visitation or punishment" meted out to those forsaking
the "principles of sound engineering" (28). Those shameful ruins, moreover,
cast a shadow over the whole profession. Until engineers "safeguar[d]" their
technologies, "man would better live as his [nomadic] ancestors did"—that
is, "in tent[s]" rather than tall buildings and with "campfire[s]" rather than
artificial "illuminant[s]" (79). More practically, these spokesmen campaigned
for stricter laws and codes to regulate future construction. The passage of a
building ordinance in July 1906 owed in part to their success in drawing public
attention to the "gaunt and ragged" ruins of certain office buildings (77).[56] Indeed, their fixation upon those abject ruins suggests almost a perverse compulsion to witness the obliteration of modern technology—a key symptom of the
"anxiety of the engineer," according to Bloch's eponymous article. Although
echoing "primitive" fears of demonic technology and the superstitious dread
of an avenging Mother Nature, the engineer's anxiety is essentially modern. It
is an expression of his lingering sense of the nothingness that lies behind all the
obsessive calculations, abstractions, and "safeguards" of "bourgeois-technical"
rationality (304–5, 308).

Engineers' gestures of contrition and self-castigation were accompanied,
however, by vehement denials that their professional honor lay in ruins. Under the aegis of recently founded bodies, such as the Technical Society of the
Pacific Coast (founded in San Francisco in 1884), and the local section of the

American Society of Civil Engineers (1905), they set about bolstering their reputations.[57] Chief among them was Charles Derleth Jr, professor of structural engineering (and later, dean of the College of Engineering) at the University of California, Berkeley. In published writings, and in public lectures accompanied by stereopticon-projected photographic slides, he reassured audiences that modern techniques and technologies had not merely survived the disaster, but were altogether vindicated by it.[58]

Derleth presented his case, however, not so much by disavowing the ruins as by reframing or resignifying them. The ruins of pipes were the result not of poor construction (the Spring Valley Water Company's pipes being of "excellent design") but rather of a natural "cataclysm" no one could have "foresee[n]." Even in their "present demolished condition," the pipes (some decades old) bespoke durability rather than fragility. Thus, far from having caused the fire, engineers had rescued the city from a much worse "water famine."[59] The earthquake had similarly confirmed the superiority of the steel skeleton over traditional brick and timber-frame construction. Glossing over the inconvenient case of City Hall, Derleth insisted that steel-frame structures—especially those with lateral framing such as the San Francisco Call Building (fig. 5.5)—had acquitted themselves well enough.[60] Even *Mining and Scientific Press* conceded that the Call's gutted but intact shell testified to the triumph of "scientific knowledge and . . . honest handiwork." This "stately skeleton" that rises like a "monolith" and "inspires" the surrounding city was the very antithesis of City Hall, it concluded, encouraging its readers to contrast photographs of the respective ruins for themselves (79, 84). The mere verticality of these downtown edifices was touted as proof of their strength and quality, especially when compared with neighboring Chinatown. Constructed primarily from wood, the labyrinthine "opium dens" and "gambling hells" of Chinatown were entirely consumed by the fire, "blaz[ing] up like tissue paper lanterns" and leaving behind "no heap of smoking ruins."[61] By contrast, even office buildings that had sustained serious damage, Derleth insisted, could easily be patched up or reclad.[62] If these were ruins, they were entirely reversible ones.

Engineers also evaded blame by differentiating between the fire and the earthquake. Buildings like the Call may have ended up gutted by the flames, Derleth claimed, but they withstood the original earth tremors "admirably."[63] If engineers had to concede their inability to render buildings fireproof, they could at least claim to have rendered them earthquake proof. In distinguishing fire from earthquake, they were joined by some of San Francisco's leading businessmen. For the commercial elite, the restoration of the city's fortunes necessitated a publicity campaign that downplayed the role of the earthquake (and by extension the possibility of a future recurrence), instead emphasizing the

Fig. 5.5. William M. McCarthy, "Ruins of Call Building," 1906. Photograph. William and Grace Mc-
Carthy Collection, California State Archives, Sacramento (1906-AC 96-07-08). William McCarthy's
voluminous amateur photographs, preserved in nine albums, more typically depicted family events
and tourist sights.

fire, a more common hazard. Insurance adjustors made a similar differentiation—albeit in reverse—denying fire damage and playing up earthquake damage, as the latter was not covered by standard policies.[64] Recently portrayed as
having spoken uncomfortable truths to politicians and businessmen, engineers
and scientists played into these campaigns of misinformation by reinscribing

the separation of "natural" and "man-made" factors despite overwhelming evidence of their mutual imbrication. Indeed, this convergence may not have been unintended. Engineers were repeatedly encouraged by the Technical Society during these years to work with the business class in spurring the region's economic growth.[65]

Engineers, business leaders, and insurance men also shared a tendency to call upon the testimony of photography. San Francisco's leading booster, Southern Pacific Railroad, commissioned panoramic shots of the ruins that would relegate earthquake damage to the distance, foregrounding the intact waterfront, and thus the healthy commercial prospects of the city (fig. 5.6). Insurance adjustors, too, summoned photographs as reliable witnesses. Given the obliteration of much physical evidence of seismic damage by the subsequent fire, adjustors solicited pictures taken in the intervening period to prove that certain buildings were already in ruins by the time the flames arrived, and thus ineligible for payouts.[66] Even seismologists relied on photographs to gauge the earthquake; the twelve-point Mercalli scale, introduced in 1902, was based not on seismometer readings (as the Richter scale would be), but on observing the physical environment.[67] This same belief in the evidentiary power of the camera led Derleth to collect 820 photographs of ruined structures, and to catalogue them according to twenty-eight different subjects in four large, leather-bound albums.[68] Close scrutiny of these pictures of steel girders and other structural members, he believed, would reveal they were twisted by the heat of the fire rather than the force of the earthquake.

The content of Derleth's photographs did not always support his faith in modern structures; several depicted how stone facades had cracked and steel cross-braces buckled from "the earth movement" itself (fig. 5.7). Nevertheless, it was his recourse to the putative objectivity of photography—and the powers of archival classification—that seemed to uphold the prowess of the expert and the authority of scientific evidence. Derleth's deployment of his photographic archive and his stereopticon projector represent a reassertion of the "will to mastery," which, as Heidegger writes, "becomes all the more urgent the more technology threatens to slip from human control."[69] Other apparatuses—precision timepieces recording the exact time and duration of the earthquake, automobiles transporting supplies and personnel, or donkey engines demolishing unsafe ruins—were similarly mobilized in last-ditch efforts to shore up technological faith.[70] These technological fixes were widely publicized in the press. The imprint of the earthquake recorded by the newly perfected seismograph appeared in general interest as well as scientific magazines. Although some might mistake these seismograms for the "weird tracings of a freakish planchette" (or Ouija board), the more technically minded found

Fig. 5.6. George Lawrence, "Photograph of San Francisco Ruins from Lawrence Captive Airship 2,000 Feet above San Francisco Bay Overlooking Waterfront, Sunset over Golden [Gat]e," 1906. Photographic print, gelatin silver, 18 x 48 inches. Library of Congress, Prints and Photographs Division, Washington, DC (LC USZ62–16640).

Fig. 5.7. "Ferry Tower, San Francisco, Earthquake Failure of Steel X [Cross] Bracing," 1906. Photograph pasted in section titled "Earthquake Destruction to Public Buildings in San Francisco," from Charles Derleth's albums of photographs of the San Francisco Earthquake and Fire, vol. 3, no. 46; Charles Derleth Papers, Bancroft Library, University of California, Berkeley.

their precision and delicacy so impressive as to "inspire a new popular respect for the achievements of modern science."[71]

The ruined city served above all as a crucial testing ground for new kinds of cameras. The motion picture companies, Edison Manufacturing Company and American Mutoscope and Biograph Company, invested large sums in the coverage of the event, producing several 360-degree panoramic actualities of the ruins. Yet Biograph's faked film of the fire, shot in its New York studios on a miniature set, proved more popular than any made on location.[72] More widely celebrated at the time was the "captive airship" launched by Chicago inventor George Lawrence to produce Southern Pacific's promotional panoramas (see fig. 5.6). In a spectacular display of technological expertise accomplished only three weeks after the disaster, he attached a massive camera (several feet in length and forty-six pounds in weight) to seventeen kites (designed for specific wind velocities), raised it two thousand feet above the ruins, triggered it by an electric current transmitted from a telephone magneto through a steel cable kite line, and finally brought it to the ground with an automatically releasing parachute.[73] The technique remained imperfect and unpredictable. Lawrence struggled to operate the shutter and added a setting sun, clouds, and various picturesque details afterward by hand. In their conventional depiction of a gently receding landscape, these panoramas are closer to nineteenth-century bird's-eye views than to the aerial abstractions of European battlefields taken ten years later. Nevertheless, newspaper photogravure supplements and souvenir pamphlets disseminated Lawrence's images, celebrating them as triumphs of the mechanical eye over the chaos of nature.[74] The intricate sequence of steps required to trigger and release his camera evoke the fanciful machines Rube Goldberg began drawing in 1914, which later included a "picture-snapping machine." Both Lawrence's and Goldberg's machines worked to restore confidence that complex—albeit unnecessarily complex—systems could function safely and smoothly, with each component leading ineluctably to the next.[75]

Such reflexive reassertions of technological prowess arguably served to divert attention from the underlying instabilities of complex systems that afflicted the emerging networked city. In so doing, they unwittingly played into the hands of businessmen opposing the postearthquake demands for greater regulation. Within three years, the 1906 ordinance requiring the bracing of new structures was substantially relaxed. And the lessons of liquidation were forgotten even sooner: within months, debris from the ruins was dumped into inlets and lagoons to make yet more unsafe "made ground" for warehouses and Southern Pacific terminal facilities.[76]

Optic Aftershocks: Snapshooting the Ruins

Few turn-of-the-century cameras were as technologically complex as Lawrence's. Six years earlier, the Eastman Kodak Company introduced an apparatus as remarkable for its simplicity as the kite camera was for its intricacy. The Kodak Brownie consisted of little more than a primitive lens, shutter release, and winding mechanism, all housed in an austere, fake-leather-covered cardboard box. Advertising logos conjoined its brand name to its defining feature, condensing its appeal to two words: "Kodak Simplicity." It was so simple that even a child could use (and afford) it, making it arguably the first children's camera.[77]

Although the introduction of the Brownie is cited as a milestone in the history of photography, it was merely the culmination of a quarter-century of efforts by George Eastman to streamline the process of taking pictures. An amateur photographer himself, Eastman had become dissatisfied with the difficulties of traditional wet-plate photography, which required considerable technical expertise to prepare the liquid collodion and develop prints. In 1879, capitalizing on Richard Maddox's earlier discovery of a dry gelatin emulsion, Eastman unveiled a machine to manufacture pre-prepared dry plates, thereby eliminating at least some of these difficulties.[78] But the mechanisms of cameras remained complex (inevitably malfunctioning at the critical moment), as did the task of loading and developing the plates. It was not until the Kodak No. 1 was introduced in 1888 that photography could genuinely be considered an undemanding, spontaneous activity. The Kodak was born out of the conjunction of three distinct innovations: the preloaded roll film (containing as many as one hundred exposures, thus surpassing the single-exposure glass plate); a lightweight camera design with basic shutter mechanism; and a film-developing and reloading service for cameras mailed back to the Rochester factory. Now relieved of the laborious tasks that preceded and succeeded the actual taking of a photograph, all the user had to do—in the words of the famous advertisement—was "Press the Button" and let Kodak "Do the Rest."[79]

The simplicity of the Kodak was thus deceptive. It remained dependent on highly complex industrial processes of film manufacturing, developing, and printing (based at the Rochester factory), and on national and international networks of distribution and marketing.[80] Although removed from sight, these processes were technological extensions of the camera—or in Heidegger's terms, part of its "equipmental totality" (109). The Kodak thus resembled those urban technologies of the period whose outward operability belied their underlying complexity. Its shutter release was one of several "pushbuttons" (a device and neologism of the 1880s) that simultaneously reduced physical effort and isolated it from the hidden machinery that performed the real work.[81] In a 1939 essay, Walter Benjamin briefly discussed the succession of inventions, beginning with the safety match in the mid-nineteenth century, that required just "one abrupt movement of the hand" to "trigge[r] a process of many steps." Whereas early telephones had magneto cranks that had to be wound with a "steady movement," later ones (introduced after 1896) required only the "lifting of a receiver" to set vast networks of communication in motion. The most significant of these activities of "switching, inserting, pressing, and the like," Benjamin claimed, was the "'snapping' of the photographer." With the snapshot camera, a "touch of the finger"—not even a whole hand—"now sufficed to fix an event for an unlimited period of time." Such hand- or finger-operated technologies arguably reached their *reductio ad absurdum* in Rube Goldberg's imagined contraptions. His machines may mobilize absurd extremes of force toward relatively modest, everyday ends, and may leave its animate and inanimate components exposed. But like the match, the telephone, or the Kodak, those complex steps are triggered with the minimum of effort. However much modern conveniences may appear to "isolat[e]" their bourgeois users from the world of machines, Benjamin argued, they also brought them "*closer* to mechanization."[82]

Through the 1890s, however, pushbuttons remained a luxury novelty beyond the reach of the masses. Although now celebrated by collectors and historians of photography, the button-operated Kodak No. 1 had limited sales, largely because it was priced at $25 (over $500 in today's currency). Only when Eastman introduced the one-dollar Brownie in 1900—as a result of further streamlining of design, cheapening of materials (cardboard instead of wood, and leatherette instead of real leather), and rationalizing of production and developing techniques—was he able to reach the masses. By the time of the earthquake, Eastman had sold over 1.2 million cameras, bringing the total number of photographers to roughly a third of the U.S. population.[83]

Although Kodak advertisements (along with photographic manuals and almanacs) encouraged these budding photographers to use the Brownie to document wholesome recreational activities such as family vacations and visits to world's fairs, its usability and reliability rendered it ideal for the nonprescribed subject of urban disaster.[84] Amid fires, crowds, and troops, its often-noted limitations—the lack of controls for adjusting focus, aperture, or shutter speed, and the cheap roll film—proved advantageous. In the time that wealthy amateurs wasted setting up tripods, inserting plates, and making adjustments, "Kodakers" could take multiple exposures, snapping away at will—an irony Rube Goldberg interpreted as poetic justice for the "poor man."[85] Thus, even before the earthquake, Kodakers had acquired a reputation (according to one San Franciscan) as rubberneckers who "get in the way of a policeman at a fire [or] . . . make [themselves] numerous in a railway accident."[86] Apparently resigned to this misappropriation of their cameras, the company announced plans—only days after the disaster—to make "every effort . . . to promptly supply the great demand for [their] products on the Coast," rebuilding their ruined San

Francisco stores "at the earliest possible date," and opening a temporary branch in Sacramento in the meantime.[87]

The presence of "Kodak Fiends" in the ruins would have caused less concern for Eastman than for locally based companies such as Southern Pacific. Many of those photographers were not in fact San Franciscans. Within days of the disaster, "immense crowds" of tourists arrived in "great transpacific liners," trains, and ferries—an influx stimulated, according to Southern Pacific, by cheap railroad ticket prices and "tourist rates for round-trip excursions" from the East Coast. With much of the tourist infrastructure that had made San Francisco a prime destination for bourgeois travelers now in ruins, temporary facilities were improvised. Makeshift hotels, restaurants, and shops were hastily erected, while those arriving by ship could return to "spend the night on board." Tourists could also procure transportation around the ruined city. Although United Railroads was at first "wholly unable to cope with the situation," it soon resumed some of its damaged streetcar lines. For a slightly higher price, enterprising San Franciscans offered special guided tours, itineraries that invariably included the desolate streets of Chinatown. "Sight-seeing trolley cars" and amphibious vessels, "ancient sea-going craft mounted on wheels and drawn by weird-looking attenuated steeds," departed from the wharf, the latter costing as much as $2 an hour, with running commentary on the ruins by the "loquacious drivers" included. Street peddlers also cashed in on this flourishing tourism, setting up vending stalls of earthquake and fire relics, of which the most popular were salvaged from Chinatown. For tourists afraid of falling debris from dynamited buildings but also wary of the exorbitant prices of peddlers, their own Kodaks offered a safer and cheaper means to obtain souvenirs of the event.[88]

It was not so much the logistical nuisance of these tourists that would have troubled Southern Pacific (although San Franciscans did complain of how "the town was overrun with . . . sightseers"), as the challenge they posed to its national publicity campaign.[89] By 1906, Kodakers were increasingly mailing their snapshots across the country, courtesy of Eastman's offer to print photographs onto postcards for 10 cents and the Post Office's reduction of the rate for noncommercial mail to 1 cent. In the earthquake's aftermath the postage rate was suspended altogether to allow impoverished survivors to contact concerned relatives and friends. Stimulated by these concessions, a flood of amateur as well as commercial "disaster postcards" depicting the ruins were printed and disseminated (fig. 5.8).[90] These postcards—along with other pictorial souvenirs—troubled civic organizations, leading newspapers, and local businesses, who hoped to restore the confidence of outside investors. "Are we not damaging the city by every one of these views we send away?" queried the *San*

Fig. 5.8. "Mrs. Wolley" [?], untitled, 1906. Amateur photographic postcard of family cooking in the street, sent to A. Mazard, Oran, Algeria. Andreas Brown collection, box 24. Research Library, The Getty Research Institute, Los Angeles, California (89.R.46). As the Post Office then allowed only the address to be written on the blank side of the card, amateurs often inscribed their descriptions of the disaster on the photograph itself, sometimes labeling the ruins or individuals depicted.

Francisco Call. "Every person owning a camera has the right to take all the pictures he desires and send them wheresoever he chooses," but such activities may "frighten people away from us."[91] Southern Pacific expressly decried the "[un]scrupulous class of sensation makers" who were magnifying the extent of the disaster. Traveling lecturers who projected hand-colored photographic slides of the ruins to audiences back east were "dwell[ing] upon" the more melodramatic aspects, and needed to be "Set Straight." As a further countermeasure, Southern Pacific issued press releases and pamphlets, and—more covertly— employed its own organs of mass publicity (such as *Sunset Magazine*) to create the impression that the city was largely unscathed.[92] The barriers erected around the burned districts and guarded by state militias—ostensibly to keep out looters—may also have been intended to curb the activities of Kodakers. Whether residents or out-of-towners, those caught photographing without a press pass risked having their cameras confiscated and their film censored—or worse, being pressed into the labor gangs clearing rubble.[93]

But these measures did little to curb the use of cameras. Unofficial photographs of the city's destruction continued to be taken by locals and tourists alike, often surreptitiously.[94] Such photographs posed a threat not only to the civic officials' and boosters' sanitized narrative but also to the engineers' framing of the ruins. Less invested financially or professionally in the city's technological ruins, Kodakers approached them as fantastical, surreal, even humorous artifacts, a world turned upside-down. Among their subjects were houses tilted over, split in two, or cut away like dolls' houses, streetcar rails bizarrely twisted in the air, and statues plunged head first into the ground (figs. 5.9 and 5.10).[95] One photographer playfully appropriated the wreckage of a United Railroads streetcar to stage the scene of a commuter with briefcase disembarking nonchalantly in the terminus of a postapocalyptic city (fig. 5.11). Contrasting with the anxiety of the engineer, these photographic witnesses appear to have experienced the breakdown of technology as a source of wonder and humor—thus corroborating the psychological observations of William James (then teaching at Stanford) that the earthquake precipitated feelings of "delight" and "excitement" rather than "fear" or "dismay."[96] The numerous snapshots and postcards of families cooking in the streets (in compliance with the mayor's proclamation) point to what another witness described as a "cheerfu[l]" acceptance of the city's "return to the days of the frontier," to an era prior to the ascendancy of modern technology.[97] This state of exhilaration in which even San Franciscans consumed the destruction, making "laughing comments on the drunken angle of the flagstaff surmounting the ferry house tower," led one writer to wonder whether he "had not made a mistake and fallen in with an excursion to Coney Island."[98] Reduced to ruins and viewed through a Kodak, modern structures could thus be reframed as giant props in some grand spectacular display. And if the city had become a stage, City Hall provided the perfect backcloth. Its ruins were appropriated as a farcical mise-en-scène for numerous family portraits (fig. 5.12).[99]

While some of these disaster photographs were formally posed portraits, many were casual impressions of ephemeral sights and incidents, that is, snapshots. Originally a hunting term for firing a shotgun without taking proper aim, the word was not applied to photography until the introduction of smaller formats (and thus shorter exposure times) around 1860. In that year Sir John Herschel celebrated the new "possibility of taking a photograph, as it were, by a snap-shot, of securing a picture in a tenth of a second," while by 1900 faster film speeds and shutter mechanisms contracted time to a hundredth of a second.[100] Instantaneous photography thus granted a certain freedom: one's finger could press the shutter release button in the instinctive, unpremeditated, almost involuntary way that a hunter pulled a trigger. Furthermore, with increased film and shutter speeds, cameras could capture mobile subjects such as horses and vehicles—and at the same time could become mobile themselves; liberated from the tripod, handheld cameras could be carried in one's pocket, drawn at

Written on photograph: ✓ An interior view after the earthquake was over. Sacramento St. Apl 18/06.

Fig. 5.9. Arnold Hunter, "An interior view after the earthquake was over, Sacramento St., Ap[ri]l 18 '06," 1906. This item is reproduced by permission of The Huntington Library, San Marino, California (photOV 10,886 [1]).

Written on postcard: J-175, S.F. Earthquake; Twisted Houses, Howard St.

Fig. 5.10. "Twisted Houses, Howard St.," 1906. Postcard (not sent). Andreas Brown collection, box 24. Research Library, The Getty Research Institute, Los Angeles, California (89.R. 46).

Fig. 5.11. [View of passenger with briefcase disembarking from wrecked United Railroads car after the earthquake], 1906. This item is reproduced by permission of The Huntington Library, San Marino, California (photPF 25851).

a moment's notice, and aimed rapidly in any direction. New cameras such as Eastman's thus cut through time and space with the power of a rifle. The very word "Kodak" was coined to evoke this explosive instantaneity. "Terse, abrupt to the point of rudeness, literally bitten off by firm and unyielding consonants at both ends," Eastman explained, this onomatopoeia "snaps like a camera shutter in your face."[101] It was this snapping of the camera lens that Benjamin believed gave "the moment a posthumous shock" ("Motifs," 132). Through this photographic fission, the continuum of time is shattered into fragments: instants or split seconds that survive in a kind of half-life on the photographic paper, just as the moment of an earthquake (5:13 a.m., April 18) persists on seismographic paper. Moreover, as with a safety match or rifle, this violent energy is unleashed at the slightest stroke of a finger.

Fig. 5.12. Family portrait in front of the ruins of City Hall, 1906. Photograph. The Hansen Collection, Museum of the City of San Francisco.

While a product of new photographic technologies, the snapshot had a certain affinity with the new conditions of urban life—or what William James called, on arriving in New York in 1907, its "permanent earthquake conditions."[102] In the 1939 essay, Benjamin goes on to compare these "tactile experiences" to the "optic" ones typical of the "big city." Whereas one's finger felt the shock of the shutter cutting through time when taking a snapshot, it was the eyes that were confronted by the barrage of images that strafed the urban landscape, such as those in metropolitan newspapers ("Motifs," 132). American readers of the "weeklies" were stunned by the way their photographs froze their subjects in undignified or unnatural poses. The "realism" of those snapshots, wrote one critic in 1902, is "so exact, so minute, that the organ of sight with which our Creator has endowed us is quite incapable of perceiving it."[103] There was also an affinity between the spasmodic snapshot and the distracted vision of city dwellers as they negotiated the crowds and vehicles that assaulted them in the streets, glancing nervously in every direction and at every intersection, while keeping one eye on the traffic lights (first introduced in Cleveland in 1914).[104] But this relationship between the mobile eye of cameras and that of pedestrians went beyond homology. Insofar as the snapshot— like the cinema—elevated these physiological shocks of the city into a "formal principle," it may be viewed functionally, as a stimulant to be administered to the jaded sensorium of city dwellers, or as an inoculation conditioning them for further shocks ("Motifs," 132).

Photographic technologies, however, cannot be reduced entirely to the function of adapting city dwellers to, or compensating them for, the enervating rhythms of modern urban life. The camera also holds out the hope, for Benjamin, of penetrating their sensory numbness, and opening up their lifeworld to critical scrutiny. The spatio-temporal shocks produced by cinematography have the potential (according to his "artwork" essay) to reduce the "prison-world" of our cities to "ruins and debris" with the "the dynamite of the tenth of a second," freeing us to re-view them afresh. So too does the ever-shrinking snapshot camera (according to his photography essay) become "ever readier to capture fleeting and secret images whose shock effect paralyzes the associative mechanisms in the beholder."[105] Optical devices may thus pierce the "protective shield" one develops against the hyperstimuli of the technologized city—a shield that prevents sensory impressions from entering one's lived, communicable "experience," condemning them "to remain in the sphere of a certain hour in one's life" ("Motifs," 115, 117).

In light of Benjamin's reflections, the impulse to collect and exchange snapshots of the San Francisco disaster manifests a desire not to evade but to assimilate an experience that—like more quotidian urban experiences—eluded the conscious mind, remaining an incoherent and incommunicable array of sensory or subsensory impressions, a "confused succession of vibrations, jars and jolts."[106] Despite—or because of—the lack of photographs of the actual forty-eight seconds of seismic shock, the subsequent snapshots of the ruins replicated that experience through their formal shocks. Objects and individuals in these snapshots tended to be out of focus (due to the fixed lenses of cameras such as the Brownie or the "camera shake" associated with handheld models), and accidentally cropped or tilted (due to their rudimentary or nonexistent viewfinders). However unorthodox compositionally, these indiscriminate snapshots were suggestive both of the shocks of everyday urban experience—the view, for instance, out of a streetcar window—and of the shock of disaster in an age of modern technology: the indiscriminate way in which it had literally shaken, split, or tilted buildings. The snapshot's randomness also extended to the way in which they were preserved in albums and scrapbooks. Unlike Derleth's systematic ordering of disaster photographs, Kodak hobbyists inserted theirs haphazardly alongside those of ordinary vacations and everyday family life, thereby creating stark juxtapositions that made the events of April 1906 appear all the more jarring.[107] Such snapshots preserved the impact of the event, retaining the power to jolt one's memory.

So thoroughly were new visual technologies integrated into the structures of perception, survivors came to view their own experiences and memories of the earthquake as quasi-photographic. According to George Malcolm Stratton, a professor of psychology and specialist in visual cognition at Berkeley, even younger eyewitnesses—who knew little about "what was happening to the civic government, . . . commerce and relief"—could recall the event as a series of precise "mental pictures." In a 1919 study of the handwritten reminiscences of over a hundred of those eyewitnesses (who were by then his students), Stratton found the disaster was registered more "vivid[ly]" in "pictorial" form than in sounds or words.[108] Borrowing from French psychologist Théodule Ribot, he labeled this intensification of visual memory through trauma "hypermnesia," the opposite of amnesia.[109] In some cases, hypermnesia was "retroactive," recording not the moment of the earthquake itself, but small, mundane details seen prior to it, such as the shape of a five-gallon can or a pair of ball-bearing skates. These apparently banal objects, exposed on the negative of the mind during this "period of about an hour of photographically literal recollection" preceding a shock, took on an ominous, almost spectral quality—as if they caused the subsequent catastrophe (481).[110] Whereas James observed how "the awful discontinuity of past and future" wrought by the earthquake left "every familiar association with material things dissevered," Stratton demonstrated precisely the opposite: that various objects and acts were rescued from the uninterrupted stream of everyday urban life, and endowed with apocalyptic meaning and photographic clarity, by the intensity of the ensuing experience.[111] Stratton also emphasized the possibility of a "concurrent hypermnesia," whereby "the person recalls in almost photographic detail the total situation at the moment of shock" (475). Again, the objects tended to be trivial and extraneous: the pattern and color of a rug, the exact position of a carpenter's bench, or the bending of some tall cypress trees glimpsed through a window as the disaster struck (476).[112] What is significant here is the instantaneous quality of these memories. The rug, bench, and trees were each captured by a rapid glance of the eye in the moment of crisis rather than by a sustained, contemplative gaze. Such hypervisual "impressions," wrote one of Stratton's subjects, were "flashes of memory" imprinted "indelibl[y]" on the mind.[113]

Stratton's research echoed a trope widely employed at the time of the disaster. Newspaper and magazine reporters in particular appealed to the epistemology of the snapshot. A reporter for *Everybody's Magazine* invoked it to characterize the random, everyday, and "rather unimportant details that struck my eyes" as he walked around the ruined city—details that could not be registered in Lawrence's panoramas or in official accounts. "A woman carrying in a cage a green and red parrot . . . a little smudge-faced girl . . . holding in her arms a blind puppy; a man with a naked torso carrying upon his head a hideous chromo; another with a mattress and cracked mirror"—all these were "little *snapshots* in my mind."[114] The aspiration of journalistic prose to the status of a visual snapshot reveals the eclipse of an earlier melodramatic mode of disaster reportage and the emergence of a more deadpan, unembellished style. But it was also an acknowledgment that only mechanical ways of seeing were adequate to the sensory intensities of a modern, technological catastrophe. Not even the novelistic skills of an Émile Zola, declared one eyewitness report, were equal to the task; this was an ordeal, agreed another, "best told by pictures."[115]

Gentlemen Photographers, Cheap Johns, and Kodak Girls: Contesting the Ruins

Not all contemporaries subscribed to the emergent epistemology of the snapshot. Such privileging of the spontaneous was anathema to serious amateurs, who believed in photography's painterly or "pictorial" possibilities. It was these gentlemanly amateurs who had dominated photography in the half-century before the earthquake. Local clubs in eastern cities were important forums providing advice, darkrooms, and exhibition space. Along these lines, the Pacific Coast Amateur Photographic Association (PCAPA) was founded by "eight gentlemen" in San Francisco in 1883, with its own affiliated journal, *Pacific Coast Photographer*. Not confined to anonymous dilettantes, these clubs incubated—and would emulate—many of the leading pictorialist photographers of the period. Alfred Stieglitz was a member of New York Camera Club and editor of its periodical *Camera Work* before founding the more exclusive Photo-Secession group in 1902, while Arnold Genthe belonged to PCAPA's successor, the California Camera Club.[116]

By 1906, however, such clubs were declining in membership and importance, a decline attributed to the Kodak revolution. Eastman's cameras, they averred, threatened to reduce photography from a worthy artistic pursuit to a frivolous diversion.[117] Most disturbing were their simple shutter release buttons, which—like other pushbuttons—augured a culture of instant gratification. In their view, "Press[ing] the Button" was almost incidental to the art of photography; what was essential was precisely "The Rest"—the preparation, developing, and printing that Kodakers let Eastman do for them.[118] Henry Adams, who took up photography in the early 1870s to capture the "spirit" of Egypt's ancient ruins, complained by the 1890s that it had become too easy ("now that it is all mechanical . . . you have fifty pictures in half an hour") and for a time renounced the pursuit altogether, becoming a self-confessed "photo-phob[e]."[119] Within Adams's elite circles, "Kodak" became a byword not merely for the debasement of photography but for the technological colonization of the urban lifeworld. In his 1906 lecture on Pragmatism, William James parodied the rationalists' idea of a world instantaneously fulfilling our desires as one mediated and circumscribed by technology: "We want water and we turn a faucet. We want a kodak-picture and we press a button. We want information and we telephone. . . . In these and similar cases, we hardly need to do more than the wishing—the world is rationally organized to do the rest." According to his brother Henry, the Kodak effect had even spread to popular literature.[120]

Gentlemanly amateurs perceived a threat to their aesthetic authority not only from "Button Pressers" (as Stieglitz called them) but also from commercial photographers.[121] By 1906, these professionals were supplying newspapers (or those able to afford the half-tone reproduction process) and photographic publishing companies catering to national and international markets as well as private customers. Their photographic wares (albums, postcards, souvenirs) were also dispensed through local junk shops, vending machines, street markets, and their own photographic parlors, or else given away as free promotional gifts in cigarette packets. These multiple outlets enabled them to cash in on the demand for ruin views even while local newspaper facilities remained in rubble.[122] This kind of commercial exploitation of the disaster alarmed the gentleman connoisseurs. In *Camera Craft* (the successor to *Pacific Coast Photographer*), they denounced the abuses of these "cheap Johns," decrying their willingness to flout aesthetic principles, peddle unsatisfactory prints, disregard the dead and dying bodies around them, and even risk their own safety. In one cautionary tale, a commercial photographer was so eager to give the public the "smoke pictures . . . they want," he ventured too close to the flames, setting fire to his tripod. Pecuniary incentives also motivated these hacks to capture "as large an area of ruins as possible on each plate." Prioritizing quantity over quality, they climbed trolley poles, ruined newspaper buildings, or even the shattered dome of City Hall to obtain that ultimate panoramic shot. Most egregious were those who plied "phony photographs," using darkroom techniques to insert flames and falling masonry to pre-1906 photographs, or disguising photographs of other disasters such as the Baltimore fire of 1904. To the consternation of *Camera Craft*, "anything showing ruins, 'went.'" If the photography of ruins was to fulfill its potential as a "most promising subjec[t]" for artistic amateurs—as one handbook hoped in 1884—it would have to be wrested from the hands of commercial photographers catering to a popular demand for the "portrayal of devastation pure and simple."[123]

Already straining to defend their aesthetic high ground from the assaults of Kodakers and "cheap Johns," the gentlemen photographers faced the encroachment of a third group: ladies with cameras. The question of whether to admit women struck at the very foundations of clubs such as the PCAPA, which, following a narrow vote in favor of the motion, dissolved in 1890, to be replaced by the California Camera Club.[124] Once enrolled, women were among the most vociferous opponents of aesthetic orthodoxy. Unwilling to exchange the confines of the bourgeois interior for the equally stifling pictorialist studio, many championed the camera's more radical and public uses. Old-school pictorialists with their soft-focus, painterly effects and stiff, artificial poses, complained the New York photographer Alice Boughton in 1905, failed to realize the medium's technological possibilities, such as giving "clear, accurate reproductions" and capturing mobile, outdoor subjects: "—running, jumping, flying appearances and *instantaneous* attitudes of bird, beast and fish, of *earthquakes* and cyclones, comets and meteors."[125] Among the women who embraced such photographic opportunities was Edith Irvine, a twenty-two-year-old from California's "Gold Country." Arriving in San Francisco within hours of the earthquake, she took at least sixty photographs, pointing her 5 x 7 glass-plate camera at dead horses, fleeing crowds, technological debris, and of course City Hall (fig. 5.13).[126]

The presence of young female photographers among the ruins threatened

Fig. 5.13. Edith Irvine, "Back of City Hall," 1906. Gelatin dry plate negative. 5 x 7 inches. Courtesy L. Tom Perry Special Collections, Harold B. Lee Library, Brigham Young University (MSS P 585).

not only prevailing aesthetic principles but also certain gender assumptions. As if to defy the expectations of motherhood (which she resisted throughout her life), Irvine appropriated that sacrosanct symbol of maternity, a baby buggy, to transport her photographic equipment around the ruins.[127] For several years, the popularization of photography had also raised concerns about women's vulnerability in public. One female club member warned that "landscape work . . . especially in cities" could expose them to unfamiliar dangers, such as "the ubiquitous small boy . . . [who] seems to rise from the earth at sight of a camera."[128] New rules of etiquette were devised, and publicized by magazines like *Ladies Home Journal*, to ensure propriety and safety for women engaging in such a public and heterosocial activity.[129] Such gender anxieties were heightened by the breakdown of social (as well as technological) mechanisms in April 1906. Edgar Cohen, writing in *Camera Craft*, expressed his unease at making the acquaintance of an attractive female photographer in the ruins.

> [I] encountered a pretty girl with a folding pocket Kodak and a look of disgust. I could tell from her actions she knew what she was about and remarked: "You find it a pretty hard game?" "Yes," she said, "I cannot do anything with it. It is too bad. I came all the way from the country to get a shot at it. Can you tell me where I can get some pretty pictures?" I said I could but they were some distance away. She had a buggy and by her invitation I went with her to find them. I commented on the characteristic independence of the American girl in accepting the company of a strange man and added that I presumed our both having cameras constituted a good reason, in California at least. In response I was informed that she belonged to the California Camera Club, that before she joined that institution she would not have done such a thing, but now, conventionalities were not allowed to count if a good picture were in sight.[130]

As if to relieve his conscience that he was not taking advantage of her photographic and sexual inexperience, Cohen cited the mitigating circumstances: that he acted on her invitation, within the relaxed moral conventions of California, and for the greater good of photography. Moreover, even after women were admitted to their clubs, male members like Cohen still deemed them aesthetic novices requiring paternal guidance.

Nevertheless, as Cohen himself acknowledged, handheld Kodaks—even in the hands of country girls—did not preclude the possibility of taking "good pictures." For all their perceived threats to aesthetic principles and gender prerogatives—embodied in the figure of the Kodak Girl, the company's advertising icon from 1893—Eastman's products were not renounced altogether.[131] On the contrary, several serious amateurs hoped such cameras would bring accident and actuality to a school of art that had grown stilted. For those tired of the pictorialist studio and society portraiture ("slave[ry] to the demands of a captious public," one amateur called it), the Kodak represented fresh subject matter and outdoor scenes, including disasters.[132] Moreover, postearthquake conditions obliged even the most committed pictorialists to adopt the hand-held camera. Even if they were able to rescue their larger, professional tripod cameras from their burning homes, those apparatuses would have been less suitable for such conditions and subject matter than the smaller cameras (especially the folding or pocket varieties) they did manage to retrieve or borrow.[133] "Viewed as photographic subject matter," another amateur wrote in *Camera Craft*, the ruined city was simply "too large for adequate portrayal; the lines of fleeing people, the scenes of activity around the burning buildings, were, on the other hand, the very best of material for the clever snapshotter."[134]

Even as they embraced the Kodak handheld camera these amateurs shunned the vulgar excesses of the snapshot. The resort to such cameras implied neither a relaxation of technical and aesthetic standards nor an acceptance of Eastman's promotion of instantaneous photography as a return to the naive, innocent eye of childhood.[135] Rather, it would enrich pictorial expression and composition. *Camera Craft* recommended they conceive of the lightweight devices as "preliminary tools," as painters use sketchbooks.[136] Such recommendations echoed avant-garde developments on the East Coast. Stieglitz was among the first art photographers to appropriate the Kodak hand camera, believing its mechanical simplicity made it less liable to break down at the decisive moment, and its blurry images conveyed action and motion. Although synonymous with the "bad work" of the "Button Pressers," it could be redeployed in more aesthetic ways. Eastman's "invention," Stieglitz claimed, might even engender "possibilities" that "the manufacturer himself did not realize" ("Hand Camera," 182–84).

The Modern Acropolis

The ruins of San Francisco thus became objects of contested meanings and contrasting pictorial approaches. But it was not just aesthetic hierarchies, professional reputations, or gender assumptions that were at stake; the future development of the city lay in the balance. In the weeks and months following the disaster, there emerged a bitter debate over how to rebuild San Francisco. The principal question was whether to follow the City Beautiful plan devised by the leading architect and urban planner Daniel Burnham.

The city's old bourgeois elite—to which most serious amateur photographers belonged—were strong advocates of the plan since its unveiling in 1904.

Having lost the mayoral elections two years earlier to Schmitz, who was backed
by the Union Labor Party and a powerful ethnic political machine, they could
reassert their authority by taking charge of reshaping the city. In espousing the
proposal for new parks and playgrounds, they could claim to be acting in the
interests of the lower classes, uplifting them through a Progressive social agenda
of physical recreation. They could also claim to be serving the city's economic
interests, by stimulating tourism, facilitating suburban growth, and lubricating
the flow of people and commodities.[137] But Burnham's vision of a "New San
Francisco" of grand civic structures, public monuments, and sweeping vistas
appealed above all to their aesthetic tastes. Humble wooden structures could
be replaced by "bold" columnated ones, and congested streets refashioned into
tree-lined boulevards, one of which was to be literally "elevated" over the surrounding warehouses (88, 179–81, 53). The plan even offered solutions to
technological eyesores in the urban landscape. Oversized or flashing electric
billboards were to be banished, and necessary fixtures (such as gas and electric
lamps) beautified by artists appointed by a municipal art commission (179).

To generate the money and influence to invite Burnham and publicize
his plan, these advocates drew on their close-knit and overlapping network
of gentleman's clubs and associations, including the California Club, Pacific
Union Club, San Francisco Art Association, Bohemian Club, and Association
for the Improvement and Adornment of San Francisco (the latter two shar-
ing the same president, ex-mayor James D. Phelan), along with various businessmen's organizations such as the Merchants' Association. Initial efforts by
these elite institutions ran up against considerable legal and logistical hurdles,
until the 1906 disaster finally presented itself as a "marvelous and unique opportunity" to implement the plan. With the fires still smoldering, Burnham
was summoned back to the city, while badge-wearing campaigners distributed
pamphlets about the "New San Francisco" in the streets.[138]

This campaign shaped the production and reception of pictorialist photographs of the ruins. Arthur Inkersley, for instance, was an outspoken supporter
in *Overland Monthly* of Burnham's remedy for "the errors . . . made in laying
out the old San Francisco" and also an active member of the California Camera Club who wrote for *Camera Craft* about his efforts to capture the ruins of
the disaster.[139] Such photographs could promote the notion of the devastated
landscape as a tabula rasa ready for an entirely new urban image. Furthermore,
rendered classically, these ruins could evoke Burnham's Beaux-Arts vision.
Artistic photographs of the broken columns and crumbing arches adorning
its seven hills (another parallel with Rome) might educate its inhabitants in
classical models of city building, thereby serving as more effective propaganda
for the plan than any pamphlets, badges, or speeches.[140] One amateur photog-

rapher, Louise Herrick Wall, described the ruins as possessing a "dignity and majesty," and a softness of coloration ("pastel shades of pink and fawn and mauve") that evoked a "beautiful city a thousand years dead — an elder Troy or Babylon."[141] But the most sustained amateur photographic exploration of the "classic artistry" of San Francisco's ruins was by the journalist John Louis Stellman. Afflicted with a "camera infatuation" since his schooldays, Stellman took over two hundred photographs of the ruins, exhibiting them as lantern slides for a lecture at the Press Club titled "The Romance of San Francisco," and publishing them as *The Vanished Ruin Era: San Francisco's Classic Artistry of Ruin Depicted in Picture and Song*. In its majestic ruin, he enthused, this "Modern Acropolis" served as an "oasis of inspiration" for its distressed inhabitants.[142]

Thus, for serious amateurs like Stellman the ruins served neither as evidence of the integrity or culpability of engineers nor as surreal or humorous material for snapshots, but as aesthetic objects to inspire, edify, and culturally legitimate their city. They substantiated the notion of a westward course of empire (whose author was invoked in the naming of the neighboring university) from ancient Athens and Rome, through London and Paris, to the New World.[143] Declaring that San Francisco's tragedy echoed those of earlier cities, and that its rebirth as a neoclassical metropolis would consummate the inexorable march of civilization from the Mediterranean to the Pacific, these advocates appealed to the Americanized version of the *translatio*. In accordance with the assumption that each successive cycle surpassed the previous one, they claimed that San Francisco's ruins were superior to earlier ones, at least in terms of their sheer quantity — measured, variously, in numbers of bricks, cubic feet of debris, or dollars of damage. In the words of a poem that circulated widely after the disaster, it had "the damndest finest ruins ever gazed on anywhere."[144]

These dreams of a renascent antiquity were disturbed, however, by the sight of gutted iron and steelwork downtown, and by the failure of many wooden structures to survive as ruins at all, especially in Chinatown, a favorite hunting ground for Orientalist photographers such as Genthe before the earthquake and Stellman afterward. Inkersley also complained about the unpicturesque gathering of debris into "neat little piles" and of refugees into "geometrically" ordered camps, and the improvising of "hideously utilarian [*sic*]" structures of wood and corrugated iron.[145] Considerable selectivity was therefore needed when depicting the ruins. In support of his conceit that the disaster had imparted an aura of "magical, if spurious, age-refinement" to this modern American city, Stellman chose structures that explicitly recalled the "time-hallowed grandeur of Athens and of Rome," such as the Strawberry Hill Observatory in Golden Gate Park (fig. 5.14), which resembled that very ruin immortalized by American travelers of Cole's generation, the Coliseum.[146] Nob Hill

Fig. 5.14. Louis John Stellman, untitled [Sweeny Observatory, after earthquake], 1906. Photographic print. 3 x 5 1/4 inches. Stellman Collection, Neg. #14,219. Courtesy of the California History Room, California State Library, Sacramento, California. When reprinting this negative for his book, *Vanished Ruin Era*, Stellman masked out the metal cable protruding from the top of the structure.

furnished particularly elegant marbled ruins. While some locals viewed the destruction of this exclusive neighborhood as a blessing (the poet Joaquin Miller suggested turning it into a public park), Genthe and his peers considered it a "rich field for [the] camera." Of all Nob Hill's ruins, their favorite was the Towne residence—or rather its only surviving feature, a marble Ionic portico (fig. 5.15). Evoking the neoclassical frontage Burnham proposed for new residences (fig. 5.16), this portico was appropriated by Genthe, Stellman, and others as a compositional device through which to frame the city as an antique ruinscape. Aestheticized by the pictorialist camera, and shot by "moonlight" to enhance its "classic beauty," the Towne portico was particularly well received by members of the pro-Burnham Bohemian Club, who christened it "The Portals of the Past," wrote poems about it, and commissioned a painted version.[147] Three blocks from the Towne house were the even more impressive ruins of the recently completed Fairmont Hotel. This latter structure, crowning the "American Acropolis" like a modern-day Parthenon, marked the "center" from which "will radiate the wonderful new city of the Western seas, the city beautiful."[148]

If the ruins of these marble edifices were ready made for the pictorialist photographer, City Hall's were rather more troublesome. Although its neoclassical design could qualify it as a "classic ruin," the domed tower was marred by the exposure of its steel skeleton, while at street level many of its Corinthian

Fig. 5.15. Louis John Stellman, "Portal of Towne Mansion, California and Taylor Streets." From *The Vanished Ruin Era: San Francisco's Classic Artistry of Ruin Depicted in Picture and Song* (San Francisco: P. Elder, 1910), facing p. 16. Stellman's accompanying poem likens the portal to a "phantom doorway" and a "living / Threshold of the Used-to-be" (16).

columns had shattered, exposing them as hollow iron cylinders filled with scraps of concrete, mortar, and brick (see fig. 5.13). The fire may (in Stellman's view) have "carved shapes of classic dignity out of structural atrocities," but it remained questionable whether it had done so in the case of City Hall.[149] For serious amateurs, its ruins denoted less engineers' professional failings than politicians' moral ones. At its conception in 1870, it was to embody the civic and civilized spirit of their growing metropolis. But over the ensuing three decades it remained unfinished, a ruin-in-reverse attesting to budget over-runs, taxpayer revolts, construction kickbacks, and spurious appropriations bills, one of which prohibited employment of nonwhite laborers. There were periods when construction was suspended altogether, prompting locals to call it "the city hall ruins," a nickname that "clung" to it until its completion in 1899.[150] The edifice was further tarnished for elite San Franciscans three years later, when Mayor Schmitz and his political accomplice Abe Ruef took over. But in the months after the earthquake, when a graft investigation was launched (and funded by none other than Phelan), the full extent of Schmitz's corruption became known—raising fresh concerns about how he and his

SUGGESTED TREATMENT FOR EXISTING DOMESTIC
STREET FRONTAGES

Fig. 5.16. "Suggested Treatment for Existing Domestic Street Frontages." Illustration from Daniel H. Burnham, *Report on a Plan for San Francisco* (published by the city, 1905), 177.

associates might expropriate and misuse funds allocated for the Burnham Plan. City Hall's collapse could thus be attributed not simply to careless construction but to moral contamination—hidden crimes now exposed as starkly as its steel substructure.[151]

But artistic amateurs did not avert their cameras from City Hall altogether, however sordid it seemed. Rather, they sought to redeem its ruins and thereby reclaim the civic authority it was intended to embody. Already Genthe and Stellman had shown how to reframe it (literally) through the neoclassical portico of the Towne house, which simultaneously softened it by relegating it to the distance. *Camera Craft* offered further guidelines for purifying this tainted ruin, and by extension the city itself, through the filter of photography. To begin with, one should not capture the whole of City Hall, as overeager reporters and naive button-pressers did. "I have seen a number of pictures made [of City Hall] by others," cautioned one contributor, "and they are spoiled for me by having the wreck of the big tower included as well. This not only distracts attention from the artistic part, but it destroys the feeling that it might be a scene in ancient Greece." Instead, contravening Diderot's rule that *ruinistes* remain faithful to time and place, the magazine recommended focusing the camera on a smaller architectural fragment, such as the isolated pair of Corinthian columns still holding up part of the entablature of the northwest portico facing Larkin Street (fig. 5.17). Furthermore, adoption of the popular hand camera need not preclude subsequent refinements. Just as de Machy transfigured a half-demolished building in Paris into a classical ruin by concealing evidence of contemporaneity (to Diderot's distaste), so could amateurs efface any signs of the modern that intruded upon their negatives. Steel beams, "telegraph wires," electric lights, the "workman" and the photographer laboring in the foreground, or the billposters the "real estate man . . . has plastered" on the remaining walls, all should be removed in the darkroom by careful retouching or cropping of the print.[152] Thus antiquated, this corner became a favorite subject for classically inspired photographers and painters such as Theodore Wores (fig. 5.18). Even reporters began to describe City Hall as having acquired a "noble . . . beauty that it had lacked when entire."[153] These efforts to beautify its ruins through photography (and poetry) echoed Burnham's earlier ideas for beautifying it through architecture and planning. His plan called for City Hall's incorporation into a larger "civic center," embellished with a colonnade and pavilions and elevated by the intersection of radiating boulevards into San Francisco's "great central *Place*" (39, 68–69, 88). City Hall thus became the crucial site in which to begin refining modernity's excesses in all its forms—be they steel and concrete constructions, Kodak hand cameras, or ethnic-based political machines.

Recycling the Ruins

No darkroom tricks, however, could shore up the fantasy of a neoclassical city rising from the ruins. Although many were themselves businessmen, the

Fig. 5.17. Edgar A. Cohen, "Larkin Street Wing, City Hall," 1906. Illustration from his article, "With a Camera in San Francisco," *Camera Craft* 12, no. 5 (1906): 191.

supporters of urban beautification had formed an uneasy alliance with other businessmen who were motivated more by short-term profits than by enduring visions. The earthquake fatally undermined this coalition, revealing deep rifts within San Francisco's upper strata. A city's rebuilding, these other businessmen believed, should proceed from immediate economic necessities. Led by the *Chronicle,* Southern Pacific, and United Railroads (which would have had to bury their unsightly wires underground), they rejected Burnham's plan as a luxury for a city whose basic infrastructure lay in ruins. It would entail exorbitant spending, prolonged deliberations, excessive legislation, and worst

Fig. 5.18. Theodore Wores, *Ruins of City Hall after the Great Earthquake and Fire*, 1908. Oil on canvas. Cantor Center for the Visual Arts, Stanford University, California.

of all, governmental intervention in the private market (to acquire private property for parks). Instead, the city should be rebuilt without delay, according to realistic and pragmatic goals and along prefire lines.[154] Even a related plan to remove Chinese residents was rejected for these reasons. A number of white San Franciscans had welcomed Chinatown's ruin as an opportunity to realize another proposal articulated prior to the earthquake, that of cleansing this central district of those ethnic others, and their associated vices, aromas, and germs. However, the efforts of a subcommittee of citizens (including Phelan) to relocate them to a more "healthy"—that is, governable—suburb were overridden by financial interests, specifically the income they generated as tourist attractions for the city and as tenants for predominantly white landlords.[155] The social ties binding the beautification societies to the commercial clubs thus came unraveled over questions of private interest. Relations were further frayed when Phelan's graft investigations extended beyond City Hall to businesses (such as Pacific Gas and Electric Company) that had offered the bribes.[156]

If the Burnham advocates had sought aesthetic inspiration from ruins that resembled (or could be made to resemble) ancient monuments, their opponents viewed them through a very different lens. To those prioritizing the instant resumption of business-as-usual, such allusions to cities of classical antiquity were misguided, given that many failed to recover from their ruins. Comparisons with Pompeii and Herculaneum were especially spurious. For one thing, an eastern capitalist objected, those "were not great cities." And furthermore, a local manufacturer added, their inhabitants did not have the "cow boy" spirit of present-day San Franciscans.[157] Rather than contemplating the ruins in aesthetic terms or sepia tones, businessmen construed them economically, in terms of income now being lost (through absence of renters or customers) or to be gained (through demolition and reconstruction). The ruins even had monetary value in themselves. According to *Sunset Magazine* (owned not coincidentally by Southern Pacific), the ruins were the "greatest junk mine that history has created out of disaster," worth $20 million in recyclable bricks and scrap metal.[158] The city's working class was successfully conscripted into this economistic way of looking. As potential construction sites, these ruins represented lucrative jobs for out-of-work laborers amounting to $175 million, *Sunset* predicted. Businessmen mobilized further working-class opposition to the Burnham Plan by playing on their fears of being displaced, like the Chinese, from their old neighborhoods.[159]

Not all opposition to the Burnham Plan derived from economic interests. For the city's engineers, it overlooked seismic safety. Whether they viewed the ruins as vindicating or discrediting pre-1906 structures, they were adamant that postfire structures would have to be based on far more stringent specifications and regulations. Initially, the choice of architect to draft the plan would have met with their approval. Burnham had pioneered new techniques of earthquake bracing two decades earlier with the headquarters for the *Chronicle*, the San Francisco newspaper that would later oppose him. With weight distributed between load-bearing masonry walls, an iron-and-steel cage, and a wooden-frame clock tower, and additional bracing provided by (horizontal and diagonal) bond iron and steel straps, the Chronicle Building was the city's "first earthquake-resistant tall building"—and it survived the earthquake, succumbing only to the fire (unlike the Call, however, its ruins collapsed soon afterward).[160] In his Beaux-Arts plan, however, Burnham neglected to address the earthquake mitigation, failing to mention the word *earthquake* even once. Even more troubling to engineers was his proposal for a "uniform cornice height" (180). Intended to give the city's buildings the architectural coherence he admired in Haussmann's Paris, these height limitations aroused strong objections from engineers committed to taller structures.[161]

While the Burnham Plan foundered largely as a result of opposition mounted by businessmen and engineers, the photographs taken by the hordes of commercial photographers and casual Kodakers also played their part. Outnumbering the gentlemanly amateurs and infringing their aesthetic rules, they aimed their lenses directly at the banal technological ruins of steel, iron, and concrete. Disseminated across the city, nation, and globe (as postcards, souvenirs, or booklets), their photographs of ruined water mains, telegraph poles, and trolley cars conveyed the need to restore basic infrastructural networks rather than indulge in architectural ornaments. Furthermore, they suggested the futility of the technocratic dream of total planning. The will to plan and control an entire cityscape—or in Burnham's words, to design a city "for all time to come"—seemed unrealistic in an age of technological complexity and urban flux (35). Thus, however much civic leaders and local companies (such as Southern Pacific) denounced the activities of unofficial photographers, these uncommissioned images ironically played into their hands. It was their failure to stem the flow of images of technological ruins that unwittingly contributed to their success in opposing Phelan's campaign. By November 1906, Burnham's vision of a City Beautiful lay in ruins.[162]

Postscript: The Fate of the Ruins

On the first anniversary of the earthquake—or "Year I, A.E."—the Fresno *Republican* celebrated the miraculous spectacle of a ruined city disappearing and a new city appearing "day by day," under the spell of those magic "wands," the pickax and the pinching bar. The rejection of the Burnham Plan, and the injection of capital from local and outside investors, insurance companies, relief donations, and congressional funds ushered in a phase of rapid demolition and reconstruction.[163] There was little chance of this modern metropolis following Naples and allowing its ruins to remain in place so that new life might blossom out of them.

The rapid disappearance of the ruins lent further poignancy and urgency to the work of the amateur photographers. As early as June 1906, Inkersley warned that "the hammer of the workman is sounding the knell of the artistic photograph."[164] While applauding the spirit of renewal, Stellman similarly lamented the apparent brevity of the "Ruin Era." The ruined temples of Athens endure "For ages historic and grim," he poeticized, but "the splendor of modern Acropolis / Was but an ephemeral spell."[165] His complaints thus echoed Tocqueville's earlier remarks about the impermanence of American ruins in an age of capitalist enterprise. In fact, Stellman suggested that economic forces of redevelopment were even more destructive than the "natural" forces of earthquake and fire. The goddess atop the dome of City Hall—who had witnessed the passing of the "human throng" and the comings and goings of "the rulers of our city," and had survived "God's mighty elements"—now lay prostrate on the ground, "despoiled" by those mere mortals, the wreckers and the vandals (fig. 5.19). Those who realized the statue was the Goddess of Progress would have recognized the vicious irony of her being dethroned and devoured by the very forces she embodied.[166] The relentless removal of such relics and the indifference of their fellow San Franciscans prompted artistic photographers to redouble their efforts to document them before it was too late. Thus, for all their aestheticism, Stellman's images of ruins were also animated by an antiquarian impulse to record their very existence. Through 1910, he used his camera as a documentary tool "to preserve" the endangered structures on photographic or printed paper (viii)—or in Baudelaire's words, "to save crumbling ruins from oblivion." Such endeavors were predicated on a disavowal of the transitoriness of photographs themselves, subject as they are to fading and deterioration. Just as the volatility of the urban landscape was condemning the earthquake remains, so would the volatility of photographic chemicals condemn their representations to obscurity. Photographs of ruins, as an earlier English writer acknowledged, are ontologically related to that which they depict.[167]

The physical ruins were not erased, however, quite as rapidly as historians (both celebratory and critical) have suggested. Some were preserved on purpose, for reasons of civic nostalgia and genteel aesthetics.[168] Through Phelan's efforts, the Portals of the Past were transplanted to Golden Gate Park as a classic folly adorning a picturesque lake, and another subject for Stellman's camera (fig. 5.20), while the Goddess of Progress's decapitated head was similarly saved from the scrap heap.[169] But other ruins persisted inadvertently, through delays in the progress of demolition and reconstruction. Depending on their political viewpoint, contemporaries blamed these delays either on the negligence of the Board of Public Works, the dilatory tactics of insurance companies, or the protests of organized labor; while the loss of titles filed in City Hall before the earthquake led to protracted property disputes.[170] But above all the absence of

Fig. 5.19. Louis John Stellman, untitled, 1906. Photographic print. 3 3/4 x 2 3/4 inches. Stellman Collection, Neg. #14,195. Courtesy of the California History Room, California State Library, Sacramento, California. This photograph of the statue of The Goddess of Progress, dethroned from the dome of City Hall by the demolition crews, also appeared in Stellman's *Vanished Ruin Era*.

Fig. 5.20. Louis John Stellman, "Portals of the Past," (n.d.). Stellman collection, Neg. #15,733a. Courtesy of the California History Room, California State Library, Sacramento, California. The entrance to the Towne mansion, relocated to Golden Gate Park, San Francisco.

a systematic and totalizing plan such as Burnham's ensured that the city would be rebuilt piecemeal and haphazardly. As in New York after 1835 and Chicago after 1871, the redevelopment of San Francisco was decidedly uneven.[171] One visitor remarked, as late as 1913, how its "buildings do not seem to have arisen simultaneously." On Market Street you see no "traces" of the disaster, but as soon as you turn off that street "the fullness of that disaster . . . comes home to you for the first time. In the rear of your hotel is an open square of melancholy ruins, below it a corner plat still waste, others beyond in rapid succession. On the side streets, fragments of 'party-walls,' a bit of crumbling arch, a stout standing chimney remind you of the San Francisco that was and that can never be again."[172] Even the city's technological infrastructure remained dilapidated for some time. In 1907, reporters still complained of the difficulty of negotiating everyday life in what was "Still a City of Ruin": its sidewalks not yet clear of obstructions, its streets not properly resurfaced or drained, its streetcar system not fully restored, its telephone switchboards understaffed, and most worryingly its water supply problems unresolved.[173] Having lost the battle for the Burnham Plan, women's urban-beautification clubs such as the Outdoor Art League now organized a Housecleaning Day to recruit workers of all classes to clear the streets of debris (fig. 5.21).

The most conspicuous of all these lingering ruins were City Hall's. Although an initial resolution to demolish and rebuild it from scratch had been

Fig. 5.21. S. D. Packscher, "Housecleaning Day," San Francisco, March 3rd, 1907. [Group portrait of Outdoor Art League?] Photograph. 5 x 7 inches. Courtesy California Historical Society, FN-19910.

Fig. 5.22. Bear Photo Co., untitled [illuminated dome of City Hall]. Dated 1906, but probably April 1907. Photograph. 9 x 7 inches. From Bear Photo Co. album, *San Francisco Earthquake & Fire* (1906), album 3, no. 147 (Bear Photo Co. no. 613). Courtesy of the California History Room, California State Library, Sacramento, California. Electrical display, illuminating the ruins of City Hall.

approved by popular vote, a subsequent bond measure to raise funds for such a project failed at the ballot, stymied again by the opposition of business interests (led by the *Chronicle*) to Burnham's revised design. It seemed as though its ruins would stand "for twenty years" as *Mining and Scientific Press* had earlier suggested—not merely as a "monument to greed and a warning to dishonest builders" (82), but also as testament to the ongoing lack of civic spirit and political consensus.[174] The city eventually razed the old structure in 1909, and voted three years later to construct the Civic Center, if only to avoid embarrassment at the upcoming Panama Pacific International Exposition. But in the interim, the old City Hall provided the setting for one last feat of technological prowess. For the anniversary of the disaster, its shattered dome and crowning goddess were bathed in "a glory of light" by two thousand "electric globes," all paid for by the San Francisco Gas and Electric Company, strung up by an electrical engineer, and activated at the touch of a pushbutton from the banquet hall of the Merchants' Association (fig. 5.22).[175]

6

The Metropolitan Life in Ruins

Architectural and Fictional Speculations in New York,
1893–1919

> Plowing through the woods, climbing over fallen columns and shattered
> building-stones, flushing a covey of loud-winged partridges, parting the bushes
> that grew thickly along the base of the wall, he now found himself in what had
> long ago been Twenty-Third Street.
>
> GEORGE ALLAN ENGLAND, *Darkness and Dawn*

Shortly after becoming New York's tallest building in 1909, the
Metropolitan Life Insurance Tower suffered a series of catastrophes
far worse than that suffered by San Francisco's skyscrapers three
years earlier. In rapid succession it was exposed to poisonous gases,
submerged under an ocean, struck by the tail of a comet, and transported back to the pre-Columbian era. Yet each time the building
somehow stayed upright. Stripped of its stone facade, reduced to
a frame of rusted steel, vacated by its white-collar occupants, even
besieged by a tribe of Native Americans or a horde of monstrous
subhumans, it nonetheless remained standing in apparent perpetuity as an effective monument to the metropolis that lay silent and
desolate around it. During these years the motif of the ruin, whose
migration we have tracked from landscape painting and travel writing to snapshot photography and mass-circulation cartoons, and

from Lake Oneida to San Francisco, became firmly identified with the emerging genre of science fiction and the skyscrapers of New York.

Although postapocalyptic cinema has by now familiarized us with the mise-en-scène of an abandoned Manhattan, for early twentieth-century readers the prospect of skyscrapers becoming ruins required a leap of imagination. How could buildings so large, expensive, new, and apparently sturdy ever become ruins? And how could steel, concrete, and glass—such seemingly unyielding and ungraceful materials—acquire the patinated surfaces and eroded forms preferred by so many theorists and connoisseurs of the ruin, from John Ruskin to Georg Simmel?[1] But above all, the notion of modern skyscrapers as antiquated ruins was belied by the economic geography of Manhattan, a metropolis growing rapidly in size, population, and wealth, while also becoming notorious for mercilessly devouring its own architectural landmarks. How could buildings become antique if their life spans were constrained by economic laws demanding the perpetual turnover of capital, and thus perpetual cycles of demolition and construction? The nineteenth-century churches and brownstones that were demolished (or threatened with demolition) to make way for high-rise, high-rent structures, had clearly failed to ripen into authentic antiquities. The question remained whether those newer structures would last any longer than, or even half as long as, those they had just supplanted. As we have seen, New Yorkers had experienced construction booms previously, especially in the 1820s and '30s. But this latest phase was distinct not only in scale and intensity but also in the degree to which new buildings seemed intended only as provisional replacements, or what the returning expatriate Henry James called "the merest of stop-gaps."[2] This apparent provisionality, as we will see, was central to James's larger sense in *The American Scene* of the impossibility of ruins in New York, and in the United States more generally. But it was also detected by many residents, from architectural critics and Progressive muckrakers to architects and engineers. Their conjectures were ultimately confirmed by the demolition of the first skyscrapers in the 1910s.

This process by which old (or even relatively recent) structures are demolished to make way for new ones, in the interests of circulating capital, has since been condensed into that succinct term, *creative destruction*. Coined in 1942 by the economist Joseph Schumpeter to refer to capitalism's capacity to reproduce itself by clearing away obsolete ideas, technologies, and businesses, the term was not applied to built landscapes until the work of Marxist urban theorists Marshall Berman and David Harvey in the 1970s and 1980s.[3] At the turn of the century, however, when social critics were more concerned with other capitalist epiphenomena (strikes, trusts, panics, or tenements), contemporaries had to draw upon their own immediate and lived sense of the spectacles of wrecking and rebuilding. Instead of superimposing a later theory, we will follow their quest for a vocabulary of their own: some metaphor, image, plot, or even tense that could express and illuminate the violent disruptions wrought by the speculative investment of capital in the urban landscape.[4]

Architectural critics, economic theorists, and literary figures were not alone in responding to these processes. The second half of this chapter will turn to the science fiction narratives (or "scientific romances" as they were then called) disseminated by the pulps (then known as "all-story magazines"). In presenting various external threats to New York (in the form of future invasions, floods, comets, or gaseous explosions), these pulp fictions were not evading the internal, contemporaneous forces of rampant real estate speculation, but confronting them from a different temporal frame. Through the perspective of postapocalyptic survivors in the ruins of New York, these narratives stripped away the skyscraper's facade of progress and timelessness, enabling their readers to evaluate its long-term impact upon the built environment. As if the skyscraper could not be understood within its own lifetime, science fiction authors represented it from the horizon of its "afterlife."

According to Walter Benjamin, it is in the "afterlife" (*Nachleben*) of a cultural object that its original value, intended meaning, and prescribed use crumble away, and its inner truths and contradictions are unmasked. Just as works of art and literature experience an afterlife in their posthumous "fame" or their subsequent reproductions and translations (the latter being the context in which he first employed this concept), so do commodities or even buildings assume an altered, posthumous existence once they have outlived their original function.[5] Both in his native Berlin and his adopted Paris, Benjamin gravitated toward recent structures that had become prematurely superseded yet lingered on in the cracks and crevices of the city. He thus directed his archaeological gaze toward sites of entertainment (panoramas, winter gardens, or waxworks) that had fallen out of fashion; monuments commemorating triumphs since overturned (as in Berlin's 1871 Victory Column); railway stations built as "gateways" to the metropolis only to be bypassed by "approach roads for motorists"; triumphal arches once marking the city's outer boundary but "today" serving as "traffic island[s]"; and above all, the Parisian shopping arcades, or *passages*, that were the height of fashion and luxury in the 1820s but were supplanted by the boulevards and *grands magasins* of the 1860s and threatened with demolition by the 1920s. In their afterlife, these varied sites confronted the modern with the archaic, the new city with remnants of the old, the commodity with its unfulfilled utopian promises, and the fashionable with reminders of fashion's obsolescence—juxtapositions powerful enough to stimulate a revolutionary awakening of the dreaming collectivity.[6] Such ruins diverged from those of Baroque allegories he had examined in *The Origin of German Tragic Drama* insofar as their transience was a function not of natural decay but of capitalist processes of artificial obsolescence: "The devaluation of the world of objects in allegory is outdone within the world of objects itself by the commodity."[7]

But whereas Benjamin sought to redeem the actual ruins of the recent past, science fiction authors rendered present skyscrapers as the imagined ruins they will have become in some deep future. To articulate what will have become of those skyscrapers is to adopt the future perfect, or "future anterior"—the tense expressing neither the past nor future, wrote the American linguist Alfred Dwight Sheffield in *Grammar and Thinking* (1912), but rather the "past *in* the future."[8] Departing from the nostalgic mood of the past perfect—those wistful recollections of what the city had been before the skyscraper—future anteriority offered an alternative perspective on the complex and obscure conditions of urban modernity. It enabled pulp authors and their readers to overturn (and thereby reveal) the city's racial, gender, and class configurations and also its temporal order. If urban and cultural criticism, from Henry James's *American Scene* to recent histories of preservation and planning, has identified American urban modernity (and postmodernity) with a flattening of time— a depthless and perpetual present in which earlier vestiges (visible in "traditional" European cities) have been completely expunged or else dissolved into simulacra—science fiction has presented more complex outcomes, in which time unfolds in multiple directions, at multiple speeds, or in nonlinear patterns.[9] In the strange light of the future interior, moreover, the present appears to contain latent traces of the archaic. Skyscrapers will not become ruins only in the deep future; they were already becoming ruins here and now.

The chief protagonist here will be one such skyscraper, the Metropolitan Life Insurance Tower. Following the recent biographies of the World Trade Center, this chapter chronicles the life history of an earlier office building.[10] It retraces what Benjamin would call its "fore-history": the various aesthetic and economic considerations contributing to the official "production" of the tower, from its conception by the company's president to its opening in 1909, when it was promoted by its brochures and agents as an icon of technological modernity. But the tower's fore-history will appear in dialectical tension with its "after-history": its popular reception by a broader public via cartoons, poems, songs, and scientific magazines, as well as its imagined death and afterlife in the pulps.[11] Both official and popular representations of this building, and both celebratory and critical accounts of New York's growing skyline in general, were bound by a single question—not so much about its aesthetic or spatial impact, but about its temporal ramifications. How long could a skyscraper expect to remain standing—a decade, a generation, a lifetime, or perhaps a millennium?

Zeppelins, Fortresses, and Collapsing Campaniles: Predicting a Skyscraper's Life Expectancy

In 1909 Metropolitan Life celebrated becoming the world's largest life insurer and completing the nation's tallest tower (fig. 6.1).[12] Designed by the architects Napoleon Le Brun & Sons as an appendage to the ten-story Home Office built in 1893, the tower was topped off at fifty stories, thus breaking through what the *Architectural Record* called "new atmospheric strata."[13] While architectural and engineering trade journals celebrated its size as the outcome of technological developments in steel-frame construction, popular magazines went further, improvising more vivid means of conveying this structure's immensity. For the cover of one issue, *Scientific American* performed the "photographic miracle of overturning" this "lofty pile," to show how it would crush all the dwellings along the upper boundary of Madison Square, sparing only "the cupola of the church on 24th street" (fig. 6.2).[14] The *Zeppelin II* airship hovering in the illustration above completes the Wellsian scene of urban bombardment, as if to suggest that only the most advanced military technologies could demolish such colossal structures. (Five years later, Japanese airships did indeed bring down this "monolith of stone and steel," in a future-war scenario published in the pulp magazine *Cavalier*.[15]) The tower's modernity resided not just in its unparalleled height but also in the advanced service technologies: rapid electric-traction elevators, powerful generators, abundant coal and water supplies, and telecommunications equipment including the station that broadcast the earliest radio concerts.[16] Again, while trade journals (and company brochures) were content to enumerate these features statistically, *Scientific American* dramatized them through another violent displacement, this time visualizing the tower being "picked up bodily and dropped on some prairie." Even in such rural isolation, "there would be practically everything needed to start a little city, including the population."[17]

The tower's technological modernity, however, would have mattered less to Metropolitan Life's directors than its embodiment of the more elusive quality of permanence. The steadfast dependability and longevity that other insurance companies conveyed through natural imagery—most famously Prudential's immovable Rock of Gibraltar, first used in 1896—was what Metropolitan Life hoped to express through architectural imagery. Brochures advertised the durable and weather-resistant cladding of white Tuckahoe marble, and the fire and rustproof concrete encasement of the steel girders.

Fig. 6.1. Metropolitan Life Insurance Company's Home Office and Tower (Le Brun & Sons, 1909). From *The Metropolitan Life Insurance Company . . .* (New York: Metropolitan Life Insurance Company, 1914), opposite p. 5.

Crowning this icon of reliability was the electric lantern installed in the apex, christened "The Light That Never Fails."[18] If anyone failed to recognize the message of permanence conveyed by the building—or by promotional images of it—company agents were to elucidate it in person when soliciting customers. At a 1915 company convention, those agents were instructed to draw on the tower's visual connotations of security and strength, and above all its correspondence to a fortress, a "modern harbour of refuge" from the "dangers of

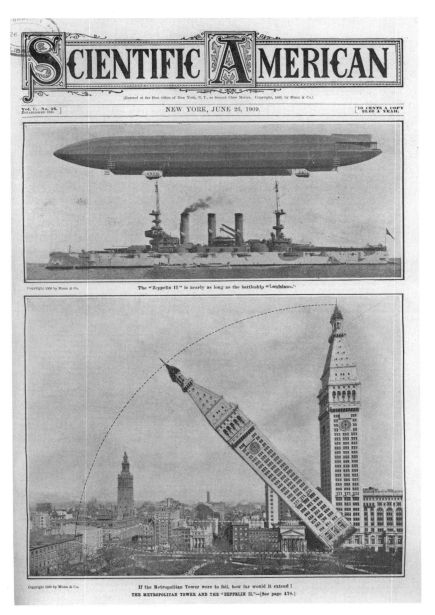

Fig. 6.2. "The Metropolitan Tower and the 'Zeppelin II,'" cover of *Scientific American* 100, no. 26 (1909): 473. "If the Metropolitan Tower were to fall, how far would it extend?"

industrial life, from the enemies of civilization, disease, crime, from all the vicissitudes and uncertainties of life."[19] This rhetoric of fortification found literal expression in a *McClure's* short story of 1915, "The Conquest of America," in which the Metropolitan Tower was commandeered as the military headquarters to defend Manhattan against a German invasion.[20]

While the trope of the modern fortress was intended to convey impregnability, it could unintentionally evoke the embattled status of big business, especially life insurance, during the Progressive Era. Only months before the tower was conceived, the insurance industry suffered unprecedented legal troubles. The Armstrong Investigation of 1905–06 charged the three leading companies—Equitable, Mutual, and New York Life—with bribery, fraud, and unlawful takeovers.[21] The court proceedings shed light on many of the aggressive strategies and schemes some insurance companies had used to lure ethnic and working-class customers away from their neighborhood cooperative societies and mutual benefit associations.[22] At the height of the investigation, even anti-Progressives like Ambrose Bierce were joining the assault. In "Insurance in Ancient America," Bierce's future historian catachrestically misconstrues insurance as a gambling game, one with the odds stacked heavily in favor of the player who owned the table. Insurance companies had flaunted and "parade[d]" their "enormous winnings"—presumably in the form of expensive buildings—as further "inducement to play against their game." In "Ashes of the Beacon," another of Bierce's satirical prospective histories, one of the first acts in the "fall of the Republic" was the violent demolition of these structures, as the "smoldering resentment of years [of insurance abuses] burst into flames, and within a week all that was left of insurance in America was the record of a monstrous and cruel delusion written in the blood of its promoters."[23] As with later fictions of the Metropolitan Tower in ruins, Bierce's account of the destruction of insurance headquarters might be read as a parody of the "folly" of insurance itself in the face of such uninsurable catastrophes. But Bierce was also exposing the conceit of architectural longevity promoted by insurance companies. Their much-vaunted towers, he suggests, would not even endure as ruins.

Metropolitan Life sought to deflect these attacks by appealing to an alternative architectural icon of longevity, the Italian Renaissance bell tower. President John Hegeman first suggested that the famous Campanile in Venice's Piazza San Marco, which had just collapsed in 1902, could be recreated in Manhattan's Madison Square on an even larger scale by adding a tower, adorned with a loggia and other Italianate motifs, to the existing Home Office Building.[24] During the Progressive Era, the Renaissance Revival style, with its civic humanist associations, was an obvious choice for companies claiming to provide public service and noblesse oblige.[25] In the aftermath of the Armstrong Investigation, Metropolitan Life's agents were encouraged to describe the new campanile as "standing out boldly and erect as a plea for righteousness and purity in business corporations," its soaring vertical lines paralleling the moral uprightness of the directors.[26] Yet the ornate exteriors and interiors of insurance campaniles and palazzos, exemplified by Metropolitan Life's lobby (fig. 6.3), also fueled their critics' disdain. For the leading insurance muckraker Burton Hendrick, these buildings' aesthetic veneer barely concealed their source, namely the surplus capital extorted from its hardworking policyholders.[27] As a committed Progressive, Hendrick did not join Bierce in denouncing insurance altogether but hoped its business practices could be reformed and regulated. Fraudulent companies needed to be held accountable in courts of law lest their opulent towers be destroyed by mobs.

Internal contradictions as well as external threats appeared to jeopardize the intended longevity of Metropolitan Life's new tower. Even if it survived the imagined violence of foreign armies, zeppelin attacks, or insurrectionary mobs, it might still succumb to the steady laws of obsolescence. With aesthetic and technological solutions to the problem of the tall building still undergoing rapid revision, even the most modern skyscraper could become quickly outmoded. Archaic European models such as Venetian campaniles were already considered retrograde by more radical architects such as Louis Sullivan, who urged his peers to follow the office building's function rather than examples from "some other land and some other time."[28] Seemingly unsurpassable technological achievements were also rapidly overshadowed by taller skyscrapers with faster elevators—in the case of the Metropolitan, after only four years, by the Woolworth Tower. And by the 1910s, as the growing congestion and darkness of downtown "canyons" led reformers to call for zoning restrictions, some predicted the obsolescence of the skyscraper altogether. In 1913, Manhattan borough president George McAneny declared that the "day of the skyscraper is passing" and existing ones would soon be "regarded as a curiosity."[29]

Even if no more were built, it was unclear exactly how long the existing ones would remain standing. Architects and engineers admitted doubts regarding a steel skeleton's lifespan. George B. Post, a pioneering architect of tall office buildings, warned by 1895 that their steel beams would suffer rust and corrosion, necessitating their dismantling before they collapse. But as those beams were "built into the walls" there was little chance of inspecting them.[30] Until the first generation of skyscrapers was demolished and their skeletons exposed, there were few visible clues to the potential life expectancy of this new architectural entity.

Fig. 6.3. The Marble Court, the Madison Avenue entrance of Metropolitan Life's 1893 Home Office Building. From *The Metropolitan Life Insurance Company . . .* (New York: Metropolitan Life Insurance Company, 1914), opposite p. 64.

The Perpetual Motion Quest, the Doctrine of the Scrap Heap, or the God of Change: Skyscrapers and Economic Obsolescence

The skyscraper's lifespan seemed to be limited by economic even more than technological and aesthetic obsolescence. From the simple perspective of supply and demand, the growth of office buildings, however spectacular, clearly lagged behind the needs of corporations. With a rapidly expanding clerical workforce—especially in insurance companies swamped with policy applications, payment slips, claim forms, and health certificates, all needing to be verified, processed, tabulated, filed, and retrieved—ever larger offices were needed to house them and faster elevators to circulate them.[31] But some observers detected a subtler form of economic obsolescence. Rather than simply a rational response to a "natural" demand for office space, the erection of newer and taller skyscrapers was essentially a self-generating process. That office construction had become a speculative game was evident in the growth and incorporation of real estate companies and also in the involvement of other businesses. Metropolitan Life had speculated extensively in real estate since 1893 when its newly created Real Estate Division took advantage of that year's panic to buy up six hundred foreclosed properties.[32] But by 1907 its speculative interests had extended to its own offices. Besides the tower's practical value as an office and symbolic value as an advertisement, it was conceived as a source of economic revenue. By renting as much as 40 percent of it to smaller companies, the directors hoped to convince their customers and critics that it would pay for itself. It may be an "advertisement," assured one director, but it was one "that costs us nothing." In fact, he confidently predicted it would "earn seven per cent on its cost."[33]

What the director failed to acknowledge were the economic constraints on a skyscraper's long-term profitability as a speculative investment. Unlike some other assets, a tall building tended to depreciate over time. Meanwhile, as taller ones were erected in neighboring blocks, the value of the land beneath it would appreciate. Before long, the burden of rising taxes—together with the expenses of insuring, maintaining, cleaning, and upgrading—would become a financial drain. At this point the structural disadvantage of buildings as fixed assets manifested itself; they cannot be relocated without being wrecked.[34] Reflecting on these constraints, a number of writers questioned the skyscraper's financial profitability over an extended period. In an 1897 article in *Scribner's Magazine* that otherwise celebrated the collective expertise of engineers, architects, and contractors in creating the tall office building, the soon-to-be-designated muckraker Lincoln Steffens lamented that it invariably "earns less year by year."[35] In contrast to Hegeman's optimistic prediction of 7 percent, Hugh Thompson estimated in *Munsey's Magazine* that "these architectural monstrosities seldom pay more than four per cent on their cost, and some of them return still less." And in the case of insurance towers, concluded muckraker Burton Hendrick, the real victims were the policyholders, who might have benefited from "other investments more advantageously made."[36]

Given this abbreviated time frame in which a skyscraper could recoup its costs and turn a profit, the superfluous ornaments introduced by aesthetically minded architects seemed all the more misguided. Clock towers, cupolas,

loggias, observation platforms, and pyramidal steeples—all of which adorned
the Metropolitan Tower—were untenantable spaces. Similarly, the narrowness
of towers like the Metropolitan subtracted from their profit margins. For real
estate experts and engineers such as George Hill, every "unnecessary" element
that architects "put into the building," indeed "every cubic foot that is used for
purely ornamental purposes beyond that needed to express its use and to make
it harmonize with others of its class," was a blatant "waste . . . perverting some
one else's money."[37] Architectural critics, in contrast, tended to view expendi-
ture on the aesthetic as long-awaited signs of "civic pride." Overlooking their
value as advertisements, Mildred Stapley applauded the "thirtieth-story loggia"
and the "terminating peak" of the Metropolitan Tower, along with the expansive lobbies of similar buildings, as a "noble sacrifice . . . of . . . office space" for
the sake of urban beautification.[38]

   But even if skyscrapers could be purged of superfluous elements, little could
be done to stem the escalating land values beneath them. Steffens concluded
that however skillfully and "almost scientific[ally]" building managers (and
real estate experts) balance the leasing price and square footage against the
price of the lot; however carefully architects offset ornament against rentable
space; and however ingeniously engineers improve the technological capacities
of tall buildings, they would always come up against the "inexorable laws of the
market." According to this "inevitable process," the "requirements of economy
and ingenuity of construction involve the solution of fresh problems, lowering
the cost of building, which entails the increase of new and higher structures;
and that carries with it higher values of the ground built on, and corresponding
lower rents," resulting in the replacement of existing structures by even higher
ones (61). So inexorable was this process, it continued even during the depression of the mid-1890s, when Steffens was writing.[39] Indeed, in such periods,
the hiring of wrecking crews becomes the only way to ensure a steady source
of tenants.

> The competition is almost desperate in some cities where there has been over-
> building in hard times. In New York the stress is such that it is said the only
> source of tenants is in the continuance of the process, as the tearing down of
> more old buildings for the next year's crop of new buildings supplies the ten-
> ants for this May's openings. (59)

Setting out to affirm the rationality of skyscraper building, Steffens unwittingly
discerned an irreconcilable contradiction at the core of New York's developing
skyline: its apparent entrapment within a "perpetual motion quest" (46).
   As a function of this process, the activities of demolition and construction

crews were no longer reliable indices of a healthy economy. If anything, the process promoted volatility. The period 1893 to 1918, although characterized by economic historians as a single cycle in the building economy, was punctuated by sharp and unpredictable minicycles lasting just two or three years.[40] And with each cycle, predictions of the skyscraper's life span grew ever shorter. Instead of claiming we are "building for all time," Hill warned in 1904, it may be "better business to say, 'We are building for fifteen years.'"[41] That rate of turnover did not abate but rather accelerated as the boom peaked around 1907–09, when the Metropolitan Tower was constructed. In the late phase of a business cycle, Harvey has shown, "last-ditch" efforts are typically made to avert a crisis of overaccumulation by "siphon[ing]" off surplus capital and labor power from the overloaded "primary circuit" of commodity production into the "secondary circuit" of long-term fixed assets such as buildings.[42] New tax laws (such as the Corporation Tax of 1909 and the Income Tax of 1913) aided and abetted this process by recognizing office buildings as assets prone to depreciation and thus eligible for tax deductions, and providing incentives to write off and rebuild.[43] Thus lubricated by bank loans and tax breaks, the skyscraper functioned as a vital but unstable component within a larger economy of planned obsolescence. Under the growing pressure to accelerate the turnover time of capital, buildings no longer followed a traditional life cycle — ripening gradually from gestation through maturity to old age — but rather the artificial, accelerated, and unpredictable cycles of speculative real estate.[44]

Given its location in Madison Square, Metropolitan Life would have expected its new tower to assume a somewhat more stable presence in the New York skyline. When the company moved there in 1890, this midtown neighborhood was still predominantly residential, with lower density, lower rents, and slower increases in land values than downtown. But with the relocation of other businesses and the completion of the Flatiron Building in 1902, Madison Square soon witnessed patterns of development and obsolescence comparable to those downtown. Correspondingly, even a midtown skyscraper could be considered a provisional structure, to be replaced in due course by a larger and more cost-effective one. As "the oldest inhabitant" of New York predicted in a contemporary cartoon, it seemed inevitable they would "pull down the Metropolitan Tower and make room for a [real?] sky-scraper" (fig. 6.4).

At the time of the tower's completion, the apparent law of perpetual motion had extinguished the lives only of older office buildings of traditional masonry construction. But it soon claimed the first skyscrapers, stimulating further concerns about their longevity. The razing of the Gillender Building in 1910 and the Tower Building in 1914 attracted widespread press attention, partly because of the reasons for their demolition. The latter, claimed the *Times*, was

IN NEWEST NEW YORK.

THE OLDEST INHABITANT: "ANOTHER OLD LANDMARK GONE AND NOW THEY'RE GOING TO PULL DOWN THE METROPOLITAN TOWER AND MAKE ROOM FOR A SKY-SCRAPER."

Fig. 6.4. "In Newest New York." Date and publication details unknown. Cartoon clipping, Metropolitan Life Tower Scrapbook, 1907–20. Courtesy of MetLife Archives.

not only the first building to rest entirely on a steel skeleton (and thus arguably New York's first skyscraper); it was also the first to be demolished purely for the sake of "reducing a tax bill," its tax assessment value having apparently exceeded the income that could be extracted through rent.[45] The spectacle of demolition was itself an object of fascination. The sheer size of such buildings (the former rising to twenty-two stories), the narrow sites, and the tight schedules (as time taken to demolish an old building was rent lost on the new one) demanded new technologies and techniques of demolition. Equipped with pneumatic guns and dynamite, a specially constructed scaffold extending over the street, a large shaft to discharge building material, and 250 men organized in day and night shifts, the foremost wrecker Jacob Volk completed the Gillender job within the forty-five days specified by the contract.[46] While Volk was perfecting the art of wrecking, architects were increasingly considering the eventual demolition of a skyscraper in their plans for its construction, making use of building materials that could be rapidly, as well as economically and efficiently, dismantled and reused.[47] But the Gillender and Tower demolitions were notable, above all, because of their recent construction; the former was just thirteen years old, the latter twenty-six. "You would think that one of these mountains of steel and brick, once put up, would be left alone for generations," complained Thompson in the 1912 article cited above. "But such is the rapid remaking of New York that even these enormous piles succumb to the god of change." Whereas Hendrick might have sympathized with the customers footing the bill, Thompson's thoughts were for professional photographers. Those specializing in "sky-line" photographs had to reshoot their panoramas "every six months."[48]

The dismantling of these skyscrapers at least provided the opportunity for which George Post had been waiting, that of inspecting their steel girders for signs of aging so as to estimate the life expectancy of other structures. In 1910 *Scientific American* reported on the lessons learned in the Gillender's ruins. A quasi-archaeological exploration revealed little evidence of metal fatigue or rust. In purely structural terms, the steel skeleton's durability and its insulation from erosion and decay under a layer of exterior cladding meant it was theoretically conceivable that "the visitor to New York five hundred or a thousand years hence [would] find the skyscrapers of today in perfect condition." But in practice their life span was dictated by the economic "doctrine of the 'scrap heap.'" As soon as "there is more profit in 'scrapping' an existing machine, plant, or building, and replacing it by another more efficient or of greater capacity," it is considered "a matter of sound business policy to send that machine to the 'junk heap' or turn the 'wrecking gang' loose upon that building." If such a doctrine were taken to its logical conclusion, *Scientific American* concluded, the future ruin of the entire city depicted by "certain imaginative magazine writers" did not seem so far-fetched.[49]

Henry James and the Impossibility of Ruins

Although the terms they coined—"doctrine of the 'scrap heap'" or "perpetual motion quest"—anticipate later critiques of creative destruction, these early critics remained largely ambivalent about, rather than overtly critical of, the skyscraper's troubled economic status. In contrast to his subsequent exposures of corporate exploitation and political corruption, Steffens's article maintained that the dilemmas of the tall office building were stimulating engineers and other experts to new heights of collaborative efficiency. The *Architectural Record* similarly rationalized the Gillender's demolition as the "economic waste ... which accompanies all progress—the substitution of new machines for old machines," as did *Scientific American* when it celebrated the technological creations borne out of destructive processes.[50] Some writers even doubted whether a skyscraper's truncated life span was a problem at all. "There are few machines that should not be replaced ... [after] ten to fifteen years," wrote Hill, and why should buildings be judged any differently? (314).

One writer who did hold architecture to higher standards and denounce the reduction of the office building to an economic problem was Henry James. Revisiting America in 1904 after a twenty-one-year absence—and thus experiencing it with that "freshness of eye" afforded a "returning absentee"—the novelist found disturbing evidence of commercialism almost everywhere, but above all in its architecture (3, 43). To James, skyscrapers were dollars writ large: the purest expression of the mercantile instinct that had consumed the country in his absence. These "monsters of the mere market" bespeak money not so much in the richness of their ornaments and wasted spaces as in their aesthetic plainness; they are a mere accumulation of floors and windows (63, 73). And as long as skyscrapers pile "window upon window"—the very features that "were going to bring in money" by providing light for "the transaction of business and the conclusion of sharp bargains"—and allow few "interspaces," they will never achieve the "grace" of European buildings, such as Italy's "comparatively windowless" campaniles (73–74, 61). Even from the East River, a distanced perspective merging them into a "whole picture" or (in a neologism of the period) "skyline," James still senses the active presence of money, as "every ... element" in the cityscape seems "backed," veritably launched as a speculative object (58, 59).[51] Indeed, the speculation has spread as far as the New Jersey shores, whose villas are also "affirming their wealth" and nothing else (11–12).

Rather than recoiling from skyscrapers on the simple grounds of the incompatibility of the economic with the aesthetic, James explores their implications for temporal experience in the metropolis. It is their contemporariness that immediately troubles him. "Impudently new" and "impudently 'novel,'" their "glory" seems almost "surprised" at itself (60). However much they resort to historical styles (such as Italian Renaissance) and traditional materials (marble), they cannot escape this newness; "no short cut of 'style,'" James observes elsewhere on his tour, "can ever successfully imitate" the effects produced by the actual "elongation of history" (50). It is a quality skyscrapers share with "so many other terrible things" (60). There is a sense of "insistent newness" not only downtown but also in the residential developments uptown (84), and indeed in the skyline as a whole, that collective "expression of things lately and currently *done*" (58). Rural landscapes prove equally lacking in historical depth. The absence of such feudal institutions as the manor and the parish, and their attendant figures, "the squire and the parson," has left a historical vacuum in the American countryside—one that unpoetic place names have done little to fill (21–22, 27). This ahistoricity of American landscapes, both rural and urban, is what defies James's attempts throughout the book to elicit any meaning from them. In an earlier work, James endorsed Nathaniel Hawthorne's famous complaint in the latter's preface to *The Marble Faun* that America had "no shadow, no antiquity, no mystery, no picturesque and gloomy wrong," and thus none of the "Ruin" on which "romance and poetry, like ivy, lichens, and wall-flowers" flourish. James added a litany of further absences: "no palaces, no castles, nor manors, nor old country-houses, nor parsonages, nor thatched cottages nor ivied ruins; no cathedrals, nor abbeys, nor little Norman churches." It is that earlier argument, about how "it takes a great deal of history to produce a little literature," that the *American Scene* dramatizes in the oxymoron of its title: the impossibility of rendering the American landscape as a picturesque or literary "scene."[52]

James does find numerous older places that give some "relief" from the "importunate newness" of America (49). There are the historical associations of Concord and Salem (190–201), and the rural remains of abandoned farmhouses and resorts in New England (14–15, 55–56). Cambridge and Boston are especially rich in timeworn buildings (49–50, 168–89), while even New York has preserved certain older structures, such as Trinity Church, Castle Garden, and City Hall, or an occasional house on Washington Square, if only "by the mercy of fate" or some "happy accident" (61, 62, 74, 87). The memories evoked by such vestiges of "the antecedent time" provide the only "escape from the ubiquitous alien," the immigrant present and future that overwhelm him from Ellis Island to Central Park (67–68, 90). They also ironically furnish him with the romantic literary material he assumed to be lacking in urbanizing America. The old house at the heart of his ghost story, "The Jolly Corner" (1909), like that of Melville's "Jimmy Rose," derives its affective powers from its defiance of urban processes of renewal. Returning to New York after decades in Europe, the narrator Spencer Brydon finds his boyhood home still standing on the corner of a street—possibly Fifth Avenue at Washington Square—that has undergone radical transformation. The "old people had mostly gone" and the "westward reaches" of the street had been "dishonoured and disfigured" by new high-rise buildings, including the narrator's other inherited property, a "tall mass of flats" currently under construction. By contrast, the old house remains unaltered, untenanted, and thus replete with memories. For Brydon, with his aversion to "beastly rent-values," this holdout's true value resides in the way its very walls, floors, and fixtures evoke—through sight, hearing, and touch—his "long-extinct youth." But this same sense of the past, confronting him in the ghostly figure of the person he might have been had he stayed in New York's mercenary milieu, will ultimately torment him into considering handing the house over to "the builders, the destroyers."[53]

James cannot quite speak of such holdouts, however, as authentic or established antiquities. He acknowledges that even that "ancient end of Fifth Avenue," with its "mild and melancholy glamour," is a product of relatively "recent history" (68), a neighborhood born less than half a century earlier. Evaluations of architectural duration in the American landscape are "comparative" at best, a word James applies repeatedly to the age value of its extant buildings (49, 68, 87). Once one has seen the newness of the Far West (the subject of a never-completed second volume), one could describe New York State (as James does on his return the following spring) as "a ripe old civilization," relatively speaking (111). But above all, it is the perpetual recourse to wreckers that compromises these *potential* ruins. In a city so committed to the construction of the new, it is only a matter of time before they go the way of other recently demolished landmarks. By 1904 many of the buildings of James's youth have disappeared, such as the "hallowed" New York University building on Washington Square, the original Metropolitan Museum, or the large church on West 14th Street which, "after passing from youth to middle age and from middle age to antiquity, has vanished as utterly as the Assyrian Empire" (71, 141–42). And James's own "birth-house" on Washington Square has been "ruthlessly suppressed" to make way for a "high, square, impersonal structure," thereby precluding "the felicities of the backward reach" experienced by Brydon (70–71). James feels these architectural losses so intensely and personally they linger on his mental map of the metropolis as absent presences, phantom limbs representing a history "amputated" from him (71).

If those landmarks that have survived (such as the Church of the Ascension on Fifth Avenue) possess any "glamour," it is on account of their "mere exemption from the 'squashed' condition" (72–73). They too seemed "doom[ed]" to imminent obliteration, a threat of "'removal' ... hover[ing] about them" (73), like that Zeppelin in *Scientific American*. Already, skyscrapers were obliterating churches, figuratively as well as literally, by rendering them invisible. Trinity Church, "once ... the pride of the town and the feature of Broadway," was among those that had since been "mercilessly deprived of their visibility" by neighboring office buildings. A half-century after Melville looked down over the city from the top of Trinity, James looked down over Trinity from the top of a skyscraper, from whose "vertiginous upper atmospheres" it seemed a "poor ineffectual thing" (61). Whether by leveling or overtopping old churches, the new landmarks inflicted a physical and symbolic violence on the city's historical fabric equivalent to that of "children stamp[ing] on snails and caterpillars" (63).

Although his rhetoric echoed antimodernists such as the neo-Gothic architect Ralph Adams Cram, who lamented how tall buildings were "crushing" neighboring churches "into ignominy," James resists the oft-made indictment of nostalgia. He is wary of becoming too attached to extant buildings and acknowledges that the sites of former buildings are "terrible traps to memory," forever "baited . . . with the cheese of association." Coeval with his own lifespan—his generation having directly witnessed their "beginnings" as well as their "ends," their "birth" and "life" as well as "death"—these bygone buildings cannot evoke that "boundless backward reach of history" James found so pleasurable about Roman ruins. Instead of the pleasure of outliving that which is ruined, they give him a disturbing sense of his own mortality—a "horrible, hateful sense of personal antiquity" not unlike that felt by Philip Hone among the ruins of Trinity Church in 1839 (142, 62–63). Neither can James easily be positioned within the nascent movement of architectural preservation.[54] At Sunnyside, Washington Irving's home in the Hudson Valley, James discovers that historic and literary landmarks are endangered as much by preservation as by demolition. Expensively and "religiously preserv[ing]" the house for tourists, "modernity" has "doomed [it] to celebrity" (117). And in another misguided act of conservation, the "pleasant promiscuous patina of time" on the marble facade of New York's City Hall has been scrubbed off (75). "The Jolly Corner" further dramatizes the vanity and futility of preservation, and its complicity with capitalism, as when Alice Staverton reminds Brydon that his "sentimental" attachment to the old house is contingent upon his "ill-gotten gains" from the new skyscraper (797). If James is guilty of nostalgia, it is a nostalgia for the very possibility of nostalgia, a longing for a time when time itself had depth and coherence.

It is not simply New York's newness, moreover, that alienates James; "new cities" are a global phenomenon, as is the renewal of old cities such as London, Paris, and Rome, "all of late so mercilessly renovated" (84). The problem is that New York's new structures function only as temporary expedients, "the merest of stop-gaps" (85; see also 12, 122), and are thus even less likely to acquire an aura of antiquity than those they replaced. "The new Paris and the new Rome," by contrast, "do at least propose, I think, to be old—one of these days" (85). Like Steffens, James thus discerned—several years before the Gillender

demolition—the temporal impermanence behind skyscrapers' expensive
and ostensibly durable facades. In part, he deduces this provisionality from
their sheer accumulation of windows, which as we have seen are financially
motivated. Thus, whereas a windowless campanile looks "supremely serene"
and exudes that sense of "long duration" evoked by other "towers or temples
or fortresses or palaces," a skyscraper with a "thousand glassy eyes" reflects
an "interested passion that, restless beyond all passions, is for ever seeking
more pliable forms" (61; emphasis added). He also intuits this process from
their collective outline; viewed from the East River, they resemble a "cluster"
of flowers, each to be "'picked,' in time, with a shears; nipped short off, by
waiting fate" (60). Architects' efforts to "gild the temporary" with expensive
ornaments betray fears of their imminent demise, as if they protest their longevity too much (84–85). Thus, if skyscrapers are "monsters" that cannibal-
ize older buildings (63), they are themselves the offspring of a larger force,
a "perpetual passionate pecuniary purpose," which in turn "derides and de-
vours them" (85). James hears the voice of this larger spirit of flux warning
of the impossibility of stasis or "rest," of the futility of "venerat[ing]" even
buildings of "fifty floors," as "there shall be immeasurably more of them, in
quantity, to tear down than of the actual past that we are now sweeping away"
(86). In describing skyscrapers as "the last word of economic ingenuity only
till another word be written," James echoes Steffens's perpetual motion quest
(61). He even gave it his own, less succinct term: "the reiterated sacrifice to
pecuniary profit" (142).

James does not reduce skyscrapers' transience to an economic logic, however. Accelerating cycles of demolition and reconstruction are symptoms of the
city's general climate of restlessness, evident in the literally breathless pace of
New Yorkers' conversations (74); the repeated relocations of Columbia College (108); the "ceaseless" "ingurgitation" of "foreign matter" into Ellis Island,
which in turn implies the infinite mutability of the "'American' character" (50,
66, 92); the urgency of the "pushing male crowd" surging through the streets
and into elevators with its "universal will to move—to move, move, move, as
an end in itself" (65, 139–40); and above all, in that monument to the "perpetually provisional," the luxury hotel (77, 80–81, 300). Just as Georg Simmel
detected a common spirit of "secret restlessness" binding cultural phenomena
as diverse as "the tumult of the metropolis, . . . the mania for traveling, . . . [or]
the wild pursuit of competition," so does James perceive an "American spirit"
linking multiple sites of experience (79). Everything in New York, indeed in
the United States, seems to "connect itself with the rest" (89).[55]

James's response to this culture of provisionality is characteristically complex. He recognizes the impossibility of any fixed standpoint outside these

scenes of restlessness, or any definite "conclusions" (93), and instead becomes a "restless analyst," immersing himself in the sensory flux and temporal contingency of metropolitan life, and mimicking it in his distracted wanderings around the city and in the circuitous digressions of his sentences (64, 82, passim). He even admonishes America for breaking its own promise of provisionality, as when it veils its skyscrapers with marble facades affecting permanence. Sounding more like Sullivan than Cram, James denounces the "cynicism" and "insincerity" of those forms as inadequately following the buildings' function as financial "stop-gaps" (84–85, 107).[56] But it is not the pretence of permanence so much as the impermanence itself that ultimately troubles James. An urban culture governed by the new and the temporary can never be "capture[d]" in art and literature, not even by the naturalism of Zola (64–65); can never become a true home (86); and can provide little in the way of "tradition," "taste," and "tranquility" (127). But above all, such a culture can never offer any sense of antiquity. The brownstone mansions and churches of the nineteenth century failed to ripen into antiques, and so it seems will the skyscrapers of the twentieth.

The Liquidity of Urban Capital: Pulp Visions

If James could not envision New York in ruins, other writers did entertain such a possibility. From the perspective of pulp-magazine science fiction, it was only as abandoned and corroded ruins that its skyscrapers' epic provisionality could, in James's term, be captured. To transform New York into a ruinscape, science fiction writers invented disasters catastrophic enough to depopulate the metropolis (or ideally the continent or planet) and thus terminate the perpetual motion quest, yet benign enough to spare the skyscrapers (or at least some of them) so they might decay gracefully thereafter.

From the genre's early years, floods offered one such scenario. *The Second Deluge*, written by the *New York Sun*'s scientific journalist Garrett P. Serviss and serialized in *Cavalier* in 1911, narrated a global disaster—the earth's collision with a "watery nebula"—from the local standpoint of New York.[57] The impact of the ensuing flood was not fully realized until the twenty-fourth and penultimate episode, when the survivors descend in a diving bell to explore the "necropolis" in "Her Ocean Tomb."

> The searchlight [of the diving bell], penetrating far through the clear water beneath [it], fell in a circle round a most remarkable object—tall, gaunt, and spectral, with huge black ribs. "Why, it's the Metropolitan tower, still standing!" cried Amos Blank. "Who would have believed it possible?" (368)

The survivors' leader Cosmo Versál explains how it remained upright under
the weight of twenty thousand feet of water.

> Although it was built so long ago [in the era of skyscrapers], it was made
> immensely strong, and well braced, and . . . it has been favored by the very
> density of that which now surrounds it, and which tends to buoy it up and
> hold it steady. But you observe that it has been stripped of the covering of
> stone. (368)[58]

The nautical metaphor of the Metropolitan Tower as a lighthouse—its electric
octagonal beacon visible from Brooklyn (where Serviss lived) and even to ships
in the bay—is here inverted.[59] No longer looking out over an ocean of urban
crowds and archipelago of city blocks, nor warning vessels away from land, the
tower has become an anchor, firmly grounded in the seabed. There could be
"nothing better" for mooring their cable, and so after "some careful maneuver-
ing" they finally "secure a satisfactory attachment to the [steel] beams of the
tower" (369).

Not confined to science fiction, floods were also evoked in nonfiction accounts to register the immensity and intensity of the city's growth. In his *Munsey's* article "The Remaking of New York," Thompson described how that city,
lacking a "plan such as had attended the birth of Washington," has "followed
the *flow* of trade currents." Since the early nineteenth century, its development
has thus been "like the ocean. It rises and falls with certain regularity, but once
in a while a mighty storm arises and sweeps everything before it. New York
has been struck again and again by these upheavals, which have changed the
whole face of the city map." Observing this latest upheaval, Thompson reiterated the *Gazette*'s earlier description of New York as "a city of modern ruins,
a perfect Baalbec of a day's growth and a day's dilapidation." Urban development, conceived here as a tide of capital on which stocks and assets are floated,
is a force for renewal and regeneration, but also for premature ruin. Manhattan
was already on the verge of becoming antique, its ruins foreshadowed as well as
erased with every act of demolition and construction.[60]

A magazine story coauthored by one of the few female science fiction writers of the period draws a more direct connection between the periodic overflowing of oceans and that of capital. In Grena Bennett and Thomas Vivian's
"The Tilting Island" (1909), the toppling of downtown skyscrapers into the
harbor and the ensuing "monster tidal wave" result from the convergence of
subterranean with man-made forces, or physical geology with capitalist geography (fig. 6.5). Witnessing the disaster as it unfolded, the Columbia geology
professor Heinrich Herman (unlike the panicking ethnic hordes) insists on a

"LOOK, MY BOY, LOOK! THE LOWER FAULT HAS BROKEN!"

Fig. 6.5. "Look, My Boy, Look! The Lower Fault Has Broken!" Illustration from Thomas J. Vivian and Grena J. Bennett, "The Tilting Island," *Everybody's Magazine* 21 (September 1909): 388.

measured deduction of its precise causes. However vast this catastrophe appears, he cannot attribute it to a single natural cause, namely the fault line in the geological crust of the island. A more immediate cause is the recent construction boom downtown. It is the sheer burden of urban capital—the weight of "twenty stories of steel, thirty stories, forty stories" that "we have massed on [one] end" of the island—that has broken the fault line and is tilting the entire island. "That is the hand of man on the edge of the plate. Do you see now?"[61] Contemporary cartoons assisted New Yorkers in picturing such scenarios. The cover of a 1902 issue of *Life* depicted lower Manhattan in 2020, some time after the weight of its buildings and fissures of its underground tunnels had caused its collapse. The only ruins visible to the balloonist sightseers are of the Brooklyn Bridge and riverfront towers (fig. 6.6). Some contemporaries were serious about such dangers. One architect cited the Metropolitan along with geologists' testimony to warn that if such towers continued to be constructed "over the fragile strata of rock upon which the city is built[,] the whole would give way to the strain and an awful catastrophe would result."[62]

Such fantasies of a sunken, tilted, or inundated Manhattan register on one level as commentaries on the pace of construction. They betray anxieties about skyscrapers' structural soundness and also about the general destabilization of Manhattan's ecological equilibrium through processes of capitalist urbanization. Man-made structures (office buildings, bridges, and tunnels) have so

SIGHTSEEING IN 1920.

The Conductor: THAT DEPRESSION DOWN THERE IS WHERE NEW YORK CITY STOOD. BUT WITH ALL ITS SKY-SCRAPERS AND UNDERGROUND TUNNELS IT SUDDENLY SUNK ONE DAY, AND THEY HAVEN'T BEEN ABLE TO FIND IT SINCE.

Fig. 6.6. "Sightseeing in 1920." Illustration on cover of *Life Magazine* 39, no. 1006 (1902): 101. The caption reads: "*The Conductor:* That depression down there is where New York City stood. But with all its sky-scrapers and underground tunnels it suddenly sunk one day, and they haven't been able to find it since."

transformed the natural landscape they resemble forces of nature, equivalent in scale and power to deluges, earthquakes, and tidal waves. The sheer weight of capital invested in the city's physical infrastructure can dislodge entire tectonic plates and landforms. But it is also the liquidity of capital—its apparent tendency to overaccumulate and unpredictably spill over into the terrain of urban construction, engulfing any obstacles in its way—that evokes the uncontainable surge of oceans. And the unevenness of its distribution, its concentration in the downtown district, can upset the balance of an entire island. Through such rhetoric and imagery, fiction and nonfiction writers (and cartoonists) of the Progressive Era thus conveyed the potentially destructive and apparently uncontrollable force of capital as it flowed across the city's grid.

Yet while reflecting on the dangers of excessive construction, these fantasies were also expressions of a culture of demolition increasingly aware of the fungability and disposability of its built environment. In his book on Charles Baudelaire, Walter Benjamin considers a similar outpouring of apocalyptic visions in nineteenth-century Paris. Beginning with Balzac's speculations about the "ruins of the bourgeoisie," historian Friedrich von Raumer's 1830 daydream about Paris one day resembling "Thebes and Babylon," and Victor Hugo's 1837 poem about the Arc de Triomphe "loom[ing] eternal and intact" over a "silent" and depopulated French "Campagna," there emerged a conception of modernity as the classical antiquity of the future that ultimately inspired the poet Baudelaire and writer Maxime du Camp in the late 1850s and '60s.[63] Although these premonitions of future ruination might be attributed to du Camp's melancholic "old age" or von Raumer's "elevated" perspective on the city from the top of Notre Dame ("what becomes most clearly recognizable from these heights," writes a later visionary of ruin, Léon Daudet, is a sense of "threat" hanging over it), Benjamin relates them to that crucial "develop[ment]" accompanying the "growth of the big cities" during the nineteenth century, namely that of "the means of razing them to the ground" (85–86). It was the large-scale demolition projects Haussmann initiated in 1859 that "evoked" such "visions of the future" (85)—or, as he puts it in *The Arcades Project*, provoked them as "symptom[s]" (97 [C7a, 4]). It now became possible to imagine the city as a "fragile" entity, "as brittle and as transparent as glass," qualities that Baudelaire rendered in *Fleurs du Mal* (*Baudelaire*, 82).

Haussmann had precipitated these visions merely by subjecting the decrepit "physiognomy" of ancient Paris to the "most modest means imaginable: spades, pickaxes, crowbars, and the like" (85). With the addition of pneumatic guns, power winches, and (occasionally) dynamite to wreckers' arsenals in early twentieth-century New York, this sense of fragility extended to structures as large and new as skyscrapers. Moreover, fantasies of ruin could *precede* the spectacles of demolition. Noting that Balzac's and Hugo's visions predate Haussmannization, Benjamin suggests that the anticipation of some kind of overhaul of Paris's congested streets "could have at least as great an effect upon a good imagination as the work of urban renewal itself" (86–87). Likewise, the anticipation of demolition accounts for the flood fantasies published prior to the Gillender's actual wrecking in 1910. In the case of New York's "incubation period," the imminence of demolition was deduced not from the problem of congestion but from the logic of economic and technological obsolescence. Like Paris's arcades, New York's skyscrapers were introduced in a period when outmoded commodities and buildings were accumulating "at a rate and on a scale that was previously unknown" as "technical progress [was] continually withdrawing newly introduced objects from circulation" (466 [N5,2]). In this context, "the monuments of the bourgeoisie," to borrow the final sentence of Benjamin's 1935 exposé of *The Arcades Project*, became recognizable "as ruins even before they have crumbled" (13)—just as the trees of Saginaw, Michigan, appeared to Tocqueville as ruins even before being felled.

Appropriately, these anticipations of ruined skyscrapers were disseminated by the pulp magazine, a medium also noted for its rapid obsolescence. These weekly and monthly magazines emerged at the turn of the century out of economies of scale introduced largely by Frank Munsey, whose offices were located in the Flatiron Building, opposite the Metropolitan Tower. By acquiring his own printing and distribution facilities and utilizing cheap wood-pulp paper, he could sell his magazines for 10 cents (the same price as the standard weekly premium for a Metropolitan Life industrial insurance policy). And much as skyscraper architects were minimizing "wasted spaces" and maximizing windows and rentable spaces, Munsey reduced the illustrations and increased the advertisements. The low price, combined with the wide range of fictional genres—encompassing pseudoscientific narratives of technological invention, alien invasion, and racial (d)evolution, as well as low-tech narratives of crime investigation, colonial adventure, and westerns—attracted a broad spectrum of readers, including women as well as men, adults as well as children, and the working class as well as middle class.[64] Yet despite rivaling the dime novel as a medium for popular fiction and forcing the middlebrow magazines to lower their prices, the pulps suffered from chronic financial precariousness and short life spans.[65] To keep pace with intense competition, Munsey alone went through as many as nine titles between 1896 and 1910; some were discontinued or sold off, others renamed or merged with other magazines.[66] There was a correspondingly high turnover of authors, with few able to secure a professional status or stable income. Even the wood-pulp paper had a notoriously short life expectancy—a problem that caused widespread concern by 1910.[67] The critic Henry Morton Robinson, writing in the 1920s, viewed the "impurities" in raw wood-pulp as proof of the cultural ephemerality and literary worthlessness of the magazines.

> In less than a month after the issue is on the stands not even the shrewdest of their own supersleuths could trace a single copy of the number carrying their yarn. No library files copies of wood-pulp. Of the millions of words the wood-pulp writer grinds out, of the hundreds of plots he concocts, nothing remains but ephemera, shadows—dead wood-pulp with an old date on the cover.[68]

It is precisely in their ephemerality, however, that the pulps resembled the city-scape they portrayed. Robinson described fiction magazines similarly to the way James described skyscrapers: as emblems of transience.

The pulp magazine industry bore an affinity with the urban landscape in its mode of distribution and consumption as well as production. Before the national subscription and mail order distribution networks of the Gernsback era, science fiction was not only published in New York but also purchased locally, in particular from street-corner vendors.[69] Small enough (at seven by ten inches) to be folded into one's coat pocket, these magazines could be read on el trains, streetcars, and subways. Even Robinson acknowledged that pulp fiction writers were something like the "*feuilletonists*" of early twentieth-century America.[70] If the *feuilleton* sections of nineteenth-century Parisian newspapers offered vignettes and sketches featuring the random details, sights, and minutiae (the *faits divers*) of that metropolis, so did Munsey's magazines register the everyday fragments of metropolitan life. His *Scrapbook* magazine consisted literally of scraps of fiction and nonfiction. "Everything that appeals to the human brain and human heart will come within the compass of THE SCRAPBOOK," Munsey announced to his readers, "fiction, . . . biography, review, philosophy, science, art, poetry, wit, humor, pathos, satire, the weird, the mystical—everything that can be classified and everything that cannot be classified. A paragraph, a little bit, a saying, an editorial, a joke, a maxim, an epigram—all these will be comprised."[71] In this and other magazines, stories were themselves fragmented. Rather than read whole, they were consumed as discrete episodes published serially over a number of months. Sometimes readers contributed to the development of a story by writing letters to the author, an activity formally integrated into the pulps with the 1911 introduction of a "reader's section" in the *Argosy*, anticipating the later phenomenon of science fiction fandom.[72] Science fiction narratives were thus products as well as expressions of the city's accelerating rhythms.

Reordering the City

In reducing the skyline to ruins, Munsey's authors opened up the possibility of exploring not just the fragility of the built environment but various other phenomena of metropolitan life, too. Along with its architectural structures, the city's social structures—its existing configurations of race, gender, and class—could be reconfigured in imaginative and unpredictable ways through the hermeneutic of ruin. This was especially the case with the emerging subgenre of the postapocalyptic "scientific romance." Whereas stories like "Tilting Island" narrated the urban catastrophe as it was occurring, the postapocalyptic romance posited the catastrophe as having already occurred prior to the narrative's inception, typically by centuries or millennia. Although thus resembling prospective history—or detective fiction, with its will to reconstruct what Ernst Bloch calls "the darkness before the beginning"—the postapocalyptic romance represented a new departure in its relative lack of interest in reconstructing the scenes, causes, or agents of urban destruction that preoccupied London, Wells, Twain, and others.[73] Its characters instead strive to grasp their new, posturban lifeworld and to survive within it.

Undated and unidentified, the apocalypse thus serves as a marker of some absolute rupture not just between the passing of one nation and the rise of another, but between history and the posthistorical, the human and the posthuman, life and afterlife. Projected beyond that apocalypse, the protagonists can neither look backward to the past (à la Bellamy), nor (as yet) look forward to any future; they can only apprehend what will have been. This paradoxical temporal dimension of future anteriority, a stock device of later science fiction, was relatively unfamiliar to contemporary readers.[74] Through such narratives, they could conceive of a time radically other to their own—one in which their racialized, gendered, and socioeconomic lifeworld will have been completely "over-turned" (following the Greek root of "catastrophe," *kata-strophe*), such that some hidden, underlying truth about urban existence is revealed or "un-veiled" (*apo-kalypsis*). This generative potential of ruination is crucial to Benjamin's methodological approach to the history of modernity, embodied in the figure of the "destructive character"—the person who "reduces" the world "to rubble, not for the sake of the rubble, but for that of the way leading through it."[75] The political implications of this strategy varied greatly, generating both radical and reactionary visions—sometimes within the same text.

An exemplar of future anteriority, and certainly the most influential postapocalyptic romance Munsey published, was George Allan England's *Darkness and Dawn*, first serialized in *Cavalier and Scrap Book* in 1911 as "The Last New Yorkers: A Weird Story of Love and Adventure in the Ruins of a Fallen

Metropolis" (fig. 6.7). This 103-episode epic opens with the hero and heroine, structural engineer Allan Stern and his stenographer Beatrice, awakening from centuries of suspended animation on the forty-eighth floor of the Metropolitan Tower. Climbing up to the observation-platform and looking out over the city, they assume they are the only survivors of some catastrophe that caused "universal ruin."[76]

> Nowhere . . . was any slightest sign of life to be discerned. Nowhere a thread of smoke arose; nowhere a sound echoed upward.
>
> Dead lay the city, between its rivers, whereon now no sail glinted in the sunlight, no tug puffed vehemently with plumy jets of steam, no liner idled at anchor or nosed its slow course out to sea. (19)

One immediately apparent transformation is that the restless flux of metropolitan life, noted by James among other visitors to New York, has been completely stilled. If utopian fiction responded to the problems of noise and overcrowding by imagining technological solutions (from telephonic music to electric walkways), postapocalyptic fiction responded by silencing and depopulating the city altogether—thus fulfilling James's fantasy about how a "truly clear New York" might have "an unsuspected charm" (69–70).[77] The contrast is particularly striking around Madison Square, which had emerged at the turn of the century as the city's public center for theater, concerts, and victory parades, and as a commercial hub of department stores and shopping arcades, including

Fig. 6.7. Inside cover of George Allan England, *Darkness and Dawn* (Boston: Small, Maynard, 1914).

the Metropolitan Life's four-hundred-foot-long marble arcade.[78] Those crowds
are now all cleared away, as the accelerated rhythms of modern social life have
been supplanted by the slower ones of nature: the sprouting of grass and vines
in the crevices of the Metropolitan's marble floor, the flow of a spring through
the square, and the growth of a forest enveloping the entire city, thereby erasing
even Central Park, as it is no longer possible to tell exactly "where it begins or
ends" (20), along with any clues to what caused the downfall. It was a landscape
in which "the future, if any such there may be, must rise from the ashes of a
crumbling past" (65).

When they explore the ruins of the Metropolitan's arcade, Allan and Beatrice are struck not only by the evacuation of its shoppers (or rather, their de-
composition into piles of dust) but also by the transformation of the commodities within it. Various items of luxury merchandise—especially those made of
cloth or other degradable materials—have become so fragile they "crumble at
the merest touch" (34). To witness this state of decay is in part to realize the
sheer depth of time, the lapse of millennia since nature "reasserted [its] dominance" (42–43), and the difficulty of procuring the necessities of life in a dead
metropolis. But the decay of those so-called consumer durables also functions
as a critique of the commodity itself. Reduced to rubble, its mythical spell is
finally dispelled. From the perspective of the future anterior, the supposedly
unique and indispensable appears undifferentiated and superfluous, the supposedly advanced and modish, antique and outmoded. The progress and modernity promised by the commodity is thus belied by the cyclical repetition of
the archaic. In describing the "dust and horrible disarray" of the furrier's shop in
the arcade as making a "sad mockery of the gold-leaf sign still visible on the window: 'Lange, Importer. All the Latest Novelties,'" England transforms the scene
into a melancholy allegory of the hollowness of the commodity form (34).

For Benjamin, such a devaluation of the commodity can in turn perform
the revolutionary task of unveiling and reawakening its hidden truth content,
namely those unfulfilled utopian wishes of an earlier generation. Similarly, England's depiction of the afterlife of commodities blasts them out of their original context of exchange and consumption, redeeming other meanings and uses
fossilized within them.[79] No longer mediated by the abstract value of money,
these objects—or at least the furs and foodstuffs sufficiently preserved in a ce-
dar chest or glass bottles—will have come to "outweigh" all the jewels and diamonds in the arcade's safes (33). Shorn of their aesthetic and exchange value,
their "use" becomes Allan's "first consideration now" (67). Unlike the scavenging capitalists in Winsor McCay's cartoon of the ruins of Wall Street (see fig.
4.6), Allan salvages gold not for its ability to store and mediate value, nor for its
"esthetic effect," but rather for its suitability as noncorrodible serving utensils

(66)—an act of creative reuse that redeems the primordial material qualities of that metal.[80] If Benjamin confronts his readers with the outmoded commodities to be found in the abandoned Parisian arcades of the recent past, England confronts his with those of an abandoned American arcade of the distant future.

This implicit critique of consumer capitalism would not have surprised readers familiar with England's background as an activist and (unsuccessful) gubernatorial candidate for the Socialist Party. During the 1890s, England worked unhappily in a New York insurance firm—an experience that, along with the Armstrong Investigation, may have motivated the choice of the Metropolitan Tower for his ruin. An attack of tuberculosis rescued him from a life of writing policies and led him to write popular novels and socialist tracts instead.[81] England's socialist views were not incidental to his stories; like London and Wells, he repeatedly employed popular fiction as a vehicle for radical politics. In *The Golden Blight* (1916), England showed how easily the dollar, and by extension the Wall Street elite controlling it, might be destroyed by a socialist scientist's discovery of a method by which gold (then the standard unit of value) could be reduced to ash. In other stories, he extrapolated from contemporary commercial practices to project dystopian futures in which the moon becomes a billboard for the projection of advertisements ("A Message from the Moon"), or air a monopolized commodity (*The Air Trust*). The latter was illustrated by the socialist artist John Sloan and dedicated—in defiance of his publishers—to the socialist leader Eugene Debs.[82]

Darkness and Dawn's anticapitalist politics were equally explicit. The urban desolation to which Allan and Beatrice awake constitutes the necessary precondition for their eventual establishment of a socialist utopia in the final episodes. Although they compare themselves with "Macaulay's lone watcher of the world-wreck on London Bridge" (22), they view the ruins not as an opportunity for picturesque aesthetics or melancholic meditations but as practical clues to rebuilding civilization upon more egalitarian foundations. Only when confronted with the daily challenges of survival does Allan question his faith in "strong individualism" and realize the value of "social cooperation"— that "the world had *been* the world merely because of the interrelations, the interdependencies of human beings in vast numbers." It is this capacity of ruination to manifest what Simmel called the "web of society" that enables Allan to "glimpse . . . the vanished social problems that had enmeshed civilization, in their true light," and thereby project an alternative future (73–74).[83] Socioeconomic analyses, of course, are subordinated to narrative developments. England is concerned less with outlining Allan's socialist vision of a cooperative civilization than with narrating the couple's racial struggle against the "Horde"—the monstrous descendents of centuries of miscegenation among the African American, Native American, and ape populations that had also survived in the ruins of New York (108)—and their subsequent transcontinental search for a community of white survivors to fulfill that vision. Nevertheless, an account of the forging of a utopian community out of the literal ruins of capitalism attracted the attention of at least one radical critic. Felix Grendon, book reviewer for the socialist *New Review*, commended this "revolutionary allegory" for its "political convictions."[84]

England articulated his critique of capitalism, however, primarily through his engineer's masculine voice. Women's rights, prominent in his political writings, are largely absent from his postapocalyptic fiction.[85] While Allan is out foraging among the commercial ruins of the fallen metropolis, Beatrice tends to remain in the tower, dedicating herself—"like the true woman she was"—to "making a real home out of the barren desolation" (66). She thus performs those indoor chores of garment making, cooking, and cleaning that defined domestic womanhood. Despite their grave situation, Allan is confident she will be delighted by "housekeeping treasures" he brings back, such as "jars of edibles," "coffee and salt," "cups and plates and a still serviceable lamp" (61–62). "Evidently," complained Grendon in his review, "feminism is a back number in 2920."[86]

England was admittedly attempting to imagine a future for American women more liberating than white-collar clerical labor. As a stenographer prior to the apocalypse, Beatrice would have gained a degree of economic, social, and sexual freedom. Metropolitan Life pioneered the recruiting of lower-middle-class, native-born, unmarried women. Outnumbering the company's male employees by 1900, these file clerks, telephone operators, and stenographers, collectively known as the Metropolitan Belles, earned wages that conferred, if not complete independence, at least the immediate pleasures of patronizing department stores, theaters, and amusement parks.[87] Cut free from the "nexus of . . . society" by the ensuing catastrophe (65), however, Beatrice undergoes a more profound transformation.

> The girl was different. . . . Was this strong woman, eager-eyed and brave, the quiet, low-voiced stenographer he remembered, busy only with her machine, her file-boxes, and her carbon-copies? Stern dared not realize the transmutation. He ventured hardly fringe it in his thoughts. (17)[88]

England presents Beatrice as liberated, able to realize character traits and inner resourcefulness suppressed by twentieth-century office work.

Along with her stenographic paraphernalia, however, Beatrice also abandons any feminist notions. Just as Allan relies on her for domestic sustenance, so does she need "his protection as never since the world began had woman needed man." Thus, "all consciousness of their former relationship—employer and employed" has entirely "vanished" (17), as they revert to a gendered division of labor. There is also a regression to Victorian morals in their deferral of passion until the seventy-sixth episode, when they discover a phonograph of a marriage ceremony preserved in the vaults of a ruined cathedral on the Hudson (484–85) (fig. 6.8). And in the final episodes, she is relieved to satisfy his wish for a male offspring, thereby fulfilling her reproductive obligations. Ultimately, the socialist reviewer Grendon excused these "curiously atavistic sentiments on sex relationships" as an aberration from England's otherwise commendable storytelling skills and "political convictions."[89] But they are in fact intimately connected, triangulated through the third category of race. Only by revitalizing and revealing their "true" gender traits will they vanquish the racialized Horde besieging the tower. Overturning the gains of twentieth-century feminists is thus the first step toward escaping from New York (fig. 6.9), discovering (in a canyon gouged out of the spot where Chicago once stood) a barbarian nation of Anglo-Saxons known as the Merucaans, and ultimately founding a white socialist utopia.[90]

The utopian transcendence of capitalist modernity in postapocalyptic romances did not always involve sexual and racial repression. At least one author reappropriated this subgenre to transcend racial, class, and gender hierarchies simultaneously. In W. E. B. Du Bois's contemporaneous short story "The Comet," the cosmic catastrophe that struck New York—indiscriminately exterminating blue- and white-collar workers, black and white, male and female—revealed not the latent racial traits of its two survivors but the arbitrariness of the very notion of racial difference.[91] As a black messenger boy for a Wall Street bank, Jim had hitherto been subjected to a regime of exploitation and exclusion. But as the only man to apparently survive the earth's collision with the comet's tail, on account of his assignment to the bank's underground vaults, he finds himself in possession of the entire metropolis, free to wander up Fifth Avenue and enter the "gorgeous, ghost-haunted halls" of a "famous hostelry" that "yesterday . . . would not have served me" (258). When he encounters the only other apparent survivor, Julia, the privileged white daughter of a Metropolitan Life executive, racial (and class) assumptions are gradually cast aside. She does not even notice "he was a Negro," nor does he think "of her as white" (259). Lacking Allan and Beatrice's sexual patience, Jim and Julia immediately ascend to the Metropolitan Life's roof, a site associated in the 1910s with illicit promiscuity among employees.[92] Standing up there in the dreamy twilight, she could no longer consider him

Fig. 6.8. "Giving the torch to Beatrice, Allan set to work. In his powerful hands the hunting-knife laid back the metal of the mysterious leaden chest." Illustration by P. J. Monahan, from George Allan England, *Darkness and Dawn* (Boston: Small, Maynard, 1914), frontispiece. Opening a time capsule in the ruins of a concrete cathedral.

Fig. 6.9. "At any moment now, one of the grey devils might hurl itself at their throats." Allan and Beatrice in Madison Park, hunted by a pack of wolves. The ruin of the Metropolitan Tower is in the background. Illustration from George Allan England, *Darkness and Dawn* (Boston: Small, Maynard, 1914), facing p. 204.

"a thing apart, a creature below, a strange outcast of another clime and blood," but instead "saw him glorified . . . her Brother Humanity incarnate, Son of God and great All-Father of the race to be" (267, 269)—while she herself has become "primal woman; mighty mother of all men to come and Bride of Life" (269). Before they can consummate their brief postapocalyptic courtship, however, they are interrupted by the arrival of rescuers from outside the city, including Julia's father and suitor, an incipient lynch mob, and Jim's wife and dead child. The apocalypse turns out to have been confined to New York, and the world without racial and class distinctions a chimerical vision. The true "catastrophe," in Benjamin's words, is the continuation of the "status quo" (*Arcades*, 473 [N9a,1]).

Published in 1920 as *Darkwater*'s final chapter, "The Comet" resonates with the larger themes in that collection of fiction, poetry, and nonfiction. Jim's memory of the intricate network of racial discrimination barring him from certain hotels and restaurants dramatizes Du Bois's sociological observation in the preceding chapter regarding the "Veil"—"tenuous, intangible," yet real—that separates Harlem, the "dark city of fifty thousand," from the rest of the metropolis (245–46). Similarly, Jim's commandeering of a Ford to drive along Central Park in search of survivors calls to mind Du Bois's earlier recollection of a white man in that park who was visibly enraged by the mere sight of "black folk [riding] by in a motor car" (33). Even the apocalyptic phrases with which Jim and Julia embrace each other echo the book's messianic references to a "Black Christ," a coming millennium of human "brotherhood," and the role of "primal woman" in ushering it in. These various black messiahs of *Darkwater* inevitably find themselves denied, rejected, or even lynched.[93] Yet ultimately Du Bois's purpose is less to outline some postmillennial vision of racial transcendence than to expose the injustices of the present. "The Comet" thus foregrounds Jim and Julia's realization that seemingly fixed racial distinctions could instantly disappear—that humanity's survival might require one to commit even that most forbidden act, interracial sex.

The choice of the Metropolitan Tower as the site of this short-lived yet powerful scene of secular "Revelation" is similarly overdetermined. As a socialist, Du Bois may have intended it to stand in for the larger economic order of urbanized capitalism, which perpetuates distinctions between "black and white," as between "rich and poor" (121). More specifically, he might be targeting Metropolitan Life for its de facto discrimination against African American customers, whom it restricted to substandard policies.[94] But Du Bois's preceding chapter also acknowledges his awe for the sublime beauty of the Manhattan skyline, and in particular the "vast grace of that Cathedral of the Purchased and Purchasing Poor, topping the world and pointing higher" (243–44).[95] During Jim and Julia's union, the tower exudes an almost mystical and metaphysical power. No longer a place of business, it becomes a divine vessel through which they channel the cosmic forces impelling them toward their apparent postracial destiny. Whatever its precise motivation, Du Bois's selection of the Metropolitan Tower for his scene of racial transcendence suggests an awareness, perhaps even a deliberate inversion, of the racial politics of the dominant science fiction authors of the Munsey era.[96] If it takes a deluge to make Serviss's protagonists realize a skyscraper's monumental solidity, and a planetary catastrophe for England's to recognize their innate gender and racial traits, a comet is needed to awaken Du Bois's white protagonist to the arbitrariness of race. Nothing less than a terrestrial collision, Du Bois ironically implies, would suffice to strip away—even temporarily—the veil of racial, as well as economic and sexual, domination enshrouding the modern metropolis.

Temporal Inversions

Writing in the future anterior allowed authors to engage not only with social relations of gender, class, and (occasionally) race, but also with temporality itself. Whereas utopian novels magically overcame contemporary contradictions by transporting readers into timeless cities of the future, and cataclysmic novels resolved them in lurid scenes of urban destruction, these scientific romances conceived a more complex temporal outcome. In the postapocalypse, time would not culminate in perfection or destruction (both implying linear trajectories), but rather unravel in multiple directions, producing that unsettling entanglement of futurity and antiquity I am calling *future anteriority*. Such scenarios resonated with the temporal experiences of the contemporary metropolis. Under the pressure of an accelerating pace of life and an intensified rate of demolition and construction, time appeared not to be collapsing into a depthless present—that incessant newness felt by James or that sense of flattened temporality evoked by more recent critics—but to be running simultaneously forward and backward, as if the city was becoming at once modern and archaic, an object of both anticipation and retrospection.[97]

Emblematic of time's transfiguration in the postapocalypse is the fate of the Metropolitan Tower's clock. When the tower opened, the company's brochures advertised its advanced chronometric system as the very epitome of modern time. Wired to slave gongs, clocks, and bells, the master clock divided the workday into abstract units of time, orchestrated the circulation of male and female employees throughout the building, and thus elevated "time-discipline" to new levels of efficiency. At the same time, this modern phenomenon of standardized and segmented time was projected outward onto the neighborhood via the electric clock on its exterior, the "largest four-dial tower clock in the world"; and to the entire city via the chimes of a seven-thousand-pound bell and the flashlights of a powerful electric lantern, all automatically coordinated with "exact synchronism."[98] From the city's "prison[s]" to the "open sea," one aspiring poet wrote, this "Clock in the Air" was an inescapable presence in New Yorkers' lives. It was, another reported, "almost synonymous with time itself." Still others referred to "Metropolitan time" as one would "railroad time," "daylight savings time," or "Western Union time."[99] Thus, in addition to telling the time, it signaled the modernization of time as such: the replacement of the varied and natural rhythms of the sun and moon by the monotonous and artificial rhythms of machines.[100] In England's postapocalypse, however, time does not simply return to its natural state. For one thing, circadian time has been irrevocably warped, as the very force of the catastrophe had reduced the length of the day by at least half an hour (188); and on the other hand, clock-time persists, both in Allan's attempted calculations and in the narrator's repeated references to the passage of minutes and hours (48, 52, passim). As if under the strain of these contradictory modes of temporality, one of the "half-ton hands" of the Metropolitan clock becomes dislodged from the tower and plummets into the street below, carving out a "vast, gaping cañon of blackness" (85).

It was not only in *Darkness and Dawn* that the Metropolitan's clock expressed a sense that time was getting out of hand. New York's daily newspapers also circulated rumors of its cataclysmic effects. According to one, pedestrians at street level were almost killed by masonry falling from the clock face. Others reported collisions in the street or bouts of amnesia, as distracted locals looked up to admire the newly installed clock.[101] On one occasion, its hands became stuck, throwing time briefly "out of joint" for the "hundreds" of New Yorkers who used it to regulate their timepieces. That stoppage was caused by a lack of lubricating oil, but in Stewart Edward White's science fiction novel *The Sign at Six* (1912), the freezing of the Metropolitan clock at 6:00 p.m. was among the first indications that a mysterious villain, known only as Monsieur X, had paralyzed the city's "entire electrical apparatus."[102]

The famous clock was involved in an even stranger catastrophe in Murray Leinster's "The Runaway Skyscraper," published in Munsey's *Argosy* in 1919. Two Metropolitan Life employees, again an engineer and his stenographer, Arthur and Estelle, realize something is amiss when "the clock on the Metropolitan Tower began to run backward. It was not a graceful proceeding. The hands had been moving onward in their customary deliberate fashion, slowly and thoughtfully, but suddenly the people in the offices near the clock's face heard an ominous creaking and groaning. There was a slight hardly discernible shiver through the tower, and then something gave with a crash. The big hands on the clock began to move backward."[103] As this rewinding of time gathers pace, Arthur, Estelle, and the other employees begin to witness the city's rapid unbuilding. Crowds recede, electric lights expire, and then—just like "old flickering motion-pictures"—the cityscape is progressively dismantled, "story by story," layer by layer, until the tower is surrounded by a forest populated by pre-Columbian Native Americans (50, 53, 58) (fig. 6.10). In response to this temporal disturbance—attributed to a flaw in the bedrock causing the skyscraper to "sink, not downward, but [backward] into the Fourth Dimension"—its occupants set about dismantling class relations, too (61). Corporate hierarchies are jettisoned as blue-collar workers emerge as the most competent leaders. With the aid of the tower's abundant resources, they survive and eventually return to the present (89–91). Leinster's time-travel narrative, like *Scientific American*'s spatial displacement of the tower onto a midwestern prairie, thus played upon the company's claim to have erected "a building that contains a city in itself."[104] England also used that phrase, "city in itself," in *Darkness and Dawn* (28), as did James in his account of skyscrapers in the *American Scene* (64).

In comparing the city's unbuilding to "old flickering motion-pictures" (53), Leinster alluded to the special temporal effects conjured by the cinematographic technique of time-lapse. Urban themes such as skyscraper construction challenged early actuality filmmakers to experiment with the speed and direction of film. By inserting a predetermined time interval between frames, they could exaggerate the speed with which a crew constructed a building. A by-product of this cinematic trick of accelerating time was an exacerbation of the already jerky (or flickering) movements of traffic and pedestrians entering the frame. In 1901 American Mutoscope and Biograph Company applied the time-lapse technique to a scene not of construction but of demolition. The razing of the Star Theatre on Broadway and 13th Street, which took approximately thirty days, was condensed into a two-minute film that was widely exhibited that year, creating the effect of a building "struck by a tornado of supernatural strength" (fig. 6.11). Audiences, moreover, did not have to wait for the dust to settle, and construction crews to arrive, to witness the spectacle of rebuilding. Another technique, performed by projectionists, was to reverse the direction of the film, transforming scenes of destruction into anticipations of (re)construction—or vice versa. Such playful exaggerations and inversions of normal temporal processes, popularized by the Lumière brothers' 1896 film *Démolition d'un mur*, fascinated spectators in American nickelodeons.[105] Furthermore, the two techniques were often combined. The catalog issued by American Mutoscope and Biograph recommended that exhibitors of its time-lapse film reverse the direction once they reached the end, hence the title

Fig. 6.10. Illustration from Murray Leinster, "The Runaway Skyscraper" (1919), reprinted in *Amazing Stories* 1, no. 3 (1926): 250. Foundation Archive of Science Fiction, University of Liverpool, England.

Demolishing and Building Up the Star Theatre. Some exhibitors may well have changed the order, showing the rebuilding of the Star Theatre first and ending with the building in fragments.[106]

It is this combination of time-lapse and reverse motion that Leinster transposes into the realm of science fiction, thereby creating a landscape of deconstructed buildings, one of which briefly appears as a ruined skeleton (53). But an additional layer of temporal complexity arises from the fact that, while the remainder of the city rapidly "disintegrate[s]" (53), the Metropolitan Tower remains intact, and the actions of its occupants continue to take place in real time. Although some science fiction critics have read this as an oversight on Leinster's part, this simultaneous bidirectionality of time is fully consistent

Fig. 6.11. Clockwise from top left: Still frames from *Demolishing and Building Up the Star Theatre* (Frederick S. Armitage, 1901), American Mutoscope & Biograph Company. Paper Print Collection, Library of Congress. Courtesy Biograph Company.

with the notion of future anteriority. Time can appear—in the cinema and in the city at large—to run forward and backward simultaneously, in accordance with the temporal paradox of the future anterior.[107] Such visions offered audiences and readers the enchantment of seeing one's city in a new and unfamiliar light, of perceiving in a few instants urban processes usually protracted over days or weeks. It was the possibility of such a condensation of time that led Benjamin to conceive of an "exciting film" that might be made from the changing map of Paris, revealing (as the flaneur does) the "unfolding of its various aspects in temporal succession," and "compress[ing] . . . a centuries-long movement of streets, boulevards, arcades, and squares into the space of half an hour" (*Arcades*, 83 [C1,9]). Whether in film or fiction, the future anterior presented an alternative way of experiencing and articulating the temporal contradictions of the built environment.

The Totemic Ruin

This unstable temporal quality is above all a feature of the ruin itself. Insofar as they represent a past that has been persisting into the present, ruins can be articulated neither in the perfect (the tense of completion) nor in the present (that of synchronicity) but only through the present perfect continuous (that of past processes that remain ongoing within the present). But the various future ruins of arcades, subways, and skyscrapers give this temporal tension an additional twist. To be projected forward to a time in which a recently completed structure will have decayed is to speak of ruin in the future perfect—or rather, the future perfect *continuous*, as it will *still* be decaying even then.[108] In *Darkness and Dawn*, the Metropolitan Tower continues to be eroded by the elements and overtaken by foliage, and is further destabilized by Allan's home-made "pulverite" bombs (195). Like Benjamin's "angel of history," the tower moves into the future backward, surveying only the "pile of debris" of the past wrought by the catastrophe known as "progress."[109]

If an aura of perishability and ephemerality is common to all ruins, here it arises not from the natural cycles of life (as in Baroque and Enlightenment articulations of the ruin) but from the artificial cycles of capitalist obsolescence. Allan reads the feeble remains of the Metropolitan Tower and other modern structures, such as Grand Central and Penn Station (built 1903 and 1910), the subway system (1904), and the Queensboro Bridge (1909), as fitting rebukes not only to the pride of American engineers (himself presumably excluded) but also to the greed of the financiers who backed them.

> "That's their engineering," gibed he, as the little boat sailed under [the ruins of the Queensboro] . . . "The old Roman bridges are good for practically eternity, but these jerry steel things, run up for profits, go to pieces in a mere thousand years! Well, the steel magnates are gone now, and their profits with them. But this junk remains as a lesson and a warning, Beta; the race to come must build better than this, and sounder, every way!" (194)

Like the crumbling commodities in the arcade, but on an even greater scale, New York's decaying architectural structures—described by Allan, as by Henry James, as having been reduced to the status of mere commodities—make a mockery of modernity's claim to novelty.

For all their fragility and ephemerality, however, these structures also express that other sense of the ruin, namely endurance. The "brute, downward-dragging, corroding, crumbling power" of *Natur*, in Simmel's terms, is still counterbalanced by the "striving upward" of *Geist*.[110] Indeed, only if "this junk remains" can it serve as a "lesson and a warning" (194). As *Scientific American* discerned in the ruins of the Gillender Building, Allan discovers that the condition of Metropolitan's "steel frame isn't too bad" (16), and is gratified to find one of his own skyscrapers well preserved (60). From the panoramic perspective of the Metropolitan's observation platform, the steel cages of ancient skyscrapers (the Park Row, the Singer, the Woolworth) were the sole discernible objects, the only holdouts still "thrusting up from the desolation" of foliage and detritus. By contrast, "almost all" of the residential buildings uptown had "crumbled in upon themselves" (20–21). The future anterior thus marks an additional temporal inversion: that of the anticipated life spans of buildings. Skyscrapers, believed by James and other critics to be more provisional than the brownstone houses and churches they were replacing, will have proved more enduring. Previously prevented from growing old, they will now have accrued that patina of age and sense of pastness for which James longed. And if the steel, concrete, and glass materials of such modern structures offended traditional connoisseurs of ruin because of their presumed inability to age gracefully and register the picturesque effects of time, it is precisely the durability of those materials that will have allowed them to remain intact; those of wood, brick, and stone have been "completely" or "practically" obliterated (60). Thus, in the same breath as lamenting the transience of modern structures, Allan delights in their persistence: "even in their overthrow, how wonderful are the works of man!" (21).

As one of the few extant monuments of capitalist modernity, the Metropolitan Tower will have become a vital link to that now ancient past. In addition to preserving Allan and Beatrice from the poisonous gases that extinguished almost all other lives, it will successfully have preserved the secrets and relics of the civilization that created it, thus serving as both time machine and time capsule. But the recovery of the forgotten meanings secreted within any defunct structure, Benjamin reminds us, requires careful excavation and interpretation. While Allan and Beatrice prove skilful at decoding them, characters in postapocalyptic narratives sometimes lack the archaeological or hermeneutic skills needed to penetrate the layers of meaning or bridge the chasm of time. Like the future historians of Ambrose's and Twain's satires, the primitive gangs inhabiting postapocalyptic New York in Van Tassel Sutphen's *The Doomsman* (1906) misconstrue its ruins, worshipping an abandoned electrical plant near Madison Square as a religious shrine.[111]

Nevertheless, the task of discerning a ruin's hidden or recalcitrant meanings, of reconstructing the totality of a culture from its surviving fragments, is aided by certain textual clues. The rural hero who explores Manhattan in *The Doomsman* discovers, in the ruins of what appears to be the New York

Public Library, some "serried shelves of books . . . and dusty tomes" containing the "secrets of the mighty past."[112] In *Darkness and Dawn*, the recovery of
an actual time capsule is what enables Allan and Beatrice to impart the lost
arts of civilization to the barbarian Merucaans. Through this fictional time
capsule, England resolves many of those practical difficulties its early advocates
encountered. The problem of how to perpetuate knowledge of the capsule's
very existence had been circumvented by disseminating golden cylinders containing a parchment roll detailing its date and exact location (444–45); and
the problem of archival decay by depositing steel records and a phonograph
(rather than perishable paper) within a hermetically sealed lead chest, placed
in turn in the crypt beneath a concrete neo-Gothic cathedral known to be
"the most massive piece of architecture this side of the pyramids" (480, 478,
447; see fig. 6.8). Like the skyscrapers themselves, such buried objects are presented as archaeological curiosities harboring some lost truth about American
urban culture.

The oracular and totemic powers bestowed upon office buildings in
Darkness and Dawn and the *Doomsman* indicate how utterly they have transcended their profane origins as commercial stopgaps erected for short-term
rents and liable to be demolished and replaced in the interests of accelerating
the turnover of capital. The very obscurity of those commercial origins enables
them to be reappropriated as objects of worship by the various postapocalyptic
tribes and hordes of New York. Just as an outmoded commodity can undergo a
transvaluation, as the hollowing-out of its exchange value and use value allows
it to gather in other uses, meanings, and affects, so too can an outmoded skyscraper come to acquire an aura of mystery and sanctity. In fact, a skyscraper's
receptiveness to such an aura is even greater than a commodity's insofar as it
never entirely gave up its claim to being treated as an object of architecture
rather than simply engineering, an aesthetic ornament rather than a financial
investment. Now, through ruination, the skyscraper will have transcended that
debate altogether and become a pure monument.

But if a ruined skyscraper can become a fragile yet lasting monument, it
will be a monument to modernity's eternal transitoriness. In other words,
the enduring truth of modern urbanism that the ruin will apocalypti-
cally unveil is paradoxically its utter failure to endure. Writing in *Scribner's*
in 1909, the leading architectural critic Montgomery Schuyler invoked
Ruskin—the very writer who had denounced modern structures for employ-
ing materials that do not decay properly—in an attempt to explain how, if
the era of corporate capitalism were to come to an end, the office buildings
it had produced would stand as testimony to it. Future historians might find
economic meaning in those surviving structures, as contemporary Ruski-

nians find spiritual meaning in the ruined Gothic cathedrals of the thirteenth century.

> These "skeletons" of our building, after the veneer of masonry had fallen from them, and they were left to assert themselves in their original crudity and starkness, before returning altogether to oxide of iron, might still be, in the majestic Ruskinian phrase, "the only witnesses that remained to us of the faith and fear of nations," the faith in the dollar toward which they so plainly aspired, the fear of "the hell of not making money."[113]

Even Lincoln Steffens conceded that the new office building "will remain, bearing in its form and plan the traces of its uses" even after its owners have gone— that it "may be finally the only remnan[t] of the other creations of modern business enterprise, the only legible chapter of the common tale" (38). While speculating about the future, Schuyler and Steffens, along with several science fiction authors, articulated a sense that skyscrapers, under the doctrine of the scrap heap, were already becoming monuments of provisionality in the present. In a description of the Parisian arcades transcribed by Benjamin, the surrealist Louis Aragon wrote: "It is only today, when the pickaxe menaces them, that they have at last become the true sanctuaries of a cult of the ephemeral" (*Arcades*, 87 [C2a,9]).

Toward the Posthuman Ruin

In April 1918, *Life*'s editor revisited those "five large paintings by Thomas Cole" hanging in the New-York Historical Society. As dispatches from the Western Front conveyed the devastation of towns and regions in Europe, *Life* departed from its usual treatment of ruins as vehicles of irreverent satire. In this new context, ruins—such as those in Cole's *The Course of Empire*—raised a more serious question about the capacity of "our civilization" to recover from such an ordeal.[1] In fact, the ruinscapes that American statesmen (including Woodrow Wilson) encountered in June 1919, when the battlefields were officially opened to visitors, were unlike any in nineteenth-century paintings. French cities like Reims and Ypres had lost prominent landmarks and were strewn with rubble, shell holes, and barbed wire, while vast swaths of countryside had become barren and depopulated. The land itself appeared ruined, scarred by artillery bombardments and trench systems, and showing few signs of any return to agriculture. In the desolate silence of the war's aftermath, one officer commented, these wastelands were "almost more lugubrious than when the scream of shells filled the air."[2]

The Great War signaled the beginning of a larger reconfiguration of the ruin that has continued to this day. Aesthetic or sentimental responses, such as those still evident after the San Francisco earthquake, would be considered ill suited to the severe devastation wrought by the total wars of the twentieth century. The ruins left behind by heavy artillery or by the air raids of subsequent wars prompted a break with the convention of the seated figure in the foreground calmly contemplating the scene and imbibing its philosophical meanings — as in the iconographic tradition cultivated by Hubert Robert, inherited by John Vanderlyn and Cole, and adapted by *Life* cartoonists and California pictorialists. Instead, they were captured in abstracted aerial photographs and in expressionist or surrealist canvases that accentuated the inhumanity of the landscape.[3] Furthermore, the Cold War threat of nuclear annihilation would prompt Americans — at least those not lulled into a false sense of security by fallout shelter programs — to imagine whole cities of blasted, irradiated ruins, indeed an entire world reduced to "one boundless Hiroshima" through Mutually Assured Destruction. Like the official photographs of Hiroshima's ruins (which, under U.S. government censorship, rarely included dead or wounded bodies), such visions of depopulated landscapes (in the words of one historian) departed from "earlier illustrations of cataclysm going back to medieval times [that] had put human victims in the foreground."[4] Even if any were to survive a nuclear apocalypse, they would be so physically and psychologically crippled that they would hardly resemble the robust, intrepid protagonists of *Darkness and Dawn*.[5] Nor was it certain that a future historian would document the follies and achievements of the departed civilization.

The abandonment of industrial infrastructure and the deterioration of urban neighborhoods in the postwar years have similarly complicated earlier attitudes toward ruins, such as the belief that future archaeologists and travelers to America would discover relics surpassing those of the Old World in grandeur. The rusted-out and boarded-up factories on the margins of cities and the crumbling housing stock of inner-city areas — products of, among other things, the withdrawal of capital, industries, and white and middle-class residents, and the destructiveness of highway construction, landlord arsons, and "race riots" — have even been compared to the grotesque ruins of modern wars.[6] Unlike the peaceful ruins in Poussin's landscapes, French theorist Antoine Picon writes, postindustrial ruinscapes are "disturbing" and "anxiety-" producing — an effect he attributes to their nondegradability; whereas traditional ruins have "surrendered themselves progressively to nature," contemporary ones are merely "relegated to obsolescence . . . like the living dead who endlessly haunt the landscape."[7] Not only are these ruins insusceptible to natural decay, they also appear resistant to economic recuperation. While some blighted areas have been gentrified, most struggle to attract new industries and investments. Boosters and activists calling for the regeneration of Newark, Detroit, or post-Katrina New Orleans, thus lack the confidence that enabled earlier generations of Americans to regard Cairo's ruins as a minor, temporary setback, or San Francisco's as harbingers of a new and better city. Even when sufficient funds are raised for the demolition of these ruins, it is rarely a prelude to new construction. Instead, once-thriving neighborhoods are returning to empty, grassy lots.

Thus, while occasionally featuring in news reports, policy debates, and academic discourses, postindustrial and urban ruins have only rarely been treated as aesthetic objects. Photographers who have recently began to tackle them—most prominently Camillo José Vergara—remain careful to acknowledge the misery of the homeless, insane, elderly, and addicted who reside there, to emphasize the unimpeachable motive of raising public awareness, and to eschew the aestheticizing styles of earlier photographers of ruin (such as Stellman).[8] Despite his repeated disclaimers and his straightforward, documentary style, several critics harbor certain misgivings about Vergara's photographic project. Some complain that his almost exclusive focus on decaying buildings displaces the human presence from these landscapes; the few African Americans in his photographs, writes one, are relegated to the background as "passive metonyms of . . . the underclass."[9] Others charge him with eliding historical responsibility, specifically that of financial and governmental institutions in causing and perpetuating these ruins.[10] Beneath these critiques lies a concern that Vergara's approach—which he acknowledges is modeled on the *vedute* of Robert, Panini, Claude, and van Ruisdael, and animated by his predilection for themes of "failure, decay, and death"—may be too "romantic and aesthetic" for such troubling subject matter.[11] Most controversial, though, was Vergara's proposal to enshrine twelve square blocks of Detroit's vacant, pre-Depression skyscrapers as a "grand national historic park of play and wonder, an urban Monument Valley," recolonized by midwestern prairie and wild animals. Although genuinely conceived as a celebration of the city's golden age of architecture and ambition, the proposal rankled not only academic critics but also local boosters concerned that such reminders of past failures would jeopardize current revitalization plans, preservationists wishing to restore and rehabilitate them as mixed-use structures, and even homeless men preferring to see them turned into shelters.[12] Yet, by the very contentiousness of his proposal, Vergara has succeeded in drawing attention to Detroit's ruins, stimulating debate about their origins and their future.

Similar objections were recently raised to the preservation and aestheticization of a more prominent ruin: that of the World Trade Center, or at least the portion of the South Tower's western facade that remained standing after the attacks. The vitriolic response of the *New Republic*'s literary editor to the *New York Times* architectural critic's passing allusion to Piranesi (among others) reveals the extent to which this ruin was viewed by many as qualitatively different from any others in history. The former considered any comparison with earlier ruins infelicitous on several grounds: the presence of bodies and emergency crews at Ground Zero ruled out the peaceful "contemplation" of "ennobling idea[s]" or the "refining sensation of beauty"; the trauma of the event demanded a direct gaze, unmediated by art-historical paradigms of picturesque decay; and the sense that the suffering was shared, that these were the "ruins of us" all, precluded the "pleasurable encounter" afforded by the ruins of *other* people or *other* times (as those of Chinatown or Nob Hill did for non-Asian or lower-class San Franciscans).[13] Many New Yorkers refused to call it a ruin at all, preferring the term "Wailing walls," or simply, "The Walls."[14] In the face of such disavowals of the historical resonances of that protruding fragment of neo-Gothic tracery (along with the building's unpopularity with architectural and urban critics from its inception), proposals to preserve it in situ proved unsuccessful. The ceremonial removal of the final steel column on May 30, 2002, was celebrated as physical proof of psychic recovery. Only by erasing those "hellish shards of steel," affirmed the *Times*, could the city and nation "deal with the tragedy."[15]

The hasty removal of the facade betrays a growing apprehension that such ruins herald a relative decline in America's imperial and economic hegemony. The subsequent curtailments of civil liberties and the military setbacks in Iraq and Afghanistan have given rise to a new outpouring of books prognosticating the *Fall of the American Empire* and *The Last Days of the American Republic*.[16] And the metastasization of debt and expansion of the financial sector have prompted similar comparisons with earlier empires.[17] As the mortgage crisis deepened, ruins began to materialize even in middle-class neighborhoods across the nation in the form of foreclosed and vacated houses. In many suburbs, entire subdivisions fell to ruin even before they were completed. Once developers, speculators, and loan brokers left one California town, the wooden frames of would-be luxury houses were left "bleaching in the sun and sand," while unfinished sidewalks leading "nowhere" sprouted weeds.[18] Such "ruins in reverse" recall the remains of earlier speculative fevers, such as the "rot[ting]" remains of Cairo's "half built houses." But if the bursting of the Jacksonian real estate bubble reverberated across the Atlantic, ruining British investors, the implosion of the subprime bubble, in this new era of globalized finance and mortgage securitization, precipitated financial turmoil across the entire globe.

Narratives of imperial decline have been accompanied by jeremiads about the declining memorial value of American architecture. Even before the financial meltdown, there were growing doubts about the capacity of celebrated works of architecture to endure as worthy memorials. On the eve of the millennium, the distinguished architectural historian Vincent Scully wondered what would remain of our "sturdiest creations" after another thousand years. While echoing the 1925 *New York Times* inquiry with which this book began, Scully's conclusions were rather more pessimistic. With the ascendancy of an "aesthetic of impermanence," twentieth-century architects renounced the age-old impulse to "buil[d] for endurance." Skyscrapers composed of little more than glass and steel, and "light-frame structures clad with plastics and other things that blow away," would fail to survive a century, let alone a millennium. This disregard for longevity has become more pronounced among recent architects like Frank Gehry, whose lightweight titanium fabrications are even more "ephemeral." The only structures that come close to the solidity and ambition of the Roman Pantheon, Scully fears, are unflattering ones, such as the "super max" prisons that are proliferating across the country, or the highways that have "torn our cities apart" and will "someday . . . be recognized as ghosts of a vast human obsession."[19]

But if contemporary architecture might not outlive us, the impact of industrial-capitalist civilization upon the environment certainly will. The recrudescence of nature, long considered fundamental to the aesthetic and philosophical pleasure of the ruin, can no longer be presumed. Even if all humans were suddenly to disappear, the journalist Alan Weisman contends in *The World without Us* (2007), many of our pernicious traces will leave their mark for millennia. Invasive, imported species such as the Chinese ailanthus tree would recolonize Manhattan's bridges, streets, and buildings more rapidly than native ones; nonbiodegradable plastic bottles, bags, and other "disposables" would continue to litter estuaries and landfills; petrochemical plants and nuclear-waste storage facilities would remain ticking time bombs; and carbon dioxide levels would not return to "prehuman levels" for a hundred thousand years.[20]

Such a scenario is presented in Alexis Rockman's painting *Manifest Destiny* (2004). Commissioned to adorn the lobby of the Brooklyn Museum of Art, this large mural depicts Brooklyn 3,000 years in the future, after the ice caps have melted, inundating all but the supports of the Brooklyn Bridge and the distant spire of the Empire State Building. While informed by architects, climatologists, and biologists, and indebted to pulp science fiction illustrators — images of that bridge in ruins date back at least to *The Last American* and *Life* magazine, and of an underwater New York to *Second Deluge* — the mural also harks back to the Hudson River School. Critical of the way those paintings legitimated beliefs in America's "manifest destiny" to exploit the continent's natural resources, Rockman nevertheless found inspiration in Cole's dissenting visions, especially *Desolation*. But unlike the heron nesting on top of Cole's solitary column, the animals that inherit Rockman's ruins do not invite reassuring sentiments about the reconciliation of nature with culture, of the kind Simmel articulated. Instead, nature itself is ruined. The water retains the deep orange glow of pollution, the creatures exhibit mutations or genetic modifications, and native species have been replaced by palm trees and tropical fish. The only native New Yorker to survive the environmental apocalypse is the humble cockroach, delicately perched on a floating oil barrel.[21]

Introduction

1. "When History Has Forgotten New York," *New York Times*, May 31, 1925, Sunday Magazine, 12.

2. On the role that discourses of urban decay have played in shaping views and policies toward American cities in the twentieth century, see Robert A. Beauregard, *Voices of Decline: The Postwar Fate of United States Cities* (Cambridge, MA, and Oxford, UK: Blackwell, 1993). For a critique of Camillo Vergara's photographs of urban ruins, see Liam Kennedy, *Race and Urban Space in American Culture* (London and New York: Routledge, 2000), 105–15. On postwar visions of destruction, see Max Page, *The City's End: Two Centuries of Fantasies, Fears, and Premonitions of New York's Destruction* (New Haven, CT: Yale University Press, 2008), 101–232.

3. Georg Simmel, "The Ruin" (1911), in *Essays on Sociology, Philosophy, and Aesthetics*, ed. Kurt H. Wolff (New York: Harper and Row, 1965), 260, 263, 266; further references cited in the text.

4. Walter Benjamin, *The Origin of German Tragic Drama*, trans. John Osborne (completed 1925, first published 1963; London and New York: Verso, 1998), 177–82; Benjamin, *The Arcades Project*, trans. Howard Eiland and Kevin McLaughlin (Cambridge, MA: Belknap Press of Harvard University Press, 2002); Ernst Bloch, "Aura of Antique Furniture, Magic of Ruins, Museum," in *The Principle of Hope*, trans. Neville Plaice, Stephen Plaice, and Paul Knight (1959; Oxford: Blackwell, 1986), 1:384–85. See also Siegfried Kracauer, "Farewell to the Linden Arcade" (1930), in Kracauer, *The Mass Ornament: Weimar Essays*, trans. and ed. Thomas Y. Levin (Cambridge, MA: Harvard University Press, 1995), 337–42. In "George Simmel" (1920–21), Kracauer refers to his mentor's essay on the ruin (along with his essay on the handle of a jug, and, I would add, that on "The Bridge and the Door") as attempts to explain "the impact these objects have on our feelings" (ibid., 229).

5. John Ruskin, "The Moral of Landscape," from the fourth volume of *Modern Painters* (1856), reprinted in *The Works of John Ruskin*, ed. E. T. Cook and Alexander Wedderburn, 39 vols. (London: G. Allen; New York: Longmans, Green, 1903–12), 5:369. Fanny Kemble, *Journal*, 2 vols. (London: Murray, 1835), 1:271.

6. Henry Nash Smith, *Virgin Land: The American West as Symbol and Myth* (1950; Cambridge, MA: Harvard University Press, 1970); R. W. B. Lewis, *The American Adam: Innocence, Tragedy, and Tradition in the Nineteenth Century* (Chicago: University of Chicago

Press, 1955). See, for example, Thoreau's yearning for "more desert sand, and . . . a wave of the Mediterranean sea" to blot out Carnac and Luxor, in "A Week on the Concord and Merrimack Rivers" (1849), in *The Writings of Henry David Thoreau*, 20 vols. (Boston and New York: Houghton Mifflin, 1906), 1:266–67.

7. Michael Kammen argues for the "dominant indifference" of Americans toward ruins "for most of the nineteenth century," and the "meaningless[ness]" of the "allegorical linkage" behind them, citing Twain's satire of "sentimental rhapsodizing over historic ruins" in *Innocents Abroad* (1869), in *Mystic Chords of Memory: The Transformation of Tradition in American Culture* (New York: Vintage Books, 1991), 53–54. For similar arguments and evidence for this view of American resistance to (and ambivalence about) the ruin, see David Lowenthal, "The Place of the Past in the American Landscape," in *Geographies of the Mind: Essays in Historical Geosophy*, ed. David Lowenthal and Martyn J. Bowden (New York: Oxford University Press, 1976), 89–117; Larzer Ziff, *Writing in the New Nation: Prose, Print, and Politics in the Early United States* (New Haven, CT: Yale University Press, 1991), 34–39.

8. Laurence Goldstein discusses Cole's *Course of Empire* in the final pages of *Ruins and Empire: The Evolution of a Theme in Augustan and Romantic Literature* (Pittsburgh: University of Pittsburgh Press, 1977), 226–31. Paul Zucker similarly cites Cole as the only exception to his claim that "the American Romantic school showed much less interest in ruins" than their European counterparts, in "Ruins—An Aesthetic Hybrid," *Journal of Aesthetics and Art Criticism* 20, no. 2 (1961): 126. Alan Wallach characterizes Cole as a Jeremiah-like figure in "Thomas Cole: Landscape and the Course of American Empire," in *Thomas Cole: Landscape into History*, ed. William H. Truettner and Alan Wallach (New Haven, CT: Yale University Press; Washington, DC: National Museum of American Art, Smithsonian Institution, 1994), 23–111. Curtis Dahl similarly recognized the convergence of a loosely affiliated "American School of Catastrophe," but confined it largely to the period 1810–45, to the region of New England, and to the traditional arts of poetry, theater, and painting ("American School of Catastrophe," *American Quarterly* 11, no. 3 [1959]: 380–90).

9. Benjamin, *Origin*, 177; see also Bloch's discussion of the Baroque ruin in *Principle of Hope*, 1:384–85. For an example of a Baroque emblem that places a skeleton within a landscape of ruins, see Susan Buck-Morss, *The Dialectics of Seeing: Walter Benjamin and the Arcades Project* (Cambridge, MA: MIT Press, 1991), 163.

10. Alois Riegl, "The Modern Cult of Monuments: Its Character and Its Origin (1903)," trans. Kurt W. Forster and Diane Ghirardo, in *Oppositions* 25 (Fall 1982): 31; further references cited in the text. Riegl's model remains compatible with subsequent art histories of the ruin, such as Paul Zucker, *Fascination of Decay: Ruins: Relic-Symbol-Ornament* (Ridgewood, NJ: Gregg Press, 1968).

11. See Peter Fritzsche, *Stranded in the Present: Modern Time and the Melancholy of History* (Cambridge, MA: Harvard University Press, 2004), especially 92–130; and Alisa Luxenberg, "Creating 'Désastres': Andrieu's Photographs of Urban Ruins in the Paris of 1871," *Art Bulletin* 80, no. 1 (1998): 113–37.

12. See, respectively, Panivong Norindr, *Phantasmatic Indochina: French Colonial Ideology in Architecture, Film, and Literature* (Durham, NC: Duke University Press, 1996), especially 18–19; Bernard S. Cohn, *Colonialism and Its Forms of Knowledge: The British in India* (Princeton, NJ: Princeton University Press, 1996), 76–105; Andrew Juniper, *Wabi Sabi: The Japanese Art of Impermanence* (North Clarendon, VT: Tuttle, 2003).

13. On the balloon-frame house as a poor ruin, see Paul Shepard, *Man in the Landscape: A Historic View of the Esthetics of Nature* (New York: Knopf, 1967), 187.

14. John Ruskin, *Seven Lamps of Architecture* (1849), in *Works*, 8:67, 68–69n; Speer's 1934 "theory of ruin-value" is discussed in Alex Scobie, *Hitler's State Architecture: The Impact of*

Classical Antiquity (University Park: Pennsylvania State University Press, 199), 93–96. See also Bloch's discussion of the ruins produced by "American terror-attacks" during the Second World War, ruins that were "without any aura" (385).

15. Philippe Hamon, *Expositions: Literature and Architecture in Nineteenth-Century France*, trans. Latia Sainson-Frank and Lisa Maguire (Berkeley: University of California Press, 1992), 58, 65n24.

16. John Ames Mitchell, *The Last American: A Fragment from the Journal of Khan-li* (New York: Frederick A. Stokes and Brother, 1889), 51. Walter Benjamin, *One-Way Street and Other Writings*, trans. Edmund Jephcott and Kingsley Shorter (London: New Left Books, 1979), 70, and *The Arcades Project*, 399 [K5a,3].

17. I am appropriating this term not only from Nietzsche's *Untimely Meditations*, but also from Benjamin's identification of Baroque allegories of skulls (and by extension ruins) with all that is "untimely" in history (*Origin*, 166).

18. As Civil War ruins appertain to issues other than that of urban modernity, they will not be discussed in this book.

19. The pleasures of antiquarianism, literary theorist Susan Stewart has argued, are contingent upon some kind of "rupture in historical consciousness . . . creating a sense that one can make one's own culture *other*—distant and discontinuous" (*On Longing: Narratives of the Miniature, the Gigantic, the Souvenir, the Collection* [Baltimore: Johns Hopkins University Press, 1984], 142).

20. Bloch, "The Anxiety of the Engineer," in *Literary Essays* (Stanford, CA: Stanford University Press, 1998), 306–7.

21. Alexis de Tocqueville, *Democracy in America*, trans. George Lawrence, ed. J. P. Mayer (1835, 1840; New York: Harper Perennial, 1988), 283–84.

22. Bloch discusses "non-contemporaneous elements"—or "remnants" that "contradic[t] the Now"—in his analysis of the rise of Nazism, *Heritage of Our Times*, trans. Neville Plaice and Stephen Plaice (1935; Berkeley: University of California Press, 1991), 108–12.

23. Robert Smithson, "A Tour of the Monuments of Passaic, New Jersey," in *Art Forum* (December 1967), reprinted in *Robert Smithson: The Collected Writings*, ed. Jack Flam (Berkeley: University of California Press, 1996), 68–74.

24. Fred Somkin characterizes the trope of the United States standing amid the ruins of earlier republican experiments (invoked by orators in the 1820s and 1830s) as a "weak attempt to orient America in historical time. All too often . . . such references were becoming conventional gestures" (*Unquiet Eagle: Memory and Desire in the Idea of American Freedom, 1815–1860* [Ithaca, NY: Cornell University Press, 1967], 89); Lowenthal describes how European ruins were, for many American travelers, "literary and visual props, picturesque devices that evoked standard enthusiasms," in "The Place of the Past," 98. William Cronon similarly describes the rhetoric of ruins adopted by urban boosters such as Logan Uriah Reavis as replete with "the stock imagery of imperial decay and rebirth" (*Nature's Metropolis: Chicago and the Great West* [New York W. W. Norton, 1991], 42). "Even at best," the literary historian Donald Ringe has written in the context of a discussion of William Cullen Bryant's poetry, "the theme of an American ruins of time is weak." Ringe, *Pictorial Mode: Space and Time in the Art of Bryant, Irving, and Cooper* (Lexington: University Press of Kentucky, 1971), 137.

25. Barbara Novak, *Nature and Culture: American Landscape and Painting, 1825–1875* (1980; New York and Oxford: Oxford University Press, 1995), 214.

26. Benjamin, *Origin*, 76–78.

27. Simmel, "The Metropolis and Mental Life" (1903), in *Simmel on Culture*, ed. David Frisby and Mike Featherstone (London: Sage, 1997), 175, 176, 181, 175, 177, 178–79. On

this article's origins as one of several lectures delivered at the German Metropolitan Exhibition, commissioned (ironically) to celebrate the modern German metropolis, see Frisby, *Cityscapes of Modernity: Critical Explorations* (Cambridge: Polity, 2001), 15–16.

28. On the German discourse of *Amerikanismus,* see Frisby, *Cityscapes of Modernity,* 17, 25, 161, 164–65. On Simmel's influence on the Chicago sociologist Robert Park, see ibid., 47. On the affinities between Simmel and the philosopher William James (and indeed his brother Henry), see Ross Posnock, *The Trial of Curiosity: Henry James, William James, and the Challenge of Modernity* (New York: Oxford University Press, 1991), 97–98 (and 179–80).

29. See, for example, Simmel's reference to "the human soul" as "that battlefield between nature . . . and spirit" ("The Ruin," 264).

30. Such a reading is suggested in the following passage: "we feel the vitality of those opposing tendencies, and—instinctively sensing these antitheses in ourselves—we notice, beyond everything merely formal and aesthetic, the significance of the configuration in whose serene unity they have their synthesis" (ibid., 261).

31. Walter Benjamin, "Paris, the Capital of the Nineteenth Century (Exposé of 1935)," in *The Arcades Project,* 4–5; this methodological approach to the history of modernity is embodied in the figure of the "destructive character," who "reduces" the world "to rubble, not for the sake of the rubble, but for that of the way leading through it ("The Destructive Character" [1931], in *Reflections: Essays, Aphorisms, Autobiographical Writings,* trans. Edmund Jephcott [New York: Schocken, 1978], 303).

Chapter 1

1. Alexis de Tocqueville, *Democracy in America,* trans. George Lawrence, ed. J. P. Mayer (1835, 1840; New York: Harper Perennial, 1988), 283–84; further references cited in the text.

2. Tocqueville recounted the Oneida ruins in his "Pocket Notebook Number 1," in *Journey to America,* trans. George Lawrence, ed. J. P. Mayer (London: Faber and Faber, 1959), 130–31 (reference to engraving their names on 130); in a letter to his sister-in-law Alexandrine de Tocqueville, dated July 25, 1831, letter packet "18," in Yale Tocqueville Manuscripts, Ms. Vault Tocqueville, B.I.a.2., Beinecke Library, Yale University; and in a longer sketch, "Cours au Lac Oneida," posthumously published and translated as "Journey to Lake Oneida," in *Journey,* 321–27, where he describes the "icy silence" (326), and mentions having read a story "many years before" called *Journey to Lake Oneida* (323); further references cited in the text. On the Tocqueville family's purchase of *Voyage d'un Allemand au Lac Onéida* (1803), the French translation of Joachim-Heinrich Campe's 1802 story, see André Jardin, *Tocqueville: A Biography,* trans. Lydia Davis and Robert Hemenway (New York: Farrar, Straus, Giroux, 1988), 123. Victor Lange traces the legend back to an earlier novel, and identifies the Frenchman as Louis des Watines, in "Visitors to Lake Oneida: An Account of the Background of Sophie von La Roche's Novel *Erscheinungen am See Oneida,*" *Symposium* 2, no. 1 (1948): especially 59–60. George Wilson Pierson claims Tocqueville and Beaumont were "acting under the spell of an extravagantly romantic idea," in *Tocqueville and Beaumont in America* (New York: Oxford University Press, 1938), 204.

3. In "Journey to Lake Oneida," Tocqueville acknowledged that "it was not chance that led us to this solitary lake. For it was the end and object of our journey" (323). Tocqueville may have decontextualized those ruins and represented them as a chance discovery out of a realization that they had been misinformed, or even duped, by the legend of the French nobleman. On the fictitiousness of the legend of these émigrés, who appear to have left France for financial reasons well before the fall of the Bastille, and to have returned after only a short stay on the island, see Pierson, *Tocqueville and Beaumont,* 201–5. Tocqueville perhaps exaggerates the extent

of the ruins in *Democracy in America*, compensating for his disappointment at the paucity of "traces" that actually remained.

4. Tocqueville, "Pocket Notebook Number 1," 130–31. Tocqueville, letter to Alexandrine, n.p. (p. 1), Beinecke.

5. See for example, Melvin Richter's reference to "that crucial chapter" as the one that "organizes Tocqueville's observations into a coherent scheme" derived from Montesquieu, in "The Uses of Theory: Tocqueville's Adaptation of Montesquieu," in *Essays in Theory and History: An Approach to the Social Sciences*, ed. Melvin Richter (Cambridge, MA: Harvard University Press, 1970), 74, 87. On the "unraveling" of his theoretical preconceptions during the early weeks of his journey, and his gradual realization of the "importance of culture to the American system," see Sheldon S. Wolin, *Tocqueville between Two Worlds: The Making of a Political and Theoretical Life* (Princeton, NJ: Princeton University Press, 2001), 102–12, 118–19, 222–25; quotations on 118, 223.

6. Tocqueville, "Extraits du voyage en Sicile" (1827), in *Oeuvres, papiers et correspondences d'Alexis de Tocqueville*, 18 vols. (Paris: Gallimard, 1951–), 5:37–54.

7. [Thomas Chandler Haliburton], *The Clockmaker; or, The Sayings and Doings of Samuel Slick, of Slickville,* 3rd series (London: Bentley, 1840), 5; the ruin in question is the abandoned lodge of the Duke of Kent in Nova Scotia, first visited by Haliburton in 1828.

8. On Tocqueville's reading of Montesquieu and Rousseau, see Richter, "The Uses of Theory," 75.

9. Charles-Louis de Montesquieu, quoted in Peter Gay, *The Enlightenment: An Interpretation*, vol. 2, *The Science of Freedom* (New York and London: W. W. Norton, 1969), 101; for similar articulations of the life cycle of nations by Condillac, d'Alembert, Voltaire, and Turgot, see ibid, 101, 109–11. For a genealogy of this idea back to the Renaissance (and beyond), see J. G. A. Pocock, *The Machiavellian Moment: Florentine Political Thought and the Atlantic Republican Tradition* (1975; Princeton, NJ: Princeton University Press, 2003); and on the concept of "fortuna" in Roman and early Christian culture, see ibid., 31–48.

10. Denis Diderot, *Diderot on Art*, vol. 2, *The Salon of 1767*, ed. John Goodman (New Haven, CT: Yale University Press, 1995), 196–97; further references cited in the text.

11. On Rousseau and Abbé Raynal's interest in Native Americans as "noble savages," see Harry Liebersohn, *Aristocratic Encounters: European Travelers and North American Indians* (Cambridge: Cambridge University Press, 1998), 25–26. There were, of course, some French intellectuals, most notably Buffon, Gobineau, and De Pauw, who saw America as the site of degeneration and decay; see Antonello Gerbi, *The Dispute of the New World: The History of a Polemic, 1750–1900*, trans. Jeremy Moyle (Pittsburgh: University of Pittsburgh Press, 1973). "Ruins," in Denis Diderot and Jean d'Alembert, eds., *Encyclopédie*, 17 vols. (1751–65), 14:433.

12. J. Hector St. John de Crèvecoeur, *Letters from an American Farmer, and Sketches of Eighteenth Century America* (1782; Harmondsworth: Penguin, 1981), 43; Marquis de Chastellux, *Travels in North-America in the Years 1780, 1781, and 1782,* 2 vols. (London: Robinson, 1787), 1:176; Viscount de Chateaubriand, *Travels in America and Italy,* 2 vols. (1827; London: Henry Colburn, 1828), 1:98. Chateaubriand did acknowledge the presence of luxury and vices, the antiquity of the forests, and the existence of indigenous ruins. For his references to the recent ruins of the revolution, see Peter Fritzsche, *Stranded in the Present: Modern Time and the Melancholy of History* (Cambridge, MA: Harvard University Press, 2004), 97–102.

13. Thomas Cole, "Essay on American Scenery," *American Monthly Magazine* 7 (1836): 9, 5, 9, 12; further references cited in the text.

14. William Cullen Bryant, "To Cole, the Painter, Departing for Europe" (1829), in *The Poetical Works of William Cullen Bryant* (New York: D. Appleton, 1916), 127–28.

15. Thomas Cole, "Verdura, or a Tale of After Time," Cole Papers, New York State Library, Box 5, Folder 8; I am indebted to the paleographer Peter Foden for assistance in deciphering and decoding this manuscript.

16. On the "four stages theory" (or "History of Civil Society") that emerged from the Scottish Enlightenment, see Drew McCoy, *The Elusive Republic: Political Economy in Jeffersonian America* (New York: W. W. Norton, 1980), 13–47; Kames and Ferguson drew more pessimistic conclusions than Adam Smith; see ibid., 35–45. Angela Miller discusses theatrical analogies in Cole's series in *Empire of the Eye: Landscape Representation and American Cultural Politics, 1825–1875* (Ithaca, NY: Cornell University Press, 1993), 32–33. The complete series is reproduced there, 27–32.

17. George Berkeley, "Verses on the Prospect of Planting Arts and Learning in America" (written 1726, published 1752), in *The Works of George Berkeley*, ed. Alexander Campbell Fraser, 4 vols. (Oxford: Clarendon Press, 1901), 4:365–66.

18. Alan Wallach, "Cole, Byron, and the Course of Empire," *Art Bulletin* 50, no. 4 (1968): 375–77.

19. *Pennsylvania Packet* (1774), quoted in Gordon Wood, *The Creation of the American Republic, 1776–1787* (Chapel Hill: University of North Carolina Press, 1969), 35. On the double meaning of the phrase "Machiavellian moment," see Pocock, *Machiavellian Moment*, viii, 554; and on the related terms of *rinnovatzione* (renewal) and *ridurre ai principii* (return to first principles), 508, 516, 545–46. For examples of political prints depicting the British Empire as a modern-day Rome in its last throes, or the American colonies as a child, see Lester C. Olson, *Emblems of American Community in the Revolutionary Era* (Washington, DC: Smithsonian Institution Press, 1991), 228–32, 125–49.

20. Thomas Jefferson, *Notes on the State of Virginia* (1785; Harmondsworth: Penguin, 1999), 171; Jefferson, letter to James Madison, December 20, 1787, in *Letters,* ed. Merrill D. Peterson (New York: Literary Classics of the United States, 1984), 918. On Jefferson's hope that spatial expansion would delay temporal development, see McCoy, *Elusive Republic,* 62, 121–22, 193–95; and on his and other republicans' opposition to large-scale manufacturing of "fineries," ibid., 59, 63, 231.

21. On Jefferson's belief that these "natural laws of social and cultural development . . . applied to America as much as to Europe," see McCoy, *Elusive Republic,* 15, 189, 203; and on his reading of the pessimistic demographic theories of Malthus and Destutt de Tracy, 191–92, 253–54. Madison similarly envisioned "in a century or a little more . . . as crowded a population in the United States as in Great Britain or France" (quoted in ibid., 255). Even Federalists who emphasized the progressive rather than ruinous effects of commerce and luxury still accepted these premises; for Hamilton's expectation of an inevitable drift away from the "republican standard," see Pocock, *Machiavellian Moment,* 530.

22. On the centrality of ancient Rome before, during, and after the Revolution, see Howard Mumford Jones, *O Strange New World: American Culture, the Formative Years* (1952; New York: Viking Press, 1964), 227–72; and Wood, *Creation of the American Republic,* 48–53.

23. John Aikin, M.D., *Letters from a Father to His Son: On Various Topics, Relative to Literature and the Conduct of Life . . .* (1793; Philadelphia: Printed by Samuel Harrison Smith, 1794), 251, 252, 258. This letter was excerpted as "On the Effect of Ruins as Objects of Sight and as Sentimental Objects," in *The New York Magazine, Or Literary Repository,* new series, vol. 1 (1796), 169–71.

24. See, for example, Allan Wallach, "Thomas Cole: Landscape and the Course of Ameri-

can Empire," in *Thomas Cole: Landscape into History*, ed. William H. Truettner and Wallach (New Haven, CT: Yale University Press, 1994), 92; and Miller, *Empire of the Eye*, 25.

25. Wallach, "Thomas Cole," 80. On this artistic hierarchy, see also William H. Gerdts, "American Landscape Painting: Critical Judgments, 1730–1845," *American Art Journal* 17, no. 1 (1985): 28–59.

26. Wallach uses the term *pessimistic* in "Thomas Cole," 95. Angela Miller identifies anti-Jacksonian references in "Thomas Cole and Jacksonian America: *The Course of Empire* as Political Allegory," *Prospects* 14 (1990): 71–72.

27. On the emergence of this new paradigm, see Wood, *Creation of the American Republic*, 391–429, 519–64, 593–615, and Wood, *The Radicalism of the American Revolution* (New York: Vintage, 1993), 229–369.

28. On the popularization of Adam Smith's work in America by the early nineteenth century, see Joyce Appleby, *Capitalism and a New Social Order: The Republicanism of the 1790s* (New York: New York University Press, 1984), 31, 50; and Appleby, *Liberalism and Republicanism in the Historical Imagination* (Cambridge, MA: Harvard University Press, 1992), 4. On the reconciliation of virtue with commerce, see Pocock, *Machiavellian Moment*, 526.

29. McCoy describes how some Americans, emboldened by the boom of the 1790s, "occasionally flirted with just such a vision of virtually endless progress toward perfection," even as they continued to invoke the older rhetoric of cyclical growth and decay (*Elusive Republic*, 170–71). See also John E. Crowley, "Classical, Anti-Classical, and Millennial Conceptions of Change in Revolutionary America," in *Classical Traditions in Early America*, ed. John W. Eadie (Ann Arbor: Center for Coördination of Ancient and Modern Studies, University of Michigan, 1976), 216, 225, 229. Appleby outlines this new "Principle of Hope" in *Capitalism and a New Social Order*, 79–105, and in *Liberalism and Republicanism*, 28–29. I subscribe here to the more consensual view that Jefferson retained his classical republicanism, and did not the endorse the capitalist goals of democratized consumption and commercialized agriculture.

30. Jones claims that by the Jacksonian period "few statesmen were convinced . . . that classical history and the classic philosophers offered guide lines to the nation" (*O Strange New World*, 266). For an example of the disavowal of antiquity, see John L. O'Sullivan, "The Great Nation of Futurity," *United States Magazine and Democratic Review* 6, no. 23 (1839): especially 427.

31. Here, my argument departs again from Appleby, who claims that the "very triumph of liberalism spelled oblivion for the intellectual traditions which had preceded it" (*Liberalism*, 29); and that the new "language" of liberalism was "totally unassimilable to the social grammar of civic humanism" (334). Instead, I follow Pocock in emphasizing the persistence of the republican "vocabulary of virtue and corruption . . . not merely as a survival slowly dying after its tap-root was cut, but with a reality and relevance to elements in American experience" (*Machiavellian Moment*, 526–27).

32. John Witherspoon, *The Dominion of Providence over the Passions of Men* (Philadelphia, 1776), in Ellis Sandoz, ed., *Political Sermons of the American Founding Era, 1730–1805*, 2 vols. (Indianapolis: Liberty Fund, 1998), 1:549.

33. David Rittenhouse, "An Oration, Delivered . . . before the American Philosophical Society, Held at Philadelphia" (1775), in William Barton, *Memoirs of the Life of David Rittenhouse* (Philadelphia: Edward Parker, 1813), 568.

34. See, for example, James Sheridan Knowles, *Knowles' Elocutionist: A First-Class Rhetorical Reader* (New York: Mowatt, 1844), 101; E. L. Magoon, *Westward Empire; or, The Great Drama of Human Progress* (New York: Harper, 1856), v, passim; John Quincy Adams, "Oration, at Plymouth, in Commemoration of the First Landing . . ." (1802), in Ebenezer Bancroft

Williston, ed., *Eloquence of the United States* (Middletown, CT: E. & H. Clark, 1827), 190, which substitutes the word "star" for "course"; and the paintings on this theme by Emmanuel Leutze, Andrew Melrose, and John Gast at midcentury.

35. "The Progress of Society," *Democratic Review* 8, no. 31 (1840): 67–68, 83–84, 85–86.

36. "Editor's Address," *American Annals of Education* 1, no. 1 (1830): 1.

37. G. W. F. Hegel, *Lectures on the Philosophy of World History: Introduction, Reason in History*, trans. H. B. Nisbet (Cambridge: Cambridge University Press, 1975), 197. If the course of empire was imagined by some Americans as continuing beyond the Pacific with the liberation of Asia, it was to do so under the aegis of America itself, the redeemer nation; see Pocock, *Macchiavellian Moment*, 542.

38. "Downfall of Nations," *Knickerbocker* 6, no. 1 (1835): 52. K. A. W., "Monuments," *Boston Lyceum* 2, no. 10 (1827): 177.

39. Daniel Webster, "The Character of Washington" (speech, 1832), in *The Works of Daniel Webster*, 6 vols. (Boston: Little, Brown, 1890), 1:231.

40. Mordecai Manuel Noah, *Oration . . .* (1817), quoted in Fred Somkin, *Unquiet Eagle: Memory and Desire in the Idea of American Freedom, 1815–1860* (Ithaca, NY: Cornell University Press, 1967), 13.

41. On the lingering suspicions, see Anders Stephanson, *Manifest Destiny: American Expansion and the Empire of Right* (New York: Hill and Wang, 1996), 18–19. On the "merg[ing]" of the jeremiad with the "language of classical republican theory," see Pocock, *Machiavellian Moment*, 511–13; quote on 513. Tuveson confirms that "there is no expectation of a universal millennium" in Berkeley's original poem, in *Redeemer Nation: The Idea of America's Millennial Role* (Chicago: University of Chicago Press, 1968), 94.

42. "Mr. Cole's Five Pictures," *New York Mirror* 14, no. 17 (1836): 135. Louis Legrand Noble, *Life and Works of Thomas Cole*, ed. Elliot S. Vesell (1853; Cambridge, MA: Belknap Press of Harvard University Press, 1964), 168, 287–88.

43. On the "evangelical" qualities of Cole's paintings, see Joshua C. Taylor, "The Religious Impulse in American Art," in *Art, Creativity, and the Sacred: An Anthology in Religion and Art*, ed. Diane Apostolos-Cappadona (New York: Continuum, 1995), 97–99.

44. Art historians such as Elizabeth Johns have read Cole's allegory as "implying that the savage state would inevitably succeed the melancholy dusk of *Desolation*" (*Painting the Dark Side: Art and the Gothic Imagination in Nineteenth-Century America* [Berkeley: University of California Press, 2004], 24). The exclusion of any human figure from *Desolation* was a conscious decision made as early as September 18, 1833; see Cole's letter to Reed on that date, in Noble, *Life and Works*, 130.

45. "Ancient Ruins," *Christian Register* (Boston) 8 (1829): 1 (emphasis in original). "The Ruin," *Western Luminary* (Lexington, KY) 4, no. 43 (1828): 337. "The Three States: Past, Present, and to Come," *Christian Index* 6, no. 12 (1832): 189.

46. S. G. W. Benjamin, "Fifty Years of American Art," *Harper's New Monthly Magazine* 59, no. 350 (1879): 254. Charles Lanman considered the last painting the "most impressive picture of this series," in "Cole's Imaginative Paintings," *Democratic Review* 12, no. 60 (1843): 600, and subsequently in *Letters from a Landscape Painter* (Boston: J. Munroe, 1845), 72. See also Joseph M. Church, "Editor's Chatter-Box," *Church's Bizarre*, June 12, 1852, 152–53.

47. "The Fine Arts: The Cole Exhibition," *The Literary World* 3, no. 62 (1848): 186. On the separate hanging of *Desolation*, see Angela Miller, "Imperial Republic: Narratives of National Expansion in American Art, 1820–1860" (PhD diss. Yale University, 1985), 85.

48. See for example the broken columns—"emblem[s] of an unfinished course of life"—in Mt. Auburn cemetery, as illustrated in Nathaniel S. Dearborn, *Dearborn's Guide through Mount*

Auburn (Boston: Dearborn, 1857), 32, 34, 35, 48, 49; quote on 48. On the commemorative uses of neoclassical imagery, see Peggy McDowell and Richard E. Meyer, *The Revival Styles in American Memorial Art* (Bowling Green, OH: Bowling Green State University Popular Press, 1994); their epigraph cites Richard Dana's 1857 paean to the "upright column" as one of several funerary symbols that represent not "decay" but "life." By the end of the century, the broken column would be rejected as "essentially unchristian" ("Editor's Easy Chair," *Harper's* 83, no. 493 [1891]: 149).

49. Barbara Franco, ed., *Masonic Symbols in American Decorative Arts* (Lexington, MA: National Heritage Museum, 1976), catalogue item 118. Chalmers Izett Paton, *Freemasonry, Its Symbolism, Religious Nature, and Law of Perfection* (London: Reeves and Turner, 1873), 168–69. On the influence of Freemasonry on Thomas Cole, see David Bjelajac, "Thomas Cole's Oxbow and the American Zion Divided," *American Art* 20, no. 1 (2006): 60–83.

50. On the masculine gendering of Doric architecture and "republican simplicity," see Roger G. Kennedy, *Greek Revival America* (New York: Stewart, Tabori, and Chang, 1989), 81. The reference to the Grecian maiden is from "Orders of Architecture: The Corinthian," *Masonic Mirror* 3, no. 29 (1827): 225.

51. Cole, letter to his parents, March 4, 1832, quoted in Noble, *Life and Works*, 114. This was Cole's second of three trips to Europe. On his inspiration from Italy's "crumbling ruins," and his conception of *The Course of Empire* in Rome, see ibid., 110–12.

52. On American artists and writers in Rome, see William Vance, *America's Rome*, 2 vols. (New Haven, CT: Yale University Press, 1991); and Theodore Stebbins, *Lure of Italy: American Artists and the Italian Experience* (Boston: Museum of Fine Arts, 1992). Acknowledging the earlier visits of Benjamin West, John Singleton Copley, and Washington Allston, Regina Soria pinpoints 1825 as the year in which this artistic migration took off, in *Dictionary of Nineteenth-Century American Artists in Italy, 1760–1914* (London: Associated University Presses, 1982), 31. On the larger impact of this and other American art colonies in Europe, see Neil Harris, *The Artist in American Society: The Formative Years, 1790–1860* (1966; Chicago: University of Chicago Press, 1982), 124–68, 284–98.

53. Thomas Jefferson, quoted in George Green Shackelford, *Thomas Jefferson's Travels in Europe, 1784–1789* (Baltimore: Johns Hopkins University Press, 1995), 103, 80, 81, 104; visiting the ruins of Bordeaux's Roman circus, Jefferson measured the bricks and analyzed their texture (119).

54. Alois Riegl, "The Modern Cult of Monuments: Its Character and Its Origin (1903)," trans. Kurt W. Forster and Diane Ghirardo, *Oppositions* 25 (Fall 1982): 22, 23 (emphasis added); further references cited in the text. Although Riegl believed age-value would become the dominant category in the twentieth century, it had emerged "long before the twentieth century" (31), initially "supported openly by a small group of aggressive artists and laymen" (34). Even in 1903, Riegl believed that it continued to exist alongside, and in tension with, historical value (34).

55. Theodore Dwight (1824), quoted in Vance, *America's Rome*, 1:73. See also the article on "Ancient Ruins" in *Christian Register*, in which the author relates the advice of his guide to the Roman ruins: "your first visit there must be made in the evening, by moonlight . . ." (1).

56. Thomas Cole, "Thoughts and Occurrences," May 22, 1838, in Cole, *The Collected Essays and Prose Sketches*, ed. Marshall Tymn (St. Paul, MN: John Colet, 1980), 157. See Cole's moonlit *Italian Coast Scene with Ruined Tower*, 1838, oil on canvas, 34 x 46 inches, National Gallery of Art, Washington, DC; and his *Aqueduct near Rome*, 1832, oil on canvas, 44 1/2 x 67 5/16 inches, Mildred Kemper Art Museum, Washington University. George Hillard (1853), quoted in Vance, *America's Rome*, 1:47.

57. See Noble, *Life and Works*, 230–31, 225, respectively.

58. Peale (1831), quoted in Vance, *America's Rome*, 1:4.

59. John Lloyd Stephens, *Incidents of Travel in Central America, Chiapas, and Yucatan* (New York: Harper, 1841). Stephens and Frederick Catherwood were "the first explorers to undertake a systematic survey of the ruins," according to Jennifer Roberts, "Landscapes of Indifference: Robert Smithson and John Lloyd Stephens in Yucatan," *Art Bulletin* 82, no. 3 (2000): 545.

60. Until it lost its monopoly in 1824, the Livingston-Fulton Company's New York–Albany boat took "at least 16 hours" and cost "as much as six to eight dollars" (Kenneth John Myers, "Art and Commerce in Jacksonian America: The Steamboat Albany Collection," *Art Bulletin* 82, no. 3 [2000]: 508, 520). As late as 1852, Nathaniel Parker Willis believed that "'Cockney annoyances' will not reach" the lower Hudson Valley ("The Highland Terrace above West Point," in *The Home Book of the Picturesque; or, American Scenery, Art, and Literature* [1852; Gainesville, FL: Scholar's Facsimiles and Reprints, 1967], 112, 110).

61. Tocqueville, "Pocket Notebook Number 1," 129. On the emergence of tourism in this period and region, see John F. Sears, *Sacred Places: American Tourist Attractions in the Nineteenth Century* (New York: Oxford University Press, 1989); Gideon Miner Davison, *The Fashionable Tour* (1822; Saratoga Springs: G. M. Davison, 1830); Theodore Dwight Jr., *The Northern Traveller* (1825; New York: Harper, 1830); Henry Gilpin, *A Northern Tour* (Philadelphia: Carey and Lea, 1825); for their publication history, see Richard Gassan, "The First American Tourist Guidebooks: Authorship and the Print Culture of the 1820s," *Book History* 8 (2005): 51–74.

62. On William Gilpin's principles and their application and popularization by British aesthetic theorists and garden designers such as Uvedale Price, Humphrey Repton, and Thomas Whately, see Malcolm Andrews, *The Search for the Picturesque: Landscape Aesthetics and Tourism in Britain, 1760–1800* (Aldershot: Scholar Press, 1989), and John Dixon Hunt, *Gardens and the Picturesque: Studies in the History of Landscape Architecture* (Cambridge, MA: MIT Press, 1992). Gilpin's clearest statement of the necessity for ruins is in *Three Essays: On Picturesque Beauty; On Picturesque Travel; and On Sketching Landscape . . .* (1792; London: Cadell and Davies, 1808), 46. He discusses the formlessness of American and Scottish landscapes in *Observations Relative Chiefly to Picturesque Beauty, Made in the Year 1776 . . .*, 2 vols. (London: Blamire, 1789), 2:112–14, 117–19; quote on 118. He also complained that America's vast lakes are ill-proportioned and thus unpicturesque, in *Observations, Relative Chiefly to Picturesque Beauty, Made in the Year 1772 . . .*, 2 vols. (London: Blamire, 1792), 1:125–26.

63. Isaac Weld, *Travels through the States of North America*, 2 vols. (1799; London: John Stockdale, 1807), 1:232. Frances Trollope, *Domestic Manners of the Americans* (1832; Harmondsworth: Penguin, 1997), 31.

64. Frances Ann Butler [Fanny Kemble], *Journal*, 2 vols. (London: Murray, 1835), 1:271. Andrews describes the picturesque as "aggressively anti-utilitarian" in *Search for the Picturesque*, 49. John Ruskin, another aesthetician who vowed never to visit the United States, considered Americans lacking in the "instinct" to which "romantic" objects such as ruins appealed ("The Moral of Landscape," in the third volume of *Modern Painters* [1843], in *The Works of John Ruskin*, ed. E. T. Cook and Alexander Wedderburn, 39 vols. [London: G. Allen, 1903–12], 5:369).

65. Harriet Martineau used the word *trollopize* in *Retrospect of Western Travel*, 3 vols. (London: Saunders and Otley, 1838), 3:219. On the American appropriation of the picturesque, see John Conron, *American Picturesque* (University Park: Pennsylvania State University Press, 2000).

66. Gilpin, *Observations . . . Made in the Year 1772*, 1:xxviii–xxix, xxv. On the "Claude glass," see Arnaud Maillet, *The Claude Glass: Use and Meaning of the Black Mirror in Western*

Art (New York: Zone, 2004). John Hill's *Drawing Book of Landscape Scenery* (New York: H. I. Megarey, 1821) included four engravings of ruins: a castle, abbey, mansion, and fort.

67. See, for example, Thomas Doughty's *Fanciful Landscape*, 1834, oil on canvas, 30 1/8 x 39 7/8 inches, National Gallery of Art, Washington, DC, which contravenes Gilpin's stipulation that artists could not go as far as "to add a magnificent castle" (*Observations . . . Made in the Year 1772*, 1: xxviii). Susan Fenimore Cooper, "A Dissolving View," in *Home Book of the Picturesque*, 79–94.

68. James Fenimore Cooper, *The Deerslayer; or, The First War-Path*, 3 vols. (London: Richard Bentley, 1841), 1:329; and Cooper, *Last of the Mohicans: A Narrative of 1757*, 3 vols. (London: John Miller, 1826), 2:146.

69. Gilpin, *Observations . . . Made in the Year 1772*, 1:70, 74–75. For a brief discussion of the folly, see Hunt, *Gardens and the Picturesque*, 181–82.

70. The ruins of Cruger's Island (originally Magdalen Island) are described in Herbert J. Spinden, "The Stephens Sculptures from Yucatan," *Natural History* 20 (1920): 381; Carl Carmer, *The Hudson* (New York and Toronto: Farrar and Rinehart, 1939), 214–15; and Roberts, "Landscapes of Indifference," 551, which refers to Cole on 565n48.

71. *New England: A Handbook for Travellers* (Boston: James R. Osgood, 1883) refers to a "picturesque and truly ancient ruin" on Cruger's Island, "imported from Italy" (347). The German immigrant William Heine painted a *View of Cruger's Island and the Catskill Mountains* in 1851. William Wade included the ruins in an 1845 panorama, also issued as a miniature folding map titled *Panorama of the Hudson River from New York to Albany* (New York: Disturnell, 1846). Fredrika Bremer, *The Homes of the New World: Impressions of America*, 2 vols. (New York: Harper, 1853), 1:36–37. Emulating Cruger, the Clews estate at Hyde Park installed a ruined arch; see Carmer, *Hudson*, 215.

72. James Feninore Cooper, *Home as Found* (1838; New York: Capricorn Books, 1961), 136, 203; further references cited in the text. Follies did not become widespread until the Gilded Age; see, for example, the ruins that St. Louis botanist Henry Shaw installed on his Tower Grove estate in 1872.

73. Tracie Felker, "First Impressions: Thomas Cole's Drawings of His 1825 Trip up the Hudson River," *American Art Journal* 24, no. 1 (1992): 60–93; Thomas Cole, *Lake with Dead Trees (Catskill)*, oil on canvas, 27 x 33 3/4 inches, Oberlin College, 1825; journal entries for July 6, 1835, and March 1843, quoted in Noble, *Life and Works*, 149, 258–61. On the connection between mountains and ruins, see Yi-Fu Tuan, "Mountains, Ruins, and the Sentiment of Melancholy," *Landscape* 14, no. 1 (1964): 27–30. On the notion of "natural antiquity," see Novak, *Nature and Culture: American Landscape and Painting, 1825–1875* (1980; New York and Oxford: Oxford University Press, 1995), 56, 59.

74. Charles Lyell, *Travels in North America*, 2 vols. (New York: Wiley and Putnam, 1845), 1:15. Susan Fenimore Cooper reported Agassiz's conclusions that "North America is, in reality, the oldest part of the earth," in "Dissolving View," 90.

75. D. J. Browne, "American Forest Trees: Sylva Americana," *North American Review* 35, no. 77 (1832): 403. The poet Charles Fenno Hoffman similarly found such forests superior to those "temples which Roman robbers have reared" and "towers in which feudal oppression has fortified itself . . ."; *A Winter in the Far West*, 2 vols. (London: Bentley, 1835), 1:193–94.

76. Washington Irving, "A Tour on the Prairies" (1835), in *The Crayon Miscellany* (Philadelphia: Lippincott, 1870), 115, 42.

77. Cole, journal entry, February 26, 1843 (in Noble, *Life and Works*, 256). On Alison's influence, see Kenneth Hafertepe, "The Enlightened Sensibility: Scottish Philosophy in American Art and Architecture" (PhD diss., University of Texas, 1986).

78. For examples of Cole's pairing of landscapes, such as *The Dream of Arcadia* with *Schroon Mountain* for the National Academy exhibition of 1838, see Vance, *America's Rome*, 1:100–105. On the hanging of paintings in between windows, see Myers, "Steamboat Albany Collection," 510.

79. On an "excursion in search of the picturesque" in the Adirondacks, Cole found two mountains, "one of a serrated outline, and the other like a lofty pyramid" (journal entry for October 7, 1835, in Noble, *Life and Works*, 151–52), which Clara Endicott Sears claims were those that would appear in *Course of Empire* (*Highlights among the Hudson River Artists* [Boston: Houghton Mifflin, 1947], 73); this claim remains unsubstantiated.

80. On Cole's visit, see Kenneth Myers, *The Catskills: Painters, Writers, and Tourists in the Mountains, 1820–1895* (Yonkers, NY: Hudson River Museum of Westchester, 1987), 45.

81. In the fifth edition of his *Northern Traveller* (1834), Dwight noted that Ticonderoga was now a "stopping plac[e]" on the Champlain steamboat route, and praised Pell's gardens (144, 148). On Ticonderoga's emergence as a site of touristic and cultural interest, see Nicholas Westbrook, "Ticonderoga in Print: Prints from the Fort Ticonderoga Museum Collection," *Imprint* 26, no. 1 (2001): 2–18. It was not until 1848, however, that the antiquarian, Benson Lossing, reclaimed Ticonderoga as primarily an American ruin of the Revolutionary War, in his *Pictorial Field-Book of the Revolution*, 2 vols. (New York: Harper, 1851–52), 1:115–25.

82. Cole superimposed this fictional scene onto his original *View near Ticonderoga* in 1829, giving it the new title, *Gelyna*, oil on canvas, 24 x 34 1/2 inches, Fort Ticonderoga Museum. Giulian C. Verplanck, "Gelyna: A Tale of Albany and Ticonderoga, Seventy Years Ago," in *Talisman for 1830* (New York: Elam Bliss, 1829), 302–35. Nathaniel Hawthorne, "Old Ticonderoga: A Picture of the Past," *American Monthly Magazine* (1836), in *Nathaniel Hawthorne: Tales and Sketches* (New York: Library of America, 1982), 386. On French aristocrats' quest for the remains of New France, see Liebersohn, *Aristocratic Encounters*, 65.

83. [Isabella Lucy Bird], *The Englishwoman in America* (London: John Murray, 1856), 134–35.

84. Theodore Dwight, "Relics of the Revolution," in *Sketches of Scenery and Manners in the United States* (New York: A. T. Goodrich, 1829), 91–92; the same sentiment is expressed in Gilpin, *Northern Tour*, 128.

85. DeWitt Clinton, *A Memoir on the Antiquities of the Western Parts of the State of New-York* (Albany: Printed by E. & E. Hosford, 1820), a version of which was delivered to the New-York Historical Society in 1811. On his contributions to archaeology, see Evan Cornog, *The Birth of Empire: DeWitt Clinton and the American Experience, 1769–1828* (New York and Oxford: Oxford University Press, 1998), 118–26. Samuel Mitchill, "The Original Inhabitants of America," in *Archaeologia Americana*, vol. 1 (Worcester, MA: American Antiquarian Society, 1820), 331. Timothy Flint, *The History and Geography of the Mississippi Valley*, 2 vols. (1832; Cincinnati: E. H. Flint, 1833), 1:133.

86. Clinton, *Memoir on the Antiquities*, 131.

87. Jefferson, *Notes on the State of Virginia*, 103; Chateaubriand, *Travels in America and Italy*, 1:156 (referring to the Ohio mounds); Tocqueville, *Democracy*, 29–30.

88. The most exhaustive of these Old World hypotheses was Josiah Priest, *American Antiquities and Discoveries in the West* (Albany, NY: Hoffman and White, 1833); the phrase "partially civilized" is from the subtitle. On Joseph Smith's theory, see Curtis Dahl, "Mound Builders, Mormons, and William Cullen Bryant," *New England Quarterly* 34, no. 2 (1961): 178–90. On their cities, see William Henry Harrison [*sic*], "A Discourse on the Aborigines of the Valley of the Ohio," in *Transactions of the Historical and Philosophical Society of Ohio, Part Second*, vol. 1 (Cincinnati: Bradbury, 1839), 223. And on barbarian invasions, see DeWitt

Clinton, "The Iroquois: Address Delivered before the New York Historical Society, Dec. 6, 1811," in *The Life and Writings of DeWitt Clinton,* ed. William W. Campbell (New York: Baker and Scribner, 1849), 265.

89. DeWitt Clinton, "Memorial . . . in Favour of a Canal Navigation between the Great Western Lakes and the Tide-Waters of the Hudson [c. 1816]," in *Memoir of DeWitt Clinton,* ed. David Hosack (New York: Seymour, 1829), 412 (emphasis added).

90. The 1840s witnessed the fastest urban growth in U.S. history (93.7 percent); see the table at www.census.gov/population/censusdata/table-4.pdf. On the demographic takeoff of the 1820s, see Paul Johnson, *Shopkeeper's Millennium: Society and Revivals in Rochester, New York, 1815–1837* (New York: Hill and Wang, 1978), 16; Johnson acknowledges that the "urban population had grown faster than the rural population between 1790 and 1810," but points out that this was only an "artificial 'windfall' urbanization created by American neutrality . . . and concentrated in a few northeastern seaports, and it stopped abruptly when the United States entered the war" (164 n. 2).

91. New York's population grew from 96,373 in 1810; 123,706 in 1820, to 202,589 in 1830; the metropolitan population (those living in cities of 50,000 or more, the standard criterion for a metropolis) was 250,246 in 1830, while the total urban population was 1,127,247; and there were thirteen cities (defined as settlements of at least 10,000) in 1820, and ninety-three by 1860 (U.S. Bureau of the Census statistics).

92. On the demographic shift beyond Albany, see Alan Taylor, *William Cooper's Town: Power and Persuasion on the Frontier of the Early American Republic* (New York: Vintage, 1995), 4. By contrast, the seaport cities of the previous century had stood "with [their] back[s] to the countryside," their merchants having "more contact with their counterparts in London and the West Indies than with farmers a few miles away" (Johnson, *Shopkeeper's Millennium,* 16).

93. "Statisticks," in *Charter and Directory of the City of Rochester* (Rochester: C. & M. Morse, 1834), 5; the 1827 *Directory* cites the "remarkable fact, that, in a population of nearly 8,000, *not one adult person is a native of the village!*" (114). The canal's route through Rochester was announced in 1819 and constructed by 1823. Utica, Syracuse, and Buffalo experienced population growths almost as dramatic: 83 percent, 282 percent, and 314 percent, respectively.

94. Thomas Cole, "Diary" (1829), quoted in Howard S. Merritt, "'A Wild Scene': Genesis of a Painting," *Baltimore Museum of Art Annual* 2 (1967): 26.

95. On classical references in town nomenclature, see Wilbur Zelinsky, "Classical Town Names in the United States: The Historical Geography of an American Idea," *Geographical Review* 57 (1967): 463–95.

96. Cole, "Diary," in Merritt, "A Wild Scene," 26.

97. Asher B. Durand, *Progress (The Advance of Civilization),* 1853, oil on canvas, 48 x 72 inches, The Warner Collection of Gulf States Paper Corporation.

98. Francis Lieber, *The Stranger in America; or, Letters to a Gentleman in Germany* (Philadelphia: Carey, Lea, and Blanchard, 1835), 287; Frederick Marryat, *Diary in America,* 3 vols. (London: Longman et al., 1839), 1:17.

99. Charles Lyell, *Principles of Geology,* 2 vols. (1830–33; Philadelphia: James Kay, 1837), 1:84. On Lyell's "discovery" of deep time, see Stephen Jay Gould, *Time's Arrow, Time's Cycle: Myth and Metaphor in the Discovery of Geological Time* (Cambridge, MA: Harvard University Press, 1987), 99–179.

100. Lyell, *Travels,* 1:17–18, 48; on the gradual process of denudation at Niagara Falls, ibid., 1:37–40. On his visit to the "Troy-Albany Capital District," where American geological science was born, see Gerald M. Friedman, "Charles Lyell in New York State," in *Lyell: The*

Past Is the Key to the Present, ed. D. J. Blundell and A. C. Scott (London: Geological Society, 1998), 71–81.

101. On this rural-urban synthesis, see James L. Machor, *Pastoral Cities: Urban Ideals and the Symbolic Landscape of America* (Madison: University of Wisconsin Press, 1987), 123–24, 128–31. The visual equivalent of such claims were lithographic bird's eye views that framed the new townscapes within larger landscapes of bucolic harmony.

102. [Hawthorne], "Sketches from Memory by a Pedestrian, No. II" *New-England Magazine* 9, no. 12 (1835): 398; further references cited in the text. Trollope, *Domestic Manners*, 292; William Leete Stone, "A Trip from New York to Niagara in 1829," *Magazine of American History* 20, no. 5 (1888): 395.

103. Jefferson, quoted in Henry Nash Smith, *Virgin Land: The American West as Symbol and Myth* (1950; Cambridge, MA: Harvard University Press, 1970), 219. Timothy Flint describes the "inverted history" witnessed when traveling *westward* (quoted in ibid., 220).

104. Captain Basil Hall, *Travels in North America*, 3 vols. (1829; Edinburgh: Cadell, 1830), 1:136; further references cited in the text. Johnson confirms that "East of the Genesee River, the fields stopped abruptly and Rochester began" (*Shopkeeper's Millenium*, 15).

105. Tocqueville, "Pocket Notebook Number 1," 130; Tocqueville, "Fortnight in the Wilds," in *Journey*, 332, 333; further references cited in the text.

106. William Leete Stone, "Narrative of the Festivities . . . ," in *Memoir . . . at the Celebration of the Completion of the New York Canals*, ed. Cadwallader D. Colden (New York: The Corporation of New York, 1825), 299.

107. Jefferson, quoted in Cornog, *Clinton*, 113.

108. Hall described how the newness of New York towns induced a "dreaming sort of feeling" in the traveler: an impression that they "had started into existence only the moment before" (*Travels*, 1:49). Rochester delayed the adoption of a city charter, remaining a "village" until 1834; see "An Act to Incorporate the City of Rochester," in *Charter and Directory*, 1–77.

109. Auguste Levasseur, *Lafayette in America in 1824 and 1825; or, Journal of a Voyage to the United States*, ed. J. D. Godman, 2 vols. (Philadelphia: Carey and Lea, 1829), 2:191.

110. Tocqueville, "Notebook E," in *Journey*, 265.

111. John Neal, "The Otter-Bag," in *The Token: A Christmas and New-Year's Present*, ed. N. P. Willis (Boston: S. G. Goodrich, 1829), 225, 226, 227; also excerpted as "The Ruins of America," *Evangelical Magazine and Gospel Advocate* [Utica], July 19, 1834, 232. John Lofland, the "Milford Bard," drew a similar comparison between the "ruins of an Indian empire" and those of the Old World, in "The Ruins of Time," *Casket* 2 (1829): 75–77; the phrase "scene of desolation" is his (77).

112. Tocqueville, "Pocket Notebook Number 1," 129, 132; Beaumont, quoted in Pierson, *Tocqueville and Beaumont*, 191.

113. Clinton, "The Iroquois," 250, 265–66.

114. Bryant, "An Indian at the Burial-Place of his Fathers," in *Poetical Works*, 58–60; quoted lines on 60; Bryant, "The Ages" (1821), in ibid., 14, 21. On the sympathies of other French aristocratic travelers for the "noble" Indians, see Liebersohn, *Aristocratic Encounters*, 61–112. Gilpin quoted Clinton's apocalyptic prediction in *Northern Tour*, p. 115. In another passage, Gilpin surveys the Mohawk Valley, once the domain of the "savage enemy" but now dominated by the Erie Canal, and wonders "how long this [current] scene is to last?" (96).

115. Cooper, *Home as Found*, 126; Hall, *Travels*, 1:162; Lyell, *Travels*, 1:48; Marryat, *Diary*, 1:178; Trollope, *Domestic Manners*, 292.

116. The urban geographer Michael Conzen has also noted this haphazardness of Ameri-

can city building, which was left to "individual energy and resourcefulness," and thus departed from "the logic of orderly, contiguous expansion" ("The Morphology of Nineteenth-Century Cities in the United States," in *Urbanization in the Americas: The Background in Comparative Perspective*, ed. W. Borah, J. Hardoy, and G. Stelter [Ottawa: National Museum of Man, 1980], 121, 125).

117. Nicolai Cikovsky Jr. and Barbara Novak have noted the frequency of tree stumps in mid-nineteenth-century American painting, but identify it as a simple emblem either of progress (of the nation) or declension (of nature); Cikovsky, "'The Ravages of the Axe': The Meaning of the Tree Stump in Nineteenth-Century American Art," *The Art Bulletin* 61, no. 4 (1979): 611–26; and Novak, "The Double-Edged Axe," *Art in America* 64 (1976): 44–50.

118. Edmund V. Gillon Jr., *Victorian Cemetery Art* (New York: Dover, 1972), figs. 161–78.

119. Gérard Genette, "Discours du récit," in *Figures III* (Paris: Éditions du Seuil 1972), 112. Toothing-stones jut out of a wall, so that a subsequent wall may be bonded to it. In the English translation, these metaphors are elided in favor of the simple term "advance mention" (Genette, *Narrative Discourse: An Essay in Method*, trans. Jane E. Lewin [Ithaca, NY: Cornell University Press, 1980], 75). This narrative device differs from "prolepsis," a more explicit reference to a future event.

120. Marryat, *Diary*, 1:153–54. Basil Hall noted how the traveler's reactions to a given scene are "modified by a host of real associations and recollections of other scenes of other voyages, in the east and in the west . . ." (*Travels*, 1:49).

121. Georg Simmel, "The Ruin" (1911), in *Essays on Sociology, Philosophy, and Aesthetics*, ed. Kurt H. Wolff (New York: Harper and Row, 1965), 265.

122. Gilpin, *Observations . . . Made in the Year 1772*, 1:69–70.

123. Cole, "Diary," in Merritt, "A Wild Scene," 26. On the construction of the Rochester aqueduct (completed 1823), see the Rochester *Directory* (1827), 120–22; and Joseph W. Barnes, "Historic Broad Street Bridge and the Erie Canal Sesquicentennial, 1825–1975," *Rochester History* 37, no. 3 (1975): 1–20.

124. "My Journal," *New-England Magazine* 9, no. 10 (1835): 274, 275, 276.

125. Canal commissioners, quoted in Barnes, "Broad Street Bridge," 7. Assembly *Documents* (1836), quoted in ibid., 6. The ruins of the aqueduct were finally swept away by the flood of 1865.

126. "Topographical Sketches: Ruins of the Genesee Bridge," *The Monthly Repository* 3, no. 4 (1832): 128.

127. Assembly *Documents* (1836), quoted in Barnes, "Broad Street Bridge," 6.

128. Clinton, "Memorial . . . in Favour of a Canal," 419.

129. *Statesman* [Pittsburgh], quoted in Richard C. Wade, *The Urban Frontier: The Rise of Western Cities, 1790–1830* (1959; Urbana: University of Illinois Press, 1996), 178–79.

130. DeWitt Clinton, letter to David Thomas (1827), quoted in Ronald E. Shaw, *Erie Water West: A History of the Erie Canal, 1792–1854* (Lexington: University Press of Kentucky, 1990), 162.

131. Blake McKelvey, *Rochester on the Genesee: The Growth of a City* (Syracuse, NY: Syracuse University Press, 1973), 36, 37; Diane Shaw, *City Building on the Eastern Frontier: Sorting the New Nineteenth-Century City* (Baltimore: Johns Hopkins University Press, 2004), 142. By 1862, Exchange Street was described as having endured a "long night of desolation, when desertion, ruin and decay seemed a power that well nigh destroyed it" ("And this was Rochester! Excerpts from the Old Citizen Letters," *Rochester History* 4, no. 1 [1942]: 17).

132. On Noah's larger career, see Jonathan D. Sarna, *Jacksonian Jew: The Two Worlds of*

Mordecai Noah (New York: Holmes and Meier, 1981); and Isaac Goldberg, *Major Noah: American-Jewish Pioneer* (New York: Knopf, 1937).

133. Noah, "Proclamation to the Jews," speech delivered at Buffalo, September 15, 1825, reprinted in "Revival of the Jewish Government," in *Wayne Sentinel* [Palmyra, NY], September 27, 1825, n.p. On the religious foundations of Ararat, see S. Joshua Kohn, "Mordecai Manuel Noah's Ararat Project and the Missionaries," *American Jewish Historical Quarterly* 55, no. 2 (1965): 162–96. For evidence of its financial motivations, see Jonathan D. Sarna, "The Roots of Ararat: An Early Letter from Mordecai M. Noah to Peter B. Porter," *American Jewish Archives* 32, no. 1 (1980): 52–58.

134. For an account of that ceremony, see "Revival of the Jewish Government"; Noah included in that speech an invitation to Native Americans to "re-unite" with their "brethren." He elaborated on this theory in his subsequent *Discourse on the Evidences of the American Indians Being the Descendants of the Lost Tribes of Israel . . .* (New York: Van Norden, 1837).

135. Noah, "Proclamation to the Jews," in "Revival of the Jewish Government." See the excoriating letter from the Grand Rabbi De Cologna to the editor of the Paris *Journal des Debats*, reprinted in *Zion's Herald*, January 25, 1826, 1. On Porter's lack of interest in the project, see Sarna, "The Roots of Ararat," 54; on the failure to attract a single settler, see ibid., 52. *Black Rock Gazette* declared his project "at an end" on January 24, 1826.

136. "The Frolic at Niagara: Mr. Doolittle's Letter to the Editor of the N. York Commercial Advertiser," *Daily National Intelligencer*, no. 5214 (1829): col. B; William Leete Stone, "From New York to Niagara," in *Holland Land Company . . .* (Buffalo: Buffalo Historical Society, 1910), 251.

137. On the touristic afterlife of this cornerstone, see Lewis F. Allen, "Founding of the City of Ararat on Grand Island—By Mordecai M. Noah," read before the [Buffalo] Historical Society, March 5, 1866, reprinted in *Buffalo Historical Society Publications* 1 (1879): 325–26. Earlier in 1866, the stone had been deposited in the Buffalo Historical Society, where it remained until 1965, at which point it was transferred to the new Grand Island Town Hall.

138. Noble E. Whitford, *History of the Canal System of the State of New York*, 2 vols. (Albany, NY: Brandow, 1906), 1:654–55. According to Pierson, Wattines [in his spelling] left the island and relocated to the northern shore of Lake Oneida circa 1793. It is not clear when exactly Watines returned to France (*Tocqueville and Beaumont*, 201–2).

139. Tocqueville, paraphrasing the woman in his letter to Alexandrine (cited above, n. 2), n.p. (p. 6), Beinecke.

Chapter 2

1. William Oliver, *Eight Months in Illinois; With Information to Emigrants* (Newcastle upon Tyne: Printed by William Andrew Mitchell, 1843), 41.

2. Charles Dickens, *American Notes for General Circulation* (1842; Harmondsworth: Penguin, 2000), 190; subsequent references cited in the text.

3. James Silk Buckingham, *The Eastern and Western States of America*, 3 vols. (London: Fisher, Son, and Co., 1842), 3:81–82.

4. William Cronon, *Nature's Metropolis: Chicago and the Great West* (New York: W. W. Norton, 1991), 23–54; further references cited in the text; Gunther Barth, *Instant Cities: Urbanization and the Rise of San Francisco and Denver* (New York: Oxford University Press, 1975), 92–127. Historians have examined how cities like St. Louis failed to become the "Great Metropolis of the West" (e.g., Jeffrey S. Adler, *Yankee Merchants and the Making of the Urban West: The Rise and Fall of Antebellum St. Louis* [Cambridge: Cambridge University Press, 1991]), but even those cities continued to grow at a reasonable rate.

5. Georg Simmel, "The Metropolis and Mental Life" (1903), in *Simmel on Culture*, ed. David Frisby and Mike Featherstone (London: Sage, 1997), 176.

6. William Glyde Wilkins speculates about Dickens's Cairo investment in *Charles Dickens in America* (London: Chapman and Hall, 1911), 210–11, a theory rejected in Jerome Meckier, *Innocent Abroad: Charles Dickens's American Engagements* (Lexington: University Press of Kentucky, 1990), 24. However, as the ledger books of Cairo's London agents, John Wright and Company, are no longer extant, one can no more disprove than prove Dickens's involvement. Dickens did have acquaintances who sustained losses; see his letter to Charles Molloy, November 28 [1840], in which he expresses fears that his former boss had "suffere[d]" from Wright's bankruptcy, in Madeline House, Graham Storey, and Kathleen Tillotson, eds., *The Letters of Charles Dickens*, 12 vols. (Oxford: Clarendon Press, 1974), 2:159.

7. See Robert Lawson-Peebles, "Dickens Goes West," in *Views of American Landscapes*, ed. Mark Gidley and Lawson-Peebles (Cambridge: Cambridge University Press, 1989), 111–28; Patricia M. Ard, "Charles Dickens and Frances Trollope: Victorian Kindred Spirits in the American Wilderness," *American Transcendental Quarterly* 7, no. 4 (1993): 293–306; and, for an argument that views the landscape descriptions as more overdetermined, Rodney S. Edgecombe, "Topographic Disaffection in Dickens's *American Notes* and *Martin Chuzzlewit*," *Journal of English and Germanic Philology* 93 (1994): 35–54.

8. See respectively, Meckier, *Innocent Abroad*, 112–19; Laura Berry, "The Body Politic and the Body Fluid: Social Expectorations and Dickens's *American Notes*," *Victorian Literature and Culture* 24 (1996): 211–27; William Sharpe, "A Pig upon the Town: Charles Dickens in New York," *Nineteenth-Century Prose* 23, no. 2 (1996): 12–24; and J. Hillis Miller, "The Sources of Dickens's Comic Art: From *American Notes* to *Martin Chuzzlewit*," *Nineteenth-Century Fiction* 24 (March 1970): 469, 470.

9. See Sidney P. Moss, *Charles Dickens' Quarrel with America* (Troy, NY: Whitston, 1984), and Meredith L. McGill, *American Literature and the Culture of Reprinting, 1834–53* (Philadelphia: University of Pennsylvania Press, 2003), 109–40.

10. See, for example, Malcolm Bradbury's confident assertion that the phrase "'general circulation' . . . no doubt referred to the American custom of literacy piracy" (*Dangerous Pilgrimages: Trans-Atlantic Mythologies and the Novel* [London: Secker and Warburg, 1995], 102); he observes, though, that "what so upset Dickens's first American visit has never really been satisfactorily explained" (99).

11. John W. Reps, *Views and Viewmakers: Lithographs of Towns and Cities in the United States and Canada . . . , 1825–1925* (Columbia: University of Missouri Press, 1984), 67, subtitle of chapter 9. Reps does acknowledge the production of more exaggerated views (ibid., 67), including Strickland's (illustrated in ibid., plate 81).

12. See also Strickland's letter of December 13, 1838, referring to their "report, plans and estimates," reprinted in the prospectus for the Cairo City and Canal Company (CCCC), *City of Cairo* ([St. Louis]: s.n., 1839), n.p., AAS; hereafter cited in the text as "Cairo prospectus." On Strickland's financial and professional struggles, especially after the Panic of 1837, which forced him to find work beyond Philadelphia and beyond architecture, see Mary N. Woods, *From Craft to Profession: The Practice of Architecture in Nineteenth-Century America* (Berkeley: University of California Press, 1999), 95–96; and Agnes Addison Gilchrist, *William Strickland: Architect and Engineer, 1788–1854* (New York: Da Capo Press, 1969), 13–14.

13. See the description of "the immense range of navigable rivers, all centering at this point" (Cairo prospectus, n.p.).

14. CCCC assured that real estate prices would soon be comparable to those of Chicago, St. Louis, Louisville, and Cincinnati (*Prospectus and Engineers' Report, Relating to the City of*

Cairo, Incorporated by the State of Illinois [St. Louis: T. Watson, 1839], 11, AAS; hereafter cited as *Report*).

15. On boosterism and the central city, see Charles N. Glaab, "Visions of Metropolis: William Gilpin and Theories of City Growth in the American West," *Wisconsin Magazine of History* 45 (1961): 21–31; and Carl Abbott, *Boosters and Businessmen: Popular Economic Thought and Urban Growth in the Antebellum Middle West* (Westport, CT: Greenwood Press, 1981), 109–25; and my discussion of Reavis in chapter 4.

16. Edward D. Mansfield, *Memoirs of the Life and Services of Daniel Drake . . .* (Cincinnati: Applegate, 1860), 118.

17. John McMurray Lansden, *A History of the City of Cairo, Illinois* (Chicago: R. R. Donnelley, 1910), 40.

18. On the warehouse that would rival any in London, see Federal Writers' Project, Works Progress Administration, *Cairo Guide* (Cairo: Cairo Public Library, 1938), 20. On the frequent flooding of new town sites along the Mississippi and the Ohio, see Timothy Mahoney, *River Towns in the Great West: The Structure of Provincial Urbanization in the American Midwest, 1820–1870* (Cambridge: Cambridge University Press, 1990), 55–86.

19. Strickland, design for a monument to Fulton (1840), in the portfolio of Strickland drawings in the Tennessee State Library; Gilchrist has found no evidence that it was ever erected (*William Strickland*, 97).

20. Blake McKelvey, *Rochester on the Genesee: The Growth of a City* (Syracuse, NY: Syracuse University Press, 1973), 36–37. Mahoney has identified circa 1830 as the moment when frontier towns, hitherto usually founded in areas of preexisting settlement, "were increasingly laid out before people arrived to use them" (*River Towns*, 90). For a typical reference to magic, see Caroline Kirkland's discussion of speculators' faith in the "necromantic power" of banks in these cities (below, p. 96). The geographer Michael Conzen reminds us that not all town founders "dreamed of starting great metropolises; in fact, "most were content to establish on the ground the makings of a county town." Nevertheless, "most nineteenth-century new town foundations in the United States were speculative . . ." ("The Morphology of Nineteenth-Century Cities in the United States," in *Urbanization in the Americas: The Background in Comparative Perspective*, ed. W. Borah, J. Hardoy, and G. Stelter [Ottawa: National Museum of Man, 1980], 127).

21. The number of blocks laid out on a plat serves as an index to the aspirations of the town founders; compared with the town plats Conzen describes ("The Morphology of Nineteenth-Century Cities in the United States," 127), Cairo's 142-block plat was particularly ambitious. Strickland's plan (see fig. 2.4) did include six open squares, a departure from the usual tendency to minimize public space and maximize profit.

22. Anthony Trollope, *North America*, 2 vols. (London: Chapman and Hall, 1862), 1:182–83; further references cited in the text. A. Stewart, "The Speculations of '34, 5, 6," *The Liberator*, April 16, 1841, 63. James Fenimore Cooper, *Home as Found* (1838; New York: Capricorn Books, 1961), 21, 101–2, 22, 105, 100, 108, 109.

23. On the deployment of metaphors of natural disaster (such as earthquakes and volcanoes) to present the 1837 Panic as divine retribution for men's moral failings, see Ann Fabian, "Speculation on Distress: The Popular Discourse of the Panics of 1837 and 1857," *Yale Journal of Criticism* 3, no. 1 (1989): 131–33; natural metaphors would also be invoked during the 1857 Panic, but would by then convey a sense of the natural laws governing markets (ibid., 137).

24. Capt. Frederick Marryat, *Diary in America*, 3 vols. (London: Longman et al., 1839), 1:59. Mrs. Mary Clavers [Caroline M. Kirkland], *A New Home—Who'll Follow? or, Glimpses of Western Life* (New York: C. S. Francis, 1839), 53–54; further references cited in the text.

Thomas L. Nicholas, *Forty Years of American Life*, 2 vols. (London: John Maxwell, 1864), 1:168; further references cited in the text.

25. Georg Simmel, "The Ruin" (1911), in *Essays on Sociology, Philosophy, and Aesthetics,* ed. Kurt H. Wolff (New York: Harper and Row, 1965), 262.

26. Ernst von Hesse-Wartegg, *Travels on the Lower Mississippi, 1879–1880*, ed. and trans. Frederic Trautmann (Columbia: University of Missouri Press, 1990), 33.

27. Edward Dicey, *Six Months in the Federal States* (London and Cambridge: Macmillan, 1863), 116–17 (emphasis added).

28. J. F. Snyder would claim that "to see Cairo was really the main object of his journey to America" ("Charles Dickens in Illinois," *Journal of the Illinois State Historical Society* 3, no. 3 [1910]: 20–21).

29. Charles Dickens, *The Life and Adventures of Martin Chuzzlewit* (1844; London: Penguin Classics, 1999), 343, 364, 484; further references cited in the text.

30. On my appropriation of the term "ruins in reverse" from Robert Smithson, "A Tour of the Monuments of Passaic, New Jersey," in *Robert Smithson: The Collected Writings*, ed. Jack Flam (Berkeley: University of California Press, 1996), 68–74, see my introduction.

31. On Browne's apparent freedom to insert details specified neither by the text itself nor by Dickens's instructions, see Michael Steig, *Dickens and Phiz* (Bloomington: Indiana University Press, 1978), 3, 8, passim.

32. On the absence of frogs in Dickens's instructions, see ibid., 69.

33. Dickens may have been referring to the opulent structure that was to replace the old Court House or the aborted bridge over the Ohio at 12th Street, both begun just before the 1837 Panic; see Ben Casseday, *The History of Louisville: From Its Earliest Settlement Till the Year 1852* (Louisville: Hull and Brother, 1852), 119, 194. Casseday describes the former as a "sublime monument of the city's folly" that "still stands an almost mouldering ruin, its half-finished grandeur constantly recalling the parable of the foolish man who 'began to build and was not able to finish'" (119).

34. On the design of Girard College's main building, and the legal difficulties that caused its completion to be delayed for fourteen years, see Henry W. Arey, *The Girard College and Its Founder* (Philadelphia: C. Sherman and Son, 1861), 44–52, 32–35, respectively.

35. Howard Gillette Jr., *Between Justice and Beauty: Race, Planning, and the Failure of Urban Policy in Washington, D.C.* (Baltimore: Johns Hopkins University Press, 1995), 2–26; L'Enfant's phrase "city of magnificent vistas" is cited in ibid., 6. Border cities such as St. Louis (and perhaps Cairo) tended to suffer from the nervousness of northeastern investors, especially during the 1850s; see Adler, *Yankee Merchants and the Making of the Urban West*, 110–44. For a history of Washington as a border city, see Carl Abbott, *Political Terrain: Washington, D.C., from Tidewater Town to Global Metropolis* (Chapel Hill: University of North Carolina Press, 1999).

36. John W. Reps, *Town Planning in Frontier America* (1965; Columbia: University of Missouri Press, 1980), 223–24, 225.

37. L'Enfant, letter to Jefferson, February 27, 1792, quoted in Gillette, *Between Justice and Beauty*, 5. On the decision to auction land straight away, see ibid., 9–12, and Reps, *Town Planning*, 224–6.

38. On loans from Holland, see Gillette, *Between Justice and Beauty*, 20–21; and on the "numerous merchant bankruptcies, [and] the collapse of four of the thirteen local banks," see James Sterling Young, *The Washington Community, 1800–1828* (New York: Columbia University Press, 1966), 24. There were calls to remove the capital in 1808 and 1814 (see respectively Gillette, *Between Justice and Beauty*, 12, and Young, *Washington Community*, 24, 51), and in

1838, Harriet Martineau reported that "the Cincinnati people are already speculating upon which of their hills or table-lands is to be the site of the new Capitol" (*Retrospect of Western Travel*, 3 vols. [London: Saunders and Otley, 1838], 1:267); see also my discussion of later calls for capital removal in chapter 4.

39. On the temporarily abandoned excavations for a city canal, the symbolic collapse of a bridge consisting of an arch of "thirteen stones inscribed for the original states," and other ruined structures in Washington circa 1800, see Young, *Washington Community*, 22–23. Congressman Griswold of Connecticut, quoted in ibid., 22.

40. Benjamin Henry Latrobe, entry for August 12, 1806, in *The Journal of Latrobe* (New York: Appleton and Company, 1905), 131. On Strickland's apprenticeship to Latrobe, see Gilchrist, *William Strickland*, 1–2. Speculative house building was encouraged by the city commissioners who relaxed building restrictions, "lowered the price of lots to purchasers who would build on them and . . . required owners to build before they could resell their lots." Many of these "jerry-built houses" remained vacant and suffered from vandalism and decay (Young, *Washington Community*, 22). Particularly notorious were the houses built by the failed land speculator, Robert Morris, which were compared to the ruins of Palmyra (Wilhelmus Bogart Bryan, *A History of the National Capital from Its Foundation* . . . , 2 vols. [New York: Macmillan, 1914], 1: 465).

41. Bryan, *History of the National Capital*, 1:618. On the covered boardwalk, see Young, *Washington Community*, 44. On the popularity in America of Volney's deist book *Les Ruines* (1791), see Paul Merrill Spurlin, *The French Enlightenment in America: Essays on the Times of the Founding Fathers* (Athens: University of Georgia Press, 1984), 134.

42. Henry Adams, *The Education of Henry Adams* (1906; Harmondsworth: Penguin, 1995), 47; further references cited in the text.

43. On the controversies surrounding the design of the Washington Monument, from its conception in 1799 to its opening in 1888, see Kirk Savage, "Self-Made Monument: George Washington and the Fight to Erect a National Monument," in *Critical Issues in Public Art: Content, Context, and Controversy*, ed. Harriet F. Senie and Sally Webster (New York: HarperCollins, 1992), 5–32; for references to it as a "stump," see 19.

44. On the popularity of slumming in Five Points after the publication of *American Notes*, see Tyler Anbinder, *Five Points: The 19th-Century New York City Neighborhood That Invented Tap Dance, Stole Elections, and Became the World's Most Notorious Slum* (New York: Free Press, 2001), 34. Dickens's account was excerpted in *The Old Brewery, and the New Mission House at Five Points; By Ladies of the Mission* (New York: Stringer and Townsend, 1854), 16–21; the 1848 founding of the mission is described at 36–41, and the "rickety" Old Brewery and its demolition in 1853, 47, 65–68. On the activities of the Ladies Home Missionary Society, see Lori D. Ginzberg, *Women and the Work of Benevolence: Morality, Politics, and Class in the Nineteenth-Century United States* (New Haven, CT: Yale University Press, 1990), 121. The tenement Dickens describes on 100–101 may well be the Old Brewery.

45. On the decline of tobacco plantations, see Avery Odelle Craven, *Soil Exhaustion as a Factor in the Agricultural History of Virginia and Maryland, 1606–1860* (1925; Columbia: University of South Carolina Press, 2006), and Carville Earle, *The Evolution of a Tidewater Settlement System: All Hallow's Parish, Maryland, 1650–1783* (Chicago: University of Chicago Press, 1975).

46. See M. Giulia Fabi, "Representing Slavery in Nineteenth-Century Britain: The Anxiety of Non / Fictional Authorship in Charles Dickens's *American Notes* and William Brown's *Clotel*," in *Images of America: Through the European Looking Glass*, ed. William L. Chew III (Brussels: VUB Press, 1997), 131.

47. Charles Ball, *Slavery in the United States: A Narrative of the Life and Adventures of Charles Ball, a Black Man* . . . (1836; New York: John S. Taylor, 1837), 51, 45–47; further references cited in the text. On the popularity and numerous reprintings of Ball's narrative, and the role of his amanuensis-editor Isaac Fisher, see William L. Andrews, *To Tell a Free Story: The First Century of Afro-American Autobiography, 1760–1865* (Urbana: University of Illinois Press, 1986), 81–84.

48. George Fitzhugh, "Trade and Panics," *De Bow's Review* 27, no. 2 (1859): 159; further references cited in the text.

49. George Fitzhugh made similar arguments against capitalist free trade in *Sociology for the South, or the Failure of Free Society* (Richmond, VA: A. Morris, 1854), 14–20, 87. On Fitzhugh's political economy, see Eugene Genovese, *The World the Slaveholders Made: Two Essays in Interpretation* (1969; Middletown, CT: Wesleyan University Press, 1988); his views were not necessarily representative of the South as a whole, or even of his native Virginian slaveholding elite (see ibid., 128). The importance of uneven development as long-term cause of sectional conflict has been acknowledged both by historians of the "modernization" school, and by neo-Marxists: see, respectively, Raimondo Luraghi, "The Civil War and the Modernization of American Society: Social Structure and Industrial Revolution in the Old South before and during the War," *Civil War History* 18, no. 3 (1972): 230–50; and Eugene Genovese, *The Political Economy of Slavery* (New York: Pantheon Books, 1965).

50. George Fitzhugh, "Wealth of the North and the South," *De Bow's Review* 23, no. 6 (1857): 587; further references cited in the text.

51. Edmund Ruffin, *Anticipations of the Future: To Serve as Lessons for the Present Time* (Richmond, VA: J. W. Randolph, 1860), 1; further references cited in the text. Ruffin was a leading advocate of scientific agricultural reform; see Ruffin, *Incidents of My Life: Edmund Ruffin's Autobiographical Essays*, ed. David F. Allmendinger Jr. (Charlottesville: University of Virginia Press, 1990); and Betty L. Mitchell, *Edmund Ruffin: A Biography* (Bloomington: Indiana University Press, 1981).

52. George Fitzhugh, "Washington City," *De Bow's* 24, no. 6 (1858): 507.

53. David R. Goldfield has challenged the myth of antebellum southerners as predominantly antiurban in *Urban Growth in the Age of Sectionalism: Virginia, 1847–1761* (Baton Rouge: Louisiana State University Press, 1977), citing Fitzhugh and De Bow on xviii, xxiii.

54. Fitzhugh, *Sociology for the South*, 136; see also Fitzhugh, "Southern Thought," *De Bow's* 23, no. 4 (1857): 337–49.

55. Col. J. Gadsden, "Commercial Spirit at the South," *De Bow's* 2, no. 2 (1846): 129–30, 132, 126–27; further references cited in the text.

56. Fitzhugh, "Washington City," 504; on the use of slaves to build the Capitol, see Jesse J. Holland, *Black Men Built the Capitol: Discovering African-American History in and around Washington, D.C.* (Guilford, CT: Globe Pequot, 2007), especially 3–4.

57. Fitzhugh, "Washington City," 503–4.

58. Charles Dickens, *Pictures from Italy and American Notes for General Circulation* (London: Chapman and Hall, 1859), 113, see also 154.

59. For a reading that treats Dickens's passage on slavery as a "substitution" for the copyright issue, see Fabi, "Representing Slavery," 132.

60. "Dickens's Notes on America," *The New Englander* 1, no. 1 (1843): 75. For the charge of accentuating the negative, see ibid., 76–77, and "Notice of New Works: American Notes for General Circulation by Charles Dickens," *Southern Literary Messenger* 9, no. 1 (1843): 61.

61. This bank is misidentified in the notes to the Penguin edition as the *First* Bank of the United States (296n2). On Strickland's copying of Stuart and Revett's illustrations of the

Parthenon, see Gilchrist, *William Strickland*, 3; see also 53–58. On the various modifications he introduced into the Greek temple form to provide the necessary security, lighting, and spatial arrangements for a bank, see his own article, "New Bank of the United States, in Philadelphia," in *The Port Folio* 12 (September 1821): 204–7, quotation on 207.

62. *New York Herald*, cited in Edmund Ruffin's journal, *The Farmers' Register* 9 (1841): 317. The depreciation of the college's shares in the Bank of the U.S. did indeed contribute to the delay; see Arey, *Girard College*, 31–32.

63. Letter dated April 24, 1842, quoted in John Forster, *The Life of Charles Dickens*, 2 vols. (1872–74; London: Chapman and Hall, 1887), 1:400.

64. Charles Dickens (with W. H. Wills), "The Old Lady in Threadneedle Street" (1850), in *Charles Dickens' Uncollected Writings from* Household Words, *1850–1859*, ed. Harry Stone (Bloomington: Indiana University Press, 1968), 122–35; page references cited in the text.

65. On the privileges accorded to the Bank of England by several Acts of Parliament, see Stephen Quinn, "Money, Finance, and Capital Markets," in *The Cambridge Economic History of Modern Britain*, vol. 1, *Industrialisation, 1700–1860*, ed. Roderick Floud and Paul Johnson (Cambridge: Cambridge University Press, 2004), especially 156.

66. On Dickens's free trade views, see Michael Sheldon, "Dickens, 'The Chimes,' and the Anti-Corn Law League," *Victorian Studies* 25 (1982): 329–53. British advocates of free trade insisted that capital, like blood, needed to circulate freely, evenly, and without artificial blockages or external tinkering; see Adam Smith's use of the trope of bodily circulation in *The Wealth of Nations, Books IV–V* (1776; Harmondsworth: Penguin, 2000), 187–88.

67. On the lingering fears of a completely unregulated circulation, even among liberal economists of the eighteenth and nineteenth centuries, see Timothy L. Alborn, "Economic Man, Economic Machine: Images of Circulation in the Victorian Money Market," in *Natural Images in Economic Thought: "Markets Read in Tooth and Claw,"* ed. Philip Mirowski (Cambridge and New York: Cambridge University Press, 1994), 174–75.

68. Parliament did make exceptions to the £5 rule, for example in 1797; see Quinn, "Money, Finance, and Capital Markets," 162.

69. On the counterfeiting and heterogeneity of paper money in this period, which prompted the publication of "bank note reporters" and "counterfeit detectors," see Stephen Mihm, *Nation of Counterfeiters: Capitalists, Con Men, and the Making of the United States* (Cambridge, MA: Harvard University Press, 2007).

70. Frederick Marryat, *Narrative of the Travels and Adventures of Monsieur Violet . . .*, 3 vols. (London: Longman, Brown, Green, and Longmans, 1843), 2:221–22.

71. Eric Helleiner, *The Making of National Money: Territorial Currencies in Historical Perspective* (Ithaca, NY: Cornell University Press, 2003), 19–41.

72. Reginald C. McGrane estimates that there were "nearly $100,000,000 of American stocks and bonds for sale in the London money market in the summer of 1839," in *Foreign Bondholders and American State Debts* (New York: Macmillan, 1935), 106.

73. According to the deal, Wright and Company would sell $1.5 million in CCCC bonds to other British investors at a commission of up to 5 percent. Lansden, *History of the City of Cairo*, 55, 170–71.

74. Joshua Bates, quoted in Smith, *Economic Aspects*, 192; *The Times*, quoted in ibid., 192.

75. Sidney George Fisher, diary entry for October 17, 1841, in *A Philadelphia Perspective: The Diary of Sidney George Fisher Covering the Years 1834–1871*, ed. Nicholas B. Wainwright (Philadelphia; Historical Society of Pennsylvania, 1967), 126. According to W. B. Smith, more than 56 percent of the Bank's shares were "in foreign hands" when it failed (*Economic Aspects of the Second Bank of the United States* [New York: Greenwood Press, 1953], 227).

76. *Cairo Guide*, 20; Snyder, "Dickens in Illinois," 21.

77. John Reps, *Cities of the Mississippi: Nineteenth-Century Images of Urban Development* (Columbia: University of Missouri Press, 1994), 4; see also Reps, *Views and Viewmakers*, 59–66.

78. McGrane, *Foreign Bondholders*, 115. The governorship of Thomas Ford (1842–46) would ensure that Illinois never went as far as to repudiate its debts entirely; see ibid., 115–25. Illinois finally resumed interest payments in July 1846.

79. On the mistrust of speculators in the western states, and the efforts of the leading British agent for loans to the states, the Baring Brothers, to reassure their investors, see McGrane, *Foreign Bondholders*, 32–33, 125.

80. Dickens's editor, John Forster, was one of the first to suggest that Martin was able to make "happy use of a bitter experience, casting off his slough of selfishness in the poisonous swamp of Eden" (*Life*, 2:75).

81. The novel is replete with dishonest and hypocritical Englishmen (Mr. Pecksniff, Jonas Chuzzlewit, Montague Tigg) and fraudulent institutions (the Anglo-Bengalee Disinterested Loan and Life Insurance Company). However, Dickens presents the various duplicities of Americans as a national condition (only Mr. Bevan is exempt), rather than one limited to certain individuals or institutions.

82. The reference to the Bank's "ruins" appears in Job R. Tyson, "Resources and Progress of Philadelphia," *De Bow's* 15, no. 1 (1853): 45.

83. [Thomas Greaves Cary], "Letter to a Lady in France on the Supposed Failure of a National Bank, the Supposed Delinquency of the National Government, the Debts of the Several States, and Repudiation; With Answers to Enquiries concerning the Books of Capt. Marryat and Mr. Dickens" (Boston: Benjamin H. Greene, 1843); references cited in the text. I am deducing Cary's Whig sympathies from the fact that he was a Boston merchant closely associated with the Lowell factories, the Mercantile Library Association, and other Whig strongholds; and from the favorable review his book received in that party's press (e.g., *North American Review* 58, no. 123 [1844], 516).

84. The notion that banks "expanded their activities without references to their true reserves, that is, specie," is the conventional claim made by Arthur Schlesinger Jr., *The Age of Jackson* (Boston: Little, Brown, 1945); Richard Hofstadter, *The American Political Tradition* (New York: Knopf, 1948); and Marvin Meyers, *The Jacksonian Persuasion* (Stanford, CA: Stanford University Press, 1960), as paraphrased by Peter Temin, *The Jacksonian Economy* (New York: Norton, 1969), 26.

85. Sean Wilentz attributes Jackson's loathing of banks and paper money to his near bankruptcy in 1795 and to the Panic of 1819, in *Andrew Jackson* (New York: Times Books, 2005), 41–42. On wildcat banks, see Mihm, *Nation of Counterfeiters*, 186.

86. "An act to establish and maintain a General system of Internal Improvements" (February 27, 1837), in *Laws of the State of Illinois* (Vandalia, IL: William Walters, 1837), 121–51; the act incorporating CCCC was approved March 1, 1837. Holbrook himself had been involved with the Illinois Central when it was a private company, acting as its treasurer, and would be criticized for using the railroad to boost his investments in Cairo; see Paul Wallace Gates, *The Illinois Central Railroad and Its Colonization Work* (Cambridge, MA: Harvard University Press, 1934), 24, 28.

87. "An Act supplemental to the 'act to establish and maintain a general system of Internal Improvements'" (1837), in *Laws of the State of Illinois*, 152. On the financing of these projects, see McGrane, *Foreign Bondholders*, 105. The crisis in Illinois in 1839–41, which resulted in the suspension of railroad and canal construction, was allegedly "precipitated by the close connection between the Illinois banks and the internal improvement schemes" (Reginald C.

McGrane, *The Panic of 1837: Some Financial Problems of the Jacksonian Era* [New York: Russell and Russell, 1965], 128). On the larger debates about state-funded public works during this period, see John Lauritz Larson, *Internal Improvement: National Public Works and the Promise of Popular Government in the Early United States* (Chapel Hill: University of North Carolina Press, 1991), 195–224.

88. The leading mid-twentieth-century historians of the Jacksonian period, Schlesinger Jr., Hofstadter, and Meyers (cited above, n. 84) similarly blamed Jackson's termination of the Second Bank. Peter Temin's *Jacksonian Economy* eventually refuted this view, pointing instead to the influx of foreign silver and gold from Europe and Mexico and the increased investments of British capital in American securities. More recent economic historians, notably Peter Rousseau, have revisited the earlier thesis, accusing Temin of being too quick to exonerate Jackson (Rousseau, "Jacksonian Monetary Policy, Specie Flows, and the Panic of 1837," *Journal of Economic History* 62, no. 2 [2002]: 457–88).

89. Cronon makes the claim that this decade marked "the most intense land speculation in American history," in *Nature's Metropolis*, 29; see also William Pooley, *The Settlement of Illinois from 1830 to 1850* (1908; PhD diss., University of Wisconsin, Madison, 1905), 564; and John Reps, *Making of Urban America* (Princeton, NJ: Princeton University Press, 1965), 361.

90. In 1839, Biddle argued that Jackson's Specie Circular had the effect of diverting gold to the western frontier, where it was "not circulated; not used," but hoarded, with ruinous implications for the Atlantic trade (quoted in Smith, *Economic Aspects*, 185).

91. Letter dated April 24, 1842, in Forster, *Life*, 1:400.

92. The Missouri senator and hard money advocate, Thomas Hart Benton, referred to "Cairo, swindling shop" as one of several synonyms for wildcat banks in a speech he gave to the U.S. Senate on January 13, 1842, warning against the new proposal of a Federal Exchequer (*The Congressional Globe* [appendix], January 1842, 65).

93. The *Democratic Review* "ascribed" the "pecuniary embarrassments of the last five years" in large part to Biddle's bank, "and its unwarrantable speculations in State stocks and cotton," among other abuses ("Currency Reform," *Democratic Review* 7, no. 26 [1840]: 167; further references cited in the text). According to Temin, the rise in the price of cotton, which can be attributed in part to Biddle's efforts, "symbolized the recovery to contemporary observers" and helped to restore the "pre-1837 credit structure" (*Jacksonian Economy*, 151). Biddle remained president until as late as March 1839, acting as advisor thereafter.

94. Temin, *Jacksonian Economy*, 152.

95. Lansden later attributed Cairo's downfall to dealings in London, in *History of the City of Cairo*, 170–71.

96. Smith, *Economic Aspects*, 216.

97. "Philadelphia Banking," *Democratic Review* 6, no. 23 (1839): 373. The same magazine argued that "the paper currency of England, under the protection of its 'Great Regulator,' that object of homage to the devout worshippers of the 'credit system,' has suffered revulsions and inflicted injuries, compared with which the evils under which we suffer are but trifles" ("Currency Reform," 185). On the "heterogeneous circulation" of various different forms of money across England during these years, see Matthew Rowlinson, "'The Scotch Hate Gold': British Identity and Paper Money," in *Nation-States and Money: The Past, Present, and Future of National Currencies*, ed. Emily Gilber and Eric Helleiner (London and New York: Routledge, 1999), 47–67.

98. For decades, the Bank has "not only failed to relieve the community, but [has] actually, by means of over-issues, produced the disasters such an institution is intended to prevent" ("Currency Reform," 189). On the failure of the Bank of England to serve as

lender and rediscounter of last resort before 1844, see Quinn, "Money, Finance, and Capital Markets," 166.

99. See Quinn, "Money, Finance, and Capital Markets," 162; and John A. Agnew, *Mastering Space: Hegemony, Territory, and International Political Economy* (London: Routledge, 1995), 26–31.

100. An American seeking a loan from the British "receives forty-seven cents on the hundred" and then loses an additional 40 percent due to the low quality of the money he receives; "thus plundered, [he] is glad to escape to the banks of the Illinois or the Mississippi with what is left" ("British Arrogance," *Democratic Review* 21, no. 112 [1847]: 325).

101. [Henry Wood?], *Change for the American Notes: In Letters from London to New York, by an American Lady* (New York: Harper, 1843), 78; further references cited in the text. The author may well have been neither American nor a lady, but rather the Yorkshireman and journalist, Henry Wood (according to the AAS catalogue). The *Democratic Review* made a similar argument: "Between February 1797, and May 1821, the British government never paid honestly, within the limits of the kingdom, one single debt; and they committed and carried out more frauds, and created more beggary and misery than they can ever compensate the world for . . ." ("British Arrogance," 325).

102. "Writings of Charles Dickens" [reprinted from *North British Review*], *Living Age* 5 (1845): 604.

103. The author's Jacksonian sympathies are clearly indicated by his/her denial of the charge of "repudiation" (78), and by the approving review of the book in the *Democratic Review* ("Change for Mr. Dickens's American Notes" 13, no. 64 [1843]:352). The Whiggish *North American Review* dismissed the book as "bad taste, bad temper, bad reasoning, and bad writing" (Review of *Change for the American Notes*, *North American Review* 58, no. 122 [1844]: 226).

104. *Conclin's New River Guide; or, A Gazetteer of All the Towns on the Western Waters* (Cincinnati: H. S. & J. Applegate, 1849), 66.

105. See John Haeger's account of how New York businessmen evaluated western land schemes, in *The Investment Frontier: New York Businessmen and the Economic Development of the Old Northwest* (Albany: State University of New York Press, 1981), 48, 61–71, 96–99, 103–4. Often town promoters were quite open about the speculative nature of their towns; see William D. Walters Jr., "The Fanciful Geography of 1836," *Old Northwest* 9 (Winter 1983–84): 339.

106. Besides the warning signs Chuzzlewit might have noticed in Scadder's land office, he also takes insufficient notice of other signs, above all the sight of a failed land speculator in New York, who it turns out had invested in Eden (274, 486). On their return journey, the genial Mr. Bevan expresses surprise that they "would go to Eden on such representations as you received" (514).

107. Chuzzlewit might thus be said to embody that mimetic tradition of "innocent or Plinian vision," which art historian Norman Bryson has termed "the Natural Attitude" to images; see Norman Bryson, *Vision and Painting: The Logic of the Gaze* (New Haven, CT: Yale University Press, 1983), 34. In investing in Eden, Mark Tapley is also of course investing in Martin Chuzzlewit, a decision that ultimately turns out to be a well-advised one (a reading suggested to me in an e-mail from Joel Brattin).

108. Strickland, who was in London at the time, was "engaged by John Wright and Company . . . to survey the land at the confluence of the Ohio and the Mississippi." Only later was he "retained as consultant engineer by Holbrook" (Gilchrist, *Strickland*, 13). American state bonds were not the only remote investments made by Wright and Company during these years; it was also the "zealous promoter of some land selling and enterprises in New Zealand

and Australasia," according to the *Circular to Bankers* issued in the aftermath of its bankruptcy (November 27, 1840), HSBC archives.

109. Governor Thomas Ford, quoted in McGrane, *Foreign Bondholders*, 116.

110. James Hall, *The West: Its Commerce and Navigation* (Cincinnati: H. W. Derby, 1848), 227–28 (emphases added); on Hall's career, see John Theodore Flanagan, *James Hall, Literary Pioneer of the Ohio Valley* (Minneapolis: University of Minnesota Press, 1941).

111. On the British debates, see John Harold Wood, *A History of Central Banking in Great Britain and the United States* (Cambridge: Cambridge University Press, 2005), 49–50, 77–81.

112. Michel Chevalier, *Society, Manners, and Politics in the United States . . .* (1836; Boston: Weeks, Jordan, and Company, 1839), 298. Because settlers "vacate house and yard and take themselves on to another place which promises more advantage," the German traveler Count Adelbert Baudissin wrote in 1854, the owners of these "half and wholly fallen-down houses . . . are often completely unknown" (quoted in Ralph Gregory, "Count Baudissin on Missouri Towns," *Bulletin of the Missouri Historical Society* 27, no. 2 [1971]: 115); see also Dickens's reference to the apparently "untenanted" decaying cabins of Eden (363).

113. [Isabella Lucy Bird], *The Englishwoman in America* (London: John Murray, 1856), 134. According to John Russell Bartlett's *Dictionary of Americanisms* (New York: Bartlett and Welford, 1848), to "chaw up" meant "to use up; demolish" (72).

114. Lansden, *History of the City of Cairo*, 58–62; John F. Stover, *History of the Illinois Central Railroad* (New York: Macmillan, 1975), 12. German geographer Friedrich Ratzel later wrote that abandoned town sites were products of intense urban and economic growth, and that "life will probably again sprout from many of the ruins," in *Sketches of Urban and Cultural Life in North America*, trans. and ed. Stewart A. Stehlin (1876; New Brunswick, NJ: Rutgers University Press, 1988), 285–95, quotation on 287.

115. Conzen, "Morphology of Nineteenth-Century Cities," 127.

116. Samuel M. Crothers, "The Mission of Humor," *Atlantic Monthly* 84, no. 503 (1899): 378 (emphasis added).

117. "When Found," *The Dickensian* 3, no. 11 (1907): 284.

Chapter 3

1. On Melville's and Fly's expedition to Illinois, see Hershel Parker, *Herman Melville: A Biography*, 2 vols. (Baltimore: Johns Hopkins University Press, 1996–), 1:164–79; and Andrew Delbanco, *Melville: His World and Work* (New York: Knopf, 2005), 32–35. Herman Melville, *The Confidence-Man* (New York: Dix, Edwards, 1857), 201. Jay Leyda was the first to identify Fly as a possible source for Bartleby, in his annotations to *The Complete Stories of Herman Melville*, ed. Jay Leyda (New York: Random House, 1949), 455; Maria Melville and Herman Melville, quoted in ibid., 455.

2. Herman Melville, "Bartleby, the Scrivener: A Story of Wall-Street," originally published in *Putnam's Monthly* 2, nos. 11, 12 (1853): 546–50, 609–16, and reprinted as "Bartleby" in *The Piazza Tales* (New York: Dix, Edwards, 1856), 31–107; references to this latter edition will be cited in the text.

3. See, respectively, Nathalia Wright, "Melville and 'Old Burton,' with 'Bartleby' as an Anatomy of Melancholy," *Tennessee Studies in Literature* 15 (1970): 1–13; Gillian Brown, "The Empire of Agoraphobia," *Representations* 20 (1987): 137–57; Kingsley Widmer, *The Ways of Nihilism: Herman Melville's Short Novels* (Los Angeles: Ward Ritchie Press, 1970), 12, 13, 120–25; Maurice Friedman, "Bartleby and the Modern Exile," in *Bartleby the Scrivener: A Symposium*, ed. Howard P. Vincent (Kent, OH: Kent State University Press, 1966), 64–81; Graham Thompson, *Male Sexuality under Surveillance: The Office in American Literature*

(Iowa City: University of Iowa Press, 2003), 3–19; Louise K. Barnett, "Bartleby as Alienated Worker," *Studies in Short Fiction* 11 (Fall 1974): 379–95; H. Bruce Franklin, "Bartleby: The Ascetic's Advent," in Dan McCall, *Melville's Short Novels: Authoritative Texts, Contexts, Criticism* (New York: Norton, 2002), 176–85.

4. Michael T. Gilmore, *American Romanticism and the Marketplace* (Chicago: University of Chicago Press, 1985), 132–45; Leo Marx, "Melville's Parable of the Walls" (1953), reprinted in *Bartleby the Inscrutable: A Collection of Commentary on Herman Melville's Tale "Bartleby the Scrivener,"* ed, M. Thomas Inge (Hamden, CT: Archon Books, 1979), 84–106.

5. Janice Stout, *Sodoms in Eden: The City in American Fiction before 1860* (Westport, CT: Greenwood Press, 1976), 136, 122. See also Marx's inclusion of Melville in "The Puzzle of Antiurbanism in Classic American Literature," in *Cities of the Mind: Images and Themes of the City in the Social Sciences*, ed. Lloyd Rodwin and Robert Hollister (New York: Plenum Press, 1984), 163–64.

6. Too often, critics construe the "Wall Street" in the subtitle as a synecdoche for the business culture of New York, or even for "America" writ large, rather than an identification of a physical locality; see Marx, "Melville's Parable," 97, and James C. Wilson, "'Bartleby': The Walls of Wall Street," *Arizona Quarterly* 37 (1981): 335–46.

7. [C. F. Daniels], editorial [no title], in *New-York Gazette and General Advertiser*, May 3, 1839, n.p. (p. 2).

8. George Foster, *New York in Slices* (New York: W. F. Burgess, 1849), 9. Walter Benjamin, *The Arcades Project*, trans. Howard Eiland and Kevin McLaughlin (Cambridge, MA: Belknap Press of Harvard University Press, 2002), 518 [P1a,2]. On the surrealist concept of "profane illumination," and Benjamin's appropriation of it, see Margaret Cohen, *Profane Illumination: Walter Benjamin and the Paris of Surrealist Revolution* (Berkeley: University of California Press, 1995).

9. Maria Guilia Amadasi Guzzo and Eugenia Equini Schneider, *Petra*, trans. Lydia G. Cochrane (Chicago: University of Chicago Press, 2002), 47, 49; Petra was not abandoned, however, until the eighth century AD (127). Nicholas Purcell, "On the Sacking of Carthage and Corinth," from *Ethics and Rhetoric: Classical Essays for Donald Russell on His 75th Birthday* (Oxford: Clarendon Press, 1995), 133–48. On the rediscovery of Carthage, see Serge Lancel, *Carthage: A History* (Oxford, UK, and Cambridge, MA: Blackwell, 1995), 428–46.

10. Henry P. Tappan, *The Growth of Cities: A Discourse Delivered before the New York Geographical Society, on the Evening of March 15, 1855* (New York: R. Craighead, 1855), 9; further references cited in the text. Tappan had just become first president of the University of Michigan; see Charles Milton Perry, *Henry Philip Tappan: Philosopher and University President* (Ann Arbor: University of Michigan Press, 1933).

11. One reference to Carthage's sewers can be found in Bishop Kip, "Recollections of John Vanderlyn, the Artist," *Atlantic Monthly* 19, no. 112 (1867): 230.

12. The previous year, lack of interest in purchasing a collection of Egyptian antiquities similarly prompted *Harper's* to warn that if New York "should by any chance be ruined, the only remains of the slightest interest to the next age would be the Astor Library, and some of the human and charitable institutions." Had Athens and Rome been as fixated upon commerce, he warned, "they would have shriveled out of history like Carthage" ("Editor's Easy Chair," *Harper's New Monthly Magazine* 9, no. 49 [1854]: 122).

13. John Lloyd Stephens's *Incidents of Travel in Egypt, Arabia Petraea and the Holy Land*, ed. Victor Wolfgang von Hagen (1837; Norman: University of Oklahoma Press, 1970); Edgar Allan Poe, "Review of Stephens's *Arabia Petraea*" (1837), in Poe, *Essays and Reviews*, ed. Gary Richard Thompson (New York: Library of America, 1984), 940; Poe, "Mellonta Tauta" (1850), in Poe, *Poetry and Tales*, ed. Patrick F. Quinn (New York: Viking Press, 1984), 871–85; further

references cited in the text. On Melville's encounter with Stephens and his book, see Hagen's introduction, xxxii, xxxiv, and Parker, *Herman Melville*, 2:317.

14. "Towering Monument to Washington that New York Began and then Forgot," *New York Times* (hereafter *NYT*), February 18, 1912, Sunday Magazine, 8; Dorothy C. Barck, "Proposed Memorials to Washington in New York City, 1802–1847," *New-York Historical Society Quarterly Bulletin* 15 (October 1931): 79–90; and Jacob Landy, "Washington Monument Project in New York," *Journal of the Society of Architectural Historians* 28, no. 4 (1969): 291–97. On the delayed completion of the Washington Monument in the capital, see chapter 2.

15. Washington Allston, *Caius Marius in the Dungeon at Minturnae* (ca. 1801–04); Morse, *Marius in Prison* (1812, location unknown); Lydia Maria Child, "Marius Amid the Ruins of Carthage," in *Readings in American Poetry*, ed. Rufus W. Griswold (New York: John C. Riker, 1843), 187–88; William Gilmore Simms, "Caius Marius," in *Poems: Descriptive, Dramatic, Legendary, and Contemplative*, 2 vols. (1853; New York: Arno Press, 1972), 2:300–311. The epigraph to this chapter is from 3:306.

16. For a brief discussion of *Marius*'s conception, exhibition, and reception, see Kenneth C. Lindsay, *The Works of John Vanderlyn: From Tammany to the Capitol* (Binghamton: University Art Gallery/State University of New York, 1970), 71–75; the painting's provenance is on 136–37.

17. *Plutarch's Lives of Illustrious Men*, trans. John Dryden, ed. A. H. Clough (Boston: Little, Brown, 1876), 306.

18. John Vanderlyn, letter to J. R. Murray, January 25, 1807, quoted in Lindsay, *Works of John Vanderlyn*, 71.

19. For the Burr reference, see Lindsay, *Works of John Vanderlyn*, 72. Vanderlyn's letter acknowledging the influence of Rome's ruins is quoted in *Albany Gallery of the Fine Arts: Catalogue of the Fourth Exhibition* (Albany, NY: Van Benthuysen, 1849), 12, in the *Marius* files, American Art Study Center, Fine Arts Museums of San Francisco. Melville viewed *Course of Empire* in New York in 1846 (Delbanco, *Melville*, 56).

20. Wyn Kelley, "Melville and John Vanderlyn: Ruin and Historical Fate from 'Bartleby' to *Israel Potter*," in *Savage Eye: Melville and the Visual Arts*, ed. Christopher Sten (Kent, OH: Kent State University Press, 1991), 122–23. On Vanderlyn's decline see "John Vanderlyn," *Putnam's* 3, no. 18 (1854): 593–95, and Kip, "Recollections," 228–35; the latter was at that time the owner of *Marius*.

21. Plutarch, *Lives*, 291.

22. See Léon Laborde, *Journey through Arabia Petraea* . . . (London: Murray, 1838).

23. "The World of New York," *Putnam's* 8, no. 46 (1856): 444. For a typical treatment of the hazards confronting a greenhorn from upstate, see George Foster, *New York by Gas-Light, and Other Urban Sketches*, ed. Stuart Blumin (1850; Berkeley: University of California Press, 1990), 178–88.

24. Charles Sellers, *The Market Revolution: Jacksonian America, 1815–1846* (New York: Oxford University Press, 1991); Melvyn Stokes and Stephen Conway, eds., *The Market Revolution in America: Social, Political, and Religious Expressions, 1800–1880* (Charlottesville: University of Virginia Press, 1996); George Rogers Taylor, *The Transportation Revolution, 1815–1860* (New York: Rinehart, 1951).

25. U.S. Bureau of the Census statistics (cities are defined there as towns with over 10,000 inhabitants; "urban" as places with over 2,500).

26. Edgar Allan Poe, *Doings of Gotham* (Pottsville, PA: Spannuth, 1929), 31.

27. Kenneth Scherzer, *The Unbounded Community: Neighborhood Life and Social Structure in New York City, 1830–1875* (Durham, NC: Duke University Press, 1992), 163–204.

28. Karen Halttunen, *Confidence Men and Painted Women: A Study of Middle-Class Culture in America, 1830–1870* (New Haven, CT: Yale University Press, 1982), 34.

29. Lyn H. Lofland, *A World of Strangers: Order and Action in Urban Public Space* (New York: Basic Books, 1973), 21, 29–55.

30. Ibid., 66–91; Halttunen, *Confidence Men*, 35–37, 39; John F. Kasson, *Rudeness and Civility: Manners in Nineteenth-Century America* (New York: Hill and Wang, 1990), 36, 43, 57–69.

31. Georg Simmel, "The Stranger," in *The Sociology of Georg Simmel*, ed. and trans. Kurt Wolff (New York: Free Press, 1950), 402–8; further references cited in the text.

32. On bachelors in boardinghouses, see Scherzer, *Unbounded Community*, 97–110, and Howard P. Chudacoff, *The Age of the Bachelor: Creating an American Subculture* (Princeton, NJ: Princeton University Press, 1999), 29–35. On Melville's initial accommodation in a "cheap boardinghouse," see Delbanco, *Melville*, 35. Walt Whitman uses the term "floating population" in *New York Dissected* (New York: Wilson, 1936), 140. On the Tombs, see Timothy J. Gilfoyle, "'America's Greatest Criminal Barracks': The Tombs and the Experience of Criminal Justice in New York City, 1838–1897," *Journal of Urban History* 29, no. 5 (2003): 525–54.

33. The reorganization of social relations in New York was belated, uneven, and protracted, because of the smaller scale of its industry and political resistance of its artisans; see Sean Wilentz, *Chants Democratic: New York City and the Rise of the American Working Class, 1788–1850* (Oxford and New York: Oxford University Press, 1984), especially 107–42, 326–59. Even Horace Greeley remarked in 1855 how "cities expand, and life becomes more and more artificial, and human relations more complicated . . ." (quoted in Edward K. Spann, *The New Metropolis: New York City, 1840–1857* [New York: Columbia University Press, 1981], 311).

34. Simmel also notes this paradox elsewhere: "The feeling of isolation [is never more intense than] . . . when one is a stranger . . . among many physically close persons, at a "party," on a train, or in the traffic of a large city" (*Sociology of Georg Simmel*, 119).

35. Georg Simmel, *The Philosophy of Money* (1907; London and New York: Routledge, 2004), 477.

36. Parker, *Herman Melville*, 1:165, 2:782. For the six years prior to 1850, Melville had lived in New York, the impact of which is described in Delbanco, *Melville*, 11, 92, 112–21.

37. Elizabeth Blackmar notes the dramatic 62 percent rise in land values during 1836 (*Manhattan for Rent, 1785–1850* [Ithaca, NY: Cornell University Press, 1989], 203). On the succession of architectural styles (from Gothic to palazzo) and materials (from brick to marble), see Lois Severini, *The Architecture of Finance: Early Wall Street* (Ann Arbor, MI: UMI Research Press, 1983).

38. The second boom "peaked in 1853–54" (Spann, *New Metropolis*, 113), exactly when "Bartleby" was published. On demand for warehouse and retail space, see Mona Domosh, *Invented Cities: The Creation of Landscape in Nineteenth-Century New York and Boston* (New Haven, CT: Yale University Press, 1996), 16; on the Croton Aqueduct, Gerard T. Koeppel, *Water for Gotham: A History* (Princeton, NJ: Princeton University Press, 2000), 139–284; on the founding of new real estate institutions, David Scobey, *Empire City: The Making and Meaning of the New York City Landscape* (Philadelphia: Temple University Press, 2002), 92, 110, 192–99; and on the 1811 Randall Plan, John Reps, *The Making of Urban America: A History of City Planning in the United States* (Princeton, NJ: Princeton University Press, 1965), 296–99.

39. David Harvey, *Paris, Capital of Modernity* (New York and London: Routledge, 2003), 125.

40. Isaac Lyon, "New York—Then and Now" (1860), in *Recollections of an Old Cartman* (Newark, NJ: Daily Journal Office, 1872), 6; further references cited in the text.

41. Philip Hone, *The Diary of Philip Hone, 1828–1851*, 2 vols., ed. Bayard Tuckerman (New York: Dodd, Mead, 1889), 1:378; further references cited in the text.

42. On the initial granting and eventual abolition of those licenses, see Graham Russell Hodges, *New York City Cartmen, 1667–1850* (New York: New York University Press, 1986), 22–26, 164–67; and on the Whig and nativist sympathies of cartmen like Lyon, 148–50, 152, 154, 169. Wilentz considers them among the "most fortunate of all" the city's manual laborers, performing work that was "regular, independent, and profitable," in *Chants Democratic*, 26 (see also 110).

43. Hone had sold this house three years earlier, in 1836 (1:203). On Hone's successes and failures as a merchant, see Spann, *New Metropolis*, 210.

44. Walter Whitman, "Tear Down and Build Up Again," *American Whig Review* 2, no. 5 (1845): 536, 537–38; "Our New Houses," *United States Democratic Review* 21, no. 113 (1847): 392.

45. "Editor's Easy Chair," *Harper's Monthly* 9, no. 50 (1854): 261, and 13, no. 74 (1856): 272–73. On the founding of *Harper's* and the development of the "discursive essay" such as Curtis's "Easy Chair," see Frank Luther Mott, *A History of American Magazines, 1741–1930*, 5 vols. (Cambridge, MA: Belknap Press of Harvard University Press, 1958–68), 2:383–84, 389. On "the short life of buildings" in nineteenth-century American cities, see Michael P. Conzen, "The Morphology of Nineteenth-Century Cities in the United States," in *Urbanization in the Americas: The Background in Comparative Perspective*, ed. W. Borah, J. Hardoy, and G. Stelter (Ottawa: National Museum of Man, 1980), 120.

46. Thomas Cole, letter to Luman Reed, September 7, 1835, quoted in Louis Legrand Noble, *Life and Works of Thomas Cole*, ed. Elliot S. Vesell (1853; Cambridge, MA: Belknap Press of Harvard University Press, 1964), 151. On Hone's purchase of his friend, Cole's, paintings, see Neil Harris, *The Artist in American Society: The Formative Years, 1790–1860* (1966; Chicago: University of Chicago Press, 1982), 105.

47. C. F. Daniels, editorial (cited above, n. 7), n.p. (p. 2). On the financial troubles of the Merchants' Exchange, see Hone's *Diary*, 2:98. His estimate that the "city in the aggregate is rebuilt . . . about once in seven years" was based on the combined effect of renovations, demolitions, and conflagrations, or "alterations, pulling down and burning up" (1:201). On my appropriation of Smithson's term, "ruins in reverse," see the introduction.

48. "Original Papers: A Return to Broadway," *Literary World* 5, no. 141 (1849): 309.

49. The *New-York Mirror* reprinted Daniels's "graphick account . . . of the 'progress of demolition' in Wall-street" in *New-York Mirror* 16, no. 47 (1839): 375, and published similar accounts complaining that New York was "a city of perpetual ruin and repair" ("The City of Modern Ruins," *New-York Mirror* 17, no. 51 [1840]: 407), and that "every street is laid in ruins" ("Modern City of Ruins," *New-York Mirror* 19, no. 20 [1841]: 159).

50. "City of Modern Ruins," 407. *The Mirror*, a weekly journal for "ladies" founded in 1823 and edited by Knickerbocker poet George Pope Morris, claimed by 1835 to have a circulation exceeding any other "literary periodical in this country" (Mott, *American Magazines*, 1:329; see also 127–28, 320–31).

51. Sam Bass Warner coined the term "walking city" in *Streetcar Suburbs: The Process of Growth in Boston, 1870–1900* (Cambridge, MA: Harvard University Press, 1962), 15–21.

52. Compared with the postbellum period, this nascent spatial differentiation was "imprecise and unstable" (Spann, *New Metropolis*, 109); "chaotic" in its continued "intermingling of wealth, ethnicity, transiency, and family status" (Scherzer, *Unbounded Community*, 33, 51); and "small-scale and spatially compact, or organized more by street than by district" (Scobey, *Empire City*, 99–100). Historians nevertheless agree on the inception of this class segregation by the 1850s (Spann, *New Metropolis*, 107; Scherzer, *Unbounded Community*, 32, 37, 40, 47, 137–60; Blackmar, *Manhattan for Rent*, 89; Domosh, *Invented Cities*, 19).

53. For a typical topography of the city, see George G. Foster, *Fifteen Minutes around New York* (New York: Dewitt and Davenport, 1849).

54. N. P. Willis, "From Saratoga. To the Julia of Some Years Ago," in *Dashes at Life with a Free Pencil* (New York: J. S. Redfield, 1845), part 4:34. On the proliferation of white-collar workers in the 1850s, see Spann, *New Metropolis*, 243–44. In 1856, the *New-York Daily Times* (hereafter *NYDT*) warned that clerks need to "live within a reasonable distance of their places of business . . ." ("High Rents," April 15, 1856, 4).

55. Stott, *Workers in the Metropolis*, 12–16, 22, 24, 32; Scherzer, *Unbounded Community*, 26, 37.

56. Whereas Hone decried in 1850 "the mania for converting Broadway into a street of shops" (2:384), *Harper's Monthly* was more approving of the "fast" transformation of lower Broadway into "a street of palaces" ("Editor's Easy Chair," *Harper's Monthly* 9, no. 50 [1854]: 260). See also Domosh, *Invented Cities*, 44, 52–53.

57. Robert Fogelson, *Downtown: Its Rise and Fall, 1880–1950* (New Haven, CT: Yale University Press, 2001), 10–12.

58. Blackmar, *Manhattan for Rent*, 48–49, 77–79, 51, 49.

59. Charles Lockwood, *Manhattan Moves Uptown* (Boston: Houghton Mifflin, 1976), 25; Severini, *Architecture of Finance*, 23–25.

60. Severini, *Architecture of Finance*, ix, 24. Martyn Bowden dates the emergence of New York's financial district slightly earlier, around 1805–10, in "Growth of the Central Districts in Large Cities," in *The New Urban History: Quantitative Explorations by American Historians*, ed. Leo Francis Schnore (Princeton, NJ: Princeton University Press, 1975), 85; either way, it preceded Boston's financial district on State Street, which did not emerge until the 1830s (ibid., 86). Even Chestnut Street, Robert E. Wright acknowledges, remained Philadelphia's "most 'fashionable' street," lined with trees, shops, and hotels (*The First Wall Street: Chestnut Street, Philadelphia, and the Birth of American Finance* [Chicago: University of Chicago Press, 2005], 2, 164)—including the hotel visited by Dickens in 1842 (see previous chapter).

61. Blackmar, *Manhattan for Rent*, 70. Contrary to the rhetoric of "separate spheres," this process did not empty the home of economic activity; women took in boarders and managed the household resources (ibid., 5, 63–68, 112). Although a startling development to antebellum Americans, this separation of business and residence came to be viewed after the Civil War as natural and inevitable, determined by the "law of progress" (Fogelson, *Downtown*, 21–23).

62. On the fear of cholera that drove elite residents out of the overcrowded lower wards, see Scherzer, *Unbounded Community*, 144–45. On architectural standardization, see Severini, *Architecture of Finance*, 36–39, 42–53, 25. This uniformity of style lasted only until 1850s, when a variety of Romanesque *palazzi* were built.

63. "The Migration of Churches," newspaper clipping in "New York City in Olden Times, consisting of newspaper cuttings arranged by Henry Onderdonk Jr., Jamaica, L.I., 1863," NYPL, IRGC Onderdonk, Local History and Genealogy Section, n.p. See also Dorothy Ganfield Fowler, *A City Church: The First Presbyterian Church in the City of New York, 1716–1976* (New York: First Presbyterian, 1981), 78–82. Melville criticized the class exclusivity of churches that relocated northward in his 1854 story "Two Temples," discussed below.

64. Woodhull quoted in Spann, *New Metropolis*, 101–2. The First Ward, which contained Wall Street, would also have declined in population had an immigrant landing depot not been established (controversially) within its bounds, at Castle Clinton in 1855; see ibid., 101–2, 155, 455n21. On the separation of commercial and residential spaces in Rochester after 1825, and the nocturnal emptiness of its business district by the 1830s, see Paul Johnson, *A Shopkeeper's Millennium: Society and Revivals in Rochester, New York, 1815–1837* (New York: Hill and Wang, 1978), 48, 52.

65. "Wall-Street," *Mirror* 17, no. 40 (1840): 319. This phenomenon was also noted in other American cities—downtown Philadelphia being "a perfect desolation after six o'clock" (quoted in Fogelson, *Downtown*, 18)—but rarely in European cities (London excepted), where "businesses and residences . . . [were] not confined to separate quarters" (ibid., 20). On the simultaneously reassuring and controlling role of the night watchman in European cities within the premodern (i.e., pre-1840) nocturnal cityscape, and his replacement by the policeman, see Joachim Schlör, *Nights in the Big City: Paris, Berlin, London, 1840–1930*, trans. Pierre Imhoff and Dafydd Roberts (London: Reaktion, 1998), 35–36, 44–46, 73–91.

66. Foster, *New York in Slices*, 97; see also his account of how Wall Street "grows rapidly vague and silent" by evening in *New York by Gas-Light*, 224. "Ears," *Harper's New Monthly* 18, no. 107 (1859): 666. On the notion of "hearing" urban space, see my article, "Echoes of the City: Spacing Sound, Sounding Space, 1888–1908," *American Literary History* 19, no. 3 (2007): 629–60.

67. Foster, *New York in Slices*, 9 (and on the busyness of Broadway in the evenings, Foster, *New York by Gaslight*, 70–76); Junius Henri Browne, *The Great Metropolis; A Mirror of New York* (Hartford, CT: American Publishing Company, 1869), 357.

68. X. Y. Z., "A City Incident," *Southern Literary Messenger* 17, no. 10 (1851): 667–69. The anonymous author reveals in the final sentence that he was staying in a hotel (669). X. Y. Z. might have been Judge John Robertson, according to Benjamin Blake Minor, *The Southern Literary Messenger, 1834–1864* (1905; Chapel Hill: University of North Carolina Press, 2007), 50. Although read in the north, the *Messenger* was staunchly southern in its political sympathies. On the commercial importance of the "regina viarum" (or "queen of roads"), see Ivana Della Portella, ed., *The Appian Way: From Its Foundation to the Middle Ages* (Los Angeles: J. Paul Getty Museum, 2004), 20–21; on Cecilia Metella's tomb, see 64–70.

69. See Harvey, *Paris, Capital of Modernity*, 125–40; see also Conzen's discussion of how "the mercantile city of the colonial period lingered well into the nineteenth century in terms of plan and lot patterns, building height, and land use" ("Morphology of Nineteenth-Century Cities," 122).

70. Lockwood, *Manhattan Moves Uptown*; Fogelson, *Downtown*.

71. Grady Clay defines the "holdout" in *Real Places: An Unconventional Guide to America's Generic Landscape* (Chicago: University of Chicago Press, 1994), 21. Urban geographer Neil Smith describes how a Lower East Side park was appropriated in the late 1980s by squatters and protestors as a "holdout" against gentrification, in *The New Urban Frontier: Gentrification and the Revanchist City* (London and New York: Routledge, 1996), 3–29; "one last stand" was the "wild west" phrase used by a reporter, quoted in ibid., 9.

72. "All Manner of Things," *Home Journal* 45, no. 195 (1849): 3; the stables were finally replaced in 1849 by law offices. "Antiquities of New-York: The Walton-Mansion—Pearl Street," *Mirror* 9, no. 37 (1832): 289; N. P. Willis, "Diary of Town Trifles," *New Mirror* 3, no. 6 (1844): 89–90; and John Disturnell, *New York as It Was and as It Is* (New York: Van Nostrand, 1876), 28.

73. James Fenimore Cooper, *New York . . . an unpublished manuscript, . . . entitled* The Towns of Manhattan (New York: Payson, 1930), 15.

74. "The Migration of Churches," n.p. On Melville's ascent to the top of Trinity's steeple in 1848, see Parker, *Herman Melville*, 1:579.

75. I am drawing here on the antinostalgic conception of the holdout in Michel de Certeau, "Ghosts in the City," in Michel de Certeau, Luce Giard, and Pierre Mayol, *Practice of Everyday Life*, vol. 2, *Living and Cooking*, trans. Timothy J. Tomasik (Minneapolis: University of Minnesota Press, 1998), 133–43.

76. On the "one family residing" in Wall Street, see *New York Express* (1841), quoted in Disturnell, *New York as It Was and as It Is*, 30. Philip Hone quoted in Lockwood, *Manhattan Moves Uptown*, 26. As late as 1878, the *Real Estate Record* found residents on lower Fifth Avenue who had "stubbornly and resolutely determined not to be removed except by the undertaker" (quoted in Fogelson, *Downtown*, 23).

77. Herman Melville, *Moby-Dick; or, The Whale* (1851; New York: Penguin, 1992), 131.

78. For Dickens's account of Five Points, see chapter 2. Willis complains about the occupation of West Broadway, a potentially desirable location for bourgeois families, by "negroes," in "Diary of Town Trifles," *New Mirror* 3, no. 6 (1844): 88. Eighty-six percent of the city's black population was still living below 14th Street in 1852. See Scherzer, *Unbounded Community*, 238n50; Leslie M. Harris, *In the Shadow of Slavery: African Americans in New York City, 1626–1863* (Chicago: University of Chicago Press, 2003), 267.

79. See David Harvey, *The Urban Experience* (Baltimore: Johns Hopkins University Press, 1989), 177–78.

80. Herman Melville, "Jimmy Rose" (1855), in *Complete Stories*, ed. Leyda, 241; further references cited in the text. The few critics who have attended to this story view the house as an amalgamation of those Melville knew in New York and Pittsfield, thus eliding the specificity of its location in a transitional street in the lower wards (see, for example, Merton M. Sealts Jr., "Ghost of Major Melvill," *New England Quarterly* 30 [1957]: 297–301).

81. Jay Leyda, in *Complete Stories*, ed. Leyda, 468. Another possible source might be the "Old Walton House" (described above p. 132).

82. "Rents Down-Town," *NYDT*, February 10, 1855, 4; "Real Estate Predictions" *NYT*, October 2, 1858, 2.

83. On the "janitors and *portiers*, the keepers of the great buildings" who were the only remaining residents of European and American financial districts, see Adna Ferrin Weber, *The Growth of Cities in the Nineteenth Century: A Study in Statistics* (1899; Ithaca, NY: Cornell University Press, 1967), 467.

84. Harvey, *Paris, Capital of Modernity*, 40–41.

85. "The Rock-City and Its Explorers," *National Magazine* 10 (1857): 395–98.

86. Spann, *New Metropolis*, 286, 289–95; on the expansion from a single horse car line in 1850 to eighteen franchises by 1875, and the resulting "horse car migration" to residential districts uptown, see Scobey, *Empire City*, 68, 70.

87. "A Death in the Family," *Graham's American Monthly Magazine* 48, no. 4 (1856): 295. Even lower Broadway had become a "major traffic problem by the 1850s" (Spann, *New Metropolis*, 278, see also 286–87). On traffic problems after 1850, see Fogelson, *Downtown*, 15–18, 30; and Scobey, *Empire City*, 139–40.

88. "The City We Live In: Wall Street," *Home Journal* 38, no. 136 (1848): 3.

89. "Billy Bowlegs in Wall Street," *NYDT*, September 27, 1852, 1; the tour was part of an effort to persuade the hostile chief to migrate from Florida to the west, perhaps by demonstrating the pace of urbanization in the east.

90. Blackmar, *Manhattan for Rent*, 168–69; Spann, *New Metropolis*, 286–90; Severini, *Architecture of Finance*, 52. Many of these proposals remained shelved until the 1850s.

91. On the equation of propertied wealth with domestic morality, see Blackmar, *Manhattan for Rent*, 109–48, 150–51; on the formation of this coalition in support of street improvements, see 158–69; on earlier regulatory ordinances, see 159.

92. Ibid., 162–64, 168. On such removals as a kind of surgical maneuver (or "cautery") that

would result in a "general development of property values," see "City Improvement," *NYDT*, July 21, 1853, 4.

93. Blackmar, *Manhattan for Rent*, 172–77. Similar projects were carried out on neighboring Chapel and Anthony streets in the mid-1830s, in the streets leveled by the fires of 1835 and 1845, and ultimately on the Bowery in 1855.

94. On the implications for the employment and residential prospects of the poor, see ibid., 162, 167–68, 176–77. According to Spann, "the fact that the Bowery extension . . . would displace many of the poor inhabitants of the Fourth Ward weighed little against the interests of $12 million in property" (*New Metropolis*, 287–88; see also 101).

95. On the emergence and definition of vagrancy, see Amy Dru Stanley, *From Bondage to Contract: Wage Labor, Marriage, and the Market in the Age of Slave Emancipation* (Cambridge and New York: Cambridge University Press, 1998), 98–137. The estimate (quoted in Scherzer, *Unbounded Community*, 87) was rough, as the "'strolling poor' that drifted in and out of cities [remained] largely invisible to keepers of public records (such as assessors' rolls)" (ibid., 21). On police stations as refuges for the homeless (less draconian, in fact, than almshouses and workhouses), see Kim Hopper, *Reckoning with Homelessness* (Ithaca, NY: Cornell University Press, 2003), 26–34.

96. See Stuart M. Blumin's introduction to Foster, *New York by Gas-Light*, especially 19–27.

97. Marshall Berman, *All That Is Solid Melts into Air: The Experience of Modernity* (London and New York: Verso, 1983), 147–55; Willis, "From Sarasota," in *Dashes*, part 4:34.

98. Baudelaire, "The Eyes of the Poor," in *Paris Spleen*, trans. Louise Varèse (1869; New York: New Directions, 1947), 52–53.

99. Willis, "From Sarasota," in *Dashes*, part 1:10, part 4:35, 9, 35.

100. Herman Melville, "Two Temples" (1854), in *Complete Stories*, ed. Leyda, "Temple First," 157. While Putnam's editors read this "temple" as a caricature of Grace Church, and thus rejected the story, Beryl Rowland has shown that many of its features are those of Trinity Church, whose steeple Melville had climbed six years earlier ("Grace Church and Melville's Story of 'The Two Temples,'" *Nineteenth-Century Fiction* 28, no. 3 [1973], 339–46).

101. Schlör refers to a "radical homelessness" that fascinated literary romantics of late nineteenth-century Paris and Berlin (and presumably horrified their bourgeois contemporaries): "Here the condition of vagabondage stands for a fundamental refusal of all ties, for the *choice of freedom*" (*Nights*, 158).

102. "The Rock-City and Its Explorers," 397. By the 1840s, the rural cemetery movement had only just begun to break the traditional habit of burying bodies in "crowded, nondescript churchyards, often surrounded by the bustle of growing cities . . ." (Harris, *The Artist in American Society*, 200).

103. "Wall-Street Church," *Mirror* 11, no. 48 (1834): 383.

104. Letter to the editor of *NYDT*, January 20 1854, 2. A proposal to extend Albany Street had first been made in 1841.

105. Mr. Tillou [*sic*—Tillon], cited in "The Extension of Albany-Street," *NYDT*, February 16, 1854, 3. At this meeting, only "owners of property, and others likely to be affected" were permitted to speak (3).

106. For several decades, the location of Allan's law office has been misidentified as 10 Wall Street; see Leyda, in *Complete Stories*, ed. Leyda, 455; Elizabeth Hardwick, "Bartleby and Manhattan," in *Bartleby in Manhattan and Other Essays* (New York: Random House, 1983), 218. My source for the proper address is *New-York Pictorial Business Directory of Wall-St. 1850* (New York: C. Lowenstrom, 1849), n.p.

107. That "somber-looking" building was eventually demolished in 1858; see "New

Insurance Buildings in Wall Street—Great Increase in Value of Wall-Street Property," *The Independent*, September 15, 1859, 8. Before it could move the cemetery, First Presbyterian had to buy back the burial vaults from their owners; the 1843 release deed authorizing it to "remove the bodies" is in that church's archives (I am indebted to its archivist David Pultz for showing me this document). In the same volume as "Bartleby," *Putnam's* published an article citing this as one of the "demolished temples" that had been "prostrat[ed] and utterly obliterat[ed]," and their tombs "ruthlessly scattered," by the commercialization of downtown ("New-York Daguerreotyped," *Putnam's* 1, no. 4, [1853]: 357–58).

108. "Gossip with Readers and Correspondents," *Knickerbocker, or New York Monthly Magazine* 24, no. 5 (1844): 477–78.

109. Review of Prof. George Bush, *Anastasis: Or the Doctrine of the Resurrection of the Body . . .* , *Knickerbocker* 24, no. 6 (1844): 572–73.

110. Michel Foucault, "Of Other Spaces" (1967 lecture), trans. Jay Miskowiec, *Diacritics* 16, no. 1 (1986): 25.

111. Barbara Foley dates Bartleby's arrival to "around 1843 or 1844" (while acknowledging that Melville interjected allusions to events from the late 1840s), in "From Wall Street to Astor Place: Historicizing Melville's 'Bartleby,'" *American Literature* 72, no. 1 (2000): 88–89. The release deed in the Presbyterian archives (cited above, n. 107) is dated February 1843.

112. The Boston *Evening Traveller* (June 3, 1856) referred to Bartleby's "ghost-like taciturnity" and the London *Athenaeum* to the "wild and ghostly power" of the *Piazza* tales as a whole; both in Brian Higgins and Hershel Parker, eds., *Herman Melville: The Contemporary Reviews* (Cambridge and New York: Cambridge University Press, 1995), 473, 481.

113. "Wall-Street Church," 383.

114. "High Rents," *NYDT*, April 15, 1856, 4.

115. Charles King, *Progress of the City of New-York, during the Last Fifty Years . . . A Lecture Delivered before the Mechanics' Society . . . on 29th December, 1851* (New York: Appleton, 1852), 10. An advertisement in *Spirit of the Times* 23, no. 7 (1853): 83, places California Express at 16 Wall Street.

116. On Gansevoort's and Allan's appointments as Examiner in Chancery, see Parker, *Herman Melville*, 1:313, 321.

117. Washington Irving, *Astoria, or Anecdotes of an Enterprise beyond the Rocky Mountains*, 2 vols. (Philadelphia: Carey, Lea, and Blanchard, 1836); Arthur D. Howden Smith, *John Jacob Astor, Landlord of New York* (Philadelphia and London: J. B. Lippincott, 1929); and on his use of the Chancery Court as many as fifty-three times between 1837 and 1848, and for the estimate of his income through rent, see Kenneth Wiggins Porter, *John Jacob Astor, Business Man*, 2 vols. (Cambridge, MA: Harvard University Press, 1931), 2:931, 939.

118. "High Rents," *The Subterranean* 3, no. 49 (1846): 2; "Reminiscences of John Jacob Astor," *New York Herald*, March 31, 1848; John D. Haeger, *John Jacob Astor, Business and Finance in the Early Republic* (Detroit: Wayne State University Press, 1991), 258. Lessees were required to pay "taxes, duties, and assessments" (Porter, *Astor*, 2:925) and erect buildings, which reverted to Astor when the lease expired (Smith, *Astor*, 257). Even Haeger, who defends Astor's business as "carefully organized," "sophisticated," and beneficial to the "public good" (249, 252), concedes that he did little "to help resolve New York's continuing housing dilemma" (260–61).

119. Melville, "Two Temples," 157. The power of the police to arrest vagrants "without process" (i.e., without warrant), and the "summary jurisdiction" of police court judges at the Halls of Justice (a.k.a. the Tombs), increased with the passage of the New York Vagrancy Act of 1880; see Gilfoyle, "The Tombs," 531, 540; and Stanley, *From Bondage to Contract*, 98–137.

120. Blackmar, *Manhattan for Rent,* 217, 220, 226, 235, 236. On the ability of eighteenth-century artisans to insert themselves into this tiered system and maintain access to and relative control over housing, see ibid., 42. The *Times* referred to the "high pressure values of 1853" in "Rents and Real Estate," February 12, 1855, 4; see also "High Rents," *NYDT,* April 15, 1856, 4; "An Alleged Case of Heartless Eviction," *NYT,* June 13, 1861, 2.

121. On tenants' lack of property, see Blackmar, *Manhattan for Rent,* 223, 241; on lease breaking, absconding, and the difficulties of litigation, 241; and on the limited social power of antebellum landlords, 217–19.

122. Charles W. McCurdy, *The Anti-Rent Era in New York Law and Politics, 1839–1865* (Chapel Hill: University of North Carolina Press, 2001). Urban tenants did occasionally sue landlords and form coalitions to protect neighborhoods (Blackmar, *Manhattan for Rent,* 218, 177, 246–48), and support the land reform movement of urban radicals (Wilentz, *Chants Democratic,* 335–43).

123. See Blackmar, *Manhattan for Rent,* 244.

124. Ibid., 240, 241, 245.

125. Scherzer reads the crowd actions in the streets of New York on Moving Day as "bold assertion[s] of working class dominion of the streets" (*Unbounded Community,* 24); while Blackmar refers to the power of the mob to intimidate landlords through "minor assaults on private property" (*Manhattan for Rent,* 84).

126. On the rights granted to squatters in western states, see Donald J. Pisani, "Squatter Law in California, 1850–1858," *Western Historical Quarterly* 25, no. 3 (1994): 285–86; and on the Pre-Emption Act of 1841, Richard White, *"It's Your Misfortune and None of My Own": A History of the American West* (Norman: University of Oklahoma Press, 1991), 139–41. Such legislation reflected either resignation to their inevitable presence or eagerness to profit from their labor in clearing the frontier.

127. On the squatters of California, the sympathy they enjoyed from the public and the police, their development of a political rhetoric of natural rights, and the Sacramento uprising of 1850, see Pisani, "Squatter Law," 278, 291–92, passim. On the San Francisco squatter riots, see "Serious Disturbances at San Francisco," *NYDT,* July 10, 1854, 1.

128. "City Squatters" *NYDT,* July 12, 1854, 4. Others called for softer tactics to resolve the squatter problem, for example an "Industrial School" that would transform those dangerous classes (or at least their children) into productive citizens; see "The 'Squatters' of the City," *NYDT,* April 19, 1854, 2. On the hope that the construction of Central Park would eliminate the problem, see Elizabeth Blackmar and Roy Rosenzweig, *The Park and the People: A History of Central Park* (Ithaca, NY: Cornell University Press, 1992), 59–91. Lockwood cites the census figure of ten thousand squatters, and the struggles to establish genteel neighborhoods there, in *Manhattan Moves Uptown,* 236–37, 242–43.

129. "The 'Squatters' of the City," 2.

130. This law declared squatting a "misdemeanor" punishable by imprisonment for up to six months and/or fine up to $500. "An Act to punish nuisances and malicious trespasses on lands," *Laws of the State of New-York* . . . (Albany: Van Benthuysen, 1857), vol. 1, chap. 396, 805–6. I have not found any earlier law.

131. Thomas W. Waterman, *A Treatise on the Law of Trespass,* 2 vols. (New York: Baker, Voorhis, and Company, 1875), 1:141, 146–47, 152.

132. Ibid., 1:149–50; John Adams, *A Treatise on the Principles and Practice of the Action of Ejectment* (4th ed.; New York: Banks, Gould, and Company, 1854), 71, 73 (see also 55–63, 551–602); and Arthur G. Sedgwick and Frederick S. Wait, *A Treatise on the Principles and*

Practice Governing the Trial of Title to Land (New York: Baker, Voorhis, and Company, 1882), 498–550.

133. Sedgwick and Wait, *Trial of Title to Land*, 505–6.

134. The notion of reward for "beneficial" use of land is refuted in Henry W. Ballantine, "Title by Adverse Possession," *Harvard Law Review* 32, no. 2 (1918): 135–39.

135. Henri Lefebvre, "The Right to the City," in *Writings on Cities*, ed. Eleanore Kofman and Elizabeth Lebas (Cambridge, MA: Blackwell, 1996), 147–59.

Chapter 4

1. Edward Gibbon, *The Autobiographies of Edward Gibbon*, ed. John Murray (London: Murray, 1896), 302; see also Gibbon's account in his *Memoirs of My Life*, ed. Georges A. Bonnard (London: Thomas Nelson and Sons, 1966), 136.

2. Of the twenty-four prospective histories (novels, short stories, or fragments), I have chosen to discuss a representative selection, encompassing well-known *and* lesser-known authors. Those not discussed or cited later in this chapter are: Bret Harte, "The Ruins of San Francisco," in *Mrs. Skaggs's Husbands, and Other Sketches* (Boston: James R. Osgood, 1873), 337–41; John McElroy, *Decline and Fall of the American Republic: Confessions of a Repentant Politician: A Story of Fifty Years Hence, Time, A.D. 1930* (Toledo: Toledo Blade, 1880); Samuel Rockwell Reed, *The War of 1886, between the United States and Great Britain* (Cincinnati: Clarke, 1882); "Sir Henry Standish Coverdale" [pseud.], *The Fall of the Great Republic, 1886–1888* (Boston: Roberts Brothers, 1885); Henry Grattan Donnelly, *The Stricken Nation* (New York: Baker, 1890); and *The Rise and Fall of the United States: A Leaf from History, A.D. 2060*, by a diplomat (London and New York: Tennyson Neely, 1898).

3. In "American Traits as Seen from Abroad," *Putnam's* 11, no. 3 (1868), Maj. Joseph Kirkland wrote that the foreigner's view is analogous to that of the "future historian" in that the "distance of space supplies in some degree the coolness and clearness that distance of time will give" (289); he also wondered whether American society was headed toward the kinds of "huge individual possessions such as marked the Decline and Fall of Rome" (299).

4. See Paul Riceour's distinction between the existence of events "in time" and "in historicality," quoted in Hayden White, *The Content of the Form: Narrative Discourse and Historical Representation* (Baltimore: Johns Hopkins University Press, 1987), 52.

5. See Randolph Starn, "Meaning Levels in the Theme of Historical Decline," *History and Theory* 14, no. 1 (1975): 1–31.

6. White, *Content of the Form*, 180–81.

7. Thomas Babington Macaulay, "Von Ranke" [Review of Von Ranke's *History of the Popes*], *Edinburgh Review* (October 1840), reprinted in Macaulay, *Critical and Historical Essays*, 3 vols. (London: Longmans, Brown, Green, and Longmans, 1843), 3:209.

8. Edward Gibbon, *The History of the Decline and Fall of the Roman Empire*, ed. J. B. Bury, 12 vols. (New York: Fred de Fau, 1906), 6:297; further references cited in the text.

9. On the classical historians, see J. G. A. Pocock, *Barbarism and Religion*, 4 vols. (Cambridge and New York: Cambridge University Press, 1999–2005), 2:17–60; on the Florentine historians of the *declinatio*, 2:153–235; and on the influence of those traditions on the first 14 chapters of volume 1 of Gibbon's *Decline and Fall*, 2:3, 419–23.

10. On Montesquieu's influence on Gibbon, see ibid., 2:210, 234; 3:441, 453.

11. See ibid., 2:424, 432–33, 437. For Gibbon, the deposition of Romulus Augustus by a "barbarian," Odoacer, in 476, marked the end of the Western Roman Empire (ibid., 3:173).

12. See ibid., 2:1, 11.

13. Pocock argues that Gibbon belongs to an English Enlightenment, "mainly Protestant in origin and character" (ibid., 1:7, 295). Confidence in the future of Western civilization was not of course shared by all Enlightenment *philosophes*, the most notable exceptions being Raynal, Diderot, and Rousseau.

14. Thomas Babington Macaulay, *History of England from the Accession of James II*, 5 vols. (London: Longman et al., 1848–59); Macaulay, "Mill on Government" [review of *Essays on Government, Jurisprudence . . .*] (1829), in *The Miscellaneous Writings, Speeches, and Poems of Lord Macaulay*, 4 vols. (London: Longmans, Green, 1880), 1:142–43.

15. Thomas Babington Macaulay, "A Speech Delivered at Edinburgh . . ." [on his election to parliament, 1852]," in *Miscellaneous Writings*, 3:442. He also "censure[d]" Gibbon (among other historians) for the "error of distorting facts to suit general principles," in "History" (1828), ibid., 1:95–96.

16. Macaulay, "Von Ranke," in *Critical and Historical Essays*, 3:209.

17. Henry George, *Progress and Poverty: An Inquiry into the Cause of Industrial Depressions and of Increase of Want with Increase of Wealth the Remedy* (1879; New York: Modern Library, 1938); references cited in the text. Publication figures from Carl Smith, *Urban Disorder and the Shape of Belief: The Great Chicago Fire, the Haymarket Bomb, and the Model Town of Pullman* (Chicago: University of Chicago Press, 1995), 212.

18. John L. Thomas, *Alternative America: Henry George, Edward Bellamy, Henry Demarest Lloyd, and the Adversary Tradition* (Cambridge, MA: Harvard University Press, 1983), 110, 114, 117.

19. On George's membership in the typographers' union, see Anna George De Mille, *Henry George: Citizen of the World* (Chapel Hill: University of North Carolina Press, 1950), 29.

20. Karl Marx, letter to Friedrich Sorge (1881), in *Karl Marx and Frederick Engels: Letters to Americans, 1848–1895* (New York: International Publishers, 1953), 129. Thomas similarly describes the Single Tax as a "utopian device" and a "piece of magic machinery," and George's strategy as "counterrevolutionary," in *Alternative America*, 118, 120, 123.

21. On his reading of the universalist historians, see Thomas, *Alternative America*, 125.

22. On the Christian millennial dream underpinning George's vision, see ibid., 123, 127, and Fred Nicklason, "Henry George: Social Gospeller," *American Quarterly* 22, no. 3 (1970): 649–64.

23. Henry George, *Social Problems* (1883; New York: Robert Schalkenbach, 1963), 1 (emphasis added); further references cited in the text.

24. Henry George, *Our Land and Land Policy* (1871; New York: Doubleday and McClure, 1902), 124.

25. Frederic Cople Jaher, *Doubters and Dissenters: Cataclysmic Thought in America, 1885–1918* (New York: Macmillan, 1964), 20.

26. Laurence Gronlund, *The Coöperative Commonwealth* (Boston: Lee and Shepard, 1884), 7–8; further references cited in the text.

27. On Haymarket, see Smith, *Urban Disorder,* 101–74; and on the Bay View Tragedy in Milwaukee, Robert Nesbit, "The Bay View Tragedy," in *Workers and Unions in Wisconsin History: A Labor History Anthology*, ed. Darryl Holter (Madison: State Historical Society of Wisconsin, 1999), 34–46.

28. Henry W. Farnham, "Progress and Poverty in Politics," *New Englander and Yale Review* 10, no. 205 (1887): 335–45. The CLU were also responding to the imprisonment of boycotters in New York the previous month. In the 1886 mayoral election, George came second to Abram Hewitt, but still received more votes than Theodore Roosevelt.

29. Anna Bowman Dodd, *The Republic of the Future; or, Socialism a Reality* (New York: Cassell, 1887), 47–49, 82–83; further references cited in the text.

30. *The Progress* (1889), quoted by (among others) Ignatius Donnelly in *Caesar's Column: A Story of the Twentieth Century* (1889; Cambridge: Belknap Press of Harvard University Press, 1960), 94.

31. Rev. E. D. M'Creary, "The Concentration of Wealth," *Christian Advocate* 66, no. 38 (1891): 618; signed, "Santa Cruz, Cal."

32. Herman E. Taubeneck, "The Concentration of Wealth, Its Cause and Results, Part I," *The Arena* 18, no. 94 (1897): 290, 300; for his specific class-based critiques of those banking acts, see Part II, which appeared in no. 95 (1897): 452–69. On Taubeneck's political career, see Lawrence Goodwyn, *The Populist Moment: A Short History of the Agrarian Revolt in America* (New York: Oxford University Press, 1978), especially 237–55.

33. Harry Thurston Peck, "The Social Advantages of the Concentration of Wealth," *The Independent* 54, no. 2787 (1902): 1051, 1053–54; Peck wrote four books on Latin literature and philology, and edited the *Harper's Dictionary of Classical Antiquities* (New York: Harper, 1897).

34. Taubeneck, "Concentration of Wealth, Part II," 468–69.

35. Dr. Joseph Rodes Buchanan, "The Coming Cataclysm of America and Europe," *The Arena* 1, no. 9 (1890): 294, 293, 296; further references cited in the text. *The Arena* was a Boston magazine that advocated social reform and women's rights.

36. Buchanan subscribed to the "spirit" of Bellamy's Nationalist movement (301, 310) and Henry Demarest Lloyd's critique of American industrialists (302 n.), but considered Donnelly's *Caesar's Column* a more accurate prediction of how the crisis would be resolved, albeit erroneously postponing it by a century (297–98). Despite his predictions about Christianity, Buchanan was well received by millenarians. *Zion's Watch Tower*, the journal of a society of Jehovah's Witnesses founded by Charles Taze Russell, himself an author of millennial prophecies, described his article as "very interesting" ("Prof. J. R. Buchanan's View," *Zion's Watch Tower and Herald of Christ's Presence* 11, no. 11 [1890]: R1246: page 8).

37. G. A. Danziger, "Labor Unions and Strikes in Ancient Rome," *Cosmopolitan* 10, no. 5 (1891): 614, 619, 616.

38. See Paul Krause, *The Battle for Homestead, 1880–1892: Politics, Culture, and Steel* (Pittsburgh: University of Pittsburgh Press, 1992), 12–25.

39. John Brisben Walker, "The 'Homestead' Object Lesson," *Cosmopolitan* 13, no. 5 (1892): 573; further references cited in the text. On Walker's career at *Cosmpolitan*, see Matthew Schneirov, *The Dream of a New Social Order: Popular Magazines in America, 1893–1914* (New York: Columbia University Press, 1994), especially 105–13.

40. Bellamy, *Looking Backward, 2000–1887* (1888; Harmondsworth: Penguin, 1982), 202.

41. Henry Demarest Lloyd, *Wealth against Commonwealth* (New York: Harper, 1894), 510. See also his earlier critiques of railroad managers as having the "callous brutality" of Roman patricians (quoted in Thomas, *Alternative America*, 4). In *The Pullman Strike* (Chicago: Kerr, 1894), the pastor who sermonized to the strikers at Pullman, William H. Carwardine, similarly warned that the nation had become fractured, "like ancient Rome, into two classes, the rich and the poor, the oppressor and the oppressed," and had failed to learn the "useful lessons" from Rome's "failures and defeats" (121).

42. Mining strikes culminating in the dispatching of troops and/or deaths of strikers during this period include: Cripple Creek, Colorado (1894), Leadville, Colorado (1896); the "Lattimer Massacre" near Hazleton, Pennsylvania (1897); Pana, Illinois (1902); Cripple Creek and Dunnville, Colorado (1903–04), culminating in the bomb explosion at Independence, Colorado (1904).

43. Jack London, *The Iron Heel* (1908; Chicago: Lawrence Hill, 1990); page references cited in the text.

44. *Iron Heel*'s hero cites the kinds of magazine articles about the growing gap between rich and poor discussed in the previous section (160–61).

45. London detailed such a scenario in his fictional account of a general strike, "The Dream of Debs," *International Socialist Review* 9, nos. 7, 8 (1909): 481–89, 561–70; quotations on 563, 568.

46. V. I. Lenin, "What Is to Be Done?" (1902), in *Collected Works*, 45 vols. (Moscow: Foreign Languages Publishing House, 1960–70), 5:347–530.

47. London's other prospective histories include: "A Curious Fragment" (1908), in *When God Laughs and Other Stories* (New York: Macmillan, 1911), 257–75, about the rise of a labor spy during a postapocalyptic age of industrial slavery, presented by the "editor" as an excerpt from a book of historical sources titled "'Historical Fragments and Sketches' . . . published in 4427, and . . . because of its accuracy and value, edited and republished by the National Committee on Historical Research" (275); "The Unparalleled Invasion" (written 1907, published 1910), in *Moon-Face, and Other Stories* (New York: Macmillan, 1919), 71–100, about an American biological attack on China, presented as an "Excerpt from Walt Mervin's 'Certain Essays in History'" (100); and *The Scarlet Plague* (New York: Macmillan, 1915), about the epidemic that decimated San Francisco (and civilization in general), as narrated sixty years later by an old professor to his grandchildren.

48. Despite the description of Ernest Everhard as a Nietzschean "superman, a blond beast," with "bulging muscles" and of native stock (8, 18, 19), London's revolutionary socialism overrides his reactionary racial and gender views here; women are assigned a prominent role in the revolutionary movement, and the "distinction between . . . native born and foreign born" seems to have diminished since the revolution (19 n.).

49. London had borrowed Wells's phrase for the title of his exposé of London poverty, *The People of the Abyss* (New York: Macmillan, 1903).

50. Others who had "caught glimpses of the shadow" include Calhoun and Lincoln (68 n.).

51. Meredith's belief in historical objectivity is evident in his critique of Avis's emotional bias: "She was too close to the events she writes about" (1); and in his call to treat twentieth-century phenomena "serious[ly]," rather than dismiss them as "laughably absurd and primitive" (39 n.), in other words to avoid (borrowing E. P. Thompson's phrase) the "massive condescension of posterity."

52. Jack London, "The Shrinkage of the Planet" (1899), in *Revolution and Other Essays* (New York: Macmillan, 1910), 155, 151; further references cited in the text.

53. Ernst Bloch, "The Conscious and Known Activity within the Not-Yet-Conscious, the Utopian Function" (1959), in *The Utopian Function of Art and Literature: Selected Essays*, trans. Jack Zipes and Frank Mecklenburg (Cambridge, MA: MIT Press, 1988), especially 103–8.

54. "Destroying the Commerce and the Harbor of New-York" *New York Times* (hereafter *NYT*), April 17, 1857, 4.

55. John G. Stevens, "The Erie Canal and Its Relations to the City of New York," *Scribner's Monthly* 15, no. 1 (1877): 117, 123–24.

56. David Scobey, *Empire City: The Making and Meaning of the New York City Landscape* (Philadelphia: Temple University Press, 2002), 135, 143.

57. Logan Uriah Reavis, *Saint Louis: The Future Great City of the World* (1867; St. Louis: St. Louis County Court, 1871), 14, 25, 45; further references cited in the text.

58. On St. Louis's failure to keep pace with Chicago, see Jeffrey S. Adler, *Yankee Merchants*

and the Making of the Urban West: The Rise and Fall of Antebellum St. Louis (Cambridge and New York: Cambridge University Press, 2002), especially 110–44.

59. Robert Luce, "Town and City Histories," *Bay State Monthly* 1, no. 5 (1884), 317–18.

60. Reavis, "The City of America," newspaper cutting [n.d.], in L. U. Reavis Collection, St. Louis Historical Society (hereafter SLHS). Reavis's publications in support of capital removal were: *The New Republic; or, The Transition Complete* (St. Louis: J. F. Torrey, 1867); *A Change of National Empire* (St. Louis: J. F. Torrey, 1869); *The National Capital Is Movable* (St. Louis: Missouri Democrat Book and Job Printing House, 1871); and *The Nation and Its Capital* (St. Louis: privately printed, 1883). See also the draft of a "Petition to Congress for the Removal of the Federal Capital," n.d., in the Reavis Collection, SLHS. The *St. Paul Press* remarked that this "Great American Capital Remover" could even persuade the Pope to relocate to the Mississippi Valley ("A Vote for Reavis," n.d., SLHS). On earlier calls for capital removal, see chapter 2.

61. Reavis (quoting Horace Greeley), *Change of National Empire*, vii. William Cronon cites this passage in *Nature's Metropolis: Chicago and the Great West* (New York: W. W. Norton, 1991), 42–43, but reads it as a simple reiteration of the "stock imagery of imperial growth and rebirth" (42), thus overlooking the more subtle variations.

62. Charles Chauncey Burr, "The Capitol at Washington," *The Old Guard* 5, no. 2 (1867): 138.

63. [Ignatius Donnelly], "The Omaha Platform [of the National People's Party]," in *A Populist Reader: Selections from the Works of American Populist Leaders*, ed. George Brown Tindall (New York: Harper and Row, 1966), 91. Donnelly, *Caesar's Column*, 284. On this novel's unexpected success see Walter Rideout's introduction, xviii–xx; on Donnelly's failed effort to found the city of Nininger, Minnesota, see Nick Yablon, "Cities in Ruin: Urban Apocalypse in American Culture, 1790–1920" (PhD diss., University of Chicago, 2002), 105–17; and on populists' use of metaphors of natural disaster such as cyclones and prairie fires, see Stuart K. Culver, "Waiting for the End of the World: Catastrophe and the Populist Myth of History," *Configurations* 3, no. 3 (1995): especially 395.

64. William Jennings Bryan, "Cross of Gold Speech," in Tindall, ed., *Populist Reader*, 210.

65. Even the agrarian populist, Donnelly, devoted much of *Caesar's Column* to the future conditions of *urban* laborers.

66. Jacob Riis, "The Tenement House Blight," *Atlantic Monthly* 83, no. 500 (1899): 761, 770–71.

67. Jacob Riis, "The Story of the Slum — Part 1," *Chicago Daily Tribune*, March 11, 1900, 37. On the terms of the Tenement House Act of 1901, and the role of other campaigners such as the Charity Organization Society of the City of New York, see Richard Plunz, *A History of Housing in New York City: Dwelling Type and Social Change in the American Metropolis* (New York: Columbia University Press, 1990), 43–49.

68. Thomas Bailey Aldrich, "Unguarded Gates," in *Unguarded Gates and Other Poems* (Boston and New York: Houghton Mifflin, 1895), 15–17; Henry Cabot Lodge, "The Restriction of Immigration" (1896) in *Speeches and Addresses, 1884–1909* (Boston and New York: Houghton Mifflin, 1909), 266, 248. A literacy requirement was eventually enacted, over President Wilson's veto, in 1917. Invasion metaphors appear in restrictionist tracts such as Frank Julian Warne, *The Immigrant Invasion* (New York: Dodd, Mead, 1913).

69. Lyman Abbott, "Danger Ahead," *The Century* 31, no. 1 (1885): 51, 57; Abbott expresses his nostalgia there for the "homogeneous" society of the early American colonies (51). His article was debated in subsequent issues, e.g., vol. 31, no. 4 (1886): 636–37; vol. 32, no. 5 (1886): 808–9.

70. Hjalmar H. Boyesen, "Dangers of Unrestricted Immigration," *Forum* 3 (July 1887): 537, 533–34, 539. On Boyesen's (limited) engagement with the immigrant experience, see Clarence A. Glasrud, "Boyesen and the Norwegian Immigration," *Norwegian-American Studies and Records* 19 (1956): 15–45.

71. John Ames Mitchell, *The Last American: A Fragment from the Journal of Khan-li* (New York: Frederick A. Stokes and Brother, 1889), 33; further references cited in the text.

72. In addition to figure 4.2, see "Sight-Seeing in 1920," *Life* 39, no. 1006 (1902): 101 (fig. 6.6 in this book); "In 1950," *Life* 51, no. 1315 (1908): 53; "1620 to 1920: Found in the Ruins of New York City," *Life* 58, no. 1506 (1911): 382. On Mitchell's role in founding *Life*, see Martha Banta, *Barbaric Intercourse: Caricature and the Culture of Conduct, 1841–1936* (Chicago: University of Chicago Press, 2003), 67–71.

73. Arthur Dudley Vinton, *Looking Further Backward* (Albany, NY: Albany Book Co., 1890), title page; further references cited in the text.

74. Sir George Tomkyns Chesney, *Battle of Dorking: Reminiscences of a Volunteer* (Edinburgh and London: William Blackwood and Sons, 1871), 3.

75. I. F. Clarke makes this assumption in *Voices Prophesying War, 1763–1984* (London: Oxford University Press, 1966), 44. In addition to the invasion fictions by Reed, "Coverdale," H. G. Donnelly, and Vinton (cited above), and Dooner, Bryce, Robinson, Benjamin, Walker, Dixon, and Wells (cited below), see also Samuel Barton, *The Battle of the Swash and the Capture of Canada* (New York: Dillingham, 1888); J. H. Palmer, *The Invasion of New York; or, How Hawaii Was Annexed* (New York: Neely, 1897); John Ulrich Giesy, *All for His Country* (New York: Macaulay, 1915); Cleveland Moffett, "The Conquest of America," *McClure's Magazine* 45, no. 1 (1915): 9–12, 85–87, continued in nos. 2, 3, 4 (1915); H. Irving Hancock, *The Invasion of the United States*, 4 vols. (Philadelphia: Henry Altemus, 1916).

76. Besides Vinton, at least two other authors imagined a Chinese invasion: Pieter Dooner, *Last Days of the Republic* (San Francisco: Alta California, 1880) and Lloyd Bryce, *A Dream of Conquest* (Philadelphia: Lippincott, 1889). The Spanish navy attacks America in Park Benjamin, "The End of New York," *Fiction Magazine*, October 31, 1881, reprinted in the anthology, *Stories by American Authors* (New York: Scribner's, 1884), 82–141.

77. Benjamin, "The End of New York," in *Stories,* 120–21, 140. See also J. Bernard Walker's description of how "the terror of the bombardment swept through the densely populated tenement-house district like the rush of a prairie fire" and triggered a "wild stampede" of "men, women, and children, Jew, Italian, Greek, and Russian, bearded rabbi and toddling child," in *America Fallen! The Sequel to the European War* (New York: Dodd, Mead, 1915), 113–14; and Rev. Thomas Dixon Jr.'s account of a German-led invasion of America, which unleashed the city's own ethnic hordes in the form of an urban insurrection beginning in the Jewish Lower East Side and spreading to other neighborhoods, in *Fall of the Nation: A Sequel to* The Birth of a Nation (New York: D. Appleton, 1916), 314–15.

78. H. G. Wells, *The War in the Air* (New York: Macmillan, 1908); references cited in the text.

79. H. G. Wells, *The Future in America: A Search after Realities* (New York and London: Harper and Brothers, 1906), 138, 147, and see also 43; Wells opposes immigration in part out of concern for the immigrants, as they were forming an exploited proletariat in America (141).

80. H. G. Wells, *Tono-Bungay* (New York: Duffield, 1908), 25; Patrick Parrinder, "H. G. Wells and the Fall of Empires," *Foundation: The Review of Science Fiction* 57 (Spring 1993): 50, 55.

81. See also Wells's subsequent discussion of *Decline and Fall*, and especially of its Antonine "prelude of splendour and tranquility," in *The Outline of History* (1920), quoted in Parrinder, "H. G. Wells," 51.

82. Wells, *Outline of History*, quoted in ibid., 51–52.

83. On Wells's reading of George, see his *Experiment in Autobiography* (New York: Macmillan, 1934), 140.

84. "The Lost Arts," *Christian* 59, no. 6 (1884): 88; "The Lost Arts," lecture in the Tabernacle, reported in *NYT*, December 2, 1852, 1; "The Lost Arts," *Circular* 3, no. 16 (1854), and "Wendell Phillips: His Lecture Last Evening on 'The Lost Arts,'" *Chicago Tribune*, January 4, 1871, 4. For the reference to the number of recitals of this "most charming lecture . . . ever delivered from an American platform," see the preface to the book edition, *The Lost Arts* (Boston: Wendell Phillips Hall Association, 1891), 3–4.

85. H. M. Alden, "Why the Ancients Had No Printing Press," *Harper's New Monthly* 37, no. 219 (1868): 397.

86. "Editors Table," *Harper's New Monthly* 10, no. 60 (1855): 836.

87. "Notes and Queries," *Harper's Weekly* 1, no. 1 (1857): 11.

88. Alexander Young, "Time the Preserver," *Religious Magazine and Monthly Review* 46, no. 6 (1871): 523, 520, 521.

89. See, for example, "The Decay of Building Stones in New York City," *Manufacturer and Builder* 15, no. 2 (1883): 43–44.

90. Judge J. A. Jameson, "Is Our Civilization Perishable?" *North American Review* 138, no. 328 (1884): 208, 212, 214.

91. "Will Future Generations Lose Historical Records of To-Day?" *NYT*, July 24, 1910, Sunday Magazine, 15.

92. For a fuller discussion of the time capsule, see Nick Yablon, "Encapsulating the Present: The 'War of the Classes' and the Birth of the Time-Capsule, 1876–1914," in Yablon, ed., *The Politics of Display: Essays in Honor of Neil Harris* (in progress). On historians' enshrinement of "objectivity" in the late nineteenth century, see Peter Novick, *That Noble Dream: The 'Objectivity Question' and the American Historical Profession* (Cambridge: Cambridge University Press, 1988), 61–108.

93. "Hint to Brickmakers," *Harper's Weekly* 11, no. 16 (1867): 733.

94. The two time capsules usually cited as the first are Westinghouse's exhibit at the New York World's Fair of 1939 and Oglethorpe University's "Crypt of Civilization" of 1940.

95. *National Republican*, 1879, quoted in C. F. Deihm, ed., *President James A. Garfield's Memorial Journal . . .* (New York: Deihm, 1882), 198. See also the account of the "Centennial Safe" (as the "Century Safe" was sometimes called) in J. S. Ingram, *The Centennial Exposition, Described and Illustrated . . .* (Philadelphia: Hubbard Bros., 1876), 722. Deihm, the wife of a publisher, took her safe around the country for two years before sealing it at the United States Capitol in 1878 ("Centennial Safe Closed," *NYT*, February 23, 1879, 1); on the durability of the safe itself, see Deihm, ed., *Garfield's Memorial Journal*, 199. Mosher had his vault embedded in the walls of Chicago's City Hall in 1885, eventually sealing ca. 10,000 photographs in it in 1889 ("For Posterity," *Chicago Daily Tribune*, February 28, 1885, 7). See *Catalogue of Memorial Photographs of Prominent Persons Whose Likenesses Will Appear in Memorial Halls at the Second Centennial . . .* (Chicago: Mosher, 1887), Chicago History Museum (hereafter CHM).

96. The Century Safe was criticized for catering to Americans' desires for "cheap fame" in Philip Quilibet, "Safe Celebrity," *The Galaxy* 22, no. 1 (1876): 125; and for having "few" "photographs of ladies" in "Centennial Safe Closed," 1. Mosher's vault was similarly described as being motivated in part by "the hope of financial reward through this wide-spread advertising of his work," in "For Posterity," 7. On Masonic cornerstone ceremonies, see Neil Harris, *Building Lives: Constructing Rites and Passage* (New Haven, CT: Yale University Press, 1999), 20–31. Macaulay's New Zealander was invoked as the potential beneficiary of the various

documents and objects placed in the cornerstones of Livingstone Missionary Hall in Nashville in 1881, and Mutual Life in New York, 1883; see, respectively, Secretary Strieby, "Address at Nashville, at the laying of the cornerstone of Livingstone Missionary Hall," *American Missionary* 35, no. 8 (1881): 233–36; and "The Critic," *The Critic* 73 (1883): 246.

97. For the Bicentennial, Deihm called for direct descendants to add their names in the space left beneath each signature, while Mosher insisted on a public reading of certain enclosed messages. Indeed, the latter's plans extended another century into the future, with the stipulation that his vault be topped up and resealed for the Tercentennial. Deihm included businessmen's testimonials in *Garfield's Memorial Journal*; Mosher nominated Marshall Field as president of his memorial project, in *Catalogue of Memorial Historical Photographs* (1883), 33.

98. Louis Ehrich, handwritten letter "To my Fellow-Townspeople of Colorado Springs in the Year 2001," Colorado Springs Century Chest Collection, Ms 0349, Tutt Library Special Collections, Colorado College (hereafter CSCCC), Folder 49, pp. 9–10. See also Ehrich, *"Posteritism": An Address Delivered at the Dedication Exercises of the Century Chest, On August 4th, 1901 . . .* (Colorado Springs: privately printed, 1901), 8, Ehrich Papers, Yale University Library.

99. Envelope of fabrics in Folder 53; hairpins in Folder 15; badges in Folders 39, 42; wax cylinders in Folder 159; photographs of urban and domestic spaces in Folder 160, CSCCC.

100. William A. Platt, "A Message on National Politics," Folder 25, p. 7; Dr. Samuel LeNord Caldwell's letter, Folder 52; Charles G. Collais, Builder and Member of Local Union #515 Carpenters and Joiners of America, letter, Folder 29, p. 9, CSCCC.

101. Besides those cited in the text, proto–time capsules were also deposited at Ramapo, New York (1876), University of Massachusetts, Amherst (1878), Palmer House Hotel, Chicago (1879), Sandwich, Massachusetts (1884), Cincinnati (1888), Cleveland (1896), Ayers, Middlesex (1898), the White House (1902), and Portland, Oregon (1903)—the latter two by Theodore Roosevelt. Mosher's vault failed to reach its terminal date when it was opened in 1908 ("Old Photographs Arouse Memories," *Tribune*, August 12, 1908, 5).

102. I am alluding here to Marx's famous remark about the repetition of history in *The Eighteenth Brumaire of Louis Napoleon*, trans. Daniel De Leon (1852; Chicago: Kerr, 1907), 5. Mitchell's prospective history was also humorous, but those of London, Wells, and Vinton were not.

103. Ambrose Bierce, "For the Ahkoond," *San Francisco Examiner*, March 18, 1888; "The Fall of the Republic: An Article from a 'Court Journal' of the Thirty-First Century," ibid., March 25, 1888; "Ashes of the Beacon: An Historical Monograph Written in 3940," ibid., February 26, 1905; these and other postapocalyptic fragments were syndicated in Hearst's *New York Journal* and *New York American*. Material from his later fragments for *Cosmopolitan*, "The Jury in Ancient America" (1905) and "Insurance in Ancient America" (1906), was incorporated into the final version of "Ashes of the Beacon," reprinted in Ambrose Bierce, *The Fall of the Republic and Other Political Satires*, ed. S. T. Joshi and David E. Schultz (Knoxville: University of Tennessee Press, 2000), 3–31; all page references are to this edition. The reference to the "curmudgeon philosopher" is in Richard O'Connor, *Ambrose Bierce: A Biography* (Boston: Little, Brown, 1967), 248; on Hearst approaching Bierce in 1887 shortly after taking over the *Examiner*, and his later transferal of Bierce to the *Cosmopolitan*, see ibid., 153, 271.

104. Bierce, "Fall of the Republic," 102.

105. Bierce, "Ashes of the Beacon," 16, 4; see also Bierce, "Insurance in Industrial America."

106. Bierce, "Ashes of the Beacon," 4. See "Translations of the Inscriptions on Foreign Blocks," in Frederick L. Harvey, *History of the Washington National Monument and of the Washington National Monument Society* (Washington, DC: Elliott, 1902), 128–29.

107. Bierce, "Inscription," in *The Devil's Dictionary* (1911), in *Collected Works of Ambrose*

Bierce, 12 vols. (New York and Washington, DC: Neale, 1909–12), 7:167–68. See my discussion of the delayed completion of the Washington Monument in chapter 2.

108. Walter Benjamin, *One-Way Street and Other Writings*, trans. Edmund Jephcott and Kingsley Shorter (London: NLB, 1979), 70; Chateaubriand, cited in Walter Benjamin, *The Arcades Project*, trans. Howard Eiland and Kevin McLaughlin (Cambridge, MA: Belknap Press of Harvard University Press, 1999), 399 [K5a,3].

109. On Bierce's critique of utopian thinkers, see Lawrence I. Berkove, "Two Impossible Dreams: Ambrose Bierce on Utopia and America," *Huntington Library Quarterly* 44, no. 4 (1981): especially 287; on his critique of feminism, social reform, and unions, see O'Connor, *Bierce*, 176, 198, 222.

110. Bierce, "Ashes of the Beacon," 26, 21, 24–25; Bierce, "Fall of the Republic," 103, 105.

111. Bierce, "Fall of the Republic," 102–3; Bierce, "Ashes of the Beacon," 6, 11–12.

112. Bierce, "Ashes of the Beacon," 5, 20; Bierce, "Fall of the Republic," 103; all further Bierce references will be to "Ashes of the Beacon."

113. In the 1888 satire, these events are dated 1897, in the later, 1905 version, the year 1995 is cited.

114. Bierce, "On Trusts," quoted in O'Connor, *Bierce*, 222. Bierce's views on labor and capital do not conform to conventional conservative models. During the depression of the mid-1890s, he sympathized with workingmen and their hopes for state-funded works projects (quoted in ibid., 221). And his view of trusts depended on whether they were "justly administered" (quoted in Berkove, "Two Impossible Dreams," 292). Nevertheless, his politics fitted uneasily in Hearst's antitrust newspaper.

115. For a brief history of their altercations, see Robert L. Gale, *An Ambrose Bierce Companion* (Westport, CT: Greenwood Press, 2001), 286–88.

116. Mark Twain, "The Secret History of Eddypus, the World-Empire" (ca. 1901–02; first published in 1972), reprinted in Twain, *The Science Fiction of Mark Twain*, ed. David Ketterer (Hamden, CT: Archon, 1984), 176–225; page references cited in the text. An outtake was published in *North American Review* (see n. 118 below). Twain's other prospective histories include: "Passage from 'Glances at History' (suppressed.) Date, 9th Century" (early 1900s), in Twain, *The Devil's Race-Track: Mark Twain's 'Great Dark' Writings*, ed. John S. Tuckey (Berkeley: University of California Press, 1980), 373–75; "Passage from 'Outlines of History' (suppressed.) Date, 9th Century" (early 1900s), ibid., 376–77; "Passage from a Lecture" (written in the early 1900s), ibid., 378–81; "History, 1,000 Years from Now" (1901), ibid., 382–83; "Extract from Article in 'The Radical,' Jan., 916" (1906), in Twain, *A Pen Warmed-Up in Hell: Mark Twain in Protest*, ed. Frederick Anderson (New York: Harper and Row, 1972), 166–68. Albert Bigelow Paine describes how "Eddypus," as the product of Twain's "vented" antipathy to Christian Science, was "not publishable matter, and really never intended as such. It was just one of the things which Mark Twain wrote to relieve mental pressure" (*Mark Twain: A Biography*, 4 vols. [New York: Harper, 1912], 3:1188); on his financial losses incurred by the failed Paige typesetter, the loss of his family home, and the death of his eldest daughter in 1896, see ibid., 3:903–14, 919–20, and 1023, respectively.

117. Twain's most famous denunciation of the American imperialist project in Cuba and the Philippines was the essay, "To the Person Sitting in Darkness," published in *North American Review* in 1901, and reprinted in Twain, *Mark Twain's Weapons of Satire: Anti-Imperialist Writings on the Philippine-American War*, ed. Jim Zwick (Syracuse, NY: Syracuse University Press, 1992), 22–39.

118. "Christian Science.—III," *North American Review* 176, no. 555 (1903): 182–83;

Twain titled this section, "V.—(Later Still.)—A Thousand Years Ago," and appended in an asterisk: "Written A.D. 2902."

119. Twain, *Science Fiction of Mark Twain*, 367n53.

120. The manuscript is nevertheless deemed more reliable than the subsequent, second-hand histories that also survived the Eddymanian raids, such as Flinder's "Glimpses of Antiquity" (181–82). Twain's interest in the time-capsule may be related to his fantasy of direct communication, evident in "Mental Telegraphy," *Harper's New Monthly* 84, no. 499 (1891): 95–104, a fantasy he ironically shared with Christian Scientists. The time capsule realized another of Twain's hopes of the period, namely for an act to preserve authors' copyright in perpetuity; included in the vault, were instructions on how the manuscript was to be reproduced and sold ("Eddypus," 196).

121. George Santayana, *The Life of Reason; or, The Phases of Human Progress*, 5 vols. (New York: Scribner's, 1905–06), 1:284. Twain may well have been contradicting Santayana when he reiterated (two years later) that "history repeats itself; . . . Not because . . . men would deliberately desire the destruction of their republic . . . but because *circumstances* which they create without suspecting what they are doing will by and by *compel* that destruction" (Twain, *Mark Twain in Eruption: Hitherto Unpublished Pages about Men and Events*, ed. Bernard DeVoto [New York: Harper, 1940], 2).

122. "Passage from a Lecture," 378–81. In the *North American Review* outtake, the ending is more final: "the Black Night shut down, never again to lift!" ("Christian Science.—III," 184; see also 181).

Chapter 5

1. Bret Harte, "The Ruins of San Francisco," in *Mrs. Skaggs' Husbands, and Other Sketches* (Boston: James R. Osgood, 1873), 337, 339, 340, 338, 340.

2. Janet E. Buerger, *French Daguerreotypes* (Chicago: University of Chicago Press, 1989), figs. 47, 24. Charles Baudelaire, "The Salon of 1859," in *Selected Writings on Art and Literature* (Harmondsworth: Penguin, 1992), 296–97. On Ruskin's initial celebration of the capacity of the daguerreotype to record "every chip of stone and stain" of architectural monuments before they fall victim to the "great public of wreckers," and his subsequent suspicion of its implications for art, see Michael Harvey, "Ruskin and Photography," *Oxford Art Journal* 7, no. 2 (1984): 25–33; quotations on 25, 26.

3. William J. Stillman, *The Acropolis of Athens, Illustrated Picturesquely and Architecturally in Photography* (London: F. S. Ellis, 1870).

4. See, respectively, Alan Trachtenberg, "Albums of War: On Reading Civil War Photographs," *Representations* 9 (Winter 1985): especially 19–26; Alisa Luxenberg, "Creating Désastres: Andrieu's Photographs of Urban Ruins in the Paris of 1871," *Art Bulletin* 80, no. 1 (1998): 113–37; Ross Miller, *American Apocalypse: The Great Fire and the Myth of Chicago* (Chicago: University of Chicago Press, 1990), 2, 93–105; Robin Kelsey, "C. C. Jones: The USGS investigation of the Charleston Earthquake," in *Archive Style: Photographs and Illustrations for U.S. Surveys, 1850–1890* (Berkeley: University of California Press, 2007), 143–89; Harold H. Strayer, *A Photographic Story of the 1889 Johnstown Flood* (Johnstown, PA: Weigel and Barber, 1992); and Patricia Bellis Bixel and Elizabeth Hayes Turner, *Galveston and the 1900 Storm: Catastrophe and Catalyst* (Austin: University of Texas Press, 2000).

5. "Largest Collection—Copyright Views of the San Francisco Fire" [advertisement for Pillsbury Picture Company, based in Oakland], *Camera Craft* 12, no. 4 (1906): n.p.

6. Edgar A. Cohen, "With a Camera in San Francisco," *Camera Craft* 12, no. 5 (1906): 183.

7. Ross Miller, *American Apocalypse*, 65. Miller argues, in Freudian-inflected terms, that

for Chicagoans (if not for newly arrived, more critical architects like Louis Sullivan), the ruins were an intolerable reminder of the "trauma," which could be "denied or overwhelmed by language" and by "the special kind of forgetting represented by the initial rebuilding" (99; see also 65, 83).

8. See Gladys Hansen and Emmet Condon, *Denial of Disaster* (San Francisco: Cameron, 1989); Ted Steinberg, "Smoke and Mirrors: The San Francisco Earthquake and Seismic Denial," in *American Disasters,* ed. Steven Biel (New York: New York University Press, 2001), 103–26.

9. H. D'Arcy Power, "Earthquake and Fire: From a Photographer's Viewpoint," *Camera Craft* 12, no. 4 (1906): 155; another amateur, Arthur Inkersley, admitted that his "first idea," even before the fire had broken out, "was to make pictures," in "An Amateur's Experience of Earthquake and Fire," *Camera Craft* 12, no. 5 (1906): 196. Arnold Genthe, *As I Remember* (1936; Salem, NH: Ayer, 1979), 89.

10. Sigmund Freud, *Inhibitions, Symptoms, and Anxiety: The Standard Edition* (New York: W. W. Norton, 1977), 102; for a Freudian reading of the mass mediation of disaster, see Patricia Mellencamp, *High Anxiety: Catastrophe, Scandal, Age, and Comedy* (Bloomington: Indiana University Press, 1992).

11. *San Francisco Chronicle,* cited in French Strother, "The Rebound of San Francisco," *The World's Work* 12, no. 3 (1906): 7779. Charles Augustus Keeler, *San Francisco through Earthquake and Fire* (San Francisco: P. Elder, 1906), 33. James Hopper, "Our San Francisco," *Everybody's Magazine* 14, no. 6 (1906): 760h.

12. Editorial in *Mining and Scientific Press*, May 5, 1906, reprinted in *After Earthquake and Fire: A Reprint of the Articles and Editorial Comment Appearing in the* Mining and Scientific Press (San Francisco: Mining and Scientific Press, 1906), 77; further references cited in text. Photograph titled "Grotesque Statuary Was Created When the Ground Shook" [CMP Box 601-03-3, stereography no. X8184]. Katherine Putnam Hooker, "Life at the Camp," Hooker Family Papers, Banc MSS 77/1 c, 63, 64.

13. Editorial in *Mining and Scientific Press*, in *After Earthquake and Fire*, 82; Hopper, "Our San Francisco," 760h.

14. J. M. Scanland, "Electrical Displays in San Francisco," *Overland Monthly and Out West Magazine* 44, no. 2 (1904): 23, 22. On the delay and budget overrun, see Frank W. Blackmar, "San Francisco's Struggle for Good Government," *Forum* 26 (January 1899): 572.

15. Scanland, "Electrical Displays," 21, 25. In fact, electrical displays promoted the adoption of electricity for everyday uses; see David E. Nye, *Electrifying America: Social Meanings of a New Technology, 1880–1940* (Cambridge, MA: MIT Press, 1990), 33–47.

16. Gray Brechin, *Imperial San Francisco: Urban Power, Earthly Ruin* (Berkeley: University of California Press, 1999), 253, 255, 263.

17. I am borrowing the term *networked city* from Joel A. Tarr and Gabriel Dupuy, eds., *Technology and the Rise of the Networked City in Europe and America* (Philadelphia: Temple University Press, 1988).

18. See, respectively, "Long Automobile Trip Ends," *San Francisco Call*, July 27, 1903, 5; "President Opens New Manila Cable," *New York Times* (hereafter *NYT*), July 5, 1903, 1; "Pacific Wireless Messages," *NYT*, February 19, 1903, 1; George Iles, *Flame, Electricity, and the Camera: Man's Progress from the First Kindling of Fire . . .* (New York: J. A. Hill, 1904), 236. San Francisco was described as the leading "telephone city" in the United States, with "one telephone to ninety-six persons," in "Telephone Statistics," *The Journal of Electricity, Power, and Gas* 16, no. 8 (1906): 266. Nye argues that "electrification increased the city's integration into a network of national institutions," in *Electrifying America*, 26.

19. On the telephone as "instrument of emergencies," see Herbert N. Casson, *The History of the Telephone* (Chicago: McClurg, 1910), 211–14; on the perceived advantages of electricity, Nye, *Electrifying America*, 2, 5, 31; on the lack of such amenities in poor and immigrant neighborhoods, ibid., 26; Mark H. Rose, *Cities of Light and Heat: Domesticating Gas and Electricity in Urban America* (University Park: Pennsylvania State University Press, 1995), 9, 72–73; and Harold L. Platt, *The Electric City: Energy and the Growth of the Chicago Area, 1880–1930* (Chicago: University of Chicago Press, 1991), 144; on utopian hopes for electricity, ibid., 60–61.

20. Jack London, "Story of an Eyewitness," *Collier's* 37, no. 6 (1906): 22; Frederick Palmer, "San Francisco in Ruins," in ibid., 13.

21. The target audience for *Mining and Scientific Press* is specified in an advertisement printed in *After Earthquake and Fire*, 194. Pursell (cited below, n. 57) compares it to *Scientific American*, in "Technical Society," 704. On the "liquefaction" of land-filled areas, see Steinberg, "Smoke and Mirrors," 106, 120.

22. On the 1838 earthquake, see Steinberg, "Smoke and Mirrors," 106.

23. Frederick Crowe, *Seeing San Francisco by Kodak: The Fourth Day after the Clock Stopped* (promotional pamphlet, L.A. Chamber of Commerce Relief Fund, 1906), caption to plate 6, HEH.

24. Edward Tenner, *Why Things Bite Back: Technology and the Revenge of Unintended Consequences* (New York: Vintage, 1997), 6, 24.

25. Wolfgang Schivelbusch, *The Railway Journey: The Industrialization of Time and Space in the Nineteenth Century* (1977; Berkeley: University of California Press, 1986), 131.

26. For references to the almighty, see Palmer, "San Francisco in Ruins," 13; and to "Mother Nature," Emma Eames, *Some Memories and Reflections* (New York: Appleton, 1927), 254, 263. But, as Carl Smith notes, the disaster was "rarely seen—especially by San Franciscans themselves—as a divine judgment upon an immoral city" ("Urban Disorder and the Shape of Belief: The San Francisco Earthquake and Fire," *Yale Review* 74 [1984]: 85). Even the majority of religious newspapers declined to see God's hand in the earthquake or fire; see "Providence and the San Francisco Disaster," *Current Literature* 40, no. 6 (1906): 649–50.

27. Ernst Bloch, "The Anxiety of the Engineer," in *Literary Essays* (Stanford, CA: Stanford University Press, 1998), 307; further references cited in the text. On *Amerikanismus,* see David Frisby, *Cityscapes of Modernity: Critical Explorations* (Cambridge: Polity, 2001), 17, 25, 161, 164–65.

28. Carolyn Marvin, *When Old Technologies Were New: Thinking about Electric Communication in the Late Nineteenth Century* (New York and Oxford: Oxford University Press, 1988), 121–22; see also Nye, *Electrifying America,* 47–48.

29. In an 1895 case against the company, the plaintiff's counsel alleged that "there is no [rail]road in the city . . . that has caused so many accidents" (*California Unreported Cases,* 7 vols. [San Francisco: Bender-Moss, 1913], 5:194). For a history of the company, see Walter Vielbaum et al., *San Francisco's Interurban to San Mateo* (Mount Pleasant, SC: Arcadia, 2005).

30. Walter Benjamin, "One-Way Street" (written 1923–26, published 1928), in *Reflections: Essays, Aphorisms, Autobiographical Writings,* trans. Edmund Jephcott, ed. Peter Demetz (New York: Schocken, 1978), 85.

31. Henry Adams, *The Education of Henry Adams* (1906; Harmondsworth: Penguin, 1995), 467. Brother Potamian and James J. Walsh, *Makers of Electricity* (New York: Fordham University Press, 1909), 148.

32. Charles Hallock, "Polarity of the Seismic Impulse," paraphrased in David Starr Jordan, "The Earthquake Rift of April, 1906," in *The California Earthquake of 1906,* ed. David Starr

Jordan (San Francisco: A. M. Robertson, 1907), 58. Hallock expounded his electromagnetic theories of worldly and otherworldly phenomena that same year, in *Luminous Bodies Here and Hereafter (The Shining Ones)* (New York: Metaphysical Publishing, 1906).

33. *New York World* (1888) and *Electrical World* (1886), both quoted in Marvin, *When Old Technologies Were New*, 119–20.

34. "Scientia" [pseud.], *The Cause of Earthquakes* (n.p.: copyright, M. C. Thompson, 1907), 9, 12.

35. Clarence Miller Jones, *From Rime to Reason; or, The Great San Francisco Earthquake Rhythmically, Orchestrally and Logically Considered* (Columbus, OH: privately printed, 1907), 11–12, 19 n. 4b; see also "Scientia," *Cause of Earthquakes*, 6.

36. On Jones's offer, see *Publishers' Weekly*, no. 1,823, January 5, 1907, 24. Paul Boyer, who traces the spread of premillennialism at the turn of the century, acknowledges that the nonmillenarian (or postmillennial) strands of American Protestantism remained dominant, in *When Time Shall Be No More: Prophecy Belief in Modern American Culture* (Cambridge, MA: Harvard University Press, 1992), 99–100.

37. Ernst Bloch, "The First Locomotive" (written 1929), in *Traces*, trans. Anthony A. Nassar (1969; Stanford, CA: Stanford University Press, 2006), 125. Wolfgang Schivelbusch similarly observes that "the more civilized the schedule and the more efficient the technology, the more catastrophic its destruction when it collapses" (*Railway Journey*, 131; see also 130, 160). "Panic of Trolley Car Passengers," *Chicago Daily Tribune*, December 14, 1895, 1.

38. Proclamation by the mayor, April 18, 1906, Broadsides collection, Banc. "The San Francisco Disaster—Honest and Dishonest Insurance. Speech of Hon. Julius Kahn, of California, in the House of Representatives . . ." (Washington, DC: s.n., 1906), 6, Banc.; James Russel Wilson, *San Francisco's Horror of Earthquake and Fire* (n.p.: Memorial Publishing, 1906), 210; Amy Kahn, Letter to Mr. Coop (April 23, 1906), Banc. MSS C-Z 75.

39. "Baltimore in Darkness," *NYT,* May 23, 1900, 2. On the separation of public lighting from the "rhythms of nature," see Wolfgang Schivelbusch, *Disenchanted Night: The Industrialisation of Light in the Nineteenth Century,* trans. Angela Davies (Oxford, New York, and Hamburg: Berg, 1988), 90–91, 96.

40. Stewart Edward White, *The Sign at Six* (Indianapolis: Bobbs-Merrill, 1912), especially 26–30.

41. "Telegraph Office on a Pole: Also How the Western Union Built a New Plant in Four Days," *Chronicle*, April 30, 1906, reprinted in *The Pandex of the Press* 4, no. 4 (1906): 78. Myrtle Robertson, eyewitness report [undated], CaHS MS 3498. On the capacity of silence to register urban transformations, see Nick Yablon, "Echoes of the City: Spacing Sound, Sounding Space, 1888–1908," *American Literary History* 19, no. 3 (2007): 629–60.

42. Michael Barkun, *Disaster and the Millennium* (New Haven, CT: Yale University Press, 1974), 178.

43. Martin Heidegger, *Being and Time*, trans. John Macquarrie and Edward Robinson (New York: Harper and Row, 1962), 99, 101; further references cited in the text.

44. Henry George, *Social Problems* (1883; New York: Robert Schalkenbach, 1963), 3, 4.

45. "Baltimore in Darkness," 2; "Paris in Darkness; Business Stopped," *NYT*, March 9, 1906, 1.

46. Thorstein Veblen, *The Engineers and the Price System* (New York: Viking Press, 1921), 52–54; he includes capitalists under the rubric of saboteurs (6–26).

47. Platt, *Electric City*, 23. "Gas Lamps Are Out," *Chicago Daily Tribune*, December 26, 1897, 14.

48. On the Spring Valley Water Company, see Brechin, *Imperial San Francisco,* 71–107; and on Pacific Gas and Electric, 250, 262–69.

49. Charles Derleth, "The Destructive Extent of the California Earthquake . . . ," in Jordan, ed., *The California Earthquake of 1906,* 128.

50. W. A. Demers, "Rube Goldberg in 'Creative Contraptions,'" in *Antiques and the Arts Online,* March 8, 2005.

51. Stephen Tobriner, *Bracing for Disaster: Earthquake-Resistant Architecture and Engineering in San Francisco, 1838–1933* (Berkeley: Heyday Books, 2006), 74. Quotation from *After Earthquake and Fire,* 28.

52. Richard L. Humphrey, "The Effects of the Earthquake and Fire on Various Structures and Structural Materials," in United States Geological Survey, *The San Francisco Earthquake and Fire . . . And Their Effects on Structures and Structural Materials,* ed. Grove Karl Gilbert (Washington, DC: Government Printing Office, 1907), 35, 36.

53. Tobriner, *Bracing for Disaster,* 95, 96.

54. Ibid., 174; Humphrey, "Effects of the Earthquake and Fire," 36.

55. Humphrey, "Effects of the Earthquake and Fire," 35. *Mining and Scientific Press* merged the issue of poor construction with political corruption (discussed below). Generally, these investigations placed the blame more on the design of the building than on the workmanship of construction crews; see Gilbert, ed., *San Francisco Earthquake,* 84–85.

56. The Building Law: Ordinance No. 31 (July 5, 1906), in *General Ordinances of the City and County of San Francisco* (1907), 208–358.

57. On the former, see Carroll W. Pursell Jr., "The Technical Society of the Pacific Coast, 1884–1914," *Technology and Culture* 17, no. 4 (1976): 702–17; on the latter, ibid., 710. There was also the Mechanic's Institute of San Francisco (founded 1855), and the Society of Structural Engineers, founded in response to the "destruction and rebuilding of the city" (712).

58. "Expert to Lecture on Recent Disaster" [newspaper not cited], August 8, 1906, and "Talks on Effects of the Quake," *Call,* August 9, 1906, pasted into Derleth's scrapbook, *The San Francisco Earthquake of April 18, 1906, and the Subsequent Conflagrations: Records Pertaining to the Disaster, and the Following Events,* 4 vols., in Charles Derleth Papers, 1865–1952, Banc MSS 91/116c, Series 3, Box 2, 1:n.p.

59. Derleth, "Destructive Extent," 177–78.

60. Ibid., 145, 141. On the deficiencies of brick constructions, see 128–33. City Hall appears only once (and in passing) in this article, and in only six of his circa 820 photographs.

61. W. W. Overton, quoted in Richard Linthicum and Trumbull White, *The Complete Story of the San Francisco Horror* (n.p.: Hubert D. Russell, 1906), 111–12.

62. Derleth, "Destructive Extent," 146–47.

63. Ibid., 141.

64. On the commercial campaign, see Steinberg, "Smoke and Mirrors," 107–9; on the insurance efforts, ibid., 111, 124n35, and see also Tobriner, *Bracing for Disaster,* 196.

65. Pursell, "Technical Society of the Pacific Coast," 717. Steinberg places engineers and scientists in a more adversarial relationship to San Francisco's businessmen in "Smoke and Mirrors," 103–26.

66. Tobriner, *Bracing for Disaster,* 196; Theodore Steinberg, *Acts of God: The Unnatural History of Natural Disaster in America* (New York: Oxford University Press, 2006), 215–16n37; on insurance disputes, see "Topics of the Day: . . . Insurance," *Literary Digest* 32, no. 18 (1906): 673.

67. Clarence Edward Dutton, *Earthquakes in the Light of the New Seismology* (London: Murray, 1904), 172–74.

68. "Photographs of the San Francisco Earthquake and Fire from the Charles Derleth Papers," Banc PIC 1958.021—fALB; included there is the business card of a dealer in "Fire and Earthquake Pictures." Architects such as Robert C. Jordan also collected photographs of the ruins; see Album 398, Boxes 1–4, HEH.

69. Martin Heidegger, "The Question concerning Technology," in *The Question concerning Technology, and Other Essays*, trans. William Lovitt (New York: Harper and Row, 1977), 5.

70. See, respectively, "The Time and Origin of the Shock," in *The California Earthquake of April 18, 1906: Report of the State Earthquake Investigation Commission*, 2 vols. (Washington, DC: Carnegie Institution, 1910), 2:3; Palmer, "San Francisco in Ruins," 13; and the photograph captioned "Razing the walls of the old Palace Hotel . . . ," in *[The New] San Francisco* (San Francisco: Cardinall-Vincent, 1908), n.p.

71. Wilbur Gleason Zeigler, *Story of the Earthquake and Fire* (San Francisco: L. C. Osteyee, 1906), n.p.; *Literary Digest* 32, no. 17 (1906): 636; the seismogram was also published in *Sunset Magazine* 17, no. 4 (1906): 203.

72. Raymond Fielding, *The American Newsreel, 1911–67* (Norman: University of Oklahoma Press, 1972), 23, 48, 42.

73. Lawrence's panoramas were published in the Southern Pacific Company's official pamphlet "San Francisco Imperishable" (San Francisco, 1906), CaHS San Francisco Miscellany/Ephemera OVBox 79, periodicals folder, which refers to the "intact" waterfront (n.p.). Simon Baker discusses the impact and sales of these photographs in "San Francisco in Ruins: The 1906 Aerial Photographs of George R. Lawrence," *Landscape* 30, no. 22 (1989): 13–14.

74. Lawrence's panoramas also appeared, for instance, in the *Los Angeles Times* on May 24, 1906.

75. On Goldberg's love of gadgets (especially cameras), despite his "constant grumblings" about mechanization, see Peter C. Marzio, *Rube Goldberg: His Life and Work* (New York: Harper and Row, 1973), 151, 177; his "picture-snapping machine" appears in ibid., 208. Note the fail-safe mechanisms included in many of Goldberg's contraptions, often in the final sentence of the instructions.

76. On the compromising of the 1906 ordinance, see Steinberg, "Smoke and Mirrors," 112, and Tobriner, *Bracing for Disaster*, 192–209. On the creation of "made ground" at Berry Street (now AT&T Park), see "Two Trains of Cars and 100 Teams Industriously Filling Four City Blocks at New Seawall with Debris from Ruins," *Call*, July 6, 1906, 7.

77. For the "Kodak Simplicity" advertisements, see Nancy Martha West, *Kodak and the Lens of Nostalgia* (Charlottesville: University of Virginia Press, 2000), plates 13, 15; see also 91, 210n11; on the 1900 Brownie, see 15. Although marketed toward children, it was also widely used by adults (88).

78. Reese Jenkins, "Technology and the Market: George Eastman and the Origins of Mass Amateur Photography," in *Technology and American History: A Historical Anthology from Technology and Culture*, ed. Stephen H. Cutcliffe and Terry S. Reynolds (Chicago: University of Chicago Press, 1997), 199–201.

79. Ibid., 202–12.

80. Ibid., 208–9, 214.

81. Marvin briefly discusses the pushbutton in *When Old Technologies Were New*, 123–24.

82. Walter Benjamin, "Some Motifs in Baudelaire," in *Baudelaire: A Lyric Poet in the Age of High Capitalism*, trans. Harry Zohn (London and New York: Verso, 1973), 131–32 (emphasis

added). On the obsolescence of crank-operated telephones, see Milton Mueller, "The Switchboard Problem: Scale, Signaling, and Organization in Manual Telephone Switching, 1877–1897," *Technology and Culture* 30, no. 3 (1989): 554–55.

83. West, *Kodak and the Lens of Nostalgia*, 23–24, 41; others estimate one in ten.

84. On Eastman's efforts to define the photographable, see West, *Kodak and the Lens of Nostalgia*, especially 36–73. On amateur photographers at world's fairs, see Julie K. Brown, *Contesting the Image: Photography and the World's Columbian Exposition* (Tucson: University of Arizona Press, 1994), 93–113.

85. In Goldberg's 1917 cartoon, "Fifty-Fifty" (in Marzio, *Rube Goldberg*, 156), the "poor man" with the box camera "env[ies] the fellow with a big camera that has a lot of complicated adjustments," but the "rich man" fails to capture his subject because he has too many "buttons to press."

86. Archibald J. Treat, presidential address at annual exhibition of the Pacific Coast Amateur Photographic Association, San Francisco, December 10/11, 1888, Treat Papers, Folder 3, CaHS. On Kodakers as "pests," see Robert Mensel, "'Kodakers Lying in Wait': Amateur Photography and the Right of Privacy in New York, 1885–1915," *American Quarterly* 43, no. 1 (1991): 24–45.

87. "Eastman Kodak Company's Pacific Coast Branch," *Camera Craft* 12, no. 4 (1906): 174.

88. "Desolation and Gloom Still in San Francisco," *NYT* (n.d., n.p.), and "Sightseers Come to View Ruins," [newspaper not cited], June 11, 1906, n.p., in Derleth's scrapbook, *The San Francisco Earthquake*, vol. 1, Derleth Papers, Banc. Railroad companies had lowered prices on the eve of the earthquake to accommodate two conventions (ibid.). On the touristic promotion of San Francisco before the earthquake, see Catherine Cocks, *Doing the Town: The Rise of Urban Tourism in the United States, 1850–1915* (Berkeley: University of California Press, 2001), 133. On the destruction of hotels and erection of makeshift stores and hotels, see Christopher Morris Douty, *The Economics of Localized Disasters: The 1906 San Francisco Catastrophe* (New York: Arno Press, 1977), 175–83.

89. Louis J. Stellman, "The Golden City," scrapbook of articles written for the *San Francisco Bulletin*, 1921, vol. 1, Louis J. Stellman Papers, CSL. On the dangers of debris and dust, see "Desolation and Gloom," n.p.

90. On the emergence of the postcard and the postal service's concessions, see Hal Morgan and Andreas Brown, *Prairie Fires and Paper Moons, The American Photographic Postcard: 1900–1920* (Boston: David R. Godine, 1981), especially xiii–xiv. The Andreas Brown Collection at the Getty contains 302 postcards categorized under "Disasters" in Box 11, and a further twenty-seven under "San Francisco earthquake, 1906" in Boxes 24/25; see also the earthquake postcards in Box 021, Folders 1, 2, CaHS.

91. "Pernicious Advertising" [editorial], *Call*, May 20, 1906, 22.

92. *San Francisco Imperishable*, n.p. "Eastern Lecturers Will Be Set Straight in the Matter" (Stockton Chamber of Commerce circular, 1906), MCSF.

93. On the military cordon, see Frank Thompson Searight, *The Doomed City* (Chicago: Laird and Lee, 1906), 39. On the forced conscription of tourists, see Frank A. Leach, *Recollections of a Newspaperman: A Record of Life and Events in California* (San Francisco: S. Levinson, 1917), 341. Even a local amateur photographer, Arthur Inkersley, was "turned back by a guard" ("An Amateur's Experience," 197).

94. With the cessation of martial law, official restrictions were relaxed, allowing freer access around the city. Souvenir hunting was also tolerated, if only because it was being "practiced by . . . sightseers, many of them people of prominence," and by state troops (Charles Morris, *The San Francisco Calamity by Earthquake and Fire . . .* [Philadelphia and Chicago: J. C. Winston, 1906], 82).

95. Photograph of upturned statue of Louis Agassiz on Stanford campus, in "San Francisco Earthquake and Fire 1906" (Photograph Album No. 25, CaHS), an anonymous leather-bound album that also contains some commercially produced photographs.

96. William James, "On Some Mental Effects of the Earthquake" (1906), reprinted in *Memories and Studies* (New York: Greenwood, 1968), 211, 216, 218.

97. "Speech of Hon. Julius Kahn," 6. For a discussion of how the San Francisco disaster was narrated (in part) as having revived San Francisco's frontier spirit, see Smith, "San Francisco Earthquake and Fire," 83–86.

98. Strother, "Rebound of San Francisco," 7779.

99. Citizens as well as tourists "flocked to be photographed in front" of the ruined City Hall (Tobriner, *Bracing for Disaster*, 192).

100. Sir J. F. W. Herschel, "Instantaneous Photography," *The Photographic News* 4, no. 88 (1860): 13.

101. Beaumont Newhall, *The History of Photography: From 1839 to the Present* (1937; New York: Museum of Modern Art, 1982), 489.

102. William James, letter to Henry James and William James Jr. (February 14, 1907), in *The Letters of William James*, ed. Henry James, 2 vols. (Boston: Atlantic Monthly, 1920), 2:264.

103. Annie Nathan Meyer, "The Snap-Shot and the Psychological Novel," *The Bookman* 15, no. 3 (1902): 260.

104. On Cleveland's traffic lights, see Clay McShane, "The Origins and Globalization of Traffic Control Signals," *Journal of Urban History* 25, no. 3 (1999): 382.

105. Walter Benjamin, "The Work of Art in the Age of Mechanical Reproduction," in *Illuminations: Essays and Reflections*, ed. Hannah Arendt, trans. Harry Zohn (New York: Schocken, 1969), 236; Benjamin, "Little History of Photography," in *Selected Writings, Volume 2: 1927–1934*, ed. Marcus Bullock and Michael Jennings, trans. Rodney Livingstone et al. (Cambridge, MA: Belknap Press, 1999), 527.

106. Joseph H. Harper, "The San Francisco Earthquake of April 18, 1906," *Journal of the Association of Engineering Societies* 40, no. 2 (1908): 87.

107. On camera shake, caused by "the least tremor," see T. Smith Baldwin, *Picture Making for Pleasure and Profit* (Chicago: Frederick J. Drake, 1903), 110. Popular and photographic magazines encouraged women especially to assemble such albums; see Elizabeth E. Siegel, "'Miss Domestic' and 'Miss Enterprise'; or, How to Keep a Photograph Album," in Patricia Buckler and Katherine Ott, *The Scrapbook in American Life* (Philadelphia: Temple University Press, 2006), 251–67. And for an example of earthquake snapshots interspersed with vacation photographs, see the anonymous Album 166, HEH.

108. George Malcolm Stratton, "Notes on Earthquake Recollections," handwritten manuscripts, George Malcolm Stratton Papers, Carton 6, Banc MSS C-B 1032, n.p.; Stratton, "Retroactive Hypermnesia, and other Emotional Effects on Memory," *Psychological Review* 26, no. 6 (1919): 483, pasted into Stratton, *Psychological Papers*, vol. 4, Stratton Papers, Banc; further references cited in the text.

109. Hypermnesia was defined in the *Dictionary of Philosophy and Psychology*, ed. James Mark Baldwin, 3 vols. (New York: Macmillan, 1902) as a disorder involving an "unusual exaltation of memory" (2:64).

110. Scolded for knocking over a flour bin the previous night, one child irrevocably associated that object with the subsequent earthquake (George Malcolm Stratton, "When Children Are in Mortal Danger," typed manuscript, Stratton Papers, Carton 1, Banc, 3–4, 8).

111. James, "On Some Mental Effects," 221. For an example of an everyday act and object

endowed with apocalyptic significance, see the tram ticket stamped 5:05 a.m. (eight minutes *before* the earthquake), framed for posterity, and preserved in CaHS San Francisco Miscellany/Ephemera OV Box 81.

112. L. Fuller's handwritten testimony, in "Recollections of the San Francisco Earthquake," Stratton Papers, Carton 6, Folder 1, Banc; Stratton, handwritten draft (material omitted from the final version), Stratton Papers, Carton 6, Banc. Another subject pointed out that "small details seem to have made a greater impression upon me than the more important incidents of the disaster" (quoted in Stratton, "When Children Are in Mortal Danger," 3).

113. Testimony of a banker's daughter, in Stratton, "When Children Are in Mortal Danger," 19.

114. Hopper, "Our San Francisco," 760b, 760f (emphasis added). See also Mary Austin's description of how "little things" such as the "red flare of a potted geranium undisturbed on a window ledge," tend to "prick themselves on the attention as the index of the greater horror," in "The Temblor: A Personal Narration," *Out West* 24, no. 6 (1906): 498.

115. On the late nineteenth-century turn from sensationalism to matter-of-fact realism, see Michael Barton, "Journalistic Gore: Disaster Reporting and Emotional Discourse in the *New York Times*, 1852–1956," in *An Emotional History of the United States*, ed. Peter N. Stearns and Jan Lewis (New York: New York University Press, 1998), 155–72. Allusion to Zola in D'Arcy Weatherbe, "First Observations of the Catastrophe," in *After Earthquake and Fire*, 45; and to "pictures," Searight, *The Doomed City*, 123.

116. Information on the PCAPA comes from the papers of Archibald Treat (MS 2170, CaHS), a founding member and later president. On Stieglitz's and Genthe's membership in amateur clubs, see Katherine Hoffman, *Stieglitz: A Beginning Light* (New Haven, CT: Yale University Press, 2004), 109–10, 113, 166–74; and Genthe, *As I Remember*, 40–41.

117. See Sarah Greenough, "The Curious Contagion of the Camera," in *On the Art of Fixing a Shadow: One Hundred and Fifty Years of Photography*, ed. Sarah Greenough, David Travis, and Joel Snyder (Washington, DC: National Gallery of Art; Chicago: Art Institute of Chicago, 1989–90), 129–55; and Greenough, "'Of Charming Glens, Graceful Glades, and Frowning Cliffs': The Economic Incentives, Social Inducements, and Aesthetic Issues of American Pictorial Photography, 1880–1902," in *Photography in Nineteenth Century America*, ed. Martha Sandweiss (New York: Abrams, 1991), 259–81, especially 277–78.

118. They also emphasized the preliminary work of selecting and composing a scene; see Walter Benn Michaels, "Action and Accident: Photography and Writing," in *The Gold Standard and the Logic of Naturalism* (Berkeley: University of California Press, 1987), especially 217–20. On the identification of the pushbutton with "popular desires for dangerously superficial pleasures," see Marvin, *When Old Technologies Were New*, 124.

119. Henry Adams, letters to Charles Milnes Gaskell (1872) and Elizabeth Cameron (1890, 1891), in *Literature and Photography—Interactions 1840–1940: A Critical Anthology*, ed. Jane M. Rabb (Albuquerque: University of New Mexico Press, 1995), 159, 161, 162. His "photo-phobia" may also be connected to his wife's 1885 suicide by ingesting photographic chemicals.

120. William James, *Pragmatism and the Meaning of Truth* (Cambridge, MA: Harvard University Press, 1975), 138–39; Henry James alluded to the Kodak as an emblem of the triumph of the "portable" in "Rostand, Romanticist," *Current Literature* 31, no. 6 (1901): 674. The following year, Meyer turned the Kodak epithet against James himself, among other realist novelists, in "The Snap-Shot and the Psychological Novel" (cited above, n. 103).

121. Alfred Stieglitz, "The Hand Camera—Its Present Importance" (1897), in *Alfred Stieglitz: Photographs and Writings*, ed. Sarah Greenough and Juan Hamilton (Washington, DC: National Gallery of Art, 1983), 182–83; further references cited in the text.

122. See the *Examiner*'s photographic supplements of May 13, May 20, and July 1, 1906 (HEH 2790). The leading commercial photographers dealing in San Francisco earthquake pictures were Charles Weidner, Edward Bear, O. F. Browning, E. E. Ford, J. D. Givens, and Hodson. Many prints bearing their signatures were taken by anonymous hired photographers. The well-known New York news photographer, Harry Coleman, refers to the high prices for authentic earthquake images back east in *Give Us a Little Smile, Baby* (New York: E. P. Dutton, 1943), 131. On photographic outlets, see Mensel, "Kodakers Lying in Wait," 32.

123. Cohen, "With a Camera in San Francisco" (cited above n. 6), 185, 187, 194, 186. Cohen may be referring to Harry Coleman, who described his "heroic" climb to the top of City Hall to obtain an "overhead view" for a supplement in the *Examiner*, in *Give Us a Little Smile, Baby*, 143–45; Coleman himself discusses "phony photographs" and "photo faking" (131). D. J. Tapley, *The New Recreation: Amateur Photography: A Practical Instructor* (New York: S. W. Green's Son, 1884), 45.

124. Peter E. Palmquist, ed., *Camera Fiends and Kodak Girls II: Sixty Selections by and about Women in Photography, 1855–1965* (New York: Midmarch Arts Press, 1995), 41.

125. Alice Boughton, "Photography, a Medium of Expression" (1905), reprinted in Peter E. Palmquist, ed., *Camera Fiends and Kodak Girls: Fifty Selections by and about Women in Photography, 1840–1930* (New York: Midmarch Arts Press, 1989), 143 (emphases added). See also Catherine Weed Barnes, "Photography from a Woman's Standpoint" (1889), ibid., 63–67.

126. Wilma Marie Plunkett, "Edith Irvine: Her Life and Photography" (master's thesis, Brigham Young University, 1989), 6, 31.

127. Ibid., 31.

128. Barnes, "Photography from a Woman's Standpoint," 64.

129. Editorial, "Kodak Manners," *Ladies Home Journal* 17, no. 4 (1900): 16.

130. Cohen, "With a Camera in San Francisco," 190.

131. On the "Kodak Girl," see West, *Kodak and the Lens of Nostalgia*, 53–60, 109–35.

132. Archibald J. Treat, "Fine Art and Photography," typed manuscript of address to the PCAPA, December 10/11, 1888 (Archibald J. Treat Papers, Folder 3 [correspondence], CaHS, MS 1877), n.p. An index of this openness to new ideas is the growing popularity by the turn of the century of Peter Henry Emerson's *Naturalistic Photography for Students of the Art* (1889; New York: Arno Press, 1973), which attacked the pictorialists of the Henry Peach Robinson school.

133. For typical accounts of cameras snatched from buildings that were burning, or about to burn, see Louis J. Stellman, typed autobiographical manuscript, Stellman Papers, Box 1989 (Folder 1), 28, CSL; Fayette J. Clute, "With Earthquake and Fire," *Camera Craft* 12, no. 4 (1906): 150; Genthe, *As I Remember*, 89.

134. Power, "Earthquake and Fire," 158. See also Cohen's realization that in these conditions "snaps were a necessity" ("With a Camera in San Francisco," 184, 192).

135. On snapshots as "indiscriminate" or "careless," see Baldwin, *Picture Making*, 109, and W. I. Lincoln Adams, "The Value of Snapshots," in *American Annual of Photography and Photographic Times Almanac for 1906* (New York: Styles and Cash, 1906), 77.

136. "Photographic Memorandums," *Camera Craft* 12, no. 4 (1906): 175–76.

137. Daniel H. Burnham, *Report on a Plan for San Francisco* (published by the city, 1905), 111–13; further references cited in the text. On its advocates' motives, see Kevin Rozario, "What Comes Down Must Go Up: Why Disasters Have Been Good for American Capitalism," in Biel, ed., *American Disasters*, 84, 86.

138. Charles Lathrop to James Duval Phelan Jr., April 30, 1906, quoted in Mansel G. Blackford, *The Lost Dream: Businessmen and City Planning on the Pacific Coast, 1890–1920*

(Columbus: Ohio State University Press, 1993), 47. On Phelan's overlapping interests, see Judd Kahn, *Imperial San Francisco: Politics and Planning in an American City, 1897–1906* (Lincoln: University of Nebraska Press, 1979), 82.

139. Arthur Inkersley, "What San Francisco Has to Start With," *Overland Monthly* 47, no. 6 (1906): 483; Inkersley, "An Amateur's Experience," 195–200.

140. On the trope of San Francisco as "Rome of the West," see Brechin, *Imperial San Francisco*, 19, 31, 106, 117, 145–151, passim.

141. Louise Herrick Wall, "Heroic San Francisco," *New Century Magazine* 72, no. 4 (1906): 590, pasted into the scrapbook, "San Francisco B.C. 1906 A.D.," Oversize San Francisco Miscellaneous, CaHS. Wall's photographs of the earthquake are in Bledsoe-Herrick Family Papers, 1750–1964, Series V, 174, Schlesinger Library, Radcliffe Institute.

142. Louis John Stellman, typed autobiographical manuscript, Stellman Papers, Box 1989 (Folder 1), 15–16, CSL; on his aspirations to being "an artist with my camera," see typed draft of introduction to *Chinatown: A Pictorial Souvenir and Guide*, 8, Stellman Papers, Box 1990, CSL. His ruin photographs are in the photography collections of CSL. See the pamphlet advertising his lectures as "picturing . . . the horror and weird grandeur of the Ruin Era that followed [the earthquake]," also in Box 1989 (Folder 5), CSL. Stellmann [*sic*], *The Vanished Ruin Era: San Francisco's Classic Artistry of Ruin Depicted in Picture and Song* (San Francisco: P. Elder, 1910), vii–viii, CaHS special collections, 1649; hereafter I will use the more common spelling of his name, Stellman.

143. On the naming of Berkeley, see Brechin, *Imperial San Francisco*, 281; and on invocations of classical antiquity, ibid., 72–75, 144–49.

144. Lawrence W. Harris, "The Damndest Finest Ruins" [After Kipling's "On the Road to Mandalay"] (San Francisco: A. B. Pierson, 1906), Poetry Broadsides Collection, CaHS .

145. Inkersley, "An Amateur's Experience," 199–200.

146. Stellman, *Vanished Ruin Era*, vii. For a typical comparison of the Observatory with the Roman Coliseum, see Edward Hungerford, *The Personality of American Cities* (New York: McBride, Nast, 1913), 303.

147. Joaquin Miller, "A Fire So Richly Fed," *Oakland Tribune*, May 6, 1906, MCSF. Genthe, "Mr. Towne's residence on California Strt. City Hall in the distance" (1906) (Banc PIC 2004.004:10—PIC); quotations from Genthe, *As I Remember*, 94. Genthe discusses this photograph, its naming by literary quipster Charles K. Field, and its painted rendering by Charles Rollo Peters (the foremost painter of California's ruined missions), in *As I Remember*, 95. R. J. Waters's photograph of the Portals appeared in Helen Throop Purdy, *San Francisco: As It Was, As It Is, And How to See It* (San Francisco: Paul Elder, 1912), opposite 50.

148. Pierre N. Beringer, "The Destruction of San Francisco," *Overland Monthly* 47, no. 5 (1906): 397–98. The phrase "American Acropolis" is used by Crowe, *Seeing San Francisco by Kodak*, caption to plate 6.

149. Stellman, *Vanished Ruin Era*, vii.

150. By the time City Hall opened in 1899, it was denounced as "a monument of extravagance and mismanagement" in "San Francisco's Struggle for Good Government," 572. On the nickname "city hall ruins," see "The City Hall: Building It Up, Tearing It Down," *Call*, April 18, 1909, 4. On "ruins in reverse," see my introduction. On city halls (including San Francisco's) as embodiments of civic ideals at certain times, and civic corruption at others, see Mary P. Ryan, "'A Laudable Pride in the Whole of Us: City Halls and Civic Materialism," *American Historical Review* 105, no. 4 (2000): 1131–70.

151. Even the *Mining and Scientific Press* editorialized that it had "collapsed miserably, because every stone of it was laid in putrid politics" and that "the great dome is stripped of its

veneer of stone as thoroughly as the iniquity of the builders stands plain to every beholder" (*After Earthquake and Fire*, 82).

152. Cohen, "With a Camera in San Francisco," 193. On the earthquake's effect on this portion of City Hall, see Gilbert, ed, *San Francisco Earthquake*, 87. On the portico's original function of conveying public accessibility, see Ryan, "Laudable Pride," 1160.

153. Hopper, "Our San Francisco," 760g.

154. See for example the editorial in the *Chronicle*, quoted in Mel Scott, *The San Francisco Bay Area: A Metropolis in Perspective* (Berkeley: University of California Press, 1959), 115. On United Railroads' opposition, see Rozario, "What Comes Down," 91.

155. On the "Passing of Chinatown," see *Literary Digest* 32, no. 18 (1906): 671–78. On the pre-1906 plan to relocate Chinatown, see John Francis Dyer, "Rebuilding Chinatown," *The World To-Day* 8, no. 5 (1905): 553–54. And on the opposition of white landlords and the Chinese themselves, see Kahn, *Imperial San Francisco*, 202–5; and Nayan Shah, *Contagious Divides: Epidemics and Race in San Francisco's Chinatown* (Berkeley: University of California Press, 2001), 152–57.

156. Brechin, *Imperial San Francisco*, 188–90.

157. Eastern capitalist, quoted in Charles Morris, *San Francisco Calamity*, 174; Guy A. Buell (a San Francisco manufacturer), letter to his Aunt Eliza Anne Ballou, April 29, 1906, manuscript collection, HEH HM 51248.

158. Barton W. Currie, "Some Reconstruction Figures," *Sunset Magazine* 17, no. 6 (1906): 314; see also Stellman, "What Becomes of San Francisco Scrap Iron and Pipe," *Chronicle*, May 26, 1907, 9. On the unions' decision not to exploit the disaster or even enforce its normal "rules" in the rebuilding period, see John Spargo, *Socialism: A Summary and Interpretation of Socialist Principles* (New York: Macmillan, 1909), 158–59.

159. Currie, "Some Reconstruction Figures," 316. On mobilizing working-class opposition to the Burnham Plan, see Rozario, "What Comes Down," 88–90.

160. Tobriner, *Bracing for Disaster*, 86–88, 124–25.

161. On engineers' opposition to height limitations, see ibid., 206.

162. For Kahn, the failure of the street widening amendment in November 1906 marks the demise of the Burnham Plan (*Imperial San Francisco*, 198–99).

163. "San Francisco One Year Later," *Coast Seaman's Journal*, May 8, 1907, MCSF. On these various financial sources, see Douty, *Economics of Localized Disasters*, 168–73, 193–207.

164. Inkersley, "An Amateur's Experience," 200.

165. Stellman, *Vanished Ruin Era*, 42.

166. See "Goddess Descends to Mother Earth," *Call*, March 12, 1909, 3; here (and in other articles), the statue (sculpted by Marion Wells) was misnamed the goddess of "liberty."

167. An English critic compared the ruins of the Paris Commune to the photographs that depicted them, in an 1872 article quoted in Luxenberg, "Creating 'Desastres,'" 130. For a Benjaminian analogy between ruins and photographs, see Eduardo Cadava, *Words of Light: Theses on the Photography of History* (Princeton, NJ: Princeton University Press, 1997), 23.

168. Rozario emphasizes rapid rebuilding in "What Comes Down," 90; and in "Making Progress: Disaster Narratives and the Art of Optimism in Modern America," in *The Resilient City: How Modern Cities Recover from Disaster*, ed. Lawrence J. Vale and Thomas J. Campanella (New York: Oxford University Press, 2005), especially 29.

169. On the preservation of "Portals of the Past," see Genthe, *As I Remember*, 95; and Purdy, *San Francisco*, 69; and see Stellman's photograph of the "Transplanted Portico" (Stellman photographs, 15,773a, CSL). The Goddess's head is now on display in City Hall.

170. See respectively, "San Francisco To-Day Still a City of Ruin," *NYT*, January 6, 1907, Sunday Magazine, 6; "Spurn Insurance Offers," *NYT*, June 3, 1906, 9; "Obstacles to Reconstruction of San Francisco," in Gilbert, ed., *San Francisco Earthquake*, 60; "A City without Records," *American Lawyer* 16, no. 3 (1908): 155–65.

171. While emphasizing the rapid rebuilding after the Chicago fire, Ross Miller acknowledges the persistence of ruins and relics into the 1880s, in *American Apocalypse*, 65, 67, 139.

172. Hungerford, *Personality of American Cities*, 303.

173. "San Francisco To-Day Still a City of Ruin," 6.

174. On the vote to replace rather than repair City Hall, see Tobriner, *Bracing for Disaster*, 192; on the failure of the bond issue, see Blackford, *Lost Dream*, 54–55. Even after demolition, the site remained marked by "foundation-leveled ruins" (Hungerford, *Personality of American Cities*, 303).

175. "Thousands Cheer Lighting of Dome of the Old City Hall," *Call*, April 19, 1907, 1; on the engineer's installation of the lights, see "City Hall Dome to Be Illuminated April 18," *Call*, April 6, 1907, 3.

Chapter 6

1. John Ruskin, *Seven Lamps of Architecture* (1849), in *The Works of John Ruskin*, ed. E. T. Cook and Alexander Wedderburn, 39 vols. (London: G. Allen; New York: Longmans, Green, 1903–12), 8:67, 68–69 n.; Georg Simmel, "The Ruin" (1911), in *Essays on Sociology, Philosophy, and Aesthetics*, ed. Kurt H. Wolff (New York: Harper and Row, 1965), 262.

2. Henry James, *The American Scene* (1907; Harmondsworth: Penguin, 1994), 85; further references cited in text.

3. Joseph Schumpeter, *Capitalism, Socialism, and Democracy* (New York: Harper, 1942), 81–86; Marshall Berman, *All That Is Solid Melts into Air: The Experience of Modernity* (London: Verso, 1983), 98–105, passim; David Harvey, *The Urban Experience* (Baltimore: Johns Hopkins University Press, 1989), 53–58, 82–83, 189–96.

4. Recently, the term *creative destruction* has become blurred through its application to various cities and periods from early nineteenth-century Paris to late twentieth-century Birmingham (Nicholas Papayanis, *Planning Paris before Haussmann* [Baltimore: Johns Hopkins University Press, 2004]; Liam Kennedy, *Remaking Birmingham: The Visual Culture of Urban Regeneration* [London and New York: Routledge, 2004], 1–10), or else posited as a consistent, inherent trait of certain cities, prototypically New York, despite the often-prolonged hiatuses in construction there. Here, I will forego that term, instead bringing into play the various phrases employed by writers at the time.

5. Walter Benjamin, "The Task of the Translator," in *Illuminations*, trans. Harry Zohn (New York: Schocken, 1968), 71; Benjamin, *The Arcades Project*, trans. Howard Eiland and Kevin McLaughlin (Cambridge, MA: Belknap Press of Harvard University Press, 2002), 460 [N2,3]; further references cited in the text.

6. Benjamin discusses Berlin's panoramas and its Victory Column in *Berlin Childhood around 1900*, trans. Howard Eiland (Cambridge, MA: Belknap Press of Harvard University Press, 2006), 42–44, 44–47; triumphal arches in *The Arcades Project*, 87 [C2a,3]; and "arcades, winter gardens, panoramas, factories, wax museums, casinos, railroad stations," in ibid., 405 [L1,3]. See also Siegfried Kracauer, "Farewell to the Linden Arcade" (1930), in Kracauer, *The Mass Ornament: Weimar Essays*, trans. and ed. Thomas Y. Levin (Cambridge, MA: Harvard University Press, 1995), 337–42.

7. Walter Benjamin, "Central Park," *New German Critique* 34 (1985): 34. On Benjamin's *Origin of German Tragic Drama*, see my introduction.

8. Alfred Dwight Sheffield, *Grammar and Thinking: A Study of the Working Conceptions in Syntax* (New York: Putnam's, 1912), diagram opposite 134 (emphasis added). This applies to both the "point" and "durative" modes of this tense: the former express a specific moment in time, as in *this building will have fallen down*, while the latter conveys a span of time, as in *this building will have been decaying* (132–33). Sheffield uses the more traditional term, "Future Perfect" (137).

9. For an account of the emergence of preservation as a response to the dehistoricizing effects of real estate, see Max Page, *The Creative Destruction of Manhattan, 1900–1940* (Chicago: University of Chicago Press, 1999), 111–43. For a similar argument about urban planning as a spatial solution to the way "capitalist city building annihilated *both* space and time," see David Scobey, *Empire City: The Making and Meaning of the New York City Landscape* (Philadelphia: Temple University Press, 2002), 87. American historians, geographers, and critics have identified timelessness in other cities and periods, such as postwar Los Angeles; see Norman M. Klein, *The History of Forgetting: Los Angeles and the Erasure of Memory* (London: Verso, 1997) and Dana Cuff, *The Provisional City: Los Angeles Stories of Architecture and Urbanism* (Cambridge, MA: MIT Press, 2000).

10. Angus K. Gillespie, *Twin Towers: The Life of New York City's World Trade Center* (New Brunswick, NJ: Rutgers University Press, 1999); Eric Darton, *Divided We Stand: A Biography of New York's World Trade Center* (New York: Basic Books, 1999). Neil Harris has recently called for greater attention to the life of buildings: see *Building Lives: Constructing Rites and Passages* (New Haven, CT: Yale University Press, 1999).

11. Benjamin discusses "fore-history" and "after-history" in *The Arcades Project*, 470 [N7a,1].

12. Metropolitan Life was the largest in terms of insurance in force; see "More Assurance in Force Than Any Other Company in the World," advertisement in *Assurance Convention Number* (1912), Box H-11 (Advertisements, 1900–1920), MLICA. Metropolitan Life began in 1866 as the National Travelers Insurance Company, changing its name two years later.

13. "Skyscraping Up to Date," *Architectural Record* 23 (January 1908): 74–75; see also "The Metropolitan Tower," *American Architect* 96 (October 1909): 125–29.

14. "The Metropolitan Tower and the 'Zeppelin II'—Two Striking Comparisons," *Scientific American* 100 (June 26, 1909): 478 and cover.

15. John Ulrich Giesy, "All for His Country," *Cavalier Magazine* 38, no. 4 to 39, no. 3 (1914), subsequently published as *All for His Country* (New York: Macaulay, 1915), quotation on 165. *Scientific American* editor, J. Bernard Walker, authored an invasion narrative himself, *America Fallen! The Sequel to the European War* (New York: Dodd, Mead, 1915), and campaigned for military rearmament.

16. The company enumerated and illustrated these features in *The Metropolitan Life Insurance Company: Its History, Its Present Position in the Insurance World, Its Home Office Building and Its Work Carried on Therein* (New York: Metropolitan Life, 1914), 43–58. On De Forest's radio station in the tower, see "Grand Opera by Wireless," *Telephony*, March 5, 1910, 293–94, Metropolitan Life Tower Scrapbook, 1907–20, MLICA.

17. "What a Skyscraper Contains," *Scientific American Supplement* 1731 (March 6, 1909): 146. See also "How the Metropolitan Life Building Would Appear If Placed in the Centre of Culebra Cut When [Panama] Canal Is Finished," *Scientific American* (n.d.), Tower Scrapbook, MLICA.

18. "The Metropolitan Life Building, New York" [n.d., n.p.], Box H-9, Folder Home Office-Tower, 1909–23, MLICA. Other protective features include automatic sprinklers and fire-alarm boxes (*Metropolitan Life Insurance Company*, 50). For an illustration of its automated

security vaults, see ibid., opposite 82. "The Light That Never Fails" appears repeatedly in promotional materials, in Box H-11 (Advertisements, 1900–1920), MLICA.

19. William Henry Atherton, speech at 1915 company convention, reprinted as *The Metropolitan Tower: A Symbol of Refuge, Warning, Love, Inspiration, Beauty, Strength* (New York: Metropolitan Life, 1915), 2–4, MLICA.

20. Cleveland Moffett, "The Conquest of America," *McClure's Magazine* 45, no. 1 (1915): 9–12, 85–87, continuing through no. 4 (1915).

21. See Morton Keller, *The Life Insurance Enterprise* (Cambridge, MA: Harvard University Press, 1963), 245–64.

22. Metropolitan Life did not introduce a tontine policy (one that paid high dividends to policyholders, provided they were still alive at the end of a stated period), but it did employ such strategies as sending agents on weekly door-to-door calls, to affect sympathy for workers' problems (Olivier Zunz, *Making America Corporate, 1870–1920* [Chicago: University of Chicago Press, 1990], 97–99). On the history of the neighborhood associations and societies, see Elizabeth Ewen, *Immigrant Women in the Land of Dollars: Life and Culture on the Lower East Side, 1890–1925* (New York: Monthly Review, 1985), 112–15.

23. Ambrose Bierce, "Ashes of the Beacon: An Historical Monograph Written in 4930" (1905), in Bierce, *The Fall of the Republic and Other Political Satires*, ed. S. T. Joshi and David E. Schultz (Knoxville: University of Tennessee Press, 2000), 20; Bierce's antipathy toward insurance predated the Armstrong Investigation; see "The Insurance Folly" (1889), ibid., 182–84.

24. See John Hegeman's montage of the original building with imaginary tower added, in MLICA. On the collapse of the original campanile, and its reconstruction in 1912, see Margaret Plant, *Venice: Fragile City, 1797–1997* (New Haven, CT: Yale University Press, 2002), 234–38.

25. Kenneth Turney Gibbs, *Business Architectural Imagery in America, 1870–1930* (Ann Arbor, MI: UMI Research Press, 1984), 93–148; Mona Domosh, *Invented Cities: The Creation of Landscape in Nineteenth-Century New York and Boston* (New Haven, CT: Yale University Press, 1996), 86–89.

26. Atherton, *Metropolitan Tower*, 6.

27. Burton J. Hendrick, *The Story of Life Insurance* (New York: McClure, Phillips, 1907), 121–23, 234–40; Hendricks's exposé first appeared in *McClure's Magazine* in 1906.

28. Louis H. Sullivan, "The Tall Office Building Artistically Considered" (1896), in *Kindergarten Chats and Other Writings* (1918; New York: Dover, 1979), 207.

29. McAneny's speech paraphrased in the *Times*, quoted in Keith Revell, "Regulating the Landscape: Real Estate Values, City Planning, and the 1916 Zoning Ordinance," in *The Landscape of Modernity: New York City, 1900–1940*, ed. David Ward and Olivier Zunz (Baltimore: Johns Hopkins University Press, 1992), 30.

30. "Limit of High Buildings," *New York Times* (hereafter *NYT*), July 14, 1895, 15.

31. See for example "Buildings Remarkable Not Alone in Height: Floor Area Essential Feature of Newest Skyscrapers," *NYT*, November 25, 1906, 21. On the Metropolitan Tower as a response to the growing company's need for efficiency, see Zunz, *Making America Corporate*, 114–16.

32. By 1905 it possessed $38 million in mortgage loans and $17.5 million in real estate assets (Louis Dublin, *A Family of Thirty Million: The Story of the Metropolitan Life Insurance Company* [New York: Metropolitan Life Insurance Co., 1943], 315, 316).

33. Haley Fiske, "Some Items about the Tower," address delivered to the Triennial Convention of 1909–10, Box H9, Home Office–Tower Folder, 1909–23, MLICA.

34. See Harvey, *The Urban Experience*, 20. On the maintenance and upgrading of large buildings during this period, see Harris, *Building Lives*, 98–113.

35. J. Lincoln Steffens, "The Modern Business Building," *Scribner's Magazine* 22, no. 1 (1897): 61; further references cited in text. The verb *muckrake* was not coined by Theodore Roosevelt until 1906. On Steffens's urban journalism during the 1890s, see Justin Kaplan, *Lincoln Steffens: A Biography* (1974; New York: Simon and Schuster, 2004), 53–65.

36. Hugh Thompson, "The Remaking of New York," *Munsey's Magazine* 47, no. 6 (1912): 904. Hendrick, *Story of Life Insurance*, 237.

37. George Hill, "The Economy of the Office Building," *Architectural Record* 15, no. 4 (1904): 313. Steffens also denounces architectural extravagance in "Modern Business Building," 54. On the "wasted spaces" debate, see Gibbs, *Business Architectural Imagery*, 131–33. Although architectural historian Carol Willis argues that the tower was the most profitable building type, yielding well-lit interiors and minimal building and servicing costs, she acknowledges that, in the case of Metropolitan Life, "a fifty story tower on a lot 75 x 85 feet was not the cheapest way to house the growing numbers of clerks and staff" (*Form Follows Finance: Skyscrapers and Skylines in New York and Chicago* [New York: Princeton Architectural Press, 1995], 24–27, 40; quotation on 43–44).

38. Mildred Stapley, "The City of Towers," *Harper's Monthly* 123, no. 737 (1911): 702; see also Montgomery Schuyler, "The Towers of Manhattan and Notes on the Woolworth Building," *Architectural Record* 33 (1913): 98–122.

39. Manuel Gottlieb observes an upturn in New York's construction industry in 1893, five years before the national construction industry (and business economy as a whole) recovered, in *Long Swings in Urban Development* (New York: Columbia University Press, 1976), 165.

40. Gottlieb claims that investment in construction in the United States has followed twenty-year "swings," disregarding the smaller cycles ("less than three years") as "[in]distinguishable from (short) business cycles" (ibid., 12–13, 59). Similarly, Brinley Thomas's detection of "long cycles" in American building activity, in *Migration and Economic Growth: A Study of Great Britain and the Atlantic Economy*, 2nd ed. (New York: Columbia University Press, 1972), is belied by his own chart, which reveals as many as eight peaks and troughs between 1893 and 1918 (176, fig. 37). Willis does emphasize the sharp fluctuations in the New York real estate market in these years as a factor that led to the enactment of a Zoning Law in 1916 to regulate those excesses (*Form Follows Finance*, 68).

41. Hill, "Economy of the Office Building," 314.

42. Harvey, *Urban Experience*, 23, 64–65, 74, 78.

43. Harris, *Building Lives*, 125–26; on "wasting assets," see Earl A. Saliers, *Depreciation: Principles and Applications* (1915; New York: Ronald, 1923), quoted in ibid., 182–83n12. Both the Corporation Tax of 1909 (which also applied to insurance companies) and the Income Tax Act of 1913 permitted deductions for depreciation; see Saliers, *Principles of Depreciation* (New York: Ronald, 1915), 81, 83; the losses incurred by demolition, unless considered as part of the cost of the new building, could be covered under the depreciation of the old building (ibid., 82–83).

44. On building life cycles, see Harris, *Building Lives*, 5, 59–60, 112–13, 163–65.

45. "First Skyscraper to Be Torn Down," *NYT*, October 29, 1913, 13.

46. See "Wrecking the Gillender Building, New York," *Engineering Record* 61 (June 11, 1910): 755–56; "Taking Down a Skyscraper," *Literary Digest* 41 (August 13, 1910): 235; "Skyscraper Going; Higher One Coming," *NYT*, April 30, 1910, 7; "Breaking Records in House-Wrecking," *NYT*, June 3, 1910, 2. The law of "perpetual motion" also demanded more rapid techniques of construction: see Montgomery Schuyler, "The Evolution of the Skyscraper,"

Scribner's 46 (September 1909): 257–71; the demolition of the Tower Building, completed in forty-five days, was the "occasion" for Schuyler's essay (257).

47. Steffens traces this trend back to the aftermath of the Chicago Fire of 1871, when American architects began to "erect structures so cheap that they could be torn down without much loss" (46).

48. Thompson, "The Remaking of New York," 904. Charles Berg and Edward H. Clark were the architects of the Gillender Building; Bradford Gilbert, that of the Tower Building.

49. "New Skyscrapers for Old," *Scientific American* 102 (May 21, 1910): 414. The Tower building's ruins yielded similar evidence about structural durability ("Life of a Skyscraper," *NYT*, July 8, 1917, 32).

50. "Wrecking a Skyscraper," *Architectural Record* 28 (1910): 76.

51. On this neologism see William R. Taylor, "New York and the Origin of the Skyline: The Commercial City as Visual Text," in *In Pursuit of Gotham: Culture and Commerce in New York* (New York and Oxford: Oxford University Press, 1992), 23–33; James uses the term on 106.

52. Nathaniel Hawthorne, *The Marble Faun* (1860; Harmondsworth: Penguin, 1990), 3; Henry James, *Hawthorne* (1879; Ithaca, NY: Cornell University Press, 1998), 34, 2.

53. Henry James, "The Jolly Corner," in *The American Novels and Stories of Henry James*, ed. F. O. Matthiessen (New York: Knopf, 1947), 796, 795, 793, 796, 797, 798, 813; further references cited in the text.

54. Ralph Adams Cram (1901), quoted in Thomas A. P. van Leeuwen, *The Skyward Trend of Thought: The Metaphysics of the American Skyscraper* (Cambridge, MA: MIT Press, 1986), 71. James discusses Roman ruins in *Italian Hours* (Boston and New York: Houghton Mifflin, 1909), especially 226–30; quotation on 455. For the view of James as nostalgic, see Page, *Creative Destruction,* 15–17, 41; and an early version of this chapter, in *American Quarterly* 56, no. 2 (2004): 308–47.

55. Georg Simmel, *The Philosophy of Money* (1907; London and New York: Routledge, 2004), 484; see also 257, 491.

56. Questioning the long-standing image of the detached aesthete scorning the commercial metropolis, some recent critics have represented James as a more ambivalent and engaged critic, who immerses himself in the provisionality and heterogeneity of the city. See Ross Posnock, *The Trial of Curiosity: Henry James, William James, and the Challenge of Modernity* (New York: Oxford University Press, 1991), 141–42, 165, passim; Collin Meissner, "'What Ghosts Will Be Left to Walk': Mercantile Culture and the Language of Art," *The Henry James Review* 21, no. 3 (2000): 246–47; David McWhirter, "'A Provision Full of Responsibilities': Senses of the Past in Henry James's Fourth Phase," in *Enacting History in Henry James: Narrative, Power, and Ethics*, ed. Gert Beulens (Cambridge: Cambridge University Press, 1997), 158. These critics underplay, in my view, James's repeated complaints about the provisional.

57. Garrett P. Serviss, "The Second Deluge," *Cavalier Magazine* (1911), reprinted as *The Second Deluge* (1912; Westport, CT: Hyperion Press, 1974); further references cited in the text.

58. For reference to "era of the skyscrapers," see ibid., 134.

59. On the electric beacon, see *Metropolitan Life Insurance Company*, 48. On Serviss as a Brooklynite, see Sam Moskowitz, ed., *Under the Moons of Mars: A History and Anthology of "The Scientific Romance" in the Munsey Magazines, 1912–1920* (New York, Chicago, and San Francisco: Holt, Rinehart, and Winston, 1970), 330. Rem Koolhaas imagines Manhattan's blocks as "dry archipelago" and its skyscrapers (especially the Metropolitan Tower) as "land-locked lighthouse[s]," in *Delirious New York: A Retroactive Manifesto for Manhattan* (1974; New York: Monacelli Press, 1994), 93, 94, 97. But as early as 1915, Metropolitan Life's agents

were encouraged to compare the tower with "those beacon towers on land, or lighthouse towers at sea" (Atherton, *The Metropolitan Tower*, 4, 5).

60. Thompson, "The Remaking of New York," 900, 894, 901, 893 (emphasis added).

61. Thomas J. Vivian and Grena J. Bennett, "The Tilting Island," *Everybody's Magazine* 21 (September 1909): 385; the ethnic hordes are on 387; the toppling of the skyscrapers and "tidal wave" are on 389.

62. Daniel P. Wiles, "Fearful Catastrophe If Mile-High Edifice Is Built: Famous Expert Tells Why Magnates Must Not Construct Dizzy Skyscrapers," unidentified newspaper clipping, Tower Scrapbook, MLICA. Laymen also expressed such fears; a convict leaving jail after several years reportedly remarked that the "whole city looks to me as though it would fall to ruins some day" ("Freed by Hughes, Flaherty Returns," *NYT*, March 26, 1907, 18).

63. Walter Benjamin, "The Paris of the Second Empire in Baudelaire" (1938), in *Charles Baudelaire: A Lyric Poet in the Era of High Capitalism*, trans. Harry Zohn (London: Verso, 1983), 84–86; further references cited in the text. The Balzac passage is cited in my epigraph to chapter 5; Hugo, cited in Benjamin, *The Arcades Project*, 94 [C6]. The theme of the future ruin dates back further, at least to Hubert Robert's 1796 painting *An Imaginary View of the Grande Galerie of the Louvre in Ruins*, oil on canvas, Musée du Louvre, Paris.

64. On Munsey's first pulp, *The Argosy*, see Frank Luther Mott, *A History of American Magazines, 1741–1930*, 5 vols. (Cambridge, MA: Belknap Press of Harvard University Press, 1958–68), 4:420–21. Munsey targeted working-class consumers in the very title of one of his pulps, *The Railroad Man's Magazine*. According to Moskowitz, *Cavalier*'s inclusion of "love stories" qualified it as a "family" rather than "men's magazine" (*Under the Moons of Mars*, 346, 347, 379). The *Argosy*'s circulation approached 500,000 by 1907, and *Cavalier and Scrapbook* 75,000 by 1913 (ibid., 329).

65. On the price cutting of middlebrow magazines and the "revolutionary" impact of the "ten-cent magazines," see Mott, *American Magazines*, 4:5–6.

66. Munsey's fiction magazines (with launch dates) were: *The Golden Argosy* (1882), *The Argosy* (1896), *All Story Magazine* (1905), *The Scrapbook* (1906), *The Railroad Man's Magazine* (1906), *The Ocean* (1907), *The Cavalier Magazine* (1908), *The Cavalier and Scrapbook* (1908), and *The Live Wire* (1908). On the crisis of the pulps circa 1910–11, see Moskowitz, *Under the Moons of Mars*, 328–29, 337.

67. The use of fragile wood-pulp paper in newspapers led the *Times* to ask, "Will Future Generations Lose Historical Records of To-day?" July 24, 1910, Sunday Magazine, 15.

68. Henry Morton Robinson, "The Wood-Pulp Racket," *Bookman* 67, no. 6 (1928): 651.

69. Some stories were even syndicated in New York's daily newspapers. *Darkness and Dawn* (discussed below) was serialized in the *Evening Mail* in 1912. *New Yorker* writer A. J. Liebling remembered waiting for his father to bring home the daily installment of this postapocalyptic narrative ("That Was New York: 'To Him She Clung,'" *New Yorker*, October 12, 1963, 143–68).

70. Robinson, "Wood-Pulp Racket," 648–49.

71. Frank A. Munsey, "Something New in Magazine Making," *The Scrap Book* 1, no. 1 (1906): 2. On the feuilletons, see Benjamin, *Baudelaire*, 27–31.

72. The *Argosy*'s reader's section was titled "The Argosy's Log-Book." Other pulps such as *Cavalier* followed suit.

73. Ernst Bloch, "A Philosophical View of the Detective Novel," in *The Utopian Function of Art and Literature: Selected Essays*, trans. Jack Zipes and Frank Mecklenburg (Cambridge, MA: MIT Press, 1996), 255; see also 249.

74. One reviewer described this literary terrain as "little trampled" ("George Allan England's 'Darkness and Dawn,'" *Bookman* 39, no. 3 [1914]: 344).

75. Walter Benjamin, "The Destructive Character" (1931), in *Reflections: Essays, Aphorisms, Autobiographical Writings*, trans. Edmund Jephcott (New York: Schocken, 1978), 303.

76. George Allan England, *Darkness and Dawn* (Boston: Small, Maynard, 1914), 13–18; further references cited in the text. It was also serialized in the *New York Evening Mail*, beginning March 4, 1912. Science fiction author H. P. Lovecraft ranked England alongside Edgar Rice Burroughs as Munsey's "supreme literary artists," and *Darkness and Dawn* as "on a par with the 'Tarzan' stories" (*H. P. Lovecraft in the Argosy: Collected Correspondence from the Munsey Magazines* [West Warwick, RI: Necronomicon Press, 1994], 36). It is not until the thirty-third episode that Allan and Beatrice discover that the catastrophe was an explosion that blew a portion of the Midwest into orbit and released poisonous gases into the atmosphere (393).

77. For a typical set of utopian solutions, see Julian Hawthorne, "June 1993," *Cosmopolitan* 14 (February 1893): 450–58. For a discussion of the will to depopulate the city as a "lashing out of the choked psyche, an attempt to 'get air,'" or as "some obscure but primal need for free space, for the silence in which the ego can cry out its mastery," see George Steiner, *In Bluebeard's Castle: Some Notes towards the Redefinition of Culture* (New Haven, CT: Yale University Press, 1971), 51–52. On anxieties about overcrowded cities, see Harris, "Utopian Fiction and Its Discontents," in *Cultural Excursions: Marketing Appetites and Cultural Tastes in Modern America* (Chicago: University of Chicago Press, 1990), 165.

78. William Taylor, "Launching a Commercial Culture: Newspaper, Magazine, and Popular Novel as Urban Baedekers," in *In Pursuit of Gotham*, 71–72; Madison Square was supplanted by Times Square during the 1910s.

79. Walter Benjamin, "Paris, the Capital of the Nineteenth Century (Exposé of 1935)," in *The Arcades Project*, 4–5.

80. Allan merely mimics the exchange of "a bushel of diamonds for a razor and a pair of scissors" (33).

81. "Illness Plucked Him from Insurance and Hurled Him into Fiction," *Literary Digest* 64 (March 6, 1920): 63–67. England's socialist writings include: *Get Together!* (New York: Wilshire, 1908), and "The Socialist Philosophy of Panics: A Non-Classic Analysis of Their Reason and Their Remedy," *The Arena* 39, no. 223 (1908): 684–70. He eventually received the Socialist Party's nomination as candidate for governor of Maine in 1912.

82. George Allan England, "A Message from the Moon," *Pearson's Magazine*, April 1907; England, *The Air Trust* (St. Louis: Phil Wager, 1915); England, *The Golden Blight* (New York: H. K. Fly, 1916).

83. Georg Simmel, "The Sociology of the Senses," in *Simmel on Culture*, ed. David Frisby and Mike Featherstone (London: Sage, 1997), 120.

84. Felix Grendon, "A Thousand Years from Now," *New Review* 2 (1914): 230–33.

85. See, for example, George Allan England, "The Leaven of Woman Suffrage 'Round the World," *Lippincott's Monthly Magazine* 85, no. 505 (1910): 123–25.

86. Grendon, "A Thousand Years from Now," 232. Another reviewer, however, described Allan and Beatrice's relationship as the kind "feminists hope marriage will some time be" ("Romance of a Depopulated New York," *NYT*, February 8, 1914, book review section, 59).

87. On Metropolitan Life's employment of women, see Zunz, *Making America Corporate*, 235. By 1915, these stenographers earned an average weekly wage of $11 (119). The company addressed contemporary concerns about the implications for sexual and social boundaries through publications such as *Rules and Regulations Governing the Office Employés of the Metropolitan Life Insurance Company of New York* (1895), MLICA; and through architectural,

spatial, and temporal arrangements that separated its male and female workers (see Angel Kwolek-Folland, *Engendering Business: Men and Women in the Corporate Office, 1870–1930* [Baltimore: Johns Hopkins University Press, 1994], 108–20). On the leisure activities of wage-earning women, see Kathy Peiss, *Cheap Amusements: Working Women and Leisure in Turn-of-the-Century New York* (Philadelphia: Temple University Press, 1986).

88. Beatrice does sometimes exercise this bravery outside the domestic sphere; see especially 135–45.

89. Grendon, "A Thousand Years from Now," 232–33.

90. On race, gender, and eugenics in early pulp fiction, see Gail Bederman, *Manliness and Civilization: A Cultural History of Gender and Race in the United States, 1880–1917* (Chicago: University of Chicago Press, 1995), 217–32; and Marianna Torgovnick, *Gone Primitive: Savage Intellects, Modern Lives* (Chicago: University of Chicago Press, 1995), 42–72. Although critics such as Mike Davis have emphasized the racist dimensions of apocalyptic fiction (*Ecology of Fear: Los Angeles and the Imagination of Disaster* [New York: Metropolitan Books, 1998], 273–356), this genre allowed considerable flexibility.

91. W. E. B. Du Bois, "The Comet," in *Darkwater: Voices from within the Veil* (1920; New York: Dover, 1969), 253–73; further references cited in text. The sighting of Halley's Comet in 1910 suggests that he wrote "The Comet" (like several other chapters of *Darkwater*) several years prior to its publication. Du Bois may also have been responding to reports of apocalyptic fears about the comet, especially among female "hysterics" and "ignorant" blacks; see "Chicago Is Terrified: Women Are Stopping Up Doors and Windows to Keep Out Cyanogen," *NYT*, May 18, 1910, 2, and "Southern Negroes in a Comet Frenzy," *NYT*, May 19, 1910, 2.

92. On the appropriation of that roof (or at least the larger roof of the Home Office Building) for heterosocial interaction, see Zunz, *Making America Corporate*, 121.

93. Compare Julia's vision of Jim as "her Brother Humanity incarnate" with *Darkwater's* opening "Credo" affirming that "all men, black and brown and white, are brothers" (3). Du Bois's feminism encompassed procreation and sexuality as well as economic independence (see especially 164–65). The "black Messiah" appears on 53–55, 105–8, 123–33. Arnold Rampersad views this "black Christ" as an essentially propagandistic device, rather than a theological claim per se (*The Art and Imagination of W. E. B. Du Bois* [Cambridge, MA: Harvard University Press, 1976], 180–81). On the centrality of this messianic trope within black nationalism, see Wilson Jeremiah Moses, *Black Messiahs and Uncle Toms: Social and Literary Manipulations of a Religious Myth* (University Park: Pennsylvania State University Press, 1982), especially 142–54. And on the intersection of Du Bois's socialism, feminism, and pan-Africanism, see Adolph L. Reed Jr., *W. E. B. Du Bois and American Political Thought: Fabianism and the Color Line* (New York: Oxford University Press, 1997).

94. Newspaper reports that Metropolitan Life stopped issuing policies to African Americans (as John Hancock did until as late as 1960) due to their "unfavorable mortality" rate remained unsubstantiated; see "The Metropolitan Life and Negro Insurance," *The Independent* 62, no. 3033 (1907): 170. Even if Metropolitan Life did accept African American policyholders, it effectively reinscribed racial discrimination by dividing its industrial policies into "standard" and "substandard" classes. African Americans tended to have access only to the latter and thus paid a higher premium while receiving fewer benefits. In 2002 Metropolitan Life finally agreed to a settlement compensating minorities for policies they held between 1901 and 1972. See "MetLife Reaches Settlements on Alleged Race-Based Policies," *Business Review*, August 30, 2002; and "In Black and White: Old Memos Lay Bare MetLife's Use of Race to Screen Customers," *Wall Street Journal*, July 24, 2001, A1, A10.

95. This may be a reference to either the Metropolitan Tower (built out of the purchase of

insurance by the poor), or the Woolworth (commonly described as a cathedral after its completion in 1913).

96. In asserting the influence on Du Bois of German literature and philosophy (especially Goethe, Schiller, and Hegel) and opera (Wagner), critics may have overlooked a more local and popular source in the Munsey magazines.

97. I am referring to Harvey's concept of "time-space compression" in *The Condition of Postmodernity: An Inquiry into the Origins of Cultural Change* (Cambridge, MA: Basil Blackwell, 1990), 240, 284–307; Stephen Kern's emphasis on synchronicity in *The Culture of Time and Space, 1880–1918* (Cambridge, MA: Harvard University Press, 1983), 11–15, passim; and Fredric Jameson's argument about the "crisis of historicity" and flattening of temporality in "Postmodernism, or the Cultural Logic of Late Capitalism," *New Left Review* 146 (1984): 53–92, among others.

98. *Metropolitan Life Insurance Company*, 47–48.

99. John Curtis Underwood, "The Clock in the Air" (n.d.), in *The Book of New York Verse*, ed. Hamilton Fish Armstrong (New York: Putnam's, 1917), 363; "The Metropolitan Clock—It's in the Movies," *Home Office* 9 (April 1920): 1, Box H10, MLICA; "Metropolitan: A Beacon to Hills," *New York Sun*, February 1922, in Box H10, MLICA. See also Sara Teasdale's poem "The Metropolitan Tower," one of several poems and songs preserved in MLICA in which this clock marks the inception of a romance.

100. For a history of the modernization of time, see Michael O'Malley, *Keeping Watch: A History of American Time* (Harmondsworth: Penguin, 1990), especially 55–98. If O'Malley posits a simple two-way choice between premodern "natural time" and modern "artificial" time, I am exploring a third notion, postapocalyptic time, or future anteriority.

101. "Biggest Clock in the World," *New York World*, February 17, 1908 (n.p.); "Tower Clock Is Wound Up; Persons in Madison Square Strain Their Necks in Looking Up at New Timepiece," unidentified newspaper clipping, n.d.; and "Gazes Skyward; Loses His Memory: Man Who Looked Up at Skyscraper Unable to Find Home . . . ," unidentified newspaper clipping, n.d.; all in Tower Scrapbook, MLICA.

102. "Tower Clock Hands Freeze," unidentified newspaper clipping [1913?], Tower Scrapbook, 1907–20, MLICA. Stewart Edward White, *The Sign at Six* (Indianapolis: Bobbs-Merrill, 1912), 24, 25.

103. Murray Leinster, "The Runaway Skyscraper," *Argosy and Railroad Man's Magazine* 105, no. 1 (1919): 59–82, reprinted in *The Best of Amazing [Stories]*, ed. Joseph Ross (New York: Doubleday, 1967), 47; further references cited in the text.

104. *Metropolitan Life Insurance Company*, 41.

105. Reference to tornado in "The Biograph as a Recorder of Current Events," *Wilson's Photographic Magazine* 38, no. 540 (1901): 473. An 1897 display of backward projection in Rochester, New York, was advertised in the newspaper as "a curious novelty" (quoted in George C. Pratt, *Spellbound in Darkness: A History of the Silent Film* [Greenwich, CT: Little, Brown, 1973], 18).

106. *American Mutoscope and Biograph Company Catalogue*, ca. 1901 (emphasis added); thanks to Tom Gunning for showing me this source and thereby confirming that *Star Theatre* was indeed projected in reverse. In the version appearing on the DVD, *Unseen Cinema: Picturing a Metropolis; New York City Unveiled* (Anthology Film Archives, 2005), the rebuilding precedes the demolishing.

107. Gernsback addressed these criticisms when reprinting "Runaway Skyscraper" in *Amazing Stories* 1, no. 3 (1926): 675.

108. See Sheffield's distinction between the "point" and "durative" modes of each tense (note 8 above).

109. Walter Benjamin, "Theses on the Philosophy of History," in *Illuminations*, 257–58.

110. Simmel, "The Ruin," 261, 263.

111. Van Tassel Sutphen, *The Doomsman* (New York and London: Harper, 1906), 125–28, 116–17.

112. Ibid., 71.

113. Schuyler, "Evolution of the Skyscraper," 258. Schuyler borrowed the first phrase about the "faith and fear of nations" from Ruskin's *The Seven Lamps*, in *Works*, 8:53; and the second, "the hell of not making money," from Thomas Carlyle, *Past and Present* (1843; Berkeley: University of California Press, 2006), 170. On Ruskin's denunciation of the iron architecture of railway stations in *Seven Lamps*, see note 1 above.

Epilogue

1. E. S. M. [Edward Sandford Martin], "Whither Bound, Sweet Earth?" *Life*. 71, no. 1850 (1918): 589.

2. Wilson (and various American ministers and advisors) visited Belgium's newly opened battlefields in June 1919 ("Wilson Deeply Moved by Belgium's Ruins," *New York Times* [hereafter *NYT*], June 20, 1919, 2). Officer cited in "May View Belgian Ruins," *NYT*, March 21, 1919, 12. On battlefield tourism, see Daniel J. Sherman, *The Construction of Memory in Interwar France* (Chicago: University of Chicago Press, 1999), 35–49.

3. See Bernd Huppauf, "Modernism and the Photographic Representation of War and Destruction," in *Fields of Vision: Essays in Film Studies, Visual Anthropology, and Photography*, ed. Leslie Deveraux and Roger Hillman (Berkeley: University of California Press, 1995), 94–126. For expressionist and surrealist ruinscapes of the First and Second World Wars, see respectively Otto Dix, *War Triptych* (1929–32), and Max Ernst, *Europe after the Rain* (1940–42). Photographers did occasionally pose soldiers, tourists, and even children among war ruins.

4. Spencer Weart, *Nuclear Fear: A History of Images* (Cambridge, MA: Harvard University Press, 1989), 238, 236.

5. See ibid., 215–40, and Robert Jay Lifton and Kai Erikson, "Nuclear War's Effect on the Mind," *NYT*, March 16, 1982, A17.

6. See, for example, Cardinal Terence Cooke, quoted in Jill Jonnes, *South Bronx Rising: The Rise, Fall, and Resurrection of an American City* (1986; New York: Fordham University Press, 2002), 264. On the Bronx's ruins, see also Marshall Berman, *All That Is Solid Melts into Air: The Experience of Modernity* (London and New York: Verso, 1983), 290–312.

7. Antoine Picon, "Anxious Landscapes: From the Ruin to Rust," *Grey Room* 1 (Fall 2000): 65–66, 76–77.

8. Camillo José Vergara, *The New American Ghetto* (New Brunswick, NJ: Rutgers University Press, 1997); Vergara, *American Ruins* (New York: Monacelli, 1999); see also Harry Skrdla, *Ghostly Ruins: America's Forgotten Architecture* (New York: Princeton Architectural Press, 2006).

9. Liam Kennedy, referring to *New American Ghetto*, in *Race and Urban Space in American Culture* (London and New York: Routledge, 2000), 108, 111.

10. Jerry Herron, "Three Meditations on the Ruins of Detroit," in *Stalking Detroit*, ed. Georgia Daskalakis, Charles Waldheim, and Jason Young (Barcelona: Actar, 2001), 25.

11. Vergara, *American Ruins*, 23, 24; Kennedy, *Race and Urban Space*, 113.

12. Vergara, *New American Ghetto*, 220; critical responses cited in ibid., 221, 223; and

in Sylvia Lewis, "What the Locals Say," *Planning* 61, no. 8 (1995): 19. Vergara also aired his proposal in several magazines (including *Metropolis*, April 1995, 36–37, and *Planning* 61, no. 8 [1995]: 18), and reiterated it in *American Ruins*, 205–6. Vergara emphasizes the celebratory intent behind the proposal, ibid., 206.

13. Leon Wieseltier, "Ruins," *New Republic* 225, no. 22 (2001): 46. Herbert Muschamp had alluded to the aesthetic tradition of the ruin in "The Commemorative Beauty of Tragic Wreckage," *NYT*, November 11, 2001, AR37.

14. Muschamp, "Commemorative Beauty," AR37.

15. "The Last Steel Column," *NYT*, May 30, 2002, A24. For an early call to preserve the facade in situ, see Philippe de Montebello, "The Iconic Power of an Artifact," *NYT*, September 25, 2001, A29; the nonprofit organization Save the Facades continued to campaign for its reinstallation as part of a larger memorial. In August 2009, the cast steel column returned to the site as a permanent museum exhibit. Critiques of the towers include Eric Darton, *Divided We Stand: A Biography of New York's World Trade Center* (New York: Basic Books, 1999).

16. See, among others, Niall Ferguson, *Colossus: The Rise and Fall of the American Empire* (Harmondsworth: Penguin, 2005), Chalmers A. Johnson, *Nemesis: The Last Days of the American Republic* (New York: Macmillan, 2006), and Cullen Murphy, *Are We Rome? The Fall of an Empire and the Fate of America* (Boston: Houghton Mifflin Harcourt, 2007).

17. Kevin Phillips, for instance, draws parallels with the decline of the Roman, Spanish, Dutch, and British empires, in *Bad Money: Reckless Finance, Failed Politics, and the Global Crisis of American Capitalism* (New York: Viking Press, 2008), 20–25, passim.

18. "In the Central Valley, the Ruins of the Housing Bust," *NYT*, August 24, 2008, BU1.

19. Vincent Scully, "Tomorrow's Ruins Today," *NYT*, Sunday Magazine, December 5, 1999, 38, 42; Scully does hope for the survival of more notable structures such as the Vietnam memorial and the Empire State Building.

20. Alan Weisman, *The World without Us* (New York: St. Martin's Press, 2007), 26–27, 112–28, 129–44, 208–10, 41; elsewhere in the book, Weisman predicts a rapid return to prehuman ecosystems.

21. Alexis Rockman, *Manifest Destiny,* 2003–04. Oil and acrylic on panel. Brooklyn Museum of Art. On Rockman's consultation with architects and scientists, and his emulation of science fiction illustrators and Hudson River School artists, including Cole, see Spencer Weart, "Spencer Weart on Depicting Global Warming," *Environmental History* 10, no. 4 (2005): 770–75.

Index

Capitalism (*continued*)
204–5; and obsolescence, 246, 252–57,
284, 286; and sectional tensions, 86–88;
transnational, 65, 81, 92, 100–103, 105;
and urbanization, 11, 12, 14, 81, 110,
131, 144–45, 158, 244–45, 264–67.
See also banks; financial panics; labor:
conflict with capital
Capital removal campaigns, 81, 168–9,
313n38, 335n60
Carnegie, Andrew, 162
Carthage (Tunisia), 55, 88, 108, 109,
110–15, 122, 147, 167, 179, 321n12
Carwardine, William H., 333n41
Cary, Thomas Greaves, 96–98, 317n83
Castle Clinton (New York City), 325n61
Castle Garden (New York City), 259
Catherwood, Frederick, 304n59
Catskills, NY, 45–46, 83–84, 88
Cavalier, 247, 263, 357n64
Cavalier and Scrap Book, 270
Cemeteries, 8, 37, 328n102, 329n107; Mt.
Auburn, *38*, 302n48
Central Labor Union, 332n28
Central Park (New York City), 143, 184, 259,
272, 278, 330n128
Century (or Centennial) Safe, 180–82, *181*,
337nn95–96, 338n97
Century Chest, 182
Champlain Canal, 47
Chancery, Court of, 119, 121, 134, 140, 141
Charleston, SC, 87, 192
Chastellux, Marquis de, 27
Chateaubriand, Francois-René de, 27, 47–48,
54, 184, 299n12
Chesney, Sir George Tomkyns, 176
Chevalier, Michel, 105
Chicago, IL, 12, 64, 147, 159, 163, 166–67,
168, 181, 182, 183, 202, 204, 275; Great
Fire of (1871), 192, 193, 240, 340n7,
352n171, 356n47
Child, Lydia Maria, 114
Childe Harold's Pilgrimage (Byron), 28
Chinatown (San Francisco), 207, 215, 229,
235–36, 292
Chinese Americans, 235–39
Christian Advocate, 160
Christian Index, 37
Christian Register, 37

Christian Science, 148, 186, 339n116,
340n120
Christianity, 4, 35–39, 41, 150, 152, 159,
161–62, 171, 180. *See also* African Meth-
odists; Christian Science; millenarianism;
millennialism
Chronicle Building (San Francisco), 236–37
Church of the Ascension (New York City),
260
Cincinnati, OH, 53, 314n38
Cinema. *See* film
Cities: antipathy toward, 3, 30, 53, 87, 108;
capital, 68, 80–83, 313n38; central, 68;
class conflict in, 148, 150, 154, 158, 159,
160, 163–67, 177, 197; in colonial era,
29, 307n92, 326n69; creative destruction of, 244–45; density of, 135–36,
177; economic decline of, 59–61, 63,
64, 66, 80, 103, 167, 195; and emergence
of downtowns, 109, 127–31, 325n60;
ethnic heterogeneity of, 148, 150,
170–71, 177, 235–36, 336n77; and
imperial decline, 27–28, 30; industrial,
87, 109, 127, 158, 200, 203; inland, 50,
168; networked, 196; as populated with
strangers, 115–19, 158, 204; population growth in, 49–50, 307nn90–91;
postwar decline of, 2, 290, 295n2; rapid
development of, 11, 12, 49–56, 80, 97,
102, 115, 117, 120–26, 237–38; as seat
of money economy, 65; sensory impact of,
15, 121, 128–30, 200, 202, 203, 220–21,
263; as signs of advanced civilization,
24, 48; slums in, 84, 126, 136–37,
158, 170, 177, 198, 336n77; southern,
87–88; spatiotemporal experience in,
15, 52, 55, 109, 220–21, 258, 262, 263,
279–80, 283; speculative (paper cities),
13, 60–61, 64, 65, 68, 69–76, 80–81,
97, 103–5, 107, 312n20; stratification
of, 109, 117, 126–28, 134, 137, 324n52,
325n61; streetcar accidents in, 200, 202;
technology in, 158, 173, 194, 196–206;
uneven development of, 12, 86, 131, 238,
240, 267, 308n116, 315n49; utopian,
158, 165, 166, 173–74; vulnerability of,
14, 65, 81, 86–87, 102, 148, 157–59,
167–71, 178–79, 197–206, 267; walking, 109, 126; as webs of interdepen-